BLACKSTONE'S GUIDE TO

The Freedom of Information Act 2000

Second edition

John Wadham and Jonathan Griffiths

OXFORD

UNIVERSITY PRESS

OXFORD
UNIVERSITY PRESS

Great Clarendon Street, Oxford OX2 6DP

Oxford University Press is a department of the University of Oxford.
It furthers the University's objective of excellence in research, scholarship,
and education by publishing worldwide in

Oxford New York

Auckland Cape Town Dar es Salaam Hong Kong Karachi
Kuala Lumpur Madrid Melbourne Mexico City Nairobi
New Delhi Shanghai Taipei Toronto

With offices in

Argentina Austria Brazil Chile Czech Republic France Greece
Guatemala Hungary Italy Japan South Korea Poland Portugal
Singapore Switzerland Thailand Turkey Ukraine Vietnam

Oxford is a registered trade mark of Oxford University Press
in the UK and in certain other countries

Published in the United States
by Oxford University Press Inc., New York

© J. Wadham and J. Griffiths 2005

The moral rights of the authors have been asserted

Crown copyright material is reproduced under Class Licence
Number CO1P0000148 with the permission of HMSO
and the Queen's Printer for Scotland

Database right Oxford University Press (maker)

First edition published by Blackstone Press in 2001
Second edition first published 2005

British Library Cataloguing in Publication Data

Data available

Library of Congress Cataloging-in-Publication Data

Wadham, John, 1952–
Blackstone's guide to the Freedom of Information Act 2000 /
John Wadham and Jonathan Griffiths.— 2nd ed.
p. cm.
ISBN 0–19–927764–8 (alk. paper)
1. Great Britain. Freedom of Information Act 2000. 2. Freedom of
information—Great Britain. 3. Government information—Great Britain.
4. Public records—Law and legislation—Great Britain. I. Title: Guide
to the Freedom of Information Act 2000. II. Title: Freedom of
Information Act 2000. III. Griffiths, Jonathan, 1965– IV. Title.
KD3756.W33 2005
342.4108'53—dc22   2004027503

1 3 5 7 9 10 8 6 4 2

Typeset by RefineCatch Limited, Bungay, Suffolk
Printed in Great Britain
on acid-free paper by
Biddles Ltd., King's Lynn

Contents—Summary

Visit the Blackstone's Guide Series Website:
www.oup.com/uk/law/practitioner/bgseries

Contents

Contents

Foreword

The Freedom of Information Act came into force on 1 January 2005. As the Act takes effect there is much for all of us to gain in moving further towards a culture where public authorities make as much information available as possible.

Public authorities must begin the process of delivering a new level of openness with the aim of rebuilding trust and improving accountability.

At the same time staff in my Office have developed practical guidance for public authorities, practitioners and individuals which will support our core function of deciding cases robustly and correctly. As the case law develops we can improve the quality of decision making in public authorities in ways which command public confidence.

In setting out to explain the Act and its context, this book contributes to the learning process which all of us who have an interest in it are now undergoing.

Richard Thomas, Information Commissioner
November 2004

Preface

The Freedom of Information Act 2000 ('the Act' throughout this Guide) represents the culmination of several decades of pressure for a statutory right of information in the United Kingdom. Increasingly, it has been understood that access to information is a prerequisite for effective popular participation in the public sphere. A series of political controversies—including the 'Arms to Iraq' and BSE affairs—have demonstrated clearly the problems which arise when information is suppressed. The fact that other jurisdictions have introduced freedom of information legislation without constitutional crisis has strengthened the case of those seeking similar legislation for the United Kingdom.

In 1997, the new Labour government entered power, having promised a Freedom of Information Act. Shortly after assuming office, the White Paper, *Your Right to Know* (1997, Cm 3818) was published. That document proposed a very liberal enactment, offering an enforceable right to a wide range of public information and restricting access in only a limited number of cases. The draft Bill which eventually emerged, however, was a pale shadow of the legislation heralded by the White Paper. It contained a greatly expanded list of exemptions to the right of access and weaker enforcement powers for the independent Information Commissioner. It was only as a result of persistent and vigorous Parliamentary pressure (largely coordinated by the Campaign for Freedom of Information) that the Act in its final form was substantially improved as a tool for obtaining access to official information.

The Act provides a right of access to information held by over 100,000 public bodies and office-holders, from central government departments to much smaller bodies such as health trusts, parish councils and schools. Under the Act, access to information held by these bodies is to be granted without significant formality, without inquiry into the motives of the applicant and at subsidised cost. This right is subject to a number of exemptions—that is provisions which, in specified circumstances, allow public authorities to refuse to communicate information (and in some cases even to refuse to confirm or deny that they are holding information). Some exemptions, such as those designed to protect the confidentiality of governmental policy discussions and personal privacy, are absolute exemptions. However, the majority of exemptions ('qualified exemptions' in this text) will only be effective where the public interest in maintaining the exemption can be demonstrated to outweigh the public interest in disclosure.

Responsibility for enforcing the right of access under the Act rests with the Information Commissioner. The Commissioner, formerly the Data Protection Commissioner, now supervises both the freedom of information regime established under the Act and the data protection regime under the Data Protection Act 1998. He is, in most cases, entitled to overrule the decisions of public authorities not to disclose information where he believes that those decisions contravene the requirements of the Act. His role, particularly in balancing the public interests in disclosure and non-disclosure, will be crucial in ensuring that the Act becomes an effective tool for public openness. Appeals from a decision of the Commissioner can be brought to the Information Tribunal.

In addition to establishing the freedom of information regime, the Act also makes significant amendments to other legislation concerning access to information. The Data Protection Act 1998 grants, amongst other things, a right of access to personal information to the 'data subject' of that information. As a result of amendment by the Act, the range of personal information available under the Data Protection Act 1998 has been substantially increased. Now all data held by public authorities, regardless of the format in which it is stored, will prima facie be available to a data subject. In addition, the existing public records regime under the Public Records Act 1958 has been transformed in order to bring it into conformity with the Act. For the first time, members of the public have an enforceable right of access to public records and are able to appeal to the Information Commissioner against decisions not to open particular public records to public scrutiny.

The Act is certainly not flawless. In particular, the extensive number and scope of exemptions to the right of access to information have been widely criticised. Nevertheless, it is likely to prove an extremely useful tool for many different kinds of applicant—individual citizens, investigative journalists, members of interest and pressure groups, commercial organisations and lawyers. The effectiveness of the Act largely depends upon the willingness of such applicants to use the mechanisms established under the Act to their fullest extent.

The aim of this Guide is to clarify the effects of a formidably complicated piece of legislation and to assist both applicants and public authorities to understand their respective rights and duties. The first three chapters provide contextual information about the rationales for freedom of information, comparable enactments in other jurisdictions and the history of legislation providing access to information in the United Kingdom. Chapters 4 to 9 seek to explain various aspects, both substantive and procedural, of the right of access to information introduced by the Act. Chapters 10 and 11 explore the relationship between the Act and the existing data protection and public records regimes respectively.

This Guide has been written at an early point in the history of comprehensive freedom of information legislation in this jurisdiction. In time, the Act will undoubtedly give rise to more detailed comparative studies of the kind available in, for example, New Zealand and Ireland (see Eagles, Taggart and Liddell, *Freedom of Information in New Zealand* (Auckland: OUP, 1992) and McDonagh, *Freedom of Information Law in Ireland* (Dublin: Round Hall, 1998)). Until that point, however, it is hoped that the Guide will assist public authorities, potential applicants and their advisors in understanding and dealing with the Act.

COMMENCEMENT OF THE ACT (s. 87)

The Freedom of Information Act received Royal Assent on 30 November 2000 and came into force in phases. Certain definitional provisions and ancillary powers (for example, the power to make regulations governing access to environmental information) came into force on the date on which the Act was passed. A number of further provisions came into force on 30 January 2001. Notably, the Data Protection Commissioner was transformed into the Information Commissioner on that date. With effect from 14 May 2001, further procedural and minor provisions of the Act have been brought into force as a result of the Freedom of Information Act 2000 (Commencement No. 1) Order 2001 (SI 2001/1637 [C 56]). Most notably, the provisions re-naming the Data Protection Tribunal as the Information Tribunal have, as a result, taken effect.

The substantive rights provided under the Act were also brought into force by delegated legislation. A considerable delay between Royal assent, 30 November 2000, and final implementation of the Act on 1 January 2005 was imposed by the government. This delay is all the more surprising since freedom of information was a manifesto commitment in the 1997 election.

However the slow implementation of the Act has had the advantage of ensuring that public authorities are ready to deal with the right to access material which came into force on 1 January. Most central government departments had to introduce publication schemes by 30 November 2002, local authorities by 28 February 2003, public authorities within the criminal justice system by 30 June 2003, the Health Service by 31 October 2003, most schools by 29 February 2004 and most others by 30 June 2004 (see Commencement Orders SI 2001/1637, SI 2002/2812 and SI 2003/2603). The creation of publication schemes has ensured that significantly more information is now available from public authorities as a matter of course and without the need for specific requests.

A number of authorities have been added and some removed from the list of those subject to the Act set out in Sch 1, Parts VI and VII. These changes were made by a number of Statutory Instruments: Additional Public Authorities (SI 2002/2623, SI 2003/1882 and SI 2004/ 938); Removal of Public Authorities (SI 2003/1883); and Excluded Welsh Authorities (SI 2002/2832).

The Information Commissioner carried out a survey of central government departments in 2003 and found that some significant steps towards open government had been taken (Freedom of Information Act 2000 Survey Findings: Central Government Departments, November 2003). The survey of all 17 central government departments, found that:

- All departments have placed their publication schemes on their website
- All departments reported existing and/or planned FOI training to raise awareness and provide guidance for staff
- The majority of departments have established cross departmental groups to manage FOI implementation
- Most departments indicated that board level responsibility had been taken for implementation of the Act.

At the time of writing, some of the regulations had not been finally laid before Parliament. The regulations concerning fees and charging, on extending the time periods for compliance (under s 10(4) and new rules for the Information Tribunal are due to be laid in early autumn). Regulations repealing statutory provisions preventing disclosure (under s 75) are due in the late autumn and regulations dealing with repeat application (under s 12(4)) are not due until 2005.

After the proofs of this book were finalized, Parliament agreed the regulations dealing with fees; the Freedom of Information and Data Protection (Appropriate Limit and Fees) Regulations 2004 No. 3244.

Acknowledgements

The authors would like to thank a number of people for their contributions to the successful completion of this book.

We would particularly like to thank Maurice Frankel and Andrew Ecclestone at the Campaign for Freedom of Information for their phenomenal work on the Act, and for their tireless work in the cause of freedom of information over the years. The scale and importance of their contribution became apparent to all of us while working on the book.

Thanks to Richard Thomas for providing the foreword.

Thanks also to Elizabeth France and her colleague at the Office of the Information Commissioner, Julia Parr, for their comments on the draft of the first edition.

Thanks also to Jim Amos at University College London for his useful comments, and to Susan Healy and Vanora Hereward at the Public Record Office for their kind help with Chapter 11.

The Freedom of Information Unit at the Home Office and subsequently at the Department of Constitutional Affairs, was a source of helpful information on the progress of the legislation.

Thanks to all staff and volunteers at Liberty who assisted in the production of the first edition, from debating the subject with us to checking the manuscript—we owe them a real debt. Particular thanks are due to Bethan Rigby who wrote substantial parts of the first edition.

As always, any mistakes are ours.

John Wadham and Jonathan Griffiths
November 2004

Tables of Statutes

Australia

Canada

European Union

Ireland

New Zealand

Scotland

Sweden

United States of America

Table of Treaties and Conventions

1

FREEDOM OF INFORMATION—AN INTRODUCTION

1.1 INTRODUCTION

This chapter has two aims. First, it seeks to provide a brief explanation of the rationales underlying freedom of information legislation. In considering legislation of constitutional significance, such as the Freedom of Information Act 2000, it is necessary to be aware of its purpose, as this will be very relevant in interpreting its provisions. The second aim of this chapter is to explore briefly the extent to which access to information can be regarded as a legally enforceable human right. If access to information is, in certain circumstances, regarded as falling within the scope of a legally recognised human right, applicants under the Act may benefit from significant advantages in seeking disclosure of information. The validity of such 'rights-based' arguments has been enhanced enormously in the United Kingdom by the passing of the Human Rights Act 1998. The relationship between the Act and the Human Rights Act is also considered at 1.4 below.

1.2 RATIONALES FOR FREEDOM OF INFORMATION LEGISLATION

1.2.1 Improvement of Democratic Processes

Freedom of information legislation is intended to improve democratic processes by giving the public greater access to information about the workings of government. This increased transparency and accountability should raise the quality of public administration. Democracy is the right of all to decide what are matters of general concern. A properly informed electorate and an accountable government are integral parts of an effective and representative democracy. John Stuart Mill aptly put the question of how citizens might be expected to 'check or encourage what they were not permitted to see' (Mill, JS, *Considerations on Representative Government* (New York: Prometheus Books, 1991, p 42)).

Free and fair elections are an essential component of a representative democracy. In the United Kingdom, the public votes in governmental elections every four or five years. Information about what the government has been doing during its term in office is essential if voters are to exercise their rights effectively. Where a government controls the supply of information to the public, there is a danger that it will avoid publishing information which may lead the electorate to vote it out of office. In this regard, Rodney Austin has cited the example of the 1983 election, prior to which the public were not fully informed about the facts behind the government's policy decision to replace the Polaris missile system with Trident missiles. The reason given for this decision was that Polaris was obsolete. However, neither Parliament nor the public was informed that, during the preceding decade, over £1,000 million had been spent updating the Polaris system, expenditure that cast doubt on the necessity for the purchase of Trident. Hence:

... a major national political issue, of crucial significance to the future defence of the United Kingdom, and over which the major parties were deeply divided, was voted upon by the electorate without full knowledge of the facts.

(Austin, R, 'Freedom of Information: the Constitutional Impact', in Jowell, J and Oliver D, *The Changing Constitution* (3rd edn, Oxford: Clarendon Press, 1994), pp 393–438)

A right of access to information helps to ensure that public authorities are held to account and thus limits the risks of complacency and maladministration. This justification for the introduction of freedom of information legislation was succinctly expressed by Lord Lester of Herne Hill in his evidence to the Select Committee on Public Administration, which considered the Draft Freedom of Information Bill in 1999:

The essence of democratic government, I suggest, lies in the ability of the electorate to make choices about who should govern or about which policies and practices they support or reject. Such choices cannot be made unless sufficient information is available ... Ultimately, information about political and government activity belongs to the people whose interests Ministers and civil servants are elected or appointed to serve.

(Select Committee on Public Administration, Third Report 1998–99, Q. 205 HC 570-I)

1.2.2 Avoiding the Need for Whistle-Blowing and Leaks

Where there is no legally enforceable right of access to information, the public must rely upon whistle-blowing or leaks as a means of discovering illegal or controversial actions by public authorities. Such reliance is unsatisfactory. The introduction of freedom of information legislation (alongside enactments such as the Public Interest Disclosure Act 1998) should help to reduce the need for such unauthorised disclosure. The effectiveness of 'whistle-blowing' as a means of promoting public access to information depends on an individual being willing to risk dismissal or even prosecution to expose wrongdoing. These serious consequences make it very difficult to rely upon individuals to inform on wrongful activity by public authorities. For example, no civil servant blew the whistle on the government's role in the Matrix Churchill case. An additional problem in relying upon such means to ensure access to information is that both whistle-blowers and those responsible for 'leaks' of information may be working to their own agendas, for example, to ensure media coverage of a particular angle of an issue. It is therefore much safer to seek to ensure that the public has access to such information through an authorised process of enquiry.

1.2.3 Accuracy of Government-held Information on Individuals

Governments hold vast and growing amounts of information on individuals. This information can affect decisions being made about them or on their behalf. The right of individuals to access such information, and correct it where necessary, is vital in allowing people to ensure that they are treated fairly in their dealings with the state. Government information on individuals can affect, for example, access to benefits, goods and services, and treatment by the police or the security services. The right to correct information regarding our 'personal data', whether publicly held or otherwise, has been available in the UK since the Data Protection Act 1984 came into force. That right, and the right of access to personal data, are currently available under the Data Protection Act 1998 and not under the Freedom of Information Act.

1.2.4 Commercial Use of Information

Information held by the public sector is increasingly in demand for commercial purposes. Data including results of surveys, government statistics, the costs of public services, and information on competitors could all prove very useful to commercial enterprises. In the United States, corporations have been among the main beneficiaries of freedom of information legislation (see Thomas, R, 'Freedom of Information—Initial Perspectives' in Beatson, J, *Constitutional Reform in the United Kingdom: Practice and Principles* (Oxford: Hart, 1998) Ch 17, p 160). The need for governments to have national information policies to ensure that such information is used as effectively as possible has been recognised by several states—see, for example, the role of the National Telecommunications and Information Administration in the US which advises the President and the public on information issues (*National Telecommunications and*

Information Administration, Annual Report 2000, US Department of Commerce, Washington, 2001).

1.3 FREEDOM OF INFORMATION AS A HUMAN RIGHT

Freedom of information is not, in its own right, generally protected under the major international human rights instruments. For example, there is no specific protection for 'the right to know' in either of the two instruments of greatest relevance to the United Kingdom, namely the United Nations International Covenant on Civil and Political Rights (ICCPR) and the European Convention on Human Rights (ECHR). The ICCPR is binding on the United Kingdom, and requires the government to report to the UN Human Rights Committee on the issues covered by the treaty every five years. The ECHR is of yet greater significance in this jurisdiction because it contains a right of individual petition and, as a result of the Human Rights Act 1998 (see 1.4 below), now forms the foundation of domestic human rights protection. The ECHR contains no specific provision granting a right of access to information. However, in certain circumstances, the right of access to information will fall within the scope of other recognised human rights, such as the right to life (Article 2) and the right to respect for private life (Article 8). In such cases, the claims of an applicant under the Act will be strengthened as a result of the Human Rights Act 1998.

Some of the different ways in which the right of access to information can be encompassed within existing articles of the ECHR are set out below. The relationship between the Act and the Human Rights Act 1998 is explored at 1.4.

1.3.1 Article 10—Freedom of Expression

The concepts of freedom of information and freedom of expression are closely entwined. It might thus be reasonably expected that the most promising means of protecting the right of access to information under the ECHR would be through Article 10, which protects freedom of expression. Indeed, the very text of Article 10(1) would seem to support this conclusion:

Everyone has the right to freedom of expression. This right shall include freedom to hold opinions and to receive and impart information and ideas without interference by public authority and regardless of frontiers. This article shall not prevent States from requiring the licensing of broadcasting, television or cinema enterprises.

Nevertheless, the European Court of Human Rights has refused to interpret Article 10 as providing individuals with a right of access to information in circumstances where there is no 'willing speaker' (ie a person or agency who might be willing to impart information to an applicant).

The public's right to receive information has been highly significant in a number of cases in which states have attempted to suppress a willing speaker's expression (see, for example, *Sunday Times v UK* (1979) 2 EHRR 245 and *Observer and Guardian v UK* (1991) 14 EHRR 153). However, in *Leander v Sweden* (1987) 9 EHRR 433, the court rejected the applicant's claim for access to government-held information which he believed had led a potential employer not to offer him a job. The Court ruled that:

Article 10 does not . . . confer on an individual a right of access to a register containing information on his personal position, nor does it embody an obligation on the Government to impart such information to the individual.

Rather it is limited to receiving information 'that others wish or may be willing to impart'. As such, unless the jurisprudence of the European Court develops further, there appears to be no scope for an applicant for information under the Freedom of Information Act 2000 to support their application with arguments based upon Article 10. Other articles of the ECHR, particularly Article 8 may, however, prove more useful in certain circumstances.

1.3.2 Article 8—Respect for Private and Family Life

The European Court of Human Rights has found that Article 8 incorporates an obligation upon public bodies to take positive steps to ensure that individuals' rights to private and family life are secured. While Article 8 does not provide a generalised right of access to all information, this positive obligation has, in certain circumstances, been found to encompass a right of access to information of particular significance to an individual's personal interests. Article 8 of the ECHR is expressed in the following terms:

1. Everyone has the right to respect for his private and family life, his home and his correspondence.

2. There shall be no interference by a public authority with the exercise of this right except such as is in accordance with the law and is necessary in a democratic society in the interests of national security, public safety or the economic well-being of the country, for the prevention of disorder or crime, for the protection of health or morals, or for the protection of the rights and freedoms of others.

The applicant in *Gaskin v United Kingdom* (1989) 12 EHRR 36, had, as a child, been in the care of his local authority. During his time in care, the local authority's social services department had built up an extensive file on him. As an adult, he applied for access to this file in order to obtain information about his childhood that was not otherwise available. Disclosure of the personal data requested would have involved the disclosure of certain third-party data concerning individuals who were involved with the applicant during his time in care. A conflict therefore arose between the applicant's right of access and the third party's right for respect of his or her private life. The local authority refused to disclose their files for this reason. The European Court found that these circumstances did not give rise to a violation of Article 10 (following *Leander v Sweden*, see 1.3.1 above). However, the applicant was successful in his argument that access to his file was an essential part of his right under Article 8 and that the local authority's blanket refusal to open its files failed to pay sufficient respect to this right. Following this case, the United Kingdom enacted legislation providing a right of access to such 'personal data' (now encompassed within the Data Protection Act 1998).

Applications for access to an applicant's own 'personal data' will not generally fall within the scope of the Act, but will instead be provided for under the Data Protection Act 1998 (see Chapter 10 below). However, the Strasbourg jurisprudence indicates that Article 8 may, in certain circumstances, also require states to provide access to information other than 'personal data'. This is perhaps demonstrated most strikingly in *Guerra v Italy* (1998) 26 EHRR 357, in which the Italian public authorities were found to have violated Article 8 in failing to inform local residents of the dangers of a chemical plant based in their neighbourhood.

Within the United Kingdom, applications for access to environmental information are generally to be handled under a specific regime. Nevertheless, the Freedom of Information Act 2000 may, in certain circumstances, be relevant to applications for environmental information (see 8.15 below). In such cases, the fact that arguments in favour of access can be supported by reference to Article 8 may be of significant assistance to the applicant. It also seems likely that applicants will seek to argue that access to other categories of information fall within the scope of the right to private and family life. These could include, for example, information about health risks from medical procedures or information about the circumstances in which relatives have suffered fatal injuries. Finally, it should be noted that the rights of third parties under Article 8 may often prevent the release of information to applicants (see Chapter 10).

1.3.3 Article 2—the Right to Life

The protection of the right to life under the ECHR also includes a positive obligation on public authorities, which may in some circumstances require the provision of information. For instance, the provision of information on health and safety may be regarded as necessary in order to ensure that an individual's life is protected. In a recent case from the European Court of Human Rights (*Oneryildiz v Turkey*, Judgment of 18 June 2002, App no 48939/99) the Court decided that failing to provide details about risks to the lives of local inhabitants from a rubbish tip was a violation of Article 2. The case concerned residents of a shantytown in Istanbul. This shantytown comprised 'a collection of slums haphazardly built on land surrounding a rubbish tip'. An expert report drawn up by the local authorities drew attention to technical problems with the tip and to the lack of measures to prevent a possible explosion of the methane gas being given off the decomposing refuse. Two years later an explosion occurred and the pile of waste engulfed a number of houses and 39 people were killed.

The Court decided that the ordinary citizen could not be expected to know the risks of methane explosions and landslides; the local authorities had that information but failed to provide it. The Court decided that in the context of the right to life the authorities had a positive duty to inform the residents of the dangers they faced. However, in circumstances where the threat to life arises from the activities of another private individual, the duty on public authorities may not be a high one (see *Osman v UK* (2000) 29 EHRR 245). Article 2 also imposes a requirement upon states to establish systems ensuring effective investigations into deaths arising in certain circumstances (see *McCann v UK* (1995) 21 EHRR 97). This obligation may require the disclosure of information and documents.

1.3.4 Article 5 (the Right to Liberty and Security) and Article 6 (the Right to a Fair Trial)

In addition to Articles 8 and 2, which seem likely to provide potential arguments for certain applicants under the Act, the right of access to information can also, in certain circumstances, fall within the scope of other articles of the ECHR. Under Article 5 ('the right to liberty and security') the right of access to a court to test the lawfulness of detention under Article 5(4) includes the right to access to documents and information (see *Weeks v UK* (1987) 10 EHRR 293). There is also, of course, a duty when placing a person under arrest to give information about the reasons for the arrest (see Article 5(2)).

Under Article 6 ('the right to a fair trial'), defendants in criminal cases also have the right to disclosure of information relevant to their trial (see Article 6(3)(a) and *Edwards v UK* (1992) 15 EHRR 417). While the Freedom of Information Act 2000 is drafted to ensure that access to information in the course of legal proceedings is handled under existing procedures rather than under the Act, it is important to remember that the exemption for information concerning investigations and proceedings (s 30) is a qualified exemption. It will, therefore, only be effective in preventing access to such information where the public interest favours non-disclosure (see 8.8). In the event of existing procedures not adequately securing the rights protected by Articles 5 or 6, an applicant may be able to argue that the public interest must be interpreted in favour of disclosure.

1.4 THE HUMAN RIGHTS ACT 1998

As a result of the Human Rights Act 1998 ('HRA 1998'), arguments based upon the requirements of the ECHR can much more readily be made in our courts.

The HRA 1998 will provide the means by which, in considering issues arising under the Freedom of Information Act 2000, the Information Commissioner, the Information Tribunal and the courts will be required to take account of the protection offered to those seeking access to information under the Convention. An exploration of some of the issues arising out of the relationship between the HRA 1998 and the Act is provided below at 1.4.2. First, however, it is necessary to set out the effects of the HRA 1998.

1.4.1 The Impact of the Human Rights Act 1998

The Human Rights Act 1998 came into force on 2 October 2000 and incorporates the European Convention on Human Rights into domestic law. Under the HRA 1998, it is unlawful for any public authority, such as the police, government departments or local councils to act incompatibly with the rights in the Convention (s 6, HRA 1998). The HRA 1998 does not directly impose duties on private individuals or companies unless they are performing public functions. For instance, a private security company will be performing a public function when looking after prisoners for the police or the courts, but not when employed to guard private premises. All courts and tribunals are public authorities for the purposes of the HRA 1998 and are therefore under a duty to respect Convention rights.

Any person who is a victim of a violation by a public authority under s 6 can use the Convention in legal proceedings (s 7(1), HRA 1998). A victim includes anyone directly affected by the actions (or omissions) of any public body. Where there has been a breach of the Convention (or even where one is about to occur), the victim of that breach is entitled to take proceedings in court. They may be able to obtain an injunction to stop the violation, force the public authority to take action or obtain damages and compensation. The HRA 1998 can also be used if a person is subject to proceedings taken against them by a public authority and, for instance, in tribunal proceedings, such as unfair dismissal proceedings.

Under the HRA 1998, legislation and the common law must be interpreted compatibly with the ECHR so far as it is possible to do so (ss 3 and 6, HRA 1998). Usually, secondary legislation (eg, statutory instruments) will be invalid to the extent that it does not comply with Convention rights. If primary legislation cannot be read in such a way as to comply with the Convention, certain higher courts are entitled to make a 'declaration of incompatibility', which allows the government to amend that law speedily to bring it into compliance (s 4).

1.4.2 The Relationship Between the Act and the Human Rights Act 1998

All the bodies subject to the Freedom of Information Act 2000 (see 4.5) will be 'public authorities' for the purposes of the Human Rights Act 1998 and are thus required to act compatibly with the ECHR. Even bodies subject to the Freedom of Information Act which have mixed private/public functions (see 4.5.1 and

4.5.2) will be subject to the HRA 1998 in respect of their public functions. The bodies responsible for enforcing the Freedom of Information Act, including the Information Commissioner, the Information Tribunal and the courts, are also public authorities for the purpose of the HRA 1998. Public authorities which are not subject to the Act (either because they are not listed in Sch 1 to the Act or because they are excluded from the Act's scope—the security and intelligence services, for example) will still be public authorities for the purposes of the HRA 1998.

In many cases, applications for access to information under the Act will not give rise to issues under the ECHR. However, in a limited number of situations, the rights contained in the ECHR may be relevant. Where the ECHR requires access to information to be granted (perhaps because, under Article 2, it is necessary for a thorough investigation of a suspicious death), it will be unlawful for a public authority to refuse to disclose that information. If a public authority were to refuse access to such information, the Information Commissioner would be obliged to interpret the Act to secure compliance with the right in question. Where a qualified exemption is at issue, this duty could be satisfied by interpreting the public interest as conclusively in favour of disclosure in such circumstances. Where access to information is sought from a public authority which is not subject to the Act, an applicant would not be able to appeal to the Information Commissioner, but would instead be obliged to bring a claim based upon the HRA 1998, s 6 in the ordinary courts.

In addition to situations in which the ECHR has a direct impact upon access to information, it is also important to note that Article 6 of the ECHR provides significant procedural protection for an individual seeking 'determination of his civil rights and obligations'. This protection includes a right to, for example, an independent, judicial determination of those rights. If the rights of an applicant under the Act could be regarded as a 'civil right' for the purposes of the Act, certain features of the Act may not satisfy the requirements of Article 6. For example, it could perhaps be argued that the ministerial veto over disclosure contained in s 53 of the Act would not, in those circumstances, comply with Article 6 and would therefore be subject to a declaration of incompatibility under the HRA 1998. The difficulty with this argument is, however, that the European Court of Human Rights is likely to regard the right of access to information under the Act as falling outside Article 6 because it is a 'pure' public law right, rather than a civil right (see Wadham J, Mountfield, H and Edmundson, A, *Blackstone's Guide to the Human Rights Act 1998* (3rd edn, Oxford: Blackstone/OUP, 2003) at 8.6.4; cf also s 56 of the Act). However, it seems strange that such an important right as freedom of information is not to be regarded as sufficiently important to attract the safeguards of Article 6.

2

FREEDOM OF INFORMATION IN EUROPE AND OTHER JURISDICTIONS

In the common-law world, the United States was the first country to introduce freedom of information legislation, in 1966. Other common-law states followed suit, including New Zealand and Australia in 1982, and Canada in 1983. Despite differences in content and implementation, these statutes bear major structural similarities. Freedom of information legislation is also common within Europe—the first country to enact such laws was Sweden in 1766, with the Freedom of the Press Act. Other European states with freedom of information legislation include Finland, Norway and Denmark (1970), France (1978), Greece (1986), Italy (1990), the Netherlands and Belgium (1991), Spain (1992), and Portugal (1993). The Council of Europe and the European Union have also recently taken steps to provide a greater degree of public access to documents.

In this chapter, the freedom of information regimes in Europe, the United States, Canada, New Zealand, Australia, Ireland and Scotland are briefly surveyed. Knowledge of these enactments is likely to be of most use to those using the Freedom of Information Act 2000 because of the significant similarities which they have with Act. While in many instances the wording of the Act differs in detail from the legislation discussed below, it is very likely that previous interpretation of these statutes will be cited in disputes concerning comparable provisions of the Act. It is likely that the principles applied in balancing the public interests in disclosure and non-disclosure in specific contexts in other jurisdictions (for example, in the case of trade secrets or economic information) will make valuable reference points for our Information Commissioner and courts.

2.1 THE COUNCIL OF EUROPE

The Council of Europe is the continent's oldest political organisation, founded in 1949. It comprises 45 countries, including 21 countries from Central and Eastern Europe. It is distinct from the 25-nation European Union, but no country has ever joined the Union without first belonging to the Council of Europe.

The Council was set up to defend human rights, parliamentary democracy and the rule of law; to develop continent-wide agreements to standardise member countries' social and legal practices; and to promote awareness of a European identity based on shared values and cutting across different cultures. Its most famous creations are the European Convention on Human Rights and the European Court of Human Rights.

The Council of Europe introduced a number of texts as early as 1970 setting out the importance of access to information from public bodies. Recently the Committee of Ministers adopted Recommendation Rec(2002)2 (http://cm.coe. int/stat/E/Public/2002/adopted_texts/recommendations/2002r2.htm) which sets out more formally the principles and procedures for access to information:

Considering the importance in a pluralistic, democratic society of transparency of public administration and of the ready availability of information on issues of public interest;

Considering that wide access to official documents, on a basis of equality and in accordance with clear rules:

- allows the public to have an adequate view of, and to form a critical opinion on, the state of the society in which they live and on the authorities that govern them, whilst encouraging informed participation by the public in matters of common interest;
- fosters the efficiency and effectiveness of administrations and helps maintain their integrity by avoiding the risk of corruption;
- contributes to affirming the legitimacy of administrations as public services and to strengthening the public's confidence in public authorities;

It recommends that: 'the utmost endeavour should be made by member states to ensure availability to the public of information contained in official documents, subject to the protection of other rights and legitimate interests'.

Member states should guarantee the right of everyone to have access, on request, to official documents held by public authorities. This principle should apply without discrimination on any ground, including that of national origin.

The recommendations also set out a list of possible exemptions but suggest that these exemptions should not prevent disclosure if there is 'an overriding interest'.

The recommendations state that applicants for documents should not have to give reasons, formalities should be kept to a minimum and applications should be dealt with promptly. The public authority should take a positive role in referring the applicant elsewhere if the document is held by another authority and should help the applicant to identify the requested document. Reasons should be given for refusing requests. Access to the documents should be by inspection or by providing a copy, whichever the applicant prefers—charges should not apply for inspecting documents and if charges are imposed for copying they should be reasonable and never more than the actual costs incurred by the authority. Applicants should have access to an independent and impartial body to deal with appeals.

These recommendations do not have any particular force but, having been drafted and agreed by such a prestigious body, they can provide a helpful principled basis for any system of freedom of information. They are likely to be used by the Council of Europe to measure any of its members' compliance with the principles. They could also be prayed in aid in relation to disputes over access to EU documents themselves (see below).

It should be noted however that it is the Council of Europe which drafts the protocols to the European Convention on Human Rights which, once signed and ratified, can add new substantive Convention rights which can subsequently be enforced in the European Court of Human Rights. However there do not appear to be any proposals to include the principles in these recommendations in such a protocol at present.

Access to the Council of Europe's own documents is best achieved via their web site (www.coe.int) although the Council does not appear to have a code for access to its own documents.

2.2 THE EUROPEAN UNION

There are special rules for obtaining access to documents from the institutions of the European Union. The organisation Statewatch has pioneered openness in the EU and more information on procedures is available from its website (www.statewatch.org/foi.htm).

Much material from EU institutions is on the websites of the Parliament (www.europarl.eu.int/home) and the Commission (http://europa.eu.int/comm/secretariat_general/sgc/acc_doc/index_en.htm).

2.2.1 The Rules of Access

The rules of access for material from the EU are set out in Regulation (EC) No 1049/2001 of 30 May 2001. Each institution of the EU has also established detailed rules on these access provisions, see The Council of the European Union, 22 November 2001, 13465/01; Bureau Decision on Public Access to European Union Parliament Documents, 29 December 2001, 2001/C 374/01 and Detailed Rules for the Application of Regulation (EC) No 1049/2001 Regarding Public Access to European Parliament, Council and Commission Documents, 31 May 2001 (all these documents are available via the Statewatch website).

The right of access applies to any citizen of the Union, anyone resident in a member state or any legal person having its registered office in a member state (Article 2(1)).

Each institution must provide a register of documents and access to this must be in an electronic form (Article 11). The institutions must also, so far as possible, make documents available in an electronic form without requiring access requests. A number of specific documents must also be published in the Official Journal (Article 13).

2.2.2 Exemptions

Access to documents will be refused if the disclosure will undermine the protection of: public security; defence and military matters; international relations; the financial, monetary or economic policy of the Community or a member state; or the privacy or integrity of the individual. Where disclosure will undermine commercial interests; court proceedings or legal advice; or the purpose of inspections, investigations and audit, a request will be refused unless there is an overriding public interest in disclosure. Access to draft and 'internal' documents will be refused if '[d]isclosure would seriously undermine the institution's decision-making process, unless there is an overriding public interest in disclosure' (Article 4(3)).

Material from member states will not be disclosed without prior consent. There are special rules for handling 'sensitive' documents, that is those documents classified as Top Secret, Secret or Confidential.

Most of the exemptions only apply during the period that the protection is justified and only for a maximum of 30 years (Article 4(7)). Exemptions relating to privacy, commercial interests and 'sensitive' documents can apply for longer than 30 years.

2.2.3 Applications

Applications have to be in writing but no reasons need to be given. There is a duty on the institution to assist the applicant in identifying the document (Article 6). Decisions on requests for documents are to be made within 15 working days. In the event of a refusal to provide a document the applicant can ask the institution to review its decision and within 15 working days either the material must be supplied or a written refusal giving reasons for the refusal must be provided (Article 8). This process of 'confirmatory applications' also requires the institution refusing documents to set out the applicant's right to initiate court proceedings or to make a complaint to the the EU's Ombudsman.

Note that these rules provide access to documents not to information, although the definition of 'document' includes content stored in electronic form or as a sound, visual or audiovisual recording (Article 3(a)).

2.2.4 Charges

Consultation of documents or obtaining copies of fewer than 20 A4 pages is free. Copies of longer documents can be the subject of a charge which must not be greater than the real cost of producing and sending the copies (Article 10).

2.2.5 Enforcement

Each institution is required to publish an annual report setting out the number of cases where access was refused, the reasons for such refusals and the number of documents not recorded in the register (Article 17). The European Ombudsman has published 'The European Code for Good Administrative Behaviour' which sets out some general principles for access to documents at Articles 22–24 (www.euro-ombudsman.eu.int/guide/en/default.htm).

The European Ombudsman can enforce the access to documents rights set out in the rules. The procedure for taking advantage of the Ombudsman service is set out at www.euro-ombudsman.eu.int/media/en/default. The European Ombudsman Statute sets out the legal basis for the Ombudsman's activities (www.euro-ombudsman.eu.int/lbasis/en/statute.htm). A complaint must be made within two years of the date on which the facts on which it is based became known to the complainant. The complainant must have first attempted to resolve the matter with the institution itself (Article 2(4)).

How to contact the European Ombudsman:

- By mail
  The European Ombudsman
  1 Avenue du Président Robert Schuman
  B.P. 403
  F-67001 Strasbourg Cedex
- By telephone
  +33 (0) 3 88 17 23 13
- By fax
  +33 (0) 3 88 17 90 62
- By e-mail
  euro-ombudsman@europarl.eu.int
- Website
  www.euro-ombudsman.eu.int

The Ombudsman procedure is considerably cheaper and faster than making an application to the European Court of Justice, Court of First Instance.

Reports setting out the effectiveness of procedures, including listing cases pending or resolved by the Court of First Instance and the Ombudsman are produced on access to documents in the EU institutions every year (see Statewatch website for links).

2.2.6 The Charter of Rights

The Charter of Rights ([2000] OJ C364/01) was promulgated at the Nice EU Council in December 2000. The question of its legal status was not resolved at that time. It was assumed that the Charter set out rather than expanded the pre-existing rights of EU citizens and that it might not be given any particular status. Keith Vaz, Minister for Europe at the time, stated that it would be 'no more legally binding than the Beano or the Sun'. The current position is that the Charter is designed to be the second part of the new EU constitution although the constitution and the Charter's place in it remain highly controversial.

Whatever its status it does include some provision on access to information and documents. Article 27 provides for workers to be provided with information from employers. This provision is taken from the revised European Social Charter (Article 21). More importantly, Article 42 states:

Any citizen of the Union, and any natural or legal person residing or having its registered office in a Member State, has right of access to European Parliament, Council and Commission documents.

This replicates Article 255 of the EC Treaty and Regulation (EC) 1049/2001 (see above). In such circumstances it is difficult to see how even an enforceable Charter would affect the right of access to documents as it does not provide any general right of access to documents from public bodies and instead restricts the right to obtaining material from EU institutions.

2.3 UNITED STATES

The US Freedom of Information Act ('USFOIA'), as passed in 1966 and subsequently amended, gives the public the right of access to records held by government agencies to which the Act applies (5 USC § 552 (1994 & Supp IV 1998)). These are all agencies and departments in the executive branch of federal government, including cabinet departments, military departments, government corporations, government controlled corporations, independent regulatory agencies and other establishments. By contrast with the Act, USFOIA also applies to the CIA and the FBI (with exemptions for operational files). It does not, however, give access to records held by Congress, the courts, or state or local governments. Access to state and local government records is available under a state's own public access laws.

Federal government documents can be accessed by anyone, not only United States citizens, and an applicant does not need to provide reasons for making a request. The duties of agencies covered by the Act include publishing information on the form, function and activities of the agency in the Federal Register. Details of the procedures for requesting information, and the fees involved in doing so, must also be listed. Requests must be acknowledged within 20 days, and a response should take 20 to 30 days. Instructions on how to make an application are published in the Citizen's Guide (*A Citizen's Guide on Using the Freedom of Information Act and the Privacy Act of 1974*, Washington, DC, United States Congress, 11 March 1999, H Rep 106–50) and more detailed information is printed annually in the Federal Register.

Areas exempt from the USFOIA under s 6(F)(b) are:

(a) material authorised to be kept secret by Presidential executive order due to national security or defence considerations;

(b) records related solely to agency personnel practices;

(c) records exempted from disclosure by statute;

(d) trade secrets or secret commercial information;

(e) inter-agency or intra-agency memorandums or letters which would not be available by law to a party other than an agency in litigation with the agency;

(f) personnel or medical records 'and similar files' if their disclosure would cause 'a clearly unwarranted invasion of privacy';

(g) information on some aspects of law enforcement;

(h) information on the regulation of financial institutions; and

(i) geological and geophysical information and data, including maps, concerning wells.

These exemptions are discretionary—the agency is not obliged to invoke them.

Unsuccessful applicants must be informed of the right to appeal through internal review. If the right to appeal is denied, the case can be heard in federal court, where the burden of proof is on the agency to justify the exemption. Following the decision in *Vaughn v Rosen* (484 F 2d 820), a practice of negotiation between the government and the applicant has developed. There is no Ombudsman or Commissioner responsible for overseeing the Act. The Privacy Act of 1974 (5 USC 552a) provides that, in general, a citizen may learn how records are collected, maintained, used, and disseminated by the Federal

Government. An individual may have access to information held by an agency about himself.

Freedom of information in the United States has in many instances been found to fall short of the original intentions of the legislation, despite reforms and the Clinton administration's apparent commitment to improving the efficacy of the USFOIA. This commitment included a memorandum sent from the President to all department and agency heads in 1993 encouraging full compliance with the Act, and the enactment of the Electronic Freedom of Information Act amendments of 1996 ('EFOIA').

The EFOIA was designed to improve the existing freedom of information law and specifically to give the public more information about the operation of government, while reducing delays in accessing information. The Act increased access to electronic records, and promoted on-line reading rooms. However, witnesses testifying before the Congress Subcommittee on Government Management, Information and Technology hearing on 'Agency Response to the EFOIA' in June 2000 reported problems not only with the implementation of the EFOIA, but with the USFOIA in general. OMB Watch, a pressure group, reported that as of November 1999 no agency had complied fully with the terms of EFOIA, and that 'overall, agency compliance with the EFOIA amendments continues to be overwhelmingly inadequate' (Patrice McDermott's evidence to the Congress Subcommittee, which can be found at www.house.gov/reform/gmit/index.htm). The Congress Subcommittee also heard evidence of severe delays in processing requests and that a broad interpretation of privacy exemptions by agencies meant that large amounts of information were withheld on the grounds that an identifiable individual was named. Both of these factors have made it difficult for reporters in particular to use the USFOIA effectively. Nevertheless, the benefits of the Act have been felt, both in specific cases and as a general support in ensuring the accountability of government. As Jane Kirkley of the Reporters' Committee for Freedom of the Press stated:

Even when journalists don't use the FOIA, it works for them. This law creates a legal presumption of openness and accountability. Given how much of a struggle it is to get access with the law in place, I can't imagine what it would be like if we didn't have that kind of legislative mandate.

> (McMasters, P, *FOIA, it's always there*, Quill 1996, Society of Professional Journalists, Indianapolis, US)

2.4 CANADA

Canada, which adopted federal freedom of information laws in 1983 under the Access to Information Act 1983, has a Westminster-style government. All provinces except Prince Edward Island have freedom of information laws, and most have commissioners to monitor and enforce these laws (see, for example,

Newfoundland—Freedom of Information Act 1981; New Brunswick—Right to Information Act 1978). FOI legislation was proposed in Prince Edward Island during the 2000–01 parliamentary session. The Access to Information Act 1983 (AIA) applies to all government departments and most agencies, including the Security Intelligence Service and the police. The right of access has, since 1989, been granted to any individual or corporation present in Canada. The government must answer all requests made under the AIA, whatever the motivation behind the request. Agencies covered by the AIA must publish information on their role, structure and policy-making practices. Fee schedules for access requests are also published. Applicants should be advised of the outcome of their request within 30 days.

Some exemptions under the AIA are mandatory and some are discretionary (AIA, ss 13–24). Mandatory exemptions, where government institutions may not disclose the information, cover confidential information from foreign governments, personal information, some third-party commercial information, and information whose disclosure is prohibited by another statute. Cabinet secrets are excluded from the AIA for 20 years, except discussion papers relating to decisions which have either been made public or were made more than four years previously. Discretionary exemptions cover information which 'could reasonably be expected to be injurious to' federal provincial affairs, foreign relations, internal and external security, the safety of individuals, the state's economic interests, law enforcement, internal government decision-making and solicitor-client privilege. Discretionary exemptions are subject to harm tests. The results of environmental tests may not be exempted. Government decisions on access may be reviewed by the Information Commissioner, a parliamentary ombudsman, with unsuccessful applicants having final recourse to a federal court, which has the power to make binding orders.

Under the Privacy Act of 1983, provision has been made for a Privacy Commissioner. The Privacy Act allows individuals access to their own records, if held by a government department covered by the Act. At the provincial level in Canada, freedom of information and privacy measures have tended to be combined in single enactments.

There have been significant benefits in having a statutory freedom of information regime in Canada. Information obtained under the AIA has revealed government audits highlighting problems at Air Canada, the operator of a plane which crashed in 1988 killing 24 people. Another release of documents under the AIA revealed a report suggesting that a government subsidy to farmers of Canadian $1 billion might have been unnecessary as many recipients were to receive separate payments from the Western Grain Stabilization Program (*The Access to Information Act: 10 Years On, 1994, The Information Commissioner of Canada* (Office of the Information Commissioner, Canada, 1994), pp 17–18). However, since the report of the Justice Committee on the workings of the Act in 1986, there have been continuing calls for reform, and in August 2000 a task force was created to review the Act. A research project run by the

School of Policy Studies at Queen's University highlighted the threat to the efficacy of Canada's freedom of information laws posed by public sector restructuring; particularly the effects of cutbacks within the public service which had led to serious delays in processing information requests, and the consequences of governmental attempts to find new revenues by selling information or raising AIA request fees (Roberts, A, *Limited Access: Assessing the Health of Canada's Freedom of Information Laws* (Queen's University, Canada 1998), p 2). This report concluded that 'evidence of increasing non-compliance suggests that a new approach to enforcement of the Act is needed'.

The Information Commissioner has also criticised the AIA. In his annual report for 1998–99, he found that:

... up to now, the Treasury Board [the President of which is responsible for the AIA] has studiously avoided its responsibilities to monitor the health of the access system, support and nurture access co-ordinators and keep under review the state of records management in government.

(Press Release, Office of the Information Commissioner of Canada, 21 July 1999)

The Information Commissioner has also frequently cited insufficient resources and obstruction by public officials as key reasons for delays in the freedom of information system (Information Commissioner's keynote address to the Conference on Access to Information Reform). The previous incumbent of the office had similarly expressed a wish to see a new attitude to freedom of information in Canada: 'the key to opening up government is . . . somehow changing the encrusted, timorous old attitudes which see openness as a threat, not an opportunity for both citizens and governments' (Information Commissioner of Canada, *Annual Report 1994–95* (Ottawa, 1995), p 4). In addition to seeking to solve these problems, calls for reform have focused on the need to abolish the Cabinet confidence exclusion, possibly replacing it with an exemption for records which would disclose Cabinet deliberations, and on the need to establish criteria for the discretionary exemptions covering policy advice to ministers or institutions (Information Commissioner's keynote address to the Conference on Access to Information Reform 1 May 2000: see www.infoweb.magi.com/~accessca).

The importance of government willingness to act within the spirit as well as the letter of freedom of information legislation, and so to change the culture of governance from one of secrecy to one of openness, is clear from the Canadian experience of freedom of information legislation.

2.5 AUSTRALIA

The Australian federal Freedom of Information Act ('AuFOIA') was enacted in 1982. Freedom of Information legislation on a similar model followed in all Australian states (New South Wales—Freedom of Information Act 1989;

Queensland—Freedom of Information Act 1992; South Australia—Freedom of Information Act 1991; Victoria—Freedom of Information Act 1982; Western Australia—Freedom of Information Act 1992; Northern Territory—Northern Territory Information Act 2002). The AuFOIA covers central government and many agencies, including the police. Certain agencies, however, are entirely excluded from the provisions of the Act—for example, the security and intelligence agencies ASIS and ASIO. This is an approach which has also been adopted under the Freedom of Information Act in the United Kingdom. Under the AuFOIA, access is available to any person, and fees are charged. An agency or minister must notify an applicant within 14 days that their request has been received, and take all reasonable steps to inform the applicant of the outcome of their request within 30 days. This may be extended by another 30 days if the agency or minister needs to consult a third party before disclosing the information (AuFOIA, s 15).

Exemptions under the AuFOIA, Part IV, apply to:

(a) information affecting national security, defence or international relations;

(b) information affecting relations with Australian States, including the Australian Capital Territory and the Northern Territory;

(c) Cabinet documents;

(d) Executive Council documents;

(e) internal working documents;

(f) information affecting the enforcement of law and the protection of public safety;

(g) documents to which secrecy provisions of enactments apply;

(h) information affecting financial or property interests of the Commonwealth;

(i) documents concerning certain operations of agencies;

(j) documents concerning personal privacy;

(k) documents subject to legal professional privilege;

(l) information relating to business affairs, etc.;

(m) documents relating to research;

(n) documents affecting the national economy;

(o) documents containing material obtained in confidence;

(p) documents the disclosure of which would be a contempt of Parliament or a contempt of court;

(q) certain documents arising out of companies and securities legislation;

(r) electoral rolls and related documents.

All exemptions are discretionary, but some are class-based and without harm tests—for example, the exemption relating to Cabinet documents. Five exemptions are subject to a public interest override, including the exemptions covering the national economy, internal working documents and departmental practices.

Some of these exemptions are potentially very broad and non-specific in scope. Ministers are able to issue certificates exempting information, a power which has frequently been exercised since 1982.

Following a refusal to supply information, an applicant has a variety of rights of appeal under the AuFOIA. He or she may request an internal review from the agency or minister in question, or an external review by the Administrative Appeals Tribunal, which can overrule the refusal if the information does not include exempt matter. The Federal Court may hear subsequent appeals on points of law.

The Privacy Act 1988 gives citizens rights regarding the use of personal information by Commonwealth and Australian Capital Territories agencies, credit providers and credit reporting agencies, any person who holds and uses tax file numbers, and any organisation which requests historic minor conviction information about an individual. Where there has been an interference with the privacy of an individual, in breach of the terms of the Privacy Act, the Privacy Commissioner can ultimately decide to dismiss or substantiate a complaint against a respondent (Privacy Act 1988, s 27).

The AuFOIA does not provide for the creation of an Information Commissioner. Instead, monitoring responsibilities under the Act were added to the existing role of the Ombudsman. Complaints about the lack of money and personnel granted to the Ombudsman have featured heavily in his annual reports on the legislation, as has criticism of government attitudes to the AuFOIA. In 1995, he reported that 'many government agencies still do not operate within the legal framework and certainly not the spirit of the Freedom of Information Act' (Commonwealth Ombudsman, *Annual Report 1994–95* (AGPS, 1995) p 35). The creation of an Information Commissioner with binding powers under the UK Act should, it is hoped, prove a more effective means of securing compliance with the new regime.

The creation of a statutory office of Freedom of Information Commissioner was one of the key recommendations of the 1995 joint Australian Law Reform Commission and Administrative Review Council report. Many submissions to the review were highly critical of the Freedom of Information regime—one describing the experience of freedom of information in Australia as one of 'frustration, delay and haphazard provision of information' (Snell, R, IP Submission 31 to Australian Law Reform Commission and Administrative Review Council, cited in Snell, R, 'Administrative Compliance and Freedom of Information in Three Jurisdictions: Australia, Canada and New Zealand', paper to conference 'FOI—One Year On' Dublin, 23 April 1999, see www.ucc.ie/ucc/depts/law/foi/conference/snellframes99.html). The report also made other recommendations for reform and, in doing so, provides a useful guide to the problems faced by a freedom of information regime after more than a decade in operation. Some of these recommendations were included in the Freedom of Information Amendment (Open Government) Bill 2000 (Bill 160, referred to the Senate Legal and Constitutional Legislation Committee on 11 October 2000;

report due). Among the most important recommendations were: the proposal to create a statutory office of Freedom of Information Commissioner, the subjecting of information communicated in confidence by an international organisation to a public interest test, the exemption of Cabinet documents for 20 years and the extension of the AuFOIA to further agencies (although not the security services). Nevertheless, the report recognised the AuFOIA as having:

... had a marked impact on the way agencies make decisions and the way they record information. Along with other elements of the administrative law package . . . the Freedom of Information Act has focused decision-makers' minds on the need to base decisions on relevant factors and to record the decision-making process . . . The knowledge that decisions and processes are open to scrutiny, including under the Freedom of Information Act, imposes a constant discipline on the public sector.

(Australian Law Reform Commission Report 77, *Open government: a review of the federal Freedom of Information Act 1982*, Commonwealth of Australia, 1995, s 2.8)

The Senate held an inquiry in April 2001 into a private member's amendment Bill designed to implement the changes but to date there have not been any changes (The Freedominfo.org Global Survey, May 2004).

2.6 NEW ZEALAND

The Official Information Act (OIA) was adopted by New Zealand in 1982. Interpretation of the OIA is based on s 5, which states that the Act should be interpreted 'in accordance with the purposes of the Act and the principle that the information shall be made available unless there is a good reason for withholding it'. The Act applies to central government, agencies, the police, the Security Intelligence Service, and most public corporations. It gives rights of access to government information, including documents and unrecorded information (for the position regarding unrecorded information under the Act, see 4.4.1).

All exemptions under the OIA are discretionary, and are subject to harm tests. The exemptions cover information the disclosure of which would be likely:

(a) to prejudice security or defence of New Zealand or the state's international relations;

(b) to prejudice the entrusting of confidential information to the Government of New Zealand on a basis of confidence by another government or international organisation;

(c) to prejudice the maintenance of the law;

(d) to endanger the safety of any person; or

(e) to damage seriously the economy of New Zealand by disclosing prematurely decisions to change or continue Government economic or financial policies.

A public interest test applies to a further 11 exemptions where disclosure may be prevented to (OIA, ss 6–9):

(a) protect personal privacy;

(b) protect trade secrets;

(c) protect information which is subject to an obligation of confidence or which any person has been or could be compelled to provide under the authority of any enactment, where the making available of the information would be likely to prejudice the supply of similar information, or information from the same source, and it is in the public interest that such information should continue to be supplied;

(d) avoid prejudice to measures protecting the health or safety of the public;

(e) avoid prejudice to the substantial economic interests of New Zealand;

(f) avoid prejudice to measures that prevent or mitigate material loss to members of the public;

(g) maintain the constitutional conventions protecting communications by or with the Sovereign or her representative, collective and individual ministerial responsibility, the political neutrality of officials, the confidentiality of advice tendered by Ministers of the Crown and officials;

(h) maintain the effective conduct of public affairs through the free and frank expression of opinions by or between Ministers or Officers and employees of any Department;

(i) maintain legal professional privilege;

(j) enable a Minister of the Crown or any Department or organisation holding the information to carry out, without prejudice or disadvantage, commercial activities or industrial negotiations; or

(k) prevent the disclosure or use of official information for improper advantage.

The OIA is enforced by an Ombudsman, who acts as an advocate for freedom of information. An appeal against a refusal to disclose information may be made to the Ombudsman and the courts. There is a collective ministerial veto on the Ombudsman's order of disclosure.

The Privacy Act 1993 features 12 information privacy principles regarding the collection, holding, use and disclosure of personal information. The Act gives individuals the right to access and request amendment of their personal information. The Act is enforced by a Privacy Commissioner, and applies to both private and public sectors.

The Official Information Act 1982 was reviewed in 1997 by the New Zealand Law Commission. The Commission found that the major problems with the OIA and its operation were the burden caused by large and broadly defined requests, tardiness in responding to requests, resistance by agencies outside the core state sector, and the absence of a coordinated approach to supervision, compliance, policy advice and education regarding the OIA. However, the Report concluded that '. . . neither these problems, nor the terms of reference, bring into question the underlying principles of the Act'. (New Zealand Law Commission

Report 40, *Review of the Official Information Act 1982*, (1997), p xi). Among the recommendations contained in the Report were measures designed to encourage dialogue between an agency and a requester and to reduce the number of requests refused on the grounds that the request would entail 'substantial collation or research'. It was also recommended that the ministerial veto and charging structure should remain, but that the Ministry of Justice should be given responsibility for ensuring 'a more co-ordinated and systematic approach to the functions of oversight, compliance, policy review, and education in relation to the Act'. It was further recommended that adequate resources should be provided to enable the Ombudsman and other institutions to complete their duties under the OIA effectively. The Commission also felt that the time limit on requests should be reduced from 20 to 15 days. The Commission's proposals have not yet been implemented (The Freedominfo.org Global Survey, May 2004).

In the Annual Report of the Ombudsman for 1999, the issue of non-compliance featured heavily:

> There appears to have been an increase in the number of cases where some Ministers and public sector agencies have failed to comply with the time requirements laid down in the legislation. Although the legislation provides no sanction for failure to comply with the time requirements, agencies should strive to ensure that they comply with the spirit and intent of the legislation by responding in a timely manner. Disregarding the spirit and intent of the legislation serves to undermine the integrity of public sector processes and public confidence in those processes.
>
> (*Annual Report of the Office of the Ombudsman, 1998–99*,
> Office of the Ombudsman, 2000, overview)

Overall, however, the experience of freedom of information seems to have been positive. It would appear that the quality of documents and information produced by public officials has also markedly improved with the advent of the OIA (see Belgrave, J, 'The Official Information Act and the Policy Process', in *The Official Information Act* (Auckland: Legal Research Foundation, 1997). The Commission's 1997 review found that: 'the widespread acceptance of the principle of open government in New Zealand is largely attributable to the Official Information Act' (New Zealand Law Commission Report 40, *Review of the Official Information Act 1982* (1997) Executive summary, p 2). It has become usual in New Zealand to disclose policy advice received by ministers once decisions have been made. The New Zealand Law Commission found that:

> Since 1982, there has been a fundamental change in attitudes to the availability of official information. Ministers and officials have learned to live with greater openness. The assumption that policy advice will eventually be released under the Act has in our view improved the quality and transparency of that advice.
>
> (New Zealand Law Commission Report 40, *Review of the Official Information Act 1982* (1997), p 5, para E18)

The Ombudsman has also highlighted the evolution of the OIA and its effect on government:

... until quite recently, the Act was mainly used to reinforce the purpose of accountability rather than of participation. Recent evidence suggests however that the main focus is slowly changing, towards recognising the benefit which follows from influencing the formulation of law and policies. In other words if laws and policies are better formulated from the beginning there will be less need to hold accountable those who administer the laws and policies.

(Sir Brian Elwood CBE—Chief Ombudsman of New Zealand, *The New Zealand Model—The Official Information Act 1982*, paper presented in August 1999 at the conference 'Freedom of Information and the Right to Know': see www.comslaw.org.au)

2.7 IRELAND

The Irish Freedom of Information Act ('IFOIA') was passed in 1997, and took effect in April 1998. It gives the public the right to access records held by government and public bodies, to correct inaccurate information held by such bodies, and to access reasons for decisions made by these bodies. It applies to central and local government, the health service, and other organisations funded by government money or loans. However, it does not cover some key bodies including the police and schools. Public bodies must also publish details of their internal practices, and produce information on how requests for information can be made. Applications for information must be acknowledged within four weeks, and fees may apply.

Under the IFOIA, Part III, ss 19–32, exempt records include those dealing with the following:

(a) meetings of the Government;

(b) deliberations of public bodies;

(c) functions and negotiations of public bodies;

(d) parliamentary and court matters;

(e) law enforcement and public safety;

(f) security, defence and international relations;

(g) information obtained in confidence;

(h) commercially sensitive information;

(i) personal information;

(j) research and natural resources;

(k) financial and economic interests of the State and public bodies; and

(l) enactments relating to non-disclosure of records.

There is no right of appeal if a minister declares a record exempt under the law enforcement or national security criteria. The exemption of Cabinet material for five years is usual, although once the decision to which the information related has been reached, the data concerned must be released.

There is a similar provision for release of statistical data in the UK Act (s 35(2)). Other mandatory exemptions apply where disclosure would breach legal professional privilege, would result in contempt of court, or is prohibited by statute. Most exemptions, however, are discretionary and subject to public interest and harm tests. Appeals against refusal, excessive fees or delay may be taken up with the body in question or the Information Commissioner, whose decision is binding. However, ministers may veto the disclosure of particularly sensitive information on law enforcement, security or international relations, and the Information Commissioner may not overturn such a veto. Nevertheless, the combination of public interest tests and the creation of an Information Commissioner with extensive powers to order disclosure make the IFOIA one of the strongest in use overseas. In general the IFOIA is non-retrospective, except in relation to personal information.

At a conference discussing the IFOLA's first year of operation, McDonagh found that overall the Act was working 'reasonably well', but that two key issues needed to be addressed. First, the scope of the Act was insufficient, excluding as it does many important public bodies such as the police and schools. Second, continuing secrecy due to the provisions of other enactments, and particularly the Official Secrets Acts, was also highlighted as a problem (McDonagh, M, *'Freedom of Information—A Promise Fulfilled?'*, conference paper at FOI—One Year On, Dublin, 23 April 1999). The Act has had positive effects: an Irish minister giving information to the UK House of Commons Select Committee on Public Administration discussing the draft Freedom of Information Bill reported that in Ireland:

the impact of the Act in government has been to make policy advice sharper, more succinct. Subjective comment and inappropriate reflections are increasingly less evident. FOI has also improved the way services are delivered to the public. Arrangements for dealing with the public are now more user-friendly, and there is a much more professional approach. It has also made Ministers think more deeply about their responsibility for individual decisions.

(House of Commons Select Committee on Public Administration
1998–99, Third Report, HC 570–I, Annex 1, para 19)

The Freedom of Information (Amendment) Act was adopted in April 2003. This was described in a recent survey (The Freedominfo.org Global Survey, May 2004) thus:

The amendment extends the time before Cabinet Documents are available from five years to ten years and expands the coverage of the exemption; allows public servants to issue unappealable certificates that deliberative processes are ongoing to prevent access and weakens the public interest test; weakens the harm test for security, defence and international relations; and allows the government to impose fees for requests and appeals. The government announced in June 2003 that it was imposing a new fee structure based in the amendment – €15 for requests, €75 for internal reviews and €150 for reviews to the Information Commissioner. The Commissioner was critical about the changes and new fees noting that 'the charges could act as a financial disincentive' of which 'the scale of charges may distort the level playing field.' The Department of Communications also began to publish the name and address of every FOI requestor on its web site along with the response, which has been criticized by the media as an effort to stop the use of FOI for investigative reporting and by the Data Protection Commissioner and civil liberties groups as threatening privacy.

2.8 SCOTLAND

2.8.1 Introduction

Scotland has its own freedom of information regime. This derives from the Freedom of Information (Scotland) Act 2002, the right of individual access came into force in January 2005.

The Act completed its passage through the Scottish Parliament on 24 April 2002 and was given Royal Assent on 28 May of the same year. Access to information is a devolved function but the Scottish Act follows the main outline of the UK Act. However, there are a number of differences which strengthen rights of access in Scotland.

In practice, the UK Act will apply to public bodies operating in Scotland where their operation is outside the powers devolved to Scotland under the Scotland Act 1998. Thus, for instance, the British Transport Police and the Ministry of Defence Police operate in Scotland but are subject to the UK Act and not the Freedom of Information (Scotland) Act. Discovering which Act applies in any set of circumstances is relatively simple because the public authorities subject to each Act do not overlap and it is clear that only those authorities listed in each Act (and any subsequent regulations) have duties under it.

The Scottish Act provides that there is a presumption of disclosure subject to exemptions and that public authorities have a duty to set up publication schemes. Publication schemes for Scottish Ministers, Parliament, local government and the police became effective in June 2004. Health service, schools and universities started in September 2004 and all remaining public authorities in November 2004.

The list of public authorities to which it applies is very wide and is set out in Sch 1 to the Scottish Act. This list can be expanded by delegated legislation.

There are two codes of practice under the scheme, one dealing with requests for information and the other with records management.

2.8.2 Differences from the UK Legislation

The Scottish legislation sets out in s 1 a right to obtain information rather than two rights as in the UK version—one to be told whether that information exists and secondly to be given that information. This might suggest that where an exemption is successfully claimed, the first of these rights will not be available. However this is cured by s 16 of the Scottish Act which provides a duty to inform an applicant that information is retained at the time that an exemption from the second right is being claimed.

The Scottish Act provides that an applicant for information can ask for a review of a request if dissatisfied with the way the public authority has dealt with it (s 20). The public authority then has 20 working days to comply with the request for a review.

The Scottish exemption from disclosure which is based on the fact that the authority intends to publish the material in the future is also different from the UK model. In the latter the exemption applies even when no specific date for publication has been decided on. The Scottish model restricts the exemption to circumstances where the publication date is less than 12 weeks from the date of the request, in addition to requiring that exemption is reasonable in all the circumstances.

The Scottish Act contains no equivalent of s 23 of the UK Act, which exempts disclosure of material originating from a secret service agency but held by an authority subject to the Act. In practice, these provisions are probably unnecessary because of the existence of other exemptions based on national security, defence and the investigation of crime in both Acts.

One important difference appears in the test to be applied in the exemptions. In the 2000 Act the test for disclosure of material relating to national security, international relations, defence, law enforcement, commercial interests and the economy is based on whether prejudice would be caused as a result of disclosure. In s 31 of the 2002 Act the test is whether disclosure would 'substantially prejudice' those other public interests. In practice, although it is likely that considerable caution will be exercised in both jurisdictions when making these assessments, the Scottish model appears to allow a much more robust regime in these circumstances and the result is likely to allow considerably more access to information. Whilst it is likely that much more of this kind of material will be held by UK authorities rather than those in Scotland, it will be sensible for those seeking such material to try the Scots first.

The combination of this difference with the absence of an equivalent of s 23 (see above) will also make it more attractive to seek materials on the secret service agencies held by other agencies in Scotland first.

One exemption in the Scottish version but not in the UK Act is that of material held by an authority for the purposes of investigating a death (s 34(2)). Another exemption missing from the UK model is the protection applied to personal information obtained as a result of the census (s 38(1)(c)).

Perhaps the most important difference between the Acts is the difference in the structure for enforcement. The Scottish Information Commissioner is not responsible for data protection issues in Scotland (the UK Information Commissioner is responsible for data protection in both regions). The Scottish Commissioner however has more responsibility for enforcement of freedom of information issues and there are fewer avenues of appeal in Scotland. The later Act does not establish the equivalent of the Information Tribunal, and the

Tribunal established for data protection in the whole of the UK has no role in freedom of information north of the border (unlike its wider role in the south). There is of course an appeal to the court on a point of law from the Scottish Commissioner. Such appeals are made to the Court of Session.

2.9 CONCLUSION

It has not been our intention to offer a detailed comparison of the Freedom of Information Act 2000 and other similar overseas regimes. In time, such detailed studies will no doubt be undertaken and will prove enormously valuable interpretative tools. Nevertheless, at this point, it is possible to make a number of comparative points. By international standards, the Act covers a wide range of bodies—central and local government, the NHS, schools and other educational institutions, the police, various other public authorities and private bodies undertaking public functions (see 4.5 below). The fact that the Act gives a right of access to 'information', rather than to the more specific 'documents', is also a benefit as this broadens its scope and efficacy (see 4.4 below).

The creation of an independent Information Commissioner with particular responsibility for overseeing the implementation of the Act, and for enforcement of the duties established under the Act, is a further strength. Evidence from the Irish experience of freedom of information has been that one of the key elements 'at the heart of a good FOI Act' is 'a powerful Information Commissioner who can review and set aside decisions by public bodies' (House of Commons Select Committee on Public Administration, Third Report, 1998–99, HC 570–I, Annex 1, para 9, evidence from Irish Minister). The creation of an offence of destroying or altering records held by a public authority with the intention of preventing disclosure of requested information under s 77 of the Act is also significant. The lack of such a sanction may have been detrimental to the freedom of information regime in Canada, where instances of deliberate destruction of documents after requests have been experienced. These led the Canadian Information Commissioner to criticise the weakness of the country's legislation in the face of such subversion (Information Commissioner of Canada, *Annual Reports*, 1995–96 and 1996–97). The Canadian Act was amended in 1999 to combat this abuse.

The Act is however comparatively weak in some other areas. One example of weakness is the blanket exclusion of the security services from the UK Act, which does nothing to enhance the accountability of those services. In the United States, New Zealand and Canada the security services fall within the scope of freedom of information, although, of course, much security information is subject to exemptions. In general, the range and scope of exemptions under the Act is wider than that generally found in the comparable enactments discussed above (see, in particular, New Zealand's Official Information Act 1982 discussed at 2.6). The class exemption covering information held for the purpose of investigations or proceedings (s 29) and the exemption preventing disclosures of information which 'would in the reasonable opinion of a qualified person be likely to prejudice the effective conduct of public affairs' (s 36(2)) are particularly controversial in this regard. The availability of a ministerial veto over certain decisions taken by the Information Commissioner (s 53) also weakens the Act by comparison with some overseas regimes—for example, compare New Zealand, which requires a collective ministerial veto.

In seeking to argue that the Act should be interpreted liberally, applicants will not be able to draw support from a statutory purpose clause. Such clauses have proven very valuable in this regard in some overseas jurisdictions. The Data Protection Registrar (now the Information Commissioner) argued strongly in favour of such a purpose clause in her evidence to the Select Committee on Public Administration in 1998. It is also important to note that it remains possible for the effectiveness of the Act to be undermined by the numerous prohibitions on the disclosure of information which remain on the statute book (see 7.9 below). In New Zealand, the Official Secrets Act and other legislation prohibiting disclosure of information was repealed as part of a coordinated move towards greater public openness (see New Zealand Law Commission Report 40, *Review of the Official Information Act 1982* (1997) para C12).

Two further valuable conclusions can be drawn from an examination of overseas experience of freedom of information. The first is that it is clear that without a significant change in governmental culture, namely a move from a culture of secrecy to one of openness, freedom of information legislation will be hampered in delivering increases in accountability and transparency. The second is that, despite flaws in the relevant legislation and its implementation in each of the states considered above, the concrete benefits of having a statutory right to know have been felt. As the Canadian Information Commissioner has concluded:

Access laws are remarkable achievements . . . [they are] becoming an essential cornerstone to a vibrant and healthy democracy. The benefits of such laws are tangible and profound; they transform the way in which public business is done . . . [T]here is . . . also greater care, frugality, integrity and honesty in government because of access laws.

(Information Commissioner's keynote address to Conference on Access to Information Reform, 1 May 2000: see www.infoweb.magi.com/~accessca)

The most recent survey of freedom of information across the globe suggests that the move to more openness is now unstoppable. 'More than 50 countries now have guaranteed their citizens the right to know what their government is up to, and more than half of these freedom of information laws passed in the last decade . . . Four countries have adopted new freedom of information laws just since the last edition of the survey was posted in September 2003.' (The Freedominfo.org Global Survey, May 2004).

3

TOWARDS FREEDOM
OF INFORMATION IN
THE UNITED KINGDOM

The delay in enacting freedom of information legislation in the United Kingdom could be regarded as indicative of a prevailing 'culture of secrecy' within public administration. This chapter aims to provide some historical context to the Freedom of Information Act 2000 by illustrating developing public concern about suppression of information prior to the Act, and to outline pre-existing laws promoting access to specific forms of information in this jurisdiction.

3.1 THE NEED FOR REFORM

In the United Kingdom, over the last few decades, a series of scandals have illustrated the existence of a 'culture of secrecy' and have indicated the desirability of freedom of information legislation to counter excessive and inappropriate secrecy in central government and other public bodies. Many such cases have concerned information concerning the security services. In 1978, in the notorious 'ABC' trial, two journalists and an ex-soldier were charged with breaching ss 1 and 2 of the Official Secrets Act 1911 (see Andrew Nicol, 'Official Secrets and Jury Vetting' [1979] Crim LR 284). Further cases in the 1980s, such as those involving civil servants Sarah Tisdall and Clive Ponting, demonstrated the substantial risks taken by whistle-blowers seeking to expose wrongdoing in public administration. Tisdall was sentenced to six months imprisonment for leaking documents to a newspaper concerning the delivery of cruise missiles to Greenham Common. Ponting believed that ministers were deliberately misleading Parliament about the sinking of an Argentinian warship. He was acquitted by a jury. The *Spycatcher* case also threw into stark relief the British government's determination to suppress all information concerning the security and intelligence services, even where that information was widely available (see *Attorney-General v Guardian Newspapers Ltd (No 2)* [1990] 1 AC 109, and *Observer & Guardian v UK* (1991) 14 EHRR 153). More recently, there have been a spate of prosecutions and civil actions brought against former security and intelligence officers, such as security service whistle-blowers David Shayler, Richard Tomlinson, 'Martyn Ingram' and Katherine Gun. These have all highlighted the lack of accountability of the security services, and illustrated the lengths to which the government may go to prevent disclosure of official information, or to ensure that potential whistle-blowers are discouraged (for details of these cases, see Liberty and Article 19, *Secrets Spies and Whistleblowers* (London: Liberty and Article 19, 2000)). Also, recent prosecutions of Tony Geraghty, Liam Clarke and the arrest of Julie-Ann Davies under s 5 of the Official Secrets Act 1989 have shown the ability and willingness of the state to seek to prevent or punish unauthorised secondary disclosure of official information.

As a result of a number of exclusions and exemptions, the Act will do very little to ensure that a more proportionate approach to the release of information concerning the security and intelligence services is adopted. However, cases such as the above have done much to indicate that many public authorities in the United Kingdom have a long-established inclination to prevent any information from reaching the public. This impression has also been heightened by a series of comparable scandals in other areas of government. The prosecution of senior executives of Matrix Churchill in 1992 for exporting arms-making equipment to Iraq collapsed when it emerged that the Government had agreed to relax the guidelines prohibiting exports of arms or arms-manufacturing equipment to Iraq without informing Parliament. Four ministers signed public interest immunity certificates regarding documents vital to the executives' defence. The case showed that ministers were prepared to allow the defendants to go to prison, rather than to allow the disclosure of documents embarrassing to the government. Sir Richard Scott conducted a public inquiry into the affair. In his report he stressed that throughout the period under investigation there was a:

... consistent undervaluing by government of the public interest that full information should be made available to Parliament. In circumstances where disclosure might be politically or administratively inconvenient, the balance struck by the government comes down, time and time again, against full disclosure.

> (Rt Hon Sir Richard Scott VC, *Report of the Inquiry into the Export of Defence Equipment and Dual-Use Goods to Iraq and Related Prosecutions* (1996), para D1. 165)

This case showed the failure of the prevailing doctrine of 'ministerial responsibility', which has often been cited as a key reason why freedom of information legislation is unnecessary. 'Ministerial responsibility' means that ministers are responsible for authorised actions undertaken by their department, and are accountable to Parliament for unauthorised actions of which they should have been aware. The Scott report stated that ministers had failed 'to give Parliament, including its Select Committees, and the public as full information as possible about the policies, decisions and actions of the Government and not to deceive or mislead Parliament and the public', as required by the guide to ministerial conduct *Questions of Procedure* (Scott Report (1996), p 1799). The 'Arms to Iraq' affair demonstrated that a culture of secrecy in government can subvert basic democratic principles.

Further concern about the inadequacy of information available to the public formed the basis of Lord Nolan's inquiry into 'Standards in Public Life'. This was set up in 1994 in order to allay public concerns over 'sleaze' and corruption among holders of public office. Lord Nolan recommended that decisions to award public contracts should be open to increased scrutiny, and that private interests relating to an MP's public duties should be registered to avoid conflicts of interest. MPs have been required since 1974 to register any sources of paid employment outside the House of Commons. Since 1995 Members must disclose the amounts of remuneration, and must inform the Parliamentary Commissioner for Standards in writing of any new or existing agreements 'involving the provision of services in his or her capacity as a Member of Parliament' (*Register of Members' Interests*, January 2000 edition, p 1). These rules are set out in the Code of Conduct for MPs, introduced in 1996 (House of Commons Paper No 688 (1995–96)).

The Macpherson report of 1998, following the enquiry into the murder of the black teenager Stephen Lawrence, specifically recommended freedom of information legislation as a means of ensuring the accountability of police services to the public. In his report, Sir William Macpherson stated that:

Seeking to achieve trust and confidence through the demonstration of fairness will not in itself be sufficient. It must be accompanied by a vigorous pursuit of openness and accountability across Police Services . . . [W]e consider it an important matter of principle that the Police Services should be open to the full provisions of a Freedom of Information Act. We see no logical grounds for a class exemption in any area.

(The Stephen Lawrence Inquiry—Report of an Inquiry by Sir William Macpherson of Cluny, 1998, Cm 4262–I, para 46.32)

The 'Arms to Africa' scandal showed that a new Labour administration was also prepared to exercise its powers to ensure that its more controversial activities were not exposed to public scrutiny. The British mercenary group Sandline was found to have breached the UN arms embargo on Sierra Leone, allegedly with the knowledge of the Foreign Office. The Foreign Affairs Select Committee of the House of Commons, which investigated the allegations, was denied access to crucial pieces of information by the Foreign Secretary, Robin Cook, who argued that release of such information would prejudice the departmental enquiry into the affair.

Finally, and most recently, the report of the Phillips inquiry into the BSE crisis showed how a Whitehall culture of secrecy, interdepartmental conflict and complacency helped cause a public health disaster. As is well known, this inquiry concerned a fatal cattle disease (bovine spongiform encephalopathy—BSE), which crossed the species barrier to infect humans with new variant Creutzfeldt-Jakob disease (vCJD). Cases of BSE in cattle had been documented since 1984 and there was increasing evidence in the following years that BSE might be able to jump the species gap. However, during this time the public were repeatedly reassured that it was safe to eat British beef by ministers and other officials. It was not until March 1996 that the government announced that vCJD had possibly been transmitted to its human victims through their consumption of infected beef in the 1980s. The Phillips report concluded that there had been 'positive censorship' early in the case; that there was 'a clear policy of restricting the disclosure of information about BSE'; that 'the witholding of information robbed those who would have had an interest in receiving it of the chance to react to it'; and that 'had there been a policy of openness rather than secrecy' this would have led 'to remedial measures being taken sooner than they were' (*The BSE Inquiry—The Report* (2000) vol 3 paras 2.175, 2.189 and 2.191; vol 1 para 180). Lord Phillips, speaking after the publication of the report, said: 'We do think, and have found, that there was what you might call a cover up in the first six months'.

The above examples indicate the importance of access to information if proper democratic scrutiny of public authorities is to take place. This series of controversies undoubtedly did a great deal to convince the public that governments could not be trusted to disclose information voluntarily and that legislation such as the Freedom of Information Act was necessary. However, in a number of the cases discussed in this section, the information in question would still not have been available if the Act had been in force. Information held by the security and intelligence services and information relating to or deriving from those services is exempt from disclosure under the Act (see 7.3 and 8.3 below). Also, information such as that at the centre of the Stephen Lawrence and BSE scandals may well be found to be covered by one of the Act's numerous exemptions from the duty to communicate information (such as s 30, for example—see 8.8 below). However, it should not be forgotten that many of the Act's exemptions are 'qualified exemptions' and will therefore only be effective where the public interest in non-disclosure outweighs the public interest in disclosure. There would seem to be considerable scope for applicants to establish that the public interest favours disclosure. Over time, it is to be hoped that the very existence of a general right of access to information will go a long way towards changing the 'culture of secrecy' described above.

3.2 EXISTING RIGHTS OF ACCESS TO INFORMATION

Despite the series of controversies described in the previous section, rights of access to information have existed prior to the coming into force of the Act in a number of specific circumstances. Some of the more significant of these rights are outlined in the remainder of this chapter.

3.2.1 Personal Information

Under the Data Protection Act 1998 ('the 1998 Act'), individuals have a right of access to data concerning themselves held by both public authorities and private bodies (s 7, DPA 1998). This Act incorporates rights of access to some types of records, such as health records and social services records, which had previously been granted under earlier legislation, such as the Access to Health Records Act 1990. The scope of the Data Protection Act 1998, and the relationship between that Act and the Freedom of Information Act, is discussed further in Chapter 10. Once the former Act is fully in force, the right to access to personal information will be amended so that all forms of such information, whether held in a structured or unstructured form, will be available from public authorities.

Under the 1998 Act, there is no right of access for relatives to the medical records of someone who has died. However, in certain circumstances, such information may be available under the Access to Health Records Act 1990. The Access to Medical Reports Act 1988 also gives an individual the right to see a report prepared by a doctor for an employer or insurer before it is sent. Credit reference agency records are available under the 1998 Act and may be corrected under the terms of the Consumer Credit Act 1974.

3.2.2 Local Government

Under the Local Government (Access to Information) Act 1985, the public may attend and receive papers for the meetings of local authorities, including those of committees and subcommittees, unless the information is exempt—for example, if personal information about an individual is being discussed. In this instance, an individual may not attend, even if he is the subject of discussion. The 1985 Act and the Public Bodies (Admission to Meetings) Act 1960 were substantially responsible for the relatively high level of access to local government information, and in particular that relating to decisions. The recently enacted Local Government Act 2000 incorporates the Local Authorities (Executive Arrangements) (Access to Information) (England) Regulations 2000 which require local authorities to:

(a) issue monthly 'Forward Plans' showing forthcoming decisions and listing related documents;

(b) give a minimum of three days prior access to reports, agendas and background papers for decisions;

(c) ensure that meetings at which a 'key decision' is to be discussed or taken are open to the public; and

(d) produce a record of such a decision and the reasoning behind it.

Further, the government have agreed to review the current level of public rights of access to meetings and information, with a view to improving it (Campaign for Freedom of Information press release, 25 July 2000, see www.cfoi.org.uk).

The National Audit Office, headed by the Comptroller and Auditor General, is responsible for auditing all Government departments and agencies, reports on which are then presented to Parliament by Order of the House of Commons. The Public Accounts Committee (PAC) investigates a further 40 or 50 of these cases a year, and issues a separate report. The government conventionally responds to this within two months, after which the PAC and Comptroller may conduct a follow-up investigation.

Local authorities are similarly audited under the supervision of the Audit Commission. The Accounts and Audit Regulations 1983 specify that during the audit of a local authority, all 'books, deeds, contracts, bills, vouchers and receipts' pertinent to the audit must be made available to the public for 15 days. The sole ground on which information can be exempted is if it concerns identifiable members of the council's staff. It has been argued that this right of access constitutes '. . . one of the most powerful access rights on the UK statute books' (Wilhelmsson, J, 'The Right to Know' in Wadham, J and Crossman, G (eds), *Your Rights* (7th edn, London: Pluto Press, 2000 p 107).

3.2.3 Environmental Information

A right of access to information about the environment held by public bodies was provided in this jurisdiction by the Environmental Information Regulations 1992. Under these regulations, information was to be made available about the condition of the environment, any conditions which impact negatively on it, and what if any measures are being taken to prevent or counter this. The 1998 Aarhus Convention, to which the UK is a signatory, is intended to increase public access to environmental information. The Act provides that the Secretary of State may make regulations to implement this convention (s 74) This power has been employed to introduce the Environmental Information Regulations 2004 (see 8.15 and App 6 below). Even prior to the introduction of the 1992 Regulations, the Environmental Protection Act 1990 granted public access to various pollution registers. The Land Registration Act 1988 gave the public access for the first time to the Land Register, ending secrecy over land ownership.

3.2.4 Litigation

The rights of access to information discussed above are some of the more significant statutory rights of access. However, it should not be forgotten that litigants have a right of access to disclosure of relevant information in the course of legal proceedings. Where proceedings are brought against a public authority, that authority may be required to disclose information which it would prefer to keep secret. The rules of disclosure in litigation do not contain the extensive list of exemptions to be found in the Act and are supported by powerful sanctions for non-compliance. However, litigation also has a number of significant disadvantages as a means of obtaining disclosure of information.

First, it is necessary to issue formal legal proceedings in order to set the process in motion. Second, where information is sought from a public authority in judicial review proceedings, the court's procedural powers to order disclosure are limited (see Lewis, C, 'Linkage between Access to Information and Judicial Review' in Beatson, J and Cripps, Y (eds), *Freedom of Expression and Freedom of Information: Essays in Honour of David Williams* (Oxford: OUP, 2000)). Thirdly, a public authority wishing to preserve the confidentiality of certain information may be entitled to refuse to disclose the information where such disclosure would damage the public interest (*Duncan v Cammell Laird* [1942] AC 624). *Conway v Rimmer* [1968] AC 910 established that on occasion the public interest might be best served by the publication of such documents, and that this needed to be balanced with possible harm to the nation resulting from disclosure. The dangers of ministerial use of public interest immunity certificates, to resist disclosure of information in proceedings on the grounds that disclosure would damage the public interest, are evident from the Matrix Churchill case. Finally, the disclosure made to the parties in litigation cannot be disclosed to others without the consent of the court, and will only become available if disclosed at the trial.

3.3 ACCESS TO INFORMATION THROUGH PARLIAMENT

In addition to the legal rights to information described above, it should not be forgotten that Parliament has very strong powers to compel public authorities to supply it with information.

3.3.1 Parliamentary Questions

Access to official information may be requested through Parliamentary Questions. On average 35,000–40,000 written or oral questions each year were asked by Members of Parliament or ministers in the late 1990s (House of Commons factsheet, series P, no 1, p 1, House of Commons Information Office, May 2000). However, ministers may refuse to answer questions—as they have done consistently in the case of questions concerning the security services or trade secrets. Once in each session, ministers may be asked if they will answer questions they had previously refused to answer. Members are advised on the admissibility of their questions by the Clerks of the House, and may refer the matter to the Speaker if they are unhappy with the advice they receive; the Speaker's decision is final. Questions in the Commons may only be asked by MPs, so members of the public are required to convince their MP of the need to ask for particular information. MPs are only entitled to ask a limited number of questions. They can only request centrally recorded government information, and local government information is therefore usually unavailable by this means. There is a cost limit on answers to written Parliamentary Questions—if the cost of a minister giving an answer is likely to exceed £550, he or she does not have to answer it.

3.3.2 Select Committees

Select committees report to the House of Commons or Lords after receiving written and oral evidence on a particular subject. Such committees may summon witnesses or documents as evidence. This system has led to increased disclosure of official information; both reports and minutes of evidence presented to select committees are published on the internet. However, the system is not without flaws—as the 'Arms to Africa' affair demonstrated. Success in obtaining information can often depend on the personalities involved, and the political unity of the committee. Committees cannot order the attendance of Members of either House, and therefore cannot compel a minister to attend to give evidence. Formal powers to summon civil servants do exist, but this has on occasion proved contentious, with ministers attending to ensure that their officials did not have to. Instances of witnesses refusing to cooperate have also been known—for example, Kevin and Ian Maxwell refused to answer questions on the Maxwell pensions affair before the Social Security Select Committee in 1992. Moreover, committees may only request written evidence or documents from the department. While this system has enhanced accountability, it is not a guaranteed method of extracting information.

3.3.3 The Parliamentary Commissioner for Administration (PCA) and Select Committee on Public Administration

The Parliamentary Commissioner for Administration (also known as the Parliamentary Ombudsman) investigates complaints about government departments made by members of the public. He may order the disclosure of evidence from departments and make recommendations on cases. The Select Committee on Public Administration considers the reports of the PCA, and considers matters relating to the quality and standards of administration provided by civil service departments and other matters relating to the civil service. See also the Open Government Code of Practice, discussed below at 3.4.1.

3.4 OPEN GOVERNMENT

In addition to the legally enforceable rights of access to information described in 3.2 above, and the Parliamentary powers to obtain disclosure of information described in 3.3, there have also been an increasing numbers of 'open government' initiatives recently. These establish procedures which are designed to promote public access to governmental, and other information, but stop short of providing legally enforceable rights of access to information. The most relevant open government initiative, in the context of the Act, has been the introduction of the Code of Practice on Access to Government Information.

3.4.1 Code of Practice on Access to Government Information

The Code of Practice on Access to Government Information was introduced in 1993 in recognition of the idea that '[o]pen government is part of an effective democracy' (White Paper, 1993, Cmnd 2290, para 1.1). The code is a non-legal instrument, and does not therefore provide a statutory right of public access to official information enforceable through the courts. The Code's five main commitments, updated in 1997, are:

(a) to supply facts and analysis with major policy decisions;

(b) to open up internal guidelines about departments' dealings with the public;

(c) to supply reasons with administrative decisions;

(d) to provide information under the Citizen's Charter about public services, what they cost, targets, performance, complaints and redress; and

(e) to respond to requests for information.

It is the final one of these commitments which is of the greatest significance to the current discussion. The Code applies to all public agencies under the jurisdiction of the Parliamentary Commissioner for Administration. There are exemptions to the obligations of public authorities to supply information under the Code. These concern, amongst other things, national security, law enforcement, internal discussion, policy advice, and nationality or immigration. Exempt information may be disclosed under the Code if the benefits to the public interest outweigh the harm that would be likely to result from disclosure.

Under the Code, queries are to be answered within 20 days, and charges made. Appeals against refusals to provide information are, in the first instance, to be taken up by the applicant with the department in question. If that approach is unsuccessful, enforcement of the Code rests with the Parliamentary

Ombudsman, who can only instigate an investigation following the referral of a complaint from an MP. Some interesting examples of unnecessary governmental secrecy have been exposed by the Ombudsman. One such case followed the refusal of the Medicines Control Agency (MCA) to release information on a drug on the grounds of commercial confidentiality. When contacted by the Ombudsman's office, the drug company, whose confidentiality the MCA was purporting to protect, was found to have no objection to the release of much of the information. The Ombudsman has also criticised the Department of Trade and Industry for failing to release a summary of information on encryption. Its refusal appeared 'to have been based on little more than an instinctive reaction to the protection of information in what is perceived to be a sensitive area' (HC 593, *The Parliamentary Ombudsman Annual Report 1999–2000*, pp 44, 46). He has also stated his general concern about the culture of secrecy elsewhere within government:

I remain concerned that, when they receive requests dealing with what are seen as sensitive or controversial areas of policy or practice, Departments too often raise the drawbridge instinctively. Much information . . . can be released in perfect safety even in such sensitive areas as national security. Some information in these areas must, of course, be carefully protected. But it is necessary to be discriminating, and not to assume automatically that no information can be released.

(HC 21, *Investigations Completed April–October 1999*)

The most significant weakness of the Code, however, is that it is not legally binding on the government departments and other bodies which it covers. The Ombudsman's recommendations do not have to be implemented, although in practice most departments comply. When the Freedom of Information Act came fully into force, this non-statutory Code was superseded. Until that point, however, it will continue to have force.

The Scottish Executive and the Welsh Assembly have had similar codes of practice since July 1999. The First Minister for Wales has made access to information a priority and has already ordered the release of Cabinet minutes six weeks after the meetings take place (First Minister's statement on Freedom of Information, 21 March 2000). The Scottish Code continued to govern this within the remit of the Scottish Executive until the Scottish Freedom of Information Act was introduced (see 2.8 above). The National Assembly for Wales will, eventually, be subject to the right of access contained in the Act.

3.4.2 Public Records

The Public Records Act 1958 (as amended) has, until the coming into force of the Act, governed access to public records (ie, records of governmental and certain other public bodies). Most public records are made available to the public 30 years after the last dated entry in the file. Some records are subject to closure for periods greater than 30 years (for discussion of the 1958 Act and of the substantial changes to the public records regime made by the Act, see Chapter 11). Some public records have, however, been made available prior to the 30-year norm established under the Act. Recently, such 'accelerated opening' has been encouraged by the Records Management Department of the Public Records Office. Individual departments may also allow privileged access to closed information to members of the public following a written application, or to researchers if they undertake not to make the information public. Following the Open Government initiative of 1992, departments were encouraged to re-examine closed or retained records to see if any could be released earlier, a move which resulted in the publication of some Prime Ministerial and Foreign Office documents.

3.4.3 Public Interest Disclosure Act 1998

The Public Interest Disclosure Act 1998 ('PIDA') came into force in Spring 1999. The PIDA forms part of the body of employment legislation and is intended to promote accountability in the workplace and to encourage employers to tackle malpractice. It does this through a combination of sanctions on the employer and protection for the whistle-blower. The PIDA applies to every factory, hospital, Whitehall department, charity, office, shop, and quango in the United Kingdom. It covers workers who raise genuine concerns about the mistreatment of patients, financial malpractice, miscarriages of justice, breach of the Civil Service Code, abuse in care, dangers to health and safety, risks to the environment, and cover-ups. The PIDA covers disclosures made internally to managers, and externally to prescribed bodies or other groups (eg, the media or the police). This last type of disclosure is only permissible if the whistle-blower: had reason to believe he would be victimised if he sought to make the disclosure internally or to a prescribed body; had good reason to believe there would be a cover-up and there was no prescribed regulator; or had already sought to raise the issue internally or with a prescribed regulator. It guarantees full compensation with the promise of penalty awards if the whistle-blower is sacked.

However, the PIDA does not extend to employees of the security and intelligence services, even when they are exposing illegal activities, although the Police Reform Act 2002 extended its remit to cover police officers from April 2004. The PIDA has already been used successfully in a number of cases (see *Bladon v ALM Medical Services*, 25 April 2000 and *Fernandes v Netcom Consultants UK*, 18 May 2000 [2000] IRLB, No 648, p 2) and is one of the most far-reaching measures of its kind in the world.

3.4.4 Internet Publication

Recently, there has been a substantial governmental effort to improve access to official information through internet publication. The 'Open Government' website, established in 1994, provides access to much government information, in line with the principles of open government and the Citizens Charter (www.open.gov.uk/services/about.htm). The Campaign for Freedom of Information has recognised and rewarded examples of good practice in this area—the BSE inquiry was, for example, given a Campaign for Freedom of Information award in 1998. On this website, frequent and detailed updates on the progress of the inquiry were made and transcripts of inquiry hearings were made available, usually within a few hours of the witness giving evidence. The inquiry also provided free access via the website to all witness statements, timetables and background information. Over 160,000 witness statements and almost 86,000 transcripts were accessed from the website, which received over 1.5 million page requests (*The BSE Inquiry—The Report, 2000*, vol 1, annex 1 para 1346).

3.4.5 Public Inquiries

Public inquiries into particular issues (for example, BSE, the murder of Stephen Lawrence, or Bloody Sunday) are ordered by the government, often as a result of political pressure. Usually chaired by a senior judge, they are funded by the government and can be extremely expensive. The BSE Inquiry for example cost around £27 million. The reports of inquiries can only make recommendations. Implementation of those recommendations is then mostly dependent on political pressure. Public inquiries can be given the power to order the attendance of witnesses and may also require the production of certain evidence.

4

ACCESS TO INFORMATION UNDER THE FREEDOM OF INFORMATION ACT—RIGHTS AND DUTIES

4.1 INTRODUCTION

The Freedom of Information Act 2000 grants a right of access to 'information' held by 'public authorities'. In this chapter, certain fundamental questions about the Act are considered. Who is entitled to exercise rights under the Act? What is the meaning of 'information' under the Act? Which persons and bodies are 'public authorities' and therefore subject to the Act? Procedural features of the regime established under the Act are discussed in Chapter 5.

4.2 RIGHTS GRANTED UNDER THE ACT

Section 1 of the Act provides that:

(1) Any person making a request for information to a public authority is entitled—
   (a) to be informed in writing by the public authority whether it holds information of the description specified in the request, and
   (b) if that is the case, to have that information communicated to him.

Thus, the Act grants two distinct rights—a right to receive confirmation or denial that information is held by a public authority (s 1(1)(a)) and a right to the communication of that information from the public authority (s 1(1)(b)). Where, in response to an application under the Act, a public authority communicates the requested information, it is deemed to have satisfied both of these rights (s 1(5)). In other circumstances, while an applicant may not be entitled to have information communicated under s 1(1)(b) because the requested information is exempt from disclosure, he or she may still be entitled to confirmation or denial that the information is held by the public authority. For example, an applicant may request access to a controversial report which is due to be published in the near future. In that case, the applicant's right to have the information contained in the report communicated to him or her may be excluded by the exemption set out in s 22 ('Information intended for future publication') (see 8.2). However, s 22 may not exempt the public authority from its duty to confirm or deny that it is holding the requested information (see s 22(2)).

The corollary of the Act's grant of these two rights to applicants is that public authorities have equivalent *duties* to confirm or deny and to communicate information. Indeed, for ease of reference, the duty placed upon public authorities by s 1(1)(a) is referred to throughout the Act as 'the duty to confirm or deny' (s 1(6)). That term is also adopted in this Guide. The duty placed upon public authorities by s 1(1)(b) is described in this text as the 'the duty to communicate information'.

4.3 WHO IS ENTITLED TO THE RIGHTS GRANTED BY THE ACT?

The duties placed upon public authorities arise when 'any person' makes a request for information to that body. The rights provided are not restricted to 'natural persons' or to persons or bodies connected with this jurisdiction. They can be enforced by individuals from this jurisdiction and abroad and by bodies enjoying only legal personality, such as companies. As a result of the Act's liberal approach to this issue, a Chinese company engaged in arms manufacture, for example, is entitled to submit a request for access to information held by the Ministry of Defence under the Act.

Unless the information in question is covered by an exemption, and as long as the appropriate procedure is followed, that information must be disclosed. Under the Act, the *motives* of the applicant in seeking the information are irrelevant (Hansard HL, 17 October 2000). This 'applicant-blind' approach is more generous than that originally adopted in the draft Freedom of Information Bill, under which a public authority would have been entitled to ask an applicant about his or her motives for requesting information under the legislation.

Given the liberality of the Act in this regard, there is no reason why a 'public authority', itself subject to the Act, should not also be entitled to benefit from the rights introduced by the Act. Indeed, given the range of persons and bodies subject to duties under the Act, it is not difficult to envisage circumstances in which a 'public authority' might wish to exercise rights under the Act. As will be seen later in this chapter, a doctor providing NHS services is, in certain circumstances, a 'public authority' for the purposes of the Act (Sch 1, paras 44, 45 and 51). Such a doctor may also wish to exercise rights under the Act in order, for example, to gain access to information held by other public authorities, such as the Medical Research Council or the Department of Health. The fact that the doctor is a 'public authority' under the Act, and is therefore subject to the duties in s 1(1), does not put him or her at any disadvantage as an applicant.

4.4 'INFORMATION' ACCESSIBLE UNDER THE ACT

4.4.1 The Requirement of Recording

As has been noted above, the rights granted under the Act are rights of access to 'information'. What then is 'information'? Some assistance in answering this question can be derived from the Act's interpretation section (s 84), which provides that:

'information' means information recorded in any form . . .

Thus, for example, a public authority is not obliged to communicate information retained only in a public official's memory. In this regard, the Act can be distinguished from New Zealand's Official Information Act 1982, which allows access to both recorded and unrecorded information (see *Commissioner of Police v Ombudsman* [1985] 1 NZLR 578 at 586).

The fact that the definition above covers information recorded 'in any form' means that, for example, requests can be made for access to written memoranda, photographs, plans, video and sound recordings and to data held on computer.

Information held in any of these forms will generally have been 'recorded'. However, it is possible that the condition will not be satisfied where information is stored only within the temporary memory of a computer or computer network.

Although information must be recorded before it falls within the scope of the Act, it is important to note that the Act provides a right to 'information' rather than to 'documents' or 'records'. This distinction is significant. As will be seen in Chapter 5, any applicant under the Act must describe the information which he or she is seeking sufficiently accurately for the public authority receiving the application to be able to identify it (ss 1(3) and 8—discussed below at 5.2.3). However, because the Act provides a right of access to 'information' and not to 'documents' or 'recordings', the applicant is not required to specify any particular document or recording.

In addition, it is important to note that a single document may consist of a number of separate 'elements' of information. Accordingly, the fact that certain information within a document may be covered by an exemption will not absolve a public authority from a duty to communicate information contained elsewhere in the document. In such cases, public authorities may be required to disclose information by means of 'redacted' documents (ie, documents in which certain exempt items of information have been obscured). For example, a record of information sought by an applicant may contain personal details relating to the person who recorded the information. Such details may well be exempt from disclosure under the Act (see, s 40 'Personal information'). However, this exemption would not cover all information contained in the record. The public authority would be obliged to disclose this non-exempt information (Hansard HL, 17 October 2000, col 931).

4.4.2 The Definition of 'Information'

Further questions concerning the meaning of 'information' in the Act are likely to arise. For example, a 'public authority' may seek to argue that it is not obliged to comply with a particular request for 'information' which it claims to have no true 'informative' value. This situation could arise, for example, where a public authority receives a request for trivial data or data which has subsequently been established to be inaccurate. There are, however, clear dangers in allowing a public authority to decide that information does not satisfy a particular qualitative threshold and therefore does not need to be disclosed. The Information Commissioner and courts are likely to prefer a more qualitatively neutral definition of 'information'. Indeed, in the course of parliamentary debate, it was indicated that inaccurate information will fall within the scope of the Act (Hansard HC, 4 April 2000, col 909).

On the other hand, an applicant may be able to argue that a public authority has failed to satisfy its duty to communicate information under the Act where the authority has communicated data which cannot be clearly interpreted. This could occur, for example, where data are recorded in a code or jargon that cannot be understood by the applicant without further explanation. It seems likely that, in a case where data disclosed do not readily reveal their meaning to a reasonable recipient, they will not 'inform' an applicant and will not, therefore, constitute 'information' for the purposes of the Act (cf s 8(2), Data Protection Act 1998).

Such a difficulty could arise where an applicant requests access to information held in an electronic format. This issue has been raised by McDonagh in her work on the Irish Freedom of Information Act 1997. She has noted that:

> . . . some records may only be accessible through the use of software and so the provision of a disk containing the record may not be sufficient to enable the requester to access it. Where the public authority owns the copyright in the software, it might be required to

give the requester a copy of such software to enable him or her to access the information or it might be required to deal with the issue by providing access to a computer on its premises through which access to the record can be gained. If, however, the software required to access the information is proprietary software, the issue is not so clear.

(McDonagh, M, *Freedom of Information Law in Ireland* (Dublin: Round Hall, 1998), p 74)

It could be argued that, under the Act, a public authority may be exempt from the duty to communicate information in such circumstances as a result of s 44 ('Prohibitions on disclosure'—in this case, the law of copyright) or s 43 ('Commercial interests'). However, such exemptions will only apply in any event where the public authority is unable to supply the information in any other form.

4.4.3 When is Information 'Held' by a Public Authority?

Under the Act, applicants have a right of access to information 'held' by a public authority. Section 3(2) of the Act provides that:

. . . information is held by a public authority if—

(a) it is held by the authority, otherwise than on behalf of another person, or
(b) it is held by another person on behalf of the authority.

In construing this provision, it is important to remember that 'information' can generally be reproduced infinitely. Thus, for example, where copies of information have been passed to a number of different public authorities, each will 'hold' that information for the purposes of the Act. There will be no need to engage in the difficult task of establishing which authority 'owns', or is most closely connected with, the information. Also, where information derives from a third party, for example, a member of the public or a company, and is communicated to a public authority, it will nevertheless be 'held' by that public authority. In this way, a public authority may hold much information which was originally 'private'. Local councils receive a considerable volume of correspondence from members of the public. Even though the information contained within that correspondence is not originally recorded by the local authority itself, it will nevertheless be 'held' by that 'public authority' for the purposes of the Act.

Conversely, in certain circumstances, it may be possible that, even where particular information can be found on the premises of a public authority, that public authority will not 'hold' the information for the purposes of the Act. For example, even if a Minister of State chooses to keep his personal diary in his departmental office, it is unlikely that the department will be regarded as 'holding' the information recorded in that diary for the purposes of the Act. The information recorded in the diary is likely to be regarded as 'held' by the Minister personally rather than in an official capacity or by the department, and will thus fall outside the ambit of the Act. This may also be true of personal e-mails sent or received by employees of a public authority, even though the e-mails are 'held' on the public authority's computer.

A more liberal definition of the circumstances under which a public authority 'holds' information applies under the Environmental Information Regulations (see Appendix 6, reg 3(2)).

4.4.4 Information Held 'on Behalf of Another Person'

In addition to the situation discussed at 4.4.3, s 3(2)(a) expressly excludes information held by a public authority 'on behalf of another person' from the scope of the Act. This provision could be regarded as covering the case of the Minister's diary discussed above. However, the use of the phrase 'on behalf of another person' seems better suited to situations where the public authority has taken information under its control and is acting as a custodian of that information. It is less apt to cover a situation where the public authority may be aware of the information in question (such as that contained in the diary) but would not properly regard itself as having power to control that information to any degree. Section 3(2)(a) is likely to be applicable where, for example, a local authority holds an archive of information belonging to another public authority for safe-keeping or where a police force holds material as a result of a seizure following a search.

It is possible that attempts may be made to use s 3(2)(a) to remove information entirely from the scope of the Act. Consider, for example, the situation of a commercial organization, Z, which provides information to a public authority. On supplying the information, Z specifies that it is to be held by the public authority 'on behalf of Z'. Z may wish to do this because, even where the information would appear to be covered by exemptions under the Act, many such exemptions can be 'trumped' by the public interest in disclosure (see below at 6.2). If Z's statement is effective in ensuring that the information is held 'on behalf of Z', there would be no need for a public authority to rely on exemptions as a means of avoiding disclosure because the information would fall outside the scope of the Act altogether. If this is the effect of s 3(2)(a), the Act would appear to be flawed. The careful balancing of interests in confidentiality and disclosure achieved by means of the exemptions in Part II of the Act would be susceptible to being by-passed entirely. It is therefore likely that the Information Commissioner and the courts will look sceptically upon such potential abuses. Instead, they are likely to focus upon the issue of whether the public authority actually has control over the information in its possession, rather than upon a verbal formula which the supplier of the information has purported to impose.

Even though such information does not fall within the scope of the Act, the Information Commissioner has suggested that a public authority's duty to offer advice and assistance to an applicant will require it to redirect any applicant for such information to the person or body to whom the information 'belongs' (see Freedom of Information Act Awareness Guidance No 12).

4.4.5 Information Held by Another Person on Behalf of a Public Authority

By contrast, where information is held by another person 'on behalf of' a public authority, that information will fall within the scope of the Act (s 3(2)(b)). The fairly typical circumstances in which a public authority stores its older records with a commercial archiving company or entrusts its legal documents to a solicitor will be covered by s 3(2)(b). Generally, such situations are unlikely to cause difficulties. However, problems could arise in the event of the third-party holder of the recorded information being unwilling, or unable, to grant access to the information. The Act provides an enforcement mechanism where public authorities refuse, or fail, to comply with their obligations under the Act (see Chapter 9). However, that procedure cannot be instigated against third-party holders of information. In order to avoid breaching their duties under the Act, it is therefore important for public authorities to ensure that third parties holding information on their behalf can be relied upon to provide the authority with that information promptly whenever a request under the Act is received.

4.4.6 A Right of Access to Information 'Held at the Time When the Request is Received'

Under s 1(4) of the Act, the information to which the right of access applies is the requested information 'held at the time when the request is received'. However, s 1(4) also provides that:

. . . account may be taken of any amendment or deletion made between that time and the time when the information is to be communicated . . ., being an amendment or deletion that would have been made regardless of the receipt of the request.

This means that, while a public authority altering or deleting information in order to avoid its duties under the Act is likely to commit a criminal offence (see 9.4.3 below), public authorities are not obliged to undo alterations or deletions made between receipt of a request and compliance with the requirements of the Act. As a result of s 1(4), an authority does not have to 'freeze' its collection of information on receipt of an application under the Act. This provision assists organisations holding large collections of information which are constantly altered and updated, for example, within computer networks.

It should be noted that s 1(4) only provides that account *may* be taken of any alteration or deletion. It does not state that the information to be communicated to the applicant should, in all cases, be the amended or deleted version. The provision will protect a public authority which is unable to provide information held at the time that a request was made, perhaps as a result of subsequent irremediable deletions or alterations. However, it does not necessarily absolve a public authority from the duty to communicate unamended or deleted information where this can be retrieved.

One rather surprising result of s 1(4), is that a public authority is not obliged to disclose information received after the time when the request was received, even where the information is readily accessible to the authority.

One of the most notable features of the Act is that it is fully retrospective. Unlike freedom of information regimes established in some other common law jurisdictions (for example, the Australian Federal Freedom of Information Act 1982 and the Irish Freedom of Information Act 1997), the Act applies to information *whenever* it was created and not only to information created after the Act's coming into force.

4.5 'PUBLIC AUTHORITIES' SUBJECT TO THE ACT

As has been indicated above, only 'public authorities' are subject to the duties established in the Act. A definition of such bodies is provided in s 3(1):

In this Act 'public authority' means—

(a) . . . any body which, any other person who, or the holder of any office which—
    (i) is listed in Schedule 1, or
    (ii) is designated by order under section 5, or
(b) a publicly-owned company . . .

Generally, in comparison with other freedom of information laws, the coverage of the Act is comprehensive. When it is fully in force, over 100,000 individuals and bodies will be subject to its provisions. The general approach adopted in the Act is to provide a finite list of public authorities which are subject to its regime. In this regard, it can be contrasted with the Human Rights Act 1998, which provides only a partial definition of the 'public authorities' subject to its requirements and relies upon courts to determine whether particular bodies satisfy the relevant definition (Human Rights Act 1998, s 6). In fact, the Human Rights Act is likely to capture more bodies than the Act. Where an approach based upon a finite list is adopted, some authorities will inevitably be omitted and the regime will only apply to them if the Secretary of State can be convinced to add them later.

The various categories of 'public authority' subject to the Act are examined in further detail at 4.5.1 below. However, it is first necessary to consider the application of the Act to public authorities within the different nations of the United Kingdom. Authorities with nation-wide powers are generally subject to the duties established by the Act. This is also the case with authorities whose primary functions relate to Wales or Northern Ireland (including the National Assembly for Wales and the Northern Ireland Assembly).

Public authorities dealing with matters falling within the competence of the Scottish Parliament are not, however, subject to the Act (s 84). A separate right of access to information held by such public authorities is provided under Scottish legislation (Freedom of Information Act (Scotland) 2002) (see 2.8 for further detail of the scope of this legislation). Under the scheme established under the two Acts, certain requests for access to information held in Scotland must be made under the Act and others must be made under the Scottish legislation. For example, a request for information held by a UK government body (or by any other body listed in Sch 1 to the Act) must be made under the Act. However, any request to any authority falling within the competence of the Scottish Parliament, such as a Scottish local authority or school, must be made under the Freedom of Information Act (Scotland) 2002. The division of responsibility between the UK and Scottish Parliaments is established under the Scotland Act 1998.

It should be noted that there are certain bodies which might, in a general sense, be described as public authorities, but are not defined as public authorities for the purpose of the Act. Information held by these bodies is not, therefore, accessible under the Act. Examples of such public authorities are the Security Service, the Secret Intelligence Service and the Royal Household.

4.5.1 Public Authorities Listed in Schedule 1

Schedule 1 contains a lengthy list of public bodies governed by the Act. Within the schedule, individual Parts list distinct categories of authority.

Part 1—General
Part I of Sch 1 lists 'core' public authorities—government departments, the House of Commons, the House of Lords, the Northern Ireland Assembly, the National Assembly for Wales and the armed forces of the Crown. Certain bodies are, however, excluded from the Act's scope. The definition of 'government department' not only excludes various Scottish bodies but also the Security Service, the Secret Intelligence Service and the Government Communications Headquarters (GCHQ) (s 84). These excluded bodies are therefore not subject to any of the obligations to provide access to information under the Act (save, to a limited degree, in relation to historical records; see 11.4.2 below). In this regard, the Act can be contrasted with freedom of information legislation in the United States, Canada and New Zealand, under which information held by the security services is not automatically excluded.

It is also important to note that the definition of 'government department' in the Act includes any 'body exercising statutory functions on behalf of the Crown' (s 84). As a result, the increasing number of governmental agencies, such as the Prison Service and the UK Passport Agency, fall within Part I.

Part II—Local Government
Part II of Sch 1 contains an extensive list of bodies responsible for local government in England, Wales and Northern Ireland; ranging from county councils and the Greater London Authority to local fire authorities, parish councils, internal drainage boards and magistrates' court committees.

Part III—The National Health Service
Part III covers authorities responsible for delivering public health services in England, Wales and Northern Ireland. The list includes not only Health Authorities and NHS trusts but also individuals providing public medical, dental, ophthalmic and pharmaceutical services 'in respect of information relating to the provision of those services' (Sch 1, paras 44, 45 and 51). Information held in recorded form by these individuals will be covered by the Act as long as it relates to the provision of NHS services.

Part IV—Schools and Other Educational Institutions
Part IV of Sch 1 lists bodies primarily responsible for the delivery of public education services in England, Wales and Northern Ireland. Generally, in England and Wales, these are the governing bodies of schools and institutions providing further and higher education. The equivalent bodies in Northern Ireland are also covered.

Other bodies responsible for the organisation and supervision of education are also subject to the Act, but are listed elsewhere in Sch 1. For example, the Department of Education and Employment falls within the scope of the Act because it is a 'government department' within Part I of Sch 1 and local education authorities (LEAs) fall within Part II. Information held by educational institutions without governing bodies (such as pupil referral units) will be obtainable by means of an application to the relevant LEA (Hansard HL, 17 October 2000, col 946). In addition, Parts VI and VII (concerning miscellaneous public authorities) include such bodies as the British Council, the Commonwealth Scholarship Commission in the United Kingdom, the School Teachers' Review Body and the Northern Ireland Higher Education Council.

Part V—Policing
Part V of Sch 1 lists bodies responsible for policing and includes police authorities in England, Wales and Northern Ireland and chief officers of police of police forces in England, Wales and Northern Ireland. It also includes the British Transport Police, the Ministry of Defence Police and any person who is responsible for nominating individuals who may be appointed as special constables by justices of the peace who is not otherwise defined as a 'public authority' under the Act. The National Criminal Intelligence Service is not listed, either here or in Part VI. However, the National Crime Squad is listed in Part VI (see below).

Parts VI and VII—Miscellaneous Public Authorities
Parts VI (General) and VII (Northern Ireland) contain very lengthy lists of miscellaneous public bodies from the Adjudicator for the Inland Revenue and Customs and Excise, via the Farm Animal Welfare Council and the Welsh Dental Committee, to the Youth Council for Northern Ireland.

Public Authorities to which the Act has Limited Application
It is important to note that, where an authority is listed in Sch 1 in relation only to information of a specified description, other information which it may hold is not subject to the Act (s 7(1)). Thus, for example, where a dentist treats some patients under the NHS and others privately, information concerning the provision of NHS services is subject to the Act but information relating to purely private work is not.

There are a number of other authorities on which the Act has limited effect. Perhaps the most noteworthy are the BBC, Channel 4, the Traffic Commissioners and the Competition Commission. In the case of such authorities, it will not always be easy to distinguish information covered by the Act from that which is not. For example, by virtue of a listing within Part VI, the British Broadcasting Corporation is governed by the Act 'in respect of information held for purposes other than those of journalism, art or literature'. In this instance, the partial coverage is not imposed in recognition of mixed private and public functions carried out by the BBC, but rather to ensure that the creative and investigative freedom of those working for the BBC is not unduly hampered by applications for disclosure of information under the Act (cf s 32 Data Protection Act 1998 and s 12 Human Rights Act 1998). There would seem to be considerable scope for dispute as to the circumstances in which information will be held for the purposes of journalism, art or literature. Given the purpose of the provision, however, it is likely that only information held in connection with specific programme-making activities will be excluded from the operation of the Act. More general information, relating to finance, management or other business activities will fall within the scope of the Act.

Amending Schedule 1 (s 4)
Under s 4 of the Act, the Secretary of State is permitted by order to add authorities to Sch 1 where two specified conditions are satisfied (s 4(1)). The first condition is that the body, or office, being considered for inclusion:

(a) is established by virtue of Her Majesty's prerogative or by an enactment or by subordinate legislation, or

(b) is established in any other way by a Minister of the Crown in his capacity as Minister or by a government department.

The second condition is that:

(a) in the case of a body, that the body is wholly or partly constituted by appointment made by the Crown, by a Minister of the Crown or by a government department, or

(b) in the case of an office, that appointments to the office are made by the Crown, by a Minister of the Crown, or by a government department.

This power will be employed where authorities have been overlooked or where new authorities are created after the passing of the Act. It can be exercised in relation to a specified person or office or in relation to a generic description of persons or offices (s 4(6)). Prior to the full coming into force of the Act, the Secretary of State has already exercised the power to bring a number of public authorities within the scope of the Act. For example, under the Freedom of Information (Additional Public Authorities) Order 2004, the Advisory Committee on Organic Standards and the Independent Review Panel for Borderline Products were, amongst other bodies, added to Part VI of Sch I.

Where the Secretary of State is considering whether to add a Welsh or Northern Ireland public authority to Sch 1 under this provision, he or she is obliged to consult the National Assembly for Wales or the First Minister and Deputy First Minister in Northern Ireland, as appropriate (s 4(7)). In accordance with the position with regard to devolved powers discussed above, the power cannot be exercised to add Scottish bodies to Sch 1 (s 4(8)).

It should be noted that the Secretary of State has no *obligation* to add authorities satisfying the relevant conditions to Sch 1. However, it is possible that prolonged failure to add a body clearly satisfying the criteria could be challenged in judicial review proceedings. Where the Secretary of State exercises the power to add authorities to Sch 1, he or she may list a body 'only in relation to information of a specified description' (s 7(2)). If an authority is listed in this limited way, it will only be subject to the provisions of the Act in respect of the information of the specified description.

Where an authority is already listed in Sch 1, the Secretary of State has the power by order to limit the application of the Act in relation to that authority to information of a specified description and the power by order to remove or amend any such existing limitation (s 7(3)). If the Secretary of State is considering making an order under s 7(3) relating to a Welsh or Northern Ireland public authority, he or she is obliged to consult relevant ministerial colleagues (s 7(4)). Concern that the power in s 7(3) was capable of being abused gave rise to Parliamentary assurances that it would not be exercised to defeat the purposes of the Act illegitimately (Hansard HL, 14 November 2000, col 182).

Where a body or office listed in Part VI or VII of Sch 1 (concerning miscellaneous public authorities) ceases to satisfy the conditions set out in s 4(1), that body or the holder of that office ceases to be a public authority for the purposes of the Act (s 4(4)). In such circumstances, the body automatically ceases to be subject to the Act. The Secretary of State, however, also has the power to remove entries relating to bodies or offices from Parts VI or Part VII where those bodies or offices have either ceased to exist or ceased to satisfy the conditions set out in s 4(1) (s 4(5)). This power exists to ensure that Parts VI and VII represent an accurate list of bodies subject to the Act and has already been exercised in a number of cases.

4.5.2 Designated Public Authorities under s 5

Authorities Exercising Public Functions
In addition to those public authorities which are publicly established and staffed and are therefore either listed in Sch 1 or capable of being added to it by order under s 4, s 5(1) empowers the Secretary of State by order to designate further persons or bodies as public authorities for the purpose of the Act. This power arises where the person or body in question:

(a) appears to the Secretary of State to exercise functions of a public nature, or

(b) is providing under a contract made with a public authority any service whose provision is a function of that authority.

On second reading in the House of Lords, Lord Falconer of Thoroton, gave some indication of the bodies which are likely to be nominated under s 5:

... [W]e are minded to consult organisations such as those running prisons under contract, or the British Board of Film Censorship, for example, about designation ...

(Hansard HL, 20 April 2000, col 825)

Organisations such as the British Board of Film Classification could be argued to be exercising 'functions of a public nature' under s 5(1)(a). The scope of that paragraph will be similar to that of s 6(3)(b) of the Human Rights Act 1998, which brings 'any person certain of whose functions are functions of a public nature' within the scope of that legislation. Private organisations such as Railtrack, Group 4 and the Press Complaints Commission are also likely candidates for designation as public authorities because they exercise functions of a public nature. At the time that the Act came fully into force, no such designations had yet been made.

Authorities Providing Services under Contract
Section 5(1)(b) covers persons or bodies providing 'contracted out' services for a public authority. For example, under this paragraph, the Secretary of State will be able to bring companies running local schools or refuse collection services in a particular area within the scope of the Act. In some cases, there will be an overlap between s 5(1)(a) and s 5(1)(b). This will be the case, for example, in relation to a company running private prisons under contract.

Any order made under s 5(1)(a) must specify those functions of the public authority which are to be brought within the scope of the Act. Only information relating to the exercise of those functions will be subject to the Act (s 7(5)). Any order made under s 5(1)(b) must specify those services provided under contract which are to be brought within the scope of the Act. Again, only information relating to the provision of those services will be subject to the Act (s 7(6)). Before making a designating order under this section, the Secretary of State is obliged to consult 'every person to whom the order relates' or their representatives (s 5(3)). Both decisions to make an order under these provisions and decisions not to designate a particular person or body under these provisions will be subject to judicial review. At the time that the Act came fully into force, no such designations had yet been made.

4.5.3 Publicly-owned Companies (s 6)

The final category of authorities subject to the Act are 'publicly-owned companies', as defined in s 6. This is the only category under which authorities automatically fall within the Act without specific reference in either Sch 1 or a subsequent Ministerial order. A company is 'publicly-owned' for the purpose of s 6 if:

(a) it is wholly owned by the Crown, or

(b) it is wholly owned by any public authority listed in Schedule 1 other than—
    (i) a government department, or
    (ii) any authority which is listed only in relation to particular information.

Such companies as Manchester Airport plc and some 'spin-off' companies established by universities will satisfy this definition. The meaning of 'wholly owned' for the purposes of this provision is provided in s 6(2). It should also be noted that the Secretary of State has a power to designate certain information held by a publicly-owned company as 'excluded information'. Such information is not subject to the duties established under the Act (s 7(7) and (8)).

4.6 PUBLICATION SCHEMES

4.6.1 Introduction

In addition to the duties to communicate information and to confirm or deny that information is held by the authority under s 1(1), every public authority subject to the Act is required to adopt, maintain and review a 'publication scheme' and to publish information in accordance with that scheme (s 19). Publication schemes are designed to ensure that public authorities take proactive steps to release information to the public. Section 19(2) sets out requirements for the contents of a public authority's publication scheme. It must:

(a) specify classes of information which the public authority publishes or intends to publish,

(b) specify the manner in which information of each class is, or is intended to be, published, and

(c) specify whether the material is, or is intended to be, available to the public free of charge or on payment.

In adopting or reviewing its publication scheme, a public authority is obliged to 'have regard to the public interest' in disclosing information to the public and in publishing reasons for decisions made by the authority (s 19(3)).

A public authority's publication scheme is intended to be a guide to the types of information that it routinely publishes, rather than a list of the actual information that is available without request under the Act. Where information is available in accordance with a publication scheme, a public authority will not usually be obliged to supply it in response to a request made under the Act. This is because the information is likely to be regarded as 'reasonably accessible to the applicant', and therefore exempt, under s 21 (s 21(3), see discussion at 7.2).

The obligations relating to publication schemes have been fully in force for all public authorities since June 2004.

4.6.2 Supervision of Publication Schemes

Publication schemes must be approved by the Information Commissioner (s 19(1)(a)). Such approval can be granted for a limited period and can be revoked on six months' notice (s 19(5) and (6)). Under s 20, the Information Commissioner may also approve 'model publication schemes' covering different classes of public authority (for example, maintained schools or parish councils). Proposals for model publication schemes can derive either from the Information Commissioner himself or from other persons (such as bodies representing the interests of particular classes of public authority). Where a model publication scheme is approved by the Information Commissioner and is adopted by a public authority without modification, that authority does not have to seek individual approval for its publication scheme (s 20(2)). This system of blanket approval will obviate the need for every GP and every school governing body to seek and retain individual approval from the Information Commissioner. In addition, such model publication schemes serve another purpose. They ensure uniformity of practice in relation to the proactive disclosure of information by public authorities. Where a public authority adopts an appropriate approved model publication scheme with modifications, it is required to seek the Information Commissioner's approval only in relation to the modifications (s 20(2)).

If the Information Commissioner refuses to approve a proposed publication scheme (or model publication scheme) or revokes approval for a publication scheme, he must give the particular public authority a statement of reasons for doing so (ss 19(7) and 20(5) and (6)). Public authorities cannot appeal to the Information Tribunal against decisions of the Information Commissioner in relation to publication schemes. Accordingly, a public body which is aggrieved by the Information Commissioner's failure to approve a publication scheme, or by a revocation of approval, will be required to instigate proceedings for judicial review. Where a public authority fails to comply with the provisions relating to publication schemes discussed above, it will have failed to comply with a requirement of Part I of the Act and could therefore be served with an enforcement notice by the Information Commissioner (s 52; see 9.2.2.3 below). In addition, the Commissioner is able to publicise default by public authorities in this regard in the annual report which he is required to provide to Parliament (s 49).

It has been confirmed that, while smaller public authorities will not necessarily be required to maintain a digitised publication scheme, the Information Commissioner will ensure that public authorities generally make appropriate use of electronic communication in their schemes (Hansard HL, 22 November 2000, col 819). He will also question any unreasonable proposals with regard to charging for copies of publication schemes (Hansard HL, 14 November 2000, col 199–200).

The Act does not regulate the level of charges that a public authority can make for the provision of the information contained in a publication scheme. Under s 19(2)(a), authorities are not obliged to specify a precise fee for supply of particular information, but simply to state *whether* a charge is made for the information. As a result, a particular publication scheme will not have to be amended whenever pricing details change. However, the Information Commissioner has emphasised that the level of charges levied under a publication scheme should be compatible with the principle of promoting public access to the information held by public authorities. He has also noted that:

It is important to recognise that the Freedom of Information Act does not give public authorities the power to charge for information. It merely provides that the publication scheme must identify whether charges will apply. The actual power to levy those charges must be provided under other legislation. A public authority that attempts to levy a charge without the power to do so will be acting ultra vires. In some cases an authority may be permitted to charge for goods and services on a cost recovery basis but would not have the power to make a profit.

Information Commissioner, *Charges under Publication Schemes* (v 1, October 2003, www.informationcommissioner.gov.uk)

In addition, it should be noted that, if information is supplied at excessive cost under a publication scheme, it may not be 'reasonably accessible' to an applicant and therefore the exemption under s 21 may not be applicable. In such circumstances, an applicant would be entitled to make an application for the information under the Act.

4.6.3 Content of Publication Schemes

The Act does not itself specify information that must be made available under a public authority's publication scheme. However, in the Parliamentary debates on the legislation, it was confirmed that manuals of guidance applied by public authorities ought generally to be made available in this way (Hansard HC, 5 April 2000, col 1118). Such manuals may be extremely valuable to applicants who wish, for example, to understand the criteria which local authorities apply in deciding applications for admission to schools or the priorities for treatment applied by a local healthcare trust.

Subsequent guidance from the Information Commissioner has suggested that the following sorts of information, amongst others, are likely to be made available under publication schemes: organisational information, agendas and minutes of meetings, targets, information concerning sources of information, circulars, reasoned decisions where those decisions are likely to affect others, information concerning the legal framework within which an authority operates, information concerning procurement and contracts entered into by the authority, and information disclosed to applicants as a result of requests made under the Act (Information Commissioner, *Publication Schemes: Guidance and Methodology*, April 2003, www.informationcommissioner.gov.uk). A good idea of the different forms of information available under publication schemes can be obtained by visiting the websites of public authorities, such as government departments or universities, or the Information Commissioner's own website.

5

APPLICATIONS FOR INFORMATION—PROCEDURE

5.1 INTRODUCTION

In this chapter, various procedural aspects of the regime introduced by the Freedom of Information Act 2000 are considered. The provisions under discussion are largely set out in ss 8–17 of the Act. However, the Act also leaves a number of procedural matters to be implemented by the Secretary of State by statutory instrument.

In addition, under s 45 of the Act, the Secretary of State is obliged to issue a Code of Practice providing guidance to public authorities on the scope of their duties under Part I of the Act. This Code provides detailed instructions to public authorities on the way in which they should respond to requests for information (see Appendix 2 for the full text of the Code of Practice on the Discharge of the Functions of Public Authorities under Part I of the Freedom of Information Act 2000—'Code of Practice under s 45').

Where a public authority fails to comply with a duty under the Act itself (for example, the duty to communicate information (s 1(1)(b)) or the duty to provide reasons for refusing a request for information (s 17)), a disappointed applicant can invoke the enforcement powers of the Information Commissioner (see Chapter 9 below). Where a public authority fails to comply with a requirement established in *regulations* made under the Act, this will generally also result in a breach of a provision of the Act itself. The Information Commissioner will again be able to enforce compliance. Failure to adhere to the Code of Practice is a different matter. Where failure to comply with a provision of the Code also constitutes a breach of the public authority's duty to provide advice and assistance (s 16; see 5.9 below), the Information Commissioner will be able to enforce compliance with that duty. However, where a breach of the Code does not also constitute a breach of duty under Part I of the Act, the Commissioner's enforcement powers are not available. While the Commissioner is required to promote good practice in accordance with the published Code of Practice under s 45 (s 47), the only sanction available to him in such circumstances is his power to issue a practice recommendation (s 48). There are no formal sanctions for failure to comply with such a practice recommendation, although a public authority ignoring a recommendation may find itself subject to adverse comment in the annual report which the Commissioner is required to lay before the Houses of Parliament (s 49) (see also Hansard HL, 17 October 2000, col 944).

5.2 FORMAL REQUIREMENTS FOR AN APPLICATION UNDER THE ACT

Requests for access to information under the Act must comply with certain formalities. These are set out in s 8(1):

In this Act ... reference to a 'request for information' is a reference to such a request which—

(a) is in writing,
(b) states the name of the applicant and an address for correspondence, and
(c) describes the information requested.

Before considering these requirements in further detail, it is important to note that the Act contains no obligation to refer specifically to the Act when making an information request. All written requests for information, including those which would formerly have been made and granted informally, are subject to the provisions of the Act.

In some instances, it may, however, be useful for an applicant to emphasise that a request for information is being made under the Act. Such emphasis is likely to remind a public authority of its obligations (for example, in relation to time-limits) under the Act. However, express reference to the Act could also lead the public authority to handle the request in accordance with more formal procedures, which are likely to include, for example, the requirement to pay a fee. In practice, public authorities are likely to ensure that all information requests are channelled through particular internal procedures in order to ensure compliance with the Act and the Code of Practice under s 45. It should be noted that the Home Office's Advisory Group on Openness has recommended that, following the coming into force of the Act, public authorities should not begin to charge for materials that they were previously willing to provide without charge.

The Act does not specify a particular individual or office-holder within public authorities to whom requests for information must be sent. This may present some difficulties for public authorities because they will be subject to duties established under the Act from the moment at which a request is received. Under the Code of Practice under s 45, public authorities are required to publish their procedures for dealing with requests for information and to include details of an address to which applicants can direct requests for information or assistance. Reference to such procedures should be made in an authority's publication scheme (Code of Practice, para 6; see Appendix 2).

5.2.1 Request for Information must be in Writing

Requests for information under the Act must be in writing (s 8(1)(a)). For the purposes of this provision, a request is to be treated as made in writing where it:

(a) is transmitted by electronic means,

(b) is received in legible form, and

(c) is capable of being used for subsequent reference.

(s 8(2))

Thus, a request for information sent by e-mail would generally satisfy this requirement. A public authority is not obliged to comply with its duties under the Act where it receives an oral request for information—for example, a request made during the course of a telephone conversation. However, in such a case, failure to advise an applicant of the need to submit a written request is likely to constitute a breach of the authority's duty to provide advice and assistance under s 16 of the Act. Both the duty to provide advice and assistance and the Code of Practice under s 45 apply to applicants for information whether or not they satisfy the formal requirements of the Act (see, s 16(1) and Hansard HL, 17 October 2000, col 945).

Where an individual is 'unable to frame their request in writing' (perhaps as a result of illiteracy, disability or illness), the Code of Practice places further specific obligations upon public authorities to ensure that assistance in framing a request is given. The Code specifies (in para 8) that appropriate assistance could include:

- advising the person that another person or agency (such as a Citizens Advice Bureau) can assist them with the application, or make the application on their behalf;
- in exceptional circumstances offering to take a note of the application over the telephone and then send the note to the applicant for confirmation (in which case the written note of the telephone request, once verified by the applicant and returned, would constitute a written request for information and the statutory time limit for reply would begin when the written confirmation was received).

Failure to act on the recommendations of the Code in this regard will not *automatically* result in a breach of s 16 because the relevant provisions of the Code state only that appropriate assistance might include the specified responses. However, a public authority would be strongly advised to implement the Code's suggestions in order to ensure compliance with s 16. Where it does comply with the Code, a public authority will automatically satisfy the duty to provide advice and assistance in this regard (s 16(2)).

5.2.2 Requirement to Provide a Name and Address for Correspondence (s 8(1)(b))

This provision is in almost all aspects self-explanatory. However, it is worth noting that the promoters of the legislation did not regard the provision of an e-mail address alone by an applicant as satisfying this requirement (Hansard HL, 14 November 2000, col 184). The reason given for this view was that a public authority which possessed information only in hard copy, rather than in electronic format, would not be able to communicate this information to an applicant who had given only an e-mail address. Again, however, on receipt of a request containing only an e-mail address, a public authority would presumably be obliged under s 16 to inform an applicant that an address in the physical world was also required.

Perhaps surprisingly, it was also suggested during debates in the House of Lords on this provision that, as a result of the 'applicant-blind' approach adopted under the Act, it was perfectly in order for an applicant to give a false name (Hansard HL, 14 November 2000, col 184). However, this may not be correct. The legislation requires 'the' name of an applicant rather than 'a' name to be stated. It is difficult to see how a false name made up for the purpose of making an application could be 'the' name of an applicant.

5.2.3 Requirement to Describe the Information Requested (s 8(1)(c))

This is the formal requirement most likely to cause practical difficulties for applicants. It is clearly imposed in order to allow a public authority to identify the specific information sought by an applicant amongst a potentially huge volume of information (cf s 7(3), Data Protection Act 1998). However, an applicant who is unfamiliar with the way in which information is retained and organised within a particular public authority will be at a significant disadvantage in describing the information that he or she is seeking. It is in relation to this paragraph that the duty to provide advice and assistance placed upon public authorities by s 16 is likely to prove most valuable to an applicant.

In addition, particular measures to enable an applicant to describe information are set out in the Code of Practice. Where an applicant fails to comply with s 8(1)(c) and, accordingly, fails to make a 'request for information' for the purposes of the Act, para 9 of the Code under s 45 obliges the relevant public authority to help the applicant to describe the information requested more clearly. Failure to comply with this obligation is again likely to constitute a breach of the duty to offer advice and assistance under s 16. A number of possible ways in which a public authority could provide assistance are listed in para 10 of the Code. This could involve, for example:

• providing an outline of the different kinds of information which might meet the terms of the request;

• providing access to detailed catalogues and indexes, where these are available, to help the applicant ascertain the nature and extent of the information held by the authority;

• providing a general response to the request setting out options for further information which could be provided on request.

Again, although failure to comply with these requirements will not automatically result in a breach of s 16, public authorities would be advised to protect themselves against proceedings for breach of that section by implementing the recommended procedures.

Paragraph 11 of the Code also makes it clear that:

applicants cannot reasonably be expected to possess identifiers such as a file reference number, or a description of a particular record, unless this information is made available by the authority for the use of applicants.

However, where, following the provision of assistance such as that described above, the applicant fails to describe the information requested 'in a way which would enable the authority to identify or locate it', the authority is not expected to seek further clarification (Code of Practice under s 45, para 12). In such circumstances, however, an authority must disclose any information relating to the application which *has* successfully identified and found. Failure to do so will constitute a breach of the duty to communicate information.

5.3 FEES

A public authority is entitled to charge a fee for complying with its duties under the Act. There is, however, no obligation upon it to charge for providing information. Where an authority wishes to make a charge, it must provide the applicant with a 'fees notice' in accordance with s 9(1):

A public authority to whom a request for information is made may, within the period for complying with section 1(1), give the applicant a notice in writing (in this Act referred to as a 'fees notice') stating that a fee of an amount specified in the notice is to be charged by the authority for complying with section 1(1).

Thus, if it is to be effective, the 'fees notice' must be in writing and must be given to the applicant within the period specified for complying with the duties under s 1(1) (see 5.4 below). If a public authority does not exercise the power to issue a fees notice, it is not entitled to claim a fee. However, it is not absolved from its duties under the Act.

Where an applicant receives a fees notice, the specified fee must be paid within three months of the giving of the notice to the applicant. If payment is not made within that period, the public authority is not obliged to comply with s 1(1). The working days between the day on which the fees notice is given to the applicant and the day on which the fee is received by the authority are disregarded in calculating whether the public authority has complied with its duty within the Act's time limits (see 5.4). In other words, the clock stops while the public authority is awaiting payment from the applicant.

Applicants could be discouraged from taking up their rights under a freedom of information regime if fees for access are set at too high a level. Accordingly, a mechanism for regulating the charging of fees by public authorities is established. Section 9(3) states that:

. . . any fee under this section must be determined by the public authority in accordance with regulations made by the Secretary of State.

The only exception to this general rule arises where another enactment makes specific provision for the level of fees to be charged in relation to a particular form of disclosure (s 9(5)). For example, the level of fee for the supply of 'office copies' of the Land Registry entry for a particular property is governed by specific regulations. The specific charging provisions will continue to apply in that case.

The draft Freedom of Information (Fees and Appropriate Limit) Regulations had already indicated that the scheme set in place by the Act was not expected to be self-financing. The Regulations provided that an applicant would be charged the full cost of the authority's 'disbursements' (such as costs for photo-copying and postage) incurred in responding to an application. However, the authority would only be able to recover 10 per cent of its costs of searching for and providing the information. It was proposed that it would not be able to charge for time spent considering whether the information is covered by an exemption.

However in a speech made on 18 October 2004 the Secretary of State for Constitutional Affairs, Lord Falconer, stated:

No individual should be priced out of the right to know. So I am pleased to announce today, that for the vast majority of cases there will be no charge for information supplied under the Freedom of Information Act. Freedom of Information really means free information. The Government will lay fees regulations before Parliament in November. There will be no charge for information that costs public bodies less than £450 to produce. And for central government, the cost ceiling will be set at £600.

In practice this means that there will be no charges below these limits for the 'search fee' but the full disbursement fee (copying etc) will still be charged. It assumed that fees above these limits will be calculated in accordance with the draft Regulations (but see 5.7 below).

In addition to providing that regulations limiting the level of fee payable can be made under the Act, s 9(4) specifies that regulations prescribing that 'no fee is to be payable in prescribed cases' can also be made. Fee 'waivers' are, in certain circumstances, a common feature of freedom of information regimes in other jurisdictions. They generally apply when there is a particular public interest in access to information (for example, because the applicant is a Member of Parliament—see the New Zealand Law Commission's *Review of the Official Information Act 1982* (Auckland, 1997), paras 146–149).

The Code of Practice issued under s 45 (see Appendix 2), para 14, recommends that the authority should try to avoid refusals based on excessive costs by indicating to the applicant what might be provided within the costs ceiling.

5.4 TIME-LIMITS FOR COMPLIANCE WITH A REQUEST FOR INFORMATION

Section 10(1) of the Act provides that:

. . . a public authority must comply with section 1(1) promptly and in any event not later than the twentieth working day following the date of receipt.

The 'date of receipt' will, in general, be the date on which the public authority receives the initial request for information. However, where the public authority has reasonably required further information in order to enable it to find the information in question, the 'date of receipt' is the date on which that further information is received by the authority (s 10(6)). Where an authority has issued a 'fees notice' (see 5.3 above), the time within which the authority is required to comply with its duties under the Act is effectively extended. This is because the period beginning with the giving of the fees notice and ending with the receipt of the fee by the authority is disregarded in calculating the period required for compliance with the request for information (s 10(2)).

A public authority is obliged to comply with a request (and not simply to 'respond') *'promptly'*. The requirement to comply with its duties not later than on the twentieth working day establishes only a maximum period. Thus, for example, if a public authority can identify requested information very easily but, nevertheless, takes 20 days to respond to the request, it may, depending upon the circumstances, be in breach of its obligation to comply 'promptly'. The Code of Practice issued under s 45 states at para 1: 'Public authorities are required to comply with all requests for information promptly and they should not delay responding until the end of the 20 working day period under section 10(1) if the information could reasonably have been provided earlier.' It should be noted that there is no specific requirement for an authority to respond expeditiously where a special need for an urgent response can be established. However, it could be argued that the requirement to respond 'promptly' should be interpreted to take account of such considerations. Thus, for example, where a journalist seeks information held by a public authority in connection with a news story of pressing public importance, a public authority may be required to take account of the time-sensitivity of the request in order to satisfy its duty to comply 'promptly'.

5.4.1 Decisions on Disclosure of Information Subject to a Qualified Exemption

Where a public authority considers that requested information is exempt from the duty to confirm or deny or the duty to communicate information as a result of an 'absolute exemption' (see Chapter 7), it must come to a decision on disclosure within the standard time-limits described above. However, where it considers that the information is covered by one of the 'qualified exemptions' (see Chapter 8), the public authority is only required to comply with its duties under Part I of the Act within 'such time as is reasonable in the circumstances' (s 10(3)). This provision recognises that the task of weighing up the relevant public interests in disclosure and non-disclosure may be a difficult task and aims to ensure that public authorities are not tempted to decide that the public interest favours continued secrecy simply because they have insufficient time to investigate the consequences of disclosure fully (see Hansard HL, 14 November 2000, col 189). In fact the Code of Practice issued under s 45 of the Act provides some helpful guidance to avoid unnecessary delays. It states at para 18:

Public authorities should aim to make *all* decisions within 20 working days, including in cases where a public authority needs to consider where the public interest lies in respect of an application for exempt information. However, it is recognised there will be some instances where it will not be possible to deal with such an application within 20 working days. Although there is no statutory time limit on the length of time the authority may take to reach a decision where the public interest must be considered, it must, under section 17(2), give an estimate of the date by which it expects to reach such a decision. In these instances, authorities are expected to give estimates which are realistic and reasonable in the circumstances of the particular case, taking account, for example, of the need to consult third parties where this is necessary. Public authorities are expected to comply with their estimates unless there are good reasons not to. If the public authority exceeds its estimate, it should apologise to the applicant and explain the reason(s) for the delay. If a public authority finds, while considering the public interest, that the estimate given is proving unrealistic, it should keep the applicant informed. Public authorities should keep a record of instances where estimates are exceeded, and where this happens more than occasionally, take steps to identify the problem and rectify it.

The authority's assessment of what is 'reasonable in the circumstances' is subject to the supervision of the Information Commissioner. In addition, it should also be noted that where a public authority has not been able to come to a decision on whether to release information covered by a 'qualified exemption' within the standard 20-day period, it must nevertheless provide the applicant with a notice stating that fact (s 10(3)).

5.4.2 Extensions of Time for Compliance

Under s 10(4) of the Act, the Secretary of State is empowered to make regulations extending the 20-day period for compliance generally or in particular cases. Such regulations cannot, however, extend the period beyond 60 days. Draft Regulations issued during the Act's progress through Parliament indicate that extensions to the period for compliance will, in certain cases, be permitted where approved by the Information Commissioner.

5.5 TRANSFERRING REQUESTS TO OTHER AUTHORITIES

Sometimes the information sought by an applicant will in fact be held by a different authority than the one receiving the original application. In such circumstances it will be insufficient for the authority receiving the application merely to say that it does not hold that information. The authority has a duty to provide advice and assistance to the applicant and to follow the Code of Practice issued under s 45 (see Appendix 2). The authority must of course provide any information it does hold itself, but para 24 of the Code states that:

If the authority to whom the original request was made believes that some or all of the information requested is held by another public authority, the authority should consider what would be the most helpful way of assisting the applicant with his or her request. In most cases this is likely to involve:

- contacting the applicant and informing him or her that the information requested may be held by another public authority;
- suggesting that the applicant re-applies to the authority which the original authority believes to hold the information;
- providing him or her with contact details for that authority.

If the authority does not know which other authority holds the information it should provide what advice it can to assist the applicant to pursue his request (para 30).

The Code of Practice also gives advice on the circumstances in which the request should be transferred to another authority. Before doing so the original authority must consult the authority it believes holds the information (para 25). Before transferring the request the authority must consider whether the applicant is likely to object to the transfer, but does not have to consult the applicant before taking that action although the applicant must be informed once this has been done (para 26). If the original authority has reasonable grounds for thinking the applicant would object to the transfer then it must obtain his or her consent before doing so.

Transfers should take place as soon as possible and once the transfer has taken place the receiving authority has the same duties to deal with the request as if the request had been made directly although time limits only run from the date of transfer (para 28).

5.6 MEANS OF COMMUNICATING INFORMATION

Under the Act, an applicant is entitled to state that he or she wishes to have information communicated in one or more specified means (s 11(1)). These are:

(a) the provision to the applicant of a copy of the information in permanent form or in another form acceptable to the applicant;

(b) the provision to the applicant of a reasonable opportunity to inspect a record containing the information; and

(c) the provision to the applicant of a digest or summary of the information in permanent form or in another form acceptable to the applicant.

Where an applicant specifies one of these methods of communication, a public authority must 'so far as reasonably practicable' give effect to that preference. Where an applicant does not specify a method of communication, a public authority is entitled to comply with a request 'by communicating information by any means which are reasonable in the circumstances' (s 11(4)). In assessing the reasonableness of a particular method of communication, the public authority is required to 'have regard to all the circumstances, including the cost of doing so' (s 11(2)). Where a public authority determines that it is not reasonably practicable to comply with an application by specified means, it is obliged to give reasons for that determination (s 11(3)).

The means of communication listed in s 11(1) give some indication of the ways in which public authorities are likely to provide information to applicants under the Act. In certain cases, one form of communication may be more appropriate than another. For example, where a request for information requires an authority to communicate information contained in a large number of documents, it may be more appropriate to allow inspection of the documents rather than to copy them for the applicant. The choice of means of communication may have significant cost consequences. In the example given above, copying all the documents would be a costly process. As 'disbursements', these costs are likely to be passed on to the applicant. In addition, certain forms of communication will be more labour-intensive than others. It could, for example, take considerably longer for an employee of a public authority to photocopy a large number of documents than to make them available for inspection. The costs of the time spent giving effect to an applicant's preference for a means of communication could therefore be a serious consideration.

Where an applicant specifies a preference for a particularly time-consuming form of communication, the public authority dealing with the request may claim either that it is not reasonably practicable to give effect to that preference or that the costs of compliance with this preference are excessive and that it is therefore not obliged to comply with the expressed preference (s 12; see below). If the public authority adopts the former course of action, it must notify the applicant of its reasons for not giving effect to his or her specified preference (s 11(3)). If it adopts the latter course of action, it would seem to be obliged only to give the applicant a notice specifying that the costs of compliance are excessive and it is therefore not obliged to satisfy the request. However, in either case, it would surely constitute a breach of the duty to provide advice and assistance if a public authority were not to explain to an applicant that the information could be provided in some other manner.

Applicants may wish to take tactical decisions when making requests for information. In addition to the issues described above, there may be other reasons for choosing to inspect records containing information rather than receiving copies or a digest. It is possible that, by inspecting documents containing the requested information, an applicant may come across further valuable information. Applicants should also beware that in other jurisdictions some public authorities appear to have swamped applicants with information in an attempt to make it harder for an applicant to identify specific relevant information—a tactic known as 'generous compliance' (see Legal Research Foundation, *The Official Information Act* (Auckland, 1997), p 35). If a public authority in this jurisdiction were to respond to a request in this way, an applicant would be able to complain to the Information Commissioner on two grounds. First, it would be able to claim that the authority has not complied with a request to communicate information in a manner which is reasonable in the circumstances (s 11(4)) and second, it could be argued that the public authority has failed to comply with its duty to offer assistance under s 16.

Various unsuccessful attempts were made in Parliament to amend the legislation to force public authorities to make greater use of electronic means of communicating information. The government argued that forcing all public authorities to respond to requests to provide information in electronic format would place an undue burden upon smaller authorities, such as parish councils and general practitioners, who would be obliged to convert records of information into digital form (Hansard HL, 14 November 2000, col 184). Nevertheless, s 11(1) refers to 'a copy of the information in permanent form or in another form acceptable to the applicant' and it therefore remains possible for an applicant to specify a preference for communication of information by electronic means. A public authority would only be required to comply with such a preference where it is reasonable to do so (s 11(1)). Where information is held in non-digital form by a small public authority, it is unlikely to be regarded as reasonable to require an authority to comply with such a preference. That will not, however, be the case where an authority already holds information in electronic format.

5.7 EXEMPTION WHERE COST OF COMPLIANCE IS EXCESSIVE

A public authority is not obliged to comply with a request for information if it estimates that the cost of complying with that request would exceed the 'appropriate limit' (s 12(1)). The Secretary of State is empowered to make regulations specifying the 'appropriate limit' (s 12(3)) and the method of estimating these costs (s 12(5)) for the purposes of this provision. If the fees for the application exceed a certain amount then the authority can refuse to disclose the material. This limit will be set out in regulations not published at the time of writing. However, in the speech by Lord Falconer referred to in 5.3 above, figures of £450 for public authorities and £600 for government departments were being suggested as the cut-off for free access and it is understood that these will be the limits that are imposed for this exemption.

Where the cost of the 'search fee' is greater than these figures the authority will be able to choose to refuse the request, charge the full fee or waive the fee. Only 'search costs' (and thus not disbursements such as copying charges or, for example, the costs of time spent deciding whether an exemption applies or not) are likely to be taken into account in calculating whether or not the limit is exceeded. Where a request could be refused in accordance with s 12, a public authority should nevertheless provide an indication of the information which could be provided within the costs ceiling.

It should be noted that, even where compliance with the duty to communicate information would be excessively expensive, a public authority is not necessarily excused from compliance with the duty to confirm or deny. A public authority will only be able to rely upon s 12 to resist compliance with the duty to confirm or deny where the costs of compliance with that duty alone exceed the 'appropriate limit' (s 12(2)). Clearly, it will often be considerably less expensive for a public authority to comply with this duty than to comply with the duty to communicate information.

Section 12(4) contains a controversial power under which the Secretary of State is able to issue regulations providing that, in certain circumstances, the costs of complying with two or more requests for information can be cumulated for the purposes of assessing whether or not the costs of compliance exceed the appropriate limits. These regulations can be made where the requests in question are submitted by one person or 'by different persons who appear to the public authority to be acting in concert or in pursuance of a campaign'.

This provision is designed to protect public authorities from the effect of campaigns aimed at disrupting the work of the authority by flooding it with a barrage of requests for information (perhaps as a protest at its activities). However, there is a danger that public authorities may claim that legitimate information-gathering exercises coordinated by interest or pressure groups will also be covered by such regulations. Where a public authority relies upon these regulations in refusing to grant requests, the Information Commissioner should interpret this limiting provision strictly. It ought to be possible for those engaged in a *bona fide* information-seeking campaign coordinated by a pressure group to demonstrate that they are primarily motivated by a desire to spread the burden of applying for information or to gain access to a wider range of information, and not by a wish to evade the costs limit. In fact the Code of Practice issued under s 45 of the Act provides some helpful guidance. It states at para 16:

Where an authority is not required to comply with a number of related requests because, under section 12(1) and regulations made under section 12(4), the cumulative cost of complying with the requests would exceed the 'appropriate limit' (ie cost threshold) prescribed in Fees Regulations, the authority should consider whether the information could be disclosed in another, more cost-effective, manner. For example, the authority should consider if the information is such that publication on the authority's website, and a brief notification of the website reference to each applicant, would bring the cost within the appropriate limit.

In some cases, a public authority may wish to comply with a request for information where the costs of compliance exceed the prescribed limit. In such circumstances, the public authority is entitled to charge for the communication of the requested information in accordance with the provisions of s 13 (unless it is in any event otherwise legally obliged to supply the information). The fees charged in such circumstances are to be assessed in accordance with regulations made by the Secretary of State.

The limit imposed by regulation 6 of the draft Freedom of Information (Fees and Appropriate Limit) Regulations 2004 is £550. The fees that can be charged for applications estimated to cost above this limit are 10% of the costs of finding and making the material available up to £550, plus all the costs above that amount plus the costs of disbursements (copying etc).

5.8 VEXATIOUS AND REPEATED REQUESTS

Under s 14(1) of the Act, a public authority is not obliged to comply with a request for information where that request is 'vexatious'. Under the Civil Procedure Rules 1998, a vexatious claim can be struck out (CPR, r 3.4) and, under s 42, Supreme Court Act 1981, a litigant who instigates proceedings habitually and without reasonable grounds can be found to be a 'vexatious litigant'. Such a 'vexatious litigant' is thereafter only entitled to instigate or continue proceedings with the permission of a High Court judge. However, 'vexatious' may have to be defined somewhat differently under the Act, which is 'applicant-blind'. The motives of the applicant for making an application under the Act are irrelevant. Section 14(1) may therefore have to be interpreted only to cover applications which can objectively be demonstrated to have been made for an improper purpose, such as frustration of the operations of a public authority.

In addition, under s 14(2), where a public authority has:

... previously complied with a request for information which was made by any person, it is not obliged to comply with a subsequent identical or substantially similar request from that person unless a reasonable interval has elapsed between compliance with the previous request and the making of the current request.

This provision may create difficulties for applicants where the fruits of a previous search have been lost or have gone astray in the post.

5.9 DUTY TO OFFER ADVICE AND ASSISTANCE

The duty to offer advice and assistance has already been referred to at a number of points in this chapter. It provides a valuable means of reinforcing the express duties placed upon public authorities and ensuring that a positive approach to openness is adopted in relation to the Act. Section 16(1) is expressed in the following terms:

It shall be the duty of a public authority to provide advice and assistance, so far as it would be reasonable to expect the authority to do so, to persons who propose to make, or have made, requests to it.

Where, in relation to the provision of advice and assistance, a public authority complies with the Code of Practice issued under s 45, it is to be taken as having complied with its duty under s 16 (s 16(2)).

5.10 FAILURE TO LOCATE INFORMATION AND PARTIAL LOCATION OF INFORMATION

It is not clear how far a public authority must go in trying to locate information because this does not seem to have been dealt with in the Act. A failure to locate information is not a refusal and apparently the notice provisions in s 17 are not applicable. The Code of Practice issued under s 45 also gives no guidance on the thoroughness of the research required before the public authority can state that it holds no such information. One can imagine that many authorities will not keep information particularly well catalogued and described, particularly material which was produced some time in the past. Obviously the duty to confirm or deny the existence of the information, set out in s 1(1)(a), applies with the usual time limit.

If the authority is able to locate part of the information, that partial information must be supplied. The Code of Practice at para 12 advises the authority to give reasons why it has not been able to locate the other part of the information requested. In fact this paragraph is designed to deal with the situation where the applicant has not been able to identify the information in such a way as to enable the authority to locate the information, but it must be assumed that reasons should be supplied whatever the cause of the failure. In practice there are a number of scenarios which might result in information not being found.

(1) The applicant is certain that the information exists and the authority cannot locate it, in which case the applicant can use the internal complaints mechanism and then ask the Commissioner to intervene. However the Commissioner cannot order disclosure of information that cannot be located. Perhaps in these circumstances this might constitute maladministration and the appropriate ombudsman could assist.

(2) The applicant and the public authority are certain that the information exists but it cannot be located. Again, although the internal complaints process and the intervention of the Commissioner may produce more rigorous searches, the only remedy for material that cannot be found is to the relevant ombudsman.

(3) If the applicant is not confident that material exists then it is unlikely that either the internal complaints mechanism, the Commission or the ombudsman will be of much help.

The Information Commissioner advises that, although poor records management is in itself not a breach of the Act, if it results in the other requirements of the Act being breached, he will consider using his enforcement powers (Awareness Guidance No 8, para 6, see www.informationcommissioner.gov.uk).

5.11 REFUSAL OF A REQUEST FOR INFORMATION

Generally, where a public authority refuses a request for information under the Act, it is required to provide an explanation of its reasons for doing so. Where it relies upon an exemption listed in Part II ('Exempt Information') of the Act, a public authority must give a notice to that effect to the applicant within the usual period for compliance under the Act (s 17(1)). This notice must specify the exemption upon which the authority is relying and state '(if that would not otherwise be apparent) why the exemption applies' (s 17(1)(c)). Where the exemption in question is a 'qualified exemption' and the public authority has not yet come to a decision whether the information should be disclosed, the notice provided to the applicant must indicate that no such decision has yet been reached (s 17(2)). If a public authority finally decides that information should not be disclosed because it is covered by a 'qualified exemption' and the public interest in non-disclosure outweighs the public interest in disclosure, it is obliged to give reasons for arriving at that decision. It must do so within 'such time as is reasonable in the circumstances' (s 17(3)). A public authority is not obliged to state why an exemption applies or why the public interest in maintaining a qualified exemption outweighs the public interest in disclosure if making such a statement would itself reveal exempt information (s 17(4)). The Code of Practice issued under s 45 of the Act provides some guidance (see Appendix 2). It states at paras 50 and 51:

50. . . . Public authorities should not (subject to the proviso in section 17(4) ie if the statement would involve the disclosure of information which would itself be exempt information) merely paraphrase the wording of the exemption. The Act also requires authorities, when withholding information (other than under an 'absolute' exemption), to state the reasons for claiming that the public interest in maintaining the exemption outweighs the public interest in disclosure. Public authorities should specify the public interest factors (for and against disclosure) which they have taken into account before reaching the decision (again, subject to the proviso in section 17(4)).

51. For monitoring purposes public authorities should keep a record of all applications where either all or part of the requested information is withheld. In addition to a record of the numbers of applications involved where information is withheld, senior managers in each public authority need information on each case to determine whether cases are being properly considered, and whether the reasons for refusals are sound. This could be done by requiring all staff who refuse a request for information to forward the details to a central point in the organisation for collation. Details of information on complaints about applications which have been refused . . . could be collected at the same central point.

In addition, where a public authority refuses to accede to a request for information on the grounds that the costs of compliance exceed the appropriate limit (s 12; see 5.7) or that a particular request is a vexatious or repeated request (s 14; see 5.8), the public authority must provide the applicant with a notice to this effect (s 17(5)). In such a case, there seems to be no further obligation to explain why the limit is exceeded or why the request is regarded as a vexatious or repeated request. Nevertheless, best practice in this regard would seem to require some such explanation. A public authority is not obliged to give any notice of refusal of a request where it is relying upon a claim that a request is a vexatious or repeated request under s 14 and where the authority has given notice of reliance upon this provision in relation to a previous request from the same applicant and it would be unreasonable to require the public authority to give further notice (s 17(6)).

Whenever a public authority gives notice that a request for information has been refused in accordance with the provisions discussed above, it is obliged to give the applicant particulars of any internal complaints procedure which it provides in relation to requests for information and particulars of the applicant's right to apply to the Information Commissioner for a decision notice (s 17(7)—for decision notices, see 9.2.2). Part XII of the Code of Practice issued under section 45 of the Act provides more detailed guidance on the complaints procedure (see Appendix 2). The Code sets out the need for the procedure to deal both with complaints about the publication scheme and with failures to deal with substantive applications properly. The Code requires that information about the authority's own complaints procedure and the right to complain to the Information Commissioner should be given to applicants when communicating any substantive decision following a request for information. Any written indication of dissatisfaction should be dealt with as a complaint.

The complaints procedure should be a fair and impartial means of dealing with handling problems and reviewing decisions taken pursuant to the Act, including decisions taken about where the public interest lies in respect of exempt information. It should be possible to reverse or otherwise amend decisions previously taken. Complaints procedures should be clear and not unnecessarily bureaucratic. They should be capable of producing a prompt determination of the complaint. (para 56)

The procedure should provide for a different person to review any original decision which is the subject of the complaint. Applicants should be provided with information about how long it will take to deal with their complaint and cases should be resolved within a reasonable time. Target times for resolving complaints should be published by public authorities. Records of complaints and their outcome should be kept and authorities should have systems for monitoring the complaints process.

Where a decision to disclose has followed a complaint, that disclosure should occur as soon as practical, and where errors have been made in the process an apology should be given and steps should be taken to avoid similar errors in future. If a decision is made to confirm a refusal to provide information then details of how to apply to the Information Commissioner should be provided to the applicant.

6

EXEMPT INFORMATION—
GENERAL ISSUES

6.1 INTRODUCTION

In common with all freedom of information legislation, the Freedom of Information Act 2000 contains a number of provisions defining particular types of information which public authorities are not obliged to disclose. These are set out in Part II of the Act (ss 21–44). Such exemptions exist because the public interest dictates that certain information should not be available to the public. It will, for example, generally be undersirable for significant threats to national security or personal privacy to arise as a result of disclosures made under freedom of information legislation. Controversially, however, the Act contains a large number of particularly extensive exemptions. Indeed, a large proportion of the criticism attracted by the Act, and the draft Bill upon which it was based, concerned the number, and scope, of the exemptions to the right of access (see, for example, Hazell, R, *Commentary on Draft Freedom of Information Bill* (London: Constitution Unit, 1999), p 17).

It is the purpose of this chapter to explain certain features of the Act which are of general application to the exemptions in Part II. In Chapters 7 and 8, the specific exempting provisions are discussed in greater detail. Chapter 7 concerns those exemptions designated 'absolute exemptions' under the Act while Chapter 8 looks in detail at those exemptions which are not 'absolute' and which, in this Guide, are accordingly described as 'qualified exemptions' (see 6.2 and 6.3 below for further explanation).

It is important to remember that, under s 1 of the Act, public authorities have two distinct duties—the duty to confirm or deny (s 1(1)(a)) and the duty to communicate information (s 1(1)(b)) (see 4.2 for further discussion of these duties). The manner in which the Act's exemptions apply to these separate duties is rather complex. As a general rule, each specific exempting provision within Part II of the Act specifies separately the circumstances in which each duty is excluded. Thus, for example, under s 41(1), a public authority does not have to communicate information where disclosure of the information would constitute an actionable breach of confidence owed to a third party. Under s 41(2), the authority is also absolved from the duty to confirm or deny where compliance with that duty constitutes an actionable breach of confidence. Circumstances may well arise where an authority is absolved from the duty to communicate information under s 41(1), but will still be required to comply with its duty to confirm or deny. For example, consider a situation where a local business has submitted details of its estimated annual profits to a local authority. Communication of that estimate of profits to a third party applicant for information could constitute an actionable breach of confidence and could, therefore, be exempt under s 41(1). However, simple confirmation or denial of the holding of that information is less likely to constitute an actionable breach of confidence and the duty to confirm or deny will not therefore necessarily be excluded under s 41(2). In many situations, public authorities will be obliged to comply with the duty to confirm or deny while, at the same time, being exempt from the duty to communicate information.

It is also important to note that none of the Act's exemptions are mandatory (cf, for example, the position under Ireland's Freedom of Information Act 1997). While disclosure of requested information may be otherwise prohibited (for example, under the Official Secrets Act 1989 or the Data Protection Act 1998), there is nothing in the Act itself to prevent the voluntary disclosure of exempt information by a public authority.

The Information Commissioner has published a series of 'Awareness Guidance' notes on the Act. Some of these provide very interesting insight into his view of the scope of a number of the exemptions to disclosure under the Act (see www.informationcommissioner.gov.uk).

6.2 ABSOLUTE EXEMPTIONS

Where information falls within the scope of an 'absolute exemption', a public authority is not obliged to communicate it to an applicant. In the case of information falling within most absolute exemptions, the authority will also be excused from the obligation to comply with the duty to confirm or deny. By contrast, where requested information falls within the scope of a 'qualified exemption', a public authority must comply with its duties under s 1(1) unless, in all the circumstances of the case, the public interest in non-disclosure outweighs the public interest in disclosure (s 2; see 6.3 below).

The absolute exemptions are listed in s 2(3). They are:

(a) information reasonably accessible by other means (s 21);

(b) information from, or relating to, certain security bodies (s 23);

(c) information contained in court records (s 32);

(d) information disclosure of which would breach Parliamentary privilege (s 34);

(e) information disclosure of which would prejudice the effective conduct of public affairs (when such information is held by the House of Commons or House of Lords) (s 36);

(f) personal information (where the applicant is the subject of the personal information and, in certain circumstances, where the applicant is a third party) (s 40);

(g) information provided in confidence (s 41); and

(h) information covered by prohibitions on disclosure (s 44).

In the case of information covered by the listed 'absolute exemptions', there is no requirement for a public authority to consider whether the public interest favours disclosure where the information falls within the scope of the exemption. The Information Commissioner's role is also restricted to an assessment of whether or not the information falls within the scope of the absolute exemption in question. He has no power to order the disclosure of the information in the 'public interest' (see Chapter 9).

The reasons for designating a particular exemption as an 'absolute', rather than a 'qualified', exemption vary from provision to provision. Some, for example, s 21 ('Information accessible to applicant by other means') and s 23 ('Information supplied by, or relating to, bodies dealing with security matters'), are included because it is assumed that the public interest can never favour disclosure of such information. Others, such as s 40 ('Personal information') and s 44 ('Prohibitions on disclosure'), are included because the disclosure of information falling within their scope is governed by other laws. A further group of exemptions, including s 32 ('Court records') and s 34 ('Parliamentary privilege'), are designated 'absolute exemptions' in order that the mechanisms introduced by the Act do not interfere unduly with the areas of responsibility of other constitutional bodies.

Two of the exempting provisions above (s 36 and s 40) confer a mixture of absolute and qualified exemption. In those cases, information will be subject to one or other type of exemption depending upon the nature of the information or, in the case of s 40, the identity of the applicant (see 8.12 and 10.4 respectively). The absolute exemption contained in s 41 ('Information provided in confidence') is anomalous because, while it is not subject to the Act's public interest balancing test, it is defined in relation to the equitable action for breach of confidence, which has its own inherent form of protection for public interest disclosure (see 7.8 below).

6.3 QUALIFIED EXEMPTIONS

6.3.1 Introduction

The term 'qualified exemption' is not used in the Act. However, it is used in this Guide to describe those exemptions which are not defined as 'absolute exemptions' within s 2 and are therefore 'qualified' in the sense that they are only effective in exempting an authority from compliance with the duty to confirm or deny where:

. . . in all the circumstances of the case, the public interest in maintaining the exclusion of the duty to confirm or deny outweighs the public interest in disclosing whether the public authority holds the information.

(s 2(1)(b))

In the case of the duty to communicate information, a qualified exemption will only be effective where:

. . . in all the circumstances of the case, the public interest in maintaining the exemption outweighs the public interest in disclosing the information.

(s 2(2)(b))

Thus, in the case of such exemptions, a public authority must first establish whether information falls within the scope of a particular exemption. Having satisfied itself that the information is covered, it must then go on to consider the competing public interests in disclosure and the maintenance of secrecy. In many cases, this is likely to prove a complex exercise and, accordingly, the Act provides additional time for public authorities to comply with their duties in such circumstances. In place of the usual 20-working-day period for compliance, the public authority is not required to comply with its duties 'until such time as is reasonable in the circumstances' (s 10(3); see 5.4.1).

This 'two-stage' approach to the application of exemptions is not uncommon in freedom of information legislation. For example, several exemptions under New Zealand's Official Information Act 1982 and the Irish Freedom of Information Act 1997 are also subject to a similar public interest assessment. The Ombudsman responsible for supervising the operation of New Zealand's freedom of information legislation has noted the infrequency with which public authorities, having established that particular information falls within an exemption, proceed to find that the public interest favours disclosure:

It is rare indeed for the holder of information once having established a prejudice [serving to exempt the information from disclosure] to then proceed to acknowledge that the reason for withholding is outweighed by the public interest.

(Sir Brian Elwood, 'The New Zealand Model—the Official Information Act', paper presented at 'FOI and the Right to Know' conference, Melbourne, August 1999)

Even if a similar pattern emerges in this jurisdiction, an applicant whose request for access to information has been refused on the grounds that a qualified exemption applies can appeal against this decision to the Information Commissioner. In considering such a complaint, the Commissioner may of course uphold the decision of the authority in question. However, it is also within his jurisdiction to decide either that the information does not fall within the scope of the exemption or, where the information does fall within the exemption, to find that the public interest favours disclosure.

6.3.2 Assessing the Public Interest

The Act provides little guidance on the factors which are relevant in an assessment of the public interest (although see s 35(4), discussed below at 8.11). This is perhaps not surprising, given the different contexts in which this issue will need to be assessed. Accordingly, issues relevant to 'public interest' disclosure are considered in connection with specific exemptions below. However, it should be noted that guidance on the public interest in disclosure of information may be found in other areas of the law (such as breach of confidence and public interest immunity) and in other jurisdictions with similar 'qualified exemptions'. In addition, some guidance on this 'public interest' assessment was provided during Parliamentary debates. It is clear, for example, that a public authority must decide the balance of public interests on an individual case-by-case basis (Hansard HL, 22 November 2000, col 831) and that the public interest will diminish over time (Hansard HL, 14 November 2000, col 224).

The Guidance Notes published by the Information Commissioner (see 6.1 above), provide advice on matters that will be relevant in assessing the public interest. The Commisssioner considers that, in general terms, the following

. . . public interest factors . . . would encourage the disclosure of information:

- furthering the understanding of and participation in the public debate of issues of the day. This factor would come into play if disclosure would allow a more informed debate of issues under consideration by the Government or a local authority.

- promoting accountability and transparency by public authorities for decisions taken by them . . . [P]lacing an obligation on authorities and officials to provide reasoned explanations for decisions made will improve the quality of decisions and administration.

- promoting accountability and transparency in the spending of public money. The public interest is likely to be served, for instance in the context of private sector delivery of public services, if the disclosure of information ensures greater competition and better value for money . . . Disclosure of information as to gifts and expenses may also assure the public of the personal probity of elected leaders and officials.

- allowing individuals and companies to understand decisions made by public authorities affecting their lives and, in some cases, assisting individuals in challenging those decisions.

- bringing to light information affecting public health and safety. The prompt disclosure of information by scientific and other experts may contribute not only to the prevention of accidents or outbreaks of disease but may also increase public confidence in official scientific advice.

(Information Commissioner, Awareness Guidance No 3,
www.informationcommissioner.gov.uk)

This list is, of course, not exhaustive and issues affecting the balance of public interests in particular contexts are discussed further in Chapter 8.

6.4 'CLASS-BASED' AND 'PREJUDICE-BASED' EXEMPTIONS

In addition to the distinction between 'absolute' and 'qualified' exemptions discussed above, exemptions under the Act can also be classified according to whether they are 'class-based' or 'prejudice-based'. The former are exemptions which are defined as including all information falling within a particular class. The latter only take effect when disclosure of the information in question would, or would be likely to, have a specified prejudicial effect. Sometimes a particular provision within Part II contains both 'class-based' exemptions and 'prejudice-based' exemptions. For example, s 27 contains a 'class-based' exemption for information which is 'confidential information obtained from a State other than the United Kingdom or from an international organization or international court' (s 27(2)). Thus, any information satisfying the definition is exempt from disclosure under the Act. It also contains a 'prejudice-based' exemption covering information disclosure of which would prejudice, or would be likely to prejudice, a variety of interests relating to international relations (s 27(1)).

6.4.1 'Class-based' Exemptions

The following exemptions contained in Part II could be described as 'class-based':

(a) information reasonably accessible by other means (s 21);

(b) information intended for future publication (s 22);

(c) information from, or concerning, certain security bodies (s 23);

(d) confidential information obtained from other states and international bodies (s 27(2));

(e) information held for the purposes of investigation and proceedings (s 30);

(f) information contained in court records (s 32);

(g) information disclosure of which would breach Parliamentary privilege (s 34);

(h) certain information relating to the formulation of government policy (s 35);

(i) information relating to communications with the Royal Family Household or relating to the conferring of honours by the Crown (s 37);

(j) information covered by regulations concerning the disclosure of environmental information (s 39);

(k) personal information (s 40);

(l) information provided in confidence (s 41);

(m) information covered by legal professional privilege (s 42);

(n) trade secrets (s 43(1));

(o) information covered by prohibitions on disclosure (s 44).

One of the criticisms most frequently made of the Act is that it contains too many 'class-based' exemptions. In general terms, under such exemptions, disclosure of information is excluded regardless of whether it would be harmful or not. There is an underlying assumption that disclosure of any information falling within their scope would inevitably be damaging. This assumption is questionable in some cases. Consider, for example, s 23, which provides a 'class-based' exemption covering all information 'directly or indirectly supplied' to a public authority by specific bodies concerned with security (including MI5) and all information which 'relates to' any such body. Clearly, there is a legitimate need to keep much information deriving from, and relating to, such bodies away from public scrutiny. However, it is questionable whether disclosure of information concerning, for example, the unforeseen escalation of costs for a new head-quarters building for MI5 would necessarily be prejudicial to the public interest.

In most cases, of course, these exemptions will only be effective where a public authority can demonstrate that, even where information falls within the exempt class, the public interest also favours continued secrecy. This will be very difficult where no prejudice would arise from disclosure. However, class-based exemptions present a particular problem for applicants where they are 'absolute' and therefore cannot be outweighed by the public interest in disclosure. A number of the 'class-based' exemptions listed above are absolute exemptions (ss 21, 23, 32, 34, 41 and, to a large extent, s 40).

6.4.2 'Prejudice-based' Exemptions

Those exemptions not listed in 6.4.1 above are 'prejudice-based' exemptions. They will only be effective in relieving a public authority of its duties to communicate information and/or to confirm or deny in relation to information which, if disclosed, would, or would be likely to, prejudice particular specified interests. For example, s 43(2) provides that:

Information is exempt information if its disclosure under this Act would, or would be likely to, prejudice the commercial interests of any person . . .

The phrasing of this exemption ('would, or would be likely to, prejudice') is to be found in most 'prejudice-based' exemptions under the Act. The only exceptions to this pattern are s 24 ('National security') and s 38 ('Health and safety'), which incorporate differently worded tests of 'prejudice' (see 8.3 and 8.14 respectively).

The use of the term 'prejudice' (as opposed to 'substantial prejudice', 'serious prejudice' or 'harm') within the majority of the exemptions covered in this section has been subject to criticism. It has been argued that the use of the term 'prejudice' reduces the burden upon a public authority seeking to establish that particular information is covered by the exemption. The use of 'serious prejudice', and possibly 'substantial prejudice', would certainly have resulted in stricter limits being placed upon the relevant exemptions. However, it is unlikely that the use of 'prejudice' rather than 'harm' will favour public authorities seeking to avoid disclosure of information. In essence, the terms are synonymous.

Anomalies may arise between the treatment of information under the Act and the treatment of the same information under the Freedom of Information Act (Scotland) 2002. Under the Scottish legislation, 'prejudice-based' exemptions generally only apply where disclosure would, or would be likely to, 'prejudice substantially' a relevant interest. However, the Act's promoters have repeatedly emphasised that alleged prejudice arising from disclosure must be 'actual, real or of substance' and not purely speculative if it is to fall within the terms of the prejudice-based exemptions in the Act (see, for example, Hansard HC, 5 April 2000, col 1067). Accordingly, the distinction seems likely to make little practical difference.

6.5 EXEMPTIONS—MISCELLANEOUS FURTHER ISSUES

So far we have considered the particular ways in which the exemptions in Part II can be categorised, and the effects of such categorisation. However, there are a number of further issues of general relevance regarding the exemptions to the rights of access to information provided in the Act.

6.5.1 Partial Disclosure of Information

Records of information, such as documents, may contain both exempt and non-exempt information. For example, a minute of a private meeting of a public authority may contain personal details relating to a specific individual. Those details may constitute 'personal data' and therefore may be exempt under s 40 ('Personal information'). However, the information in the rest of the minute may not fall within the scope of any of the Act's exemptions. In such circumstances, the public authority is required to 'redact' those parts of the minute which are exempt from disclosure and must communicate the non-exempt information to the applicant. Unlike freedom of information legislation in some other jurisdictions (see, for example, Australia's federal Freedom of Information Act 1982, s 22, and Ireland's Freedom of Information Act 1997, s 13), there is no express provision to this effect in the Act. However, a public authority's obligation to make partial disclosure in this way derives from the fact that the Act imposes duties in relation to 'information' rather than 'records' or 'documents' (see 4.4.1 above). Accordingly, all non-exempt information must be communicated. Confirmation of this interpretation of the Act was provided during Parliamentary debates on the provision (Hansard HL, 17 October 2000, col 931).

6.5.2 No 'Reverse Freedom of Information'

Many of the exemptions in Part II of the Act exist to protect the rights and interests of third parties. Examples of such exemptions are s 38 ('Health and safety'), s 40 ('Personal information'), s 41 ('Information provided in confidence') and s 43 ('Commercial interests'). In many cases, public authorities will be required to decide whether or not to disclose information in circumstances where the person or body with the strongest interest in non-disclosure is a third party rather than the authority itself. For example, a third party may have provided information to a public authority which it regards as a trade secret (and is therefore covered by s 43(1)). However, it may not necessarily be obvious to the public authority that the information is in fact a 'trade secret'.

Where a question arises as to whether or not information is covered by a 'prejudice-based' exemption, the task of the public authority is likely to prove yet more difficult. It will not, for example, always be easy for a public authority to establish whether disclosure of particular information would, or would be likely to, prejudice the commercial interests of a third party (under s 43(2)). In such circumstances, a third party may, with some justification, be concerned that its interests will not be adequately protected by the authority. For this reason, many overseas jurisdictions have incorporated 'reverse freedom of information' procedures of one form or another (see, for example, the Australian Freedom of Information Act 1982, s 27, and the Canadian Access to Information Act 1982, s 28). Under such provisions, a public authority must typically consult third parties affected by disclosure prior to release of information. Third parties may also be entitled to challenge a public authority's decision to disclose information affecting their interests.

The Act has no such formal 'reverse freedom of information' procedures. It imposes no legal obligation upon a public authority to consult affected third parties and, where a public authority proposes to release information affecting the interests of third parties, those third parties have no means of preventing this under the Act. However, the Code of Practice issued under s 45 specifies circumstances in which the Lord Chancellor considers it advisable for a public authority to consult third parties following receipt of a request for information (paras 31–40).

Where disclosure of information cannot be made without the consent of a third party (perhaps because disclosure by the authority would breach an obligation of confidence), the Code advises a public authority, where practicable, to consult the third party with a view to seeking such consent (para 33). A public authority should also consult a third party where consultation would help the authority either to decide (i) whether disclosure falls within one of the Act's exemptions or (ii) where the public interest lies in a particular case (para 35). The Code also specifies circumstances under which consultation is unnecessary because, for example, the cost of consultation would be disproportionate or where consultation is likely to have no real effect on the authority's decision on disclosure (paras 36–38). In all cases, it is emphasised that, even where consultation takes place, responsibility for taking a decision on disclosure rests with the public authority and does not pass to the third party (para 40).

Breaches of the Code do not give rise to enforceable sanctions under the Act unless such breaches also constitute failure to comply with the duties established in Part I of the Act. Where a third party wishes to prevent the disclosure of information, it will have to rely on other causes of action. For example, if a third party considers that a public authority owes it an obligation of confidence in relation to particular information and that the authority is proposing to release that information without permission, the authority will have to seek an interlocutory injunction restraining the authority from committing a breach of confidence (see Griffiths, J, 'Recapturing Liberating Information—The Relationship between the United Kingdom's Freedom of Information Act 2000 and Private Law Restraints on Disclosure' in Torremans, P (ed), *Copyright and Human Rights* (Kluwer Law International, 2004)).

6.5.3 Duty to Give Reasons for Non-Disclosure of Information

Where a public authority claims that information is covered by an exemption and therefore that it does not have to comply with the duty to communicate information or the duty to confirm or deny, it must, under s 17(1), give the applicant a notice which:

(a) states the fact that the public authority is relying upon an exemption in denying disclosure;

(b) specifies the exemption in question; and

(c) states (if that would not otherwise be apparent) why the exemption applies.

This duty to give a statement explaining the reasons for a denial of disclosure does not apply where such a statement 'would involve the disclosure of information which would itself be exempt information' (s 17(4)). Thus, for example, if a public authority relies upon the exemption in s 24 ('National security') to resist disclosure of information, it would not necessarily have to explain why a threat to national security would be likely to arise from a particular disclosure. A duty to do so would entirely defeat the purpose of the exemption itself.

6.5.4 Challenges to Public Authorities' Reliance Upon Exemptions

The mechanisms for challenging public authorities' reliance upon the Act's exemptions are discussed in Chapter 9 below. At this point, however, it is worth pausing a moment to consider where the burden of proof lies when such a challenge is made. In the case of claims based upon the 'qualified exemptions', a public authority will only be entitled to resist disclosure where, 'in all the circumstances of the case', the public interest in non-disclosure outweighs the public interest in disclosure (s 2(1)(b) and s 2(2)(b)). The wording of these provisions suggests that the burden of proof in such cases should fall upon the public authority. Indeed, it would seem appropriate to place the burden of proof in all such cases upon the public authority seeking to rely upon an exempting provision. However, in other jurisdictions, there has been a reluctance to employ formal evidential doctrines, such as the burden of proof in proceedings before a Commissioner or Ombudsman (*Commissioner of Police v Ombudsman* [1985] 1 NZLR 578). The absence of a purpose clause favouring disclosure in the Act and the fact that the right of access to information will only rarely constitute a legally recognised human right (see Chapter 1) also make it more difficult for an applicant to argue that any doubts as to the application of an exemption should be resolved in his or her favour.

7

ABSOLUTE EXEMPTIONS

7.1 INTRODUCTION

This chapter further examines those exemptions designated 'absolute exemptions'—that is, exemptions which are not subject to any assessment of the public interest. For a discussion of the distinctions between 'absolute' and 'qualified' exemptions, see 6.2 and 6.3 above.

7.2 INFORMATION REASONABLY ACCESSIBLE BY OTHER MEANS

7.2.1 Introduction

Section 21(1) of the Freedom of Information Act 2000 provides that:

Information which is reasonably accessible to members of the public otherwise than under section 1 is exempt information.

The underlying rationale for this exemption is obvious. If information can reasonably be obtained by other means, there is no need to bring the formal access right under the Act into play. It is, however, an unusual exemption because it excludes the duty to communicate information but not the duty to confirm or deny. This structure has presumably been chosen for the exemption because, while there may be good reasons for exempting a public authority from the duty to communicate information under the Act where that information is otherwise reasonably accessible, there is unlikely to be any good reason for exempting that authority from the duty to expend the minimum amount of effort required simply to confirm or deny whether it holds such information. Indeed, in such circumstances, a breach of the duty to provide advice and assistance under the Act (s 16) may be committed by a public authority which, on providing confirmation or denial, fails to explain how the information in question is otherwise available.

A number of different types of information can be caught by this exemption. For example, it will cover information which the public authority or any other person is obliged to publish under other legislation, such as the Local Government Act 1972 or the Environmental Protection Act 1990. The exemption may also apply where information is made available by a third party, such as a commercial publisher, or where a public authority provides information without legislative obligation. In this latter case, however, information will not be covered by the exemption unless it is made available in accordance with the authority's publication scheme (s 21(3)). Public authorities are thereby encouraged to ensure that their publication schemes have comprehensive coverage of all information proactively disclosed.

7.2.2 When will Information be Reasonably Accessible?

Section 21 will only apply where information is *reasonably* accessible by other means. Information which is made available by a public authority or a third party in accordance with a legislative obligation is deemed to be reasonably accessible to the applicant 'whether free of charge or on payment' (s 21(2)(b)). Thus, for example, even though the Land Registry charges fees for the provision of copies of entries in the Land Register, the information within those copies will still fall within this exemption. The only circumstance in which this rule will not apply is where the information disclosed in accordance with a statutory obligation is available only on inspection.

In all cases other than those covered by s 21(2)(b), it will be necessary to determine whether information is *reasonably* available in the particular context. The Act confirms that information *may* be reasonably accessible, even though it is accessible only on payment of a fee (s 21(2)(a)). However, the use of the term 'may' indicates that information accessible only on payment of an unreasonably high fee will not be covered by s 21. Thus, for example, consider a situation where a public authority arranges for publication of research data by a commercial publisher. In principle, any applications to the public authority for access to that information could be covered by s 21. The exemption is not restricted to information available directly from the public authority itself. However, it would be possible for the applicant to argue that the level of fee charged for access by the third party was too high for the information to be regarded as reasonably accessible. The Information Commissioner has provided an example of a situation in which the level of charge may take information outside the scope of this exemption:

[A] public authority may be asked for information contained in its annual report. It may not be reasonable to require the applicant to purchase a copy of the report if the request is only for a small amount of the information contained in it.

(Information Commissioner, Freedom of Information Awareness Guidance No 6,
Information Reasonably Accessible to the Applicant by Other Means,
www.informationcommissioner.gov.uk)

In considering the reasonableness of the fee, it should be noted that s 21 only applies where information is otherwise reasonably accessible 'to the applicant'. Account ought therefore to be taken of the individual applicant's means. Information that may be reasonably accessible to a large corporation may not be reasonably accessible to a person with limited financial resources.

Where a public authority claims that information is available under its publication scheme, and therefore that s 21 is applicable, an applicant will be able to challenge the level of fee under that scheme. The Act does not otherwise contain any specific regulation of the fees chargeable for access under such schemes. This will, however, surely be an issue that the Information Commissioner will regard as relevant in deciding whether or not to approve a publication scheme or a model publication scheme under ss 19 and 20.

The Information Commissioner may also be required to consider factors other than cost in assessing the application of s 21. For example, if, in response to a request for information, a public authority were to state that information is available for inspection at a particular office in Cornwall at restricted times only, an applicant living in Northumberland may be able to argue that the information is not reasonably accessible to him or her. Again, the fact that s 21 refers to information which is 'reasonably accessible to the applicant' is significant here. The applicant's location, means, ability to understand English and physical condition, as well as the nature of the information disclosed, will all be relevant in an assessment of whether information is reasonably accessible by such means. This interpretation of s 21 was confirmed during Parliamentary debates on the provision (see Hansard HC, 5 April 2000, col 1035).

Many public authorities now make increasingly effective use of the Internet as a means of disseminating information. As this form of publication becomes even more prevalent, applicants may be able to argue that, where information is not distributed in this form, it is not reasonably accessible for the purposes of s 21. However, at present, this argument is unlikely to be effective in relation to information held by many public authorities. During the Act's progress through Parliament, Government ministers were concerned to ensure that smaller public authorities, such as school governing bodies and parish councils, should not be under an obligation to make information available digitally under the Act. In addition, while it may be possible to argue that government departments should be required to make much newly produced information available on-line, they would surely not be required to digitise all existing information currently held in other forms.

Conversely, if a public authority were only to publish particular information in digital form, an applicant without access to the necessary technology may still be able to argue that the information is not reasonably accessible to him or her. The force of this argument is likely to diminish in future.

7.2.3 Duty to Offer Advice and Assistance

It should be remembered that a public authority is obliged to offer advice and assistance to persons proposing to, or making, requests for information (s 16). In the circumstances considered in this section, this duty is surely likely to require authorities to explain to an applicant how to obtain information from another source.

7.3 INFORMATION SUPPLIED BY, OR CONCERNING, CERTAIN SECURITY BODIES

7.3.1 Scope of the Exemption

Information is exempt from the duty to communicate information if it 'was directly or indirectly supplied to the public authority by', or 'relates to' any of a number of listed bodies with security functions. These bodies, set out in s 23(3) of the Act, are:

(a) the Security Service (MI5);

(b) the Secret Intelligence Service (MI6);

(c) the Government Communications Headquarters (GCHQ);

(d) the Special Forces (for example, the SAS);

(e) the Tribunal established under the Regulation of Investigatory Powers Act 2000;

(f) the Tribunal established under the Interception of Communications Act 1985;

(g) the Tribunal established under the Security Service Act 1989;

(h) the Tribunal established under the Intelligence Services Act 1994;

(i) the Security Vetting Appeals Panel;

(j) the Security Commission;

(k) the National Criminal Intelligence Service; and

(l) the Service Authority for the National Criminal Intelligence Service.

These bodies are not themselves 'public authorities' for the purposes of the Act and therefore, in any event, an applicant is not entitled to seek information directly from them. The purpose of s 23 is to cover information that has been supplied by or relates to any of these bodies but is held by another public authority subject to the Act. The information does not have to *originate* from the listed body. This exemption is based upon the premise that it cannot be in the public interest for any such information to be accessible under the Act. This premise is questionable. For example, there seems little reason why a blanket exemption should apply to information revealing that new premises built to house one or other of the services included in the list above had greatly exceeded budget. Indeed, it might be strongly argued that it would be in the public interest to have access to such information. However, as such information would clearly 'relate to' the relevant service, s 23 would be satisfied.

Concerns about the over-extensive nature of this provision are exacerbated by extensions of the role of some of these services into areas traditionally associated with ordinary police forces, such as action against drug crime and money laundering (for example, under the Security Service Act 1996, s 1).

7.3.2 Certificates under s 23

Under s 23(2), a Minister of the Crown is able to certify that specified information 'was directly or indirectly supplied by, or relates to' any of the bodies covered by this exemption. Such a certificate is to be taken as 'conclusive evidence of that fact', subject to the possibility of appeal to the Information Tribunal. On appeal, the Information Tribunal is entitled to substitute its own view as to whether the requested information is covered by the exemption (s 60; see 9.3.3). It would appear that such certificates must be issued in relation to specific requested information rather than prospectively in relation to general classes of information (cf s 24(4) discussed at 8.3.2). During Parliamentary debates on this provision, it was suggested by Lord Falconer of Thoroton for the Government that the information that a certificate has been signed would not itself be exempt from disclosure under the Act (Hansard HL, 19 October 2000, col 1259). This assertion is open to question because any such certificate would clearly 'relate to' one of the listed bodies in the broadest sense of that phrase. Nevertheless, the statement will perhaps encourage courts to interpret this vague and potentially expansive provision in a restrictive manner.

Under s 23(5), the duty to confirm or deny does not apply if compliance with that duty would involve the disclosure of any information (whether or not already recorded) which was either supplied by, or relates to, one of the listed bodies. The impact of this provision is not entirely clear. It is difficult to see how simple confirmation or denial, provided by a public authority other than those listed in s 23, could be regarded as 'supplied' (directly or otherwise) by a listed body. However, it could be argued by a public authority that any such confirmation or denial 'relates to' one of the relevant bodies in a general sense. Acceptance of that argument would mean that the duty to confirm or deny would effectively never apply under s 23. Nevertheless, Parliament did not choose expressly to exempt this duty in its entirety (cf ss 21 and 43(1) where the duty to confirm or deny is entirely excluded). This discrepancy may encourage the Information Commissioner and courts to interpret s 23(5) restrictively. Under a restrictive interpretation, the only confirmations or denials which would be exempt would be those which, in the context of the application for information or of information otherwise available, would directly reveal the involvement of one of the listed bodies. Even if this restrictive interpretation is adopted, public authorities will in any event be able to rely upon s 24 where compliance with the duties of disclosure under the Act would endanger national security (see 8.3).

7.3.3 Information in Historical Records in a Public Record Office (s 64(2))

It should be noted that, where information is contained in a 'historical record' (see 11.1 for a definition) in the Public Record Office or the Public Record Office of Northern Ireland, s 23 ceases to function as an absolute exemption. Thus, even if information within the hands of the PRO was supplied by, or relates to, one of the listed security bodies, it will only be exempt from the duty to disclose where the public interest in continued secrecy outweighs the public interest in disclosure.

7.4 INFORMATION CONTAINED IN COURT RECORDS

Courts and tribunals are not themselves 'public authorities' for the purposes of the Act (although bodies responsible for the administration of the justice system, such as the Lord Chancellor's Department and the Council of Tribunals, are covered by the Act). Accordingly, this exemption applies only to information held by other public bodies. The purpose of s 32 (and of the exclusion of courts and tribunals from the ambit of the Act) is to ensure that the disclosure of information within the legal process continues to be governed by courts and tribunals themselves.

Section 32(1) provides that:

Information held by a public authority is exempt information if it is held only by virtue of being contained in—

(a) any document filed with, or otherwise placed in the custody of, a court for the purposes of proceedings in a particular cause or matter,

(b) any document served upon, or by, a public authority for the purposes of proceedings in a particular cause or matter, or

(c) any document created by—
    (i) a court, or
    (ii) a member of the administrative staff of a court,
for the purposes of proceedings in a particular cause or matter.

This would, for example, cover formal pleadings served by, or upon, a government department. In addition to pleadings, it also covers information contained in other formal court documents such as summonses, witness statements, affidavits and skeleton arguments.

It is important to note that this exemption is only effective where information is held only by virtue of being contained in the specified court records. Thus, for example, where a public authority enters into a written contract with a third party and, subsequently, that contract is appended to pleadings in court proceedings, the contract will not itself be covered by s 32. The public authority does not hold it only by virtue of its being contained in the pleadings.

For the purposes of s 32, 'court' is defined to include any tribunal or body exercising the judicial power of the State (s 32(4)(a)). This definition is the same as that which applies under the Contempt of Court Act 1981, s 19. Bodies such as Mental Health Review Tribunals and Employment Tribunals are regarded as exercising the judicial power of the state. However, those which exercise purely administrative functions, such as a local rating court, are not (*Attorney-General v BBC* [1981] AC 303). It should nevertheless be noted that s 32(4)(a) is phrased to '*include* any tribunal or body exercising the judicial power of the State' [emphasis added]. Accordingly, it may be possible to argue that this definition extends to cover courts or tribunals that do not actually exercise the judicial power of *this* state, such as the European Court of Justice or the European Court of Human Rights.

Under s 32(2), information is exempt from the duty to communicate where it is held only by virtue of being contained in:

(a) any document placed in the custody of a person conducting an inquiry or arbitration, for the purposes of the inquiry or arbitration, or

(b) any document created by a person conducting an inquiry or arbitration, for the purposes of the inquiry or arbitration.

'Inquiry' and 'arbitration' in this context refer only to inquiries and arbitrations conducted in accordance with specified statutory provisions (s 32(4)).

It should be noted that s 32 applies only to information contained in documents relating to 'proceedings in a particular cause or matter'. Other information of more general application to the legal process will not be covered by the provision. Thus, for example, a public authority would not be entitled to rely on s 32(1) in seeking to resist disclosure of a statistical analysis of conviction rates for particular offences in particular courts. In addition, information contained in certain other documents relating to litigation would not seem to fall within the scope of s 32. For example, where a public authority litigant holds draft documentation or a letter before action, this information will often not have been 'served' and would not therefore seem to be covered by the exemption (although it may be covered by s 42—see 8.17 below).

Under s 32(3), the duty to confirm or deny is excluded entirely in relation to information falling within either s 32(1) or (2). Thus a public authority is not required to confirm or deny whether it holds information held only by virtue of being contained in a document falling within those provisions. This seems unnecessarily broad in the light of the exemption's purpose outlined above.

7.5 DISCLOSURES WHICH WOULD INFRINGE PARLIAMENTARY PRIVILEGE

7.5.1 Introduction

A public authority is exempt from the obligation to communicate information where such exemption is necessary to avoid an infringement of 'the privileges of either House of Parliament' (s 34(1) and (2)). This exemption preserves Parliament's sole power to control its own business, specifically in relation to the disclosure of information. An infringement of Parliamentary privilege would, for example, be likely to arise if a public authority were to make a premature disclosure of the report of a Parliamentary Select Committee or to reveal the private deliberations of such a Committee. Accordingly, where a public authority holds such information, it will be exempt from the obligation to disclose it as a result of s 34. For discussion of the scope of Parliamentary privilege, see Coppel, P, *Information Rights* (London: Sweet & Maxwell, 2004), pp 569–573.

Under s 34(2), the duty to confirm or deny is excluded where exemption from that duty is required to avoid an infringement of the privileges of either House of Parliament. Simple confirmation or denial that particular information is held is clearly less likely to infringe Parliamentary privilege than disclosure of the information itself. However, s 34(2) will apply where the very existence of particular information cannot be disclosed without breach of privilege.

7.5.2 Certificates under s 34(4)

Where the Speaker of the House of Commons (in relation to the privileges of the Commons) or the Clerk of the Parliaments (in relation to the privileges of the Lords) certifies that exemption under s 34 is necessary in order to avoid a breach of Parliamentary privilege, such certificate is to be regarded as 'conclusive evidence of that fact' (s 34(3)). There is no statutory mechanism for appeal against the issue of such a certificate. This is in accordance with the general principle that decisions taken by Parliamentary officers are not subject to judicial review. Nevertheless, while Parliament has sole authority to determine whether a breach of privilege has occurred, it does not have authority to create new forms of Parliamentary privilege and the courts are entitled to define the scope of existing Parliamentary privileges. Thus, s 34(3) should be construed so that a certificate signed by the Speaker or the Clerk of the Parliaments is only to be regarded as conclusive evidence of the fact that a particular disclosure would infringe an established privilege and not as conclusive evidence of the scope of Parliamentary privilege.

7.6 DISCLOSURES PREJUDICING THE EFFECTIVE CONDUCT OF PUBLIC AFFAIRS—INFORMATION HELD BY THE HOUSE OF COMMONS OR THE HOUSE OF LORDS

Under s 36 of the Act, information is exempt from disclosure where, in the reasonable opinion of a 'qualified person' its disclosure would prejudice, or would be likely to prejudice, certain specified interests relating to public affairs (such as the 'collective responsibility of Ministers of the Crown' or 'the free and frank provision of advice'). In most circumstances, the exemption contained in s 36 is a 'qualified exemption' and will therefore only apply where, in all the circumstances of the case, the public interest in non-disclosure outweighs the public interest in disclosure of the information. Accordingly, the provision is discussed in greater detail at 8.12. However, where information is held by the House of Commons or the House of Lords, s 36 is an absolute exemption. It is likely to be relied upon in relation to disclosures which, while not actually breaching Parliamentary privilege, would otherwise prejudice the effective conduct of Parliamentary business (see the examples given at Hansard HL, 17 October 2000, col 902).

In the case of information held by the Houses of Parliament, the 'qualified person' for the purpose of s 36 is the Speaker (in the case of the House of Commons) and the Clerk to the Parliaments (in the case of the House of Lords) (s 36(5)). Where, on an application for information made to either of the Houses of Parliament, the relevant 'qualified person' certifies that compliance with the duties to communicate information or to confirm or deny would have any of the prejudicial effects specified in s 36, that certificate is to be taken as conclusive evidence of that fact. Thus, again, there is no opportunity to challenge the application of the exemption when its benefit is claimed by one of the Houses of Parliament. Such a restriction upon access to a court could, in other circumstances, be regarded as incompatible with Article 6(1) of the European Convention on Human Rights and therefore would raise issues under the Human Rights Act 1998 (see, for example, *Osman v UK* (2000) 29 EHRR 245). However, it should be noted that Article 6 is concerned only with rights of a private law nature. Without further development of the jurisprudence on this Article, a statutory right of access to information held by a public authority is unlikely to possess the personal, economic or individual characteristics of the private law sphere and will thus not constitute a 'civil right' within Article 6(1) (see Wadham, J, Mountfield, H and Edmundson, A, *Blackstone's Guide to the Human Rights Act 1998* (3rd edn, Oxford: Blackstone/OUP, 2003), pp 140–142).

7.7 PERSONAL INFORMATION

Under s 40 of the Act, public authorities are, in general, exempt from the Act's duty to provide access to 'personal data' (as defined in the Data Protection Act 1998).

Where an application for information constituting 'personal data' is made by the 'data subject' (ie, the person who is the subject of the data), that information will be covered by the exemption in s 40(1) and will automatically be channelled through the access procedures established under the Data Protection Act 1998.

Where an application for information is made by someone other than the 'data subject', disclosure of that information will often constitute a breach of the Data Protection Act and consequently the public authority will usually be exempt from its duties under the Act as a result of s 40(2).

Generally, the exemptions in both s 40(1) and s 40(2) are absolute exemptions. They are considered in further detail in Chapter 10.

7.8 INFORMATION PROVIDED IN CONFIDENCE

7.8.1 Introduction

Section 41(1) of the Act provides that:

Information is exempt information if—

(a) it was obtained by the public authority from any other person (including another public authority), and

(b) the disclosure of the information to the public (otherwise than under this Act) by the public authority holding it would constitute a breach of confidence actionable by that or any other person.

It is important to note that this exemption only covers information received from *another* body or person in confidence and does not apply to all material which a public authority itself regards as confidential. It is also important to note that information falling within s 41 may also be exempt from disclosure under other provisions of the Act, such as s 40 (personal information), s 43(1) (trade secrets) or s 30(2) (confidential sources).

The scope of s 41 is defined by reference to the equitable action for breach of confidence. In order fully to understand its scope, it is necessary to understand how that form of action operates. A summary of the most significant aspects of the law of breach of confidence is therefore given below (see Bently, L & Sherman, B, *Intellectual Property Law* (2nd edn, Oxford: OUP, 2004), pp 993–1051, for further analysis). While s 41 is classed as an 'absolute exemption' under the Act, its classification as such is rather misleading, because the action for breach of confidence itself contains an inherent 'public interest' limitation.

The use of the term 'actionable' in s 41(b) does not mean that the exemption will apply whenever a public authority would *arguably* breach a duty of confidence by disclosing information. It only applies when disclosure would actually constitute a breach of confidence (Hansard HL, 25 October 2000, cols 415–16).

7.8.2 Breach of Confidence

An action for breach of confidence can be brought to prevent the disclosure of commercial, personal and official information of a confidential nature. The most frequently cited definition of the necessary constituents for the action was given by Megarry J in *Coco v AN Clark (Engineers) Ltd* [1969] RPC 41 at 47:

In my judgment, three elements are normally required if, apart from contract, a case of breach of confidence is to succeed. First, the information itself . . . must 'have the necessary quality of confidence about it'. Secondly, that information must have been imparted in circumstances importing an obligation of confidence. Thirdly, there must be an unauthorised use of that information to the detriment of the person communicating it.

Thus, information which is in the 'public domain', or has not been treated as confidential by its originator, will not have the necessary quality of confidence. However, information which has been subject only to restricted disclosure may still remain subject to an obligation of confidence (see *Attorney-General v Guardian Newspapers Limited (No 2)* [1990] 1 AC 109). Public authorities frequently hold confidential information. This could include, for example, commercial information supplied to a regulatory authority under a statutory obligation, information provided to the authority by one of its employees, or information supplied by an informant to a local police force.

The circumstances under which an *obligation* of confidence (the second requirement referred to in the definition above) can arise also vary widely. At the simplest level, an obligation of confidence expressly imposed by a confidant and expressly accepted by a recipient of information will create an obligation of confidence in equity, and possibly in contract also. However, in other cases, the obligation will arise as a result of the relationship between parties (for example, that between doctor and patient or lawyer and client) or will be implied from the circumstances in which a particular disclosure is made (see, for example, *Hellewell v Chief Constable of Derbyshire* [1995] 1 WLR 804). As the obligation is equitable in nature, it is capable of binding someone other than the original recipient of confidential information where that subsequent recipient knows or ought to know that the information in question has been disclosed in breach of confidence. A public authority will thus not only be under an obligation of confidence where it has accepted information on the express understanding that it will remain confidential—as, for example, in the case of information supplied in response to a public consultation exercise. It will also be bound by an obligation of confidence where the circumstances in which it receives information suggest that that information is to be held confidentially or that it has previously been disclosed in breach of a confidential duty owed to another. This will even be the case where information is supplied to the public authority by someone other than the person to whom the obligation of confidence was originally owed.

Interestingly, recent cases concerning media intrusions into the lives of celebrities suggest that the obligation of confidence will exist whenever a person comes into possession of information which he or she ought, from the context or nature of the information, to realise is confidential (see, for example, *Campbell v MGN Ltd* [2004] 2WLR 1232, HL). The action for breach of confidence may therefore cover situations where a public authority has in its possession any information which a reasonable person would regard as confidential in quality.

7.8.3 The Public Interest 'Defence'

As mentioned above, s 41 is a rather anomalous 'absolute exemption' because the action for breach of confidence contains its own 'public interest' test. A court will not enforce an obligation of confidence where to do so would be contrary to the public interest. This means, for example, that a person seeking to enforce a confidence will not be able to do so where the information reveals some form of 'iniquity' on his or her part (see *Gartside v Outram* (1856) 26 LJ Ch 113). Indeed, in certain cases, courts have refused to enforce an obligation of confidence where there is some other 'just cause or excuse' for disclosing the information in question (see *Lion Laboratories v Evans* [1984] 2 All ER 417).

In cases concerning this public interest 'defence', courts have emphasised that their task is to balance the public interest in honouring an obligation of confidence in a particular case with the public interest in disclosing the information in question (see *X v Y* [1988] 2 All ER 417). As such, the exercise which they are conducting is very similar to that which will have to be performed by the Information Commissioner and courts in determining the public interest in relation to 'qualified exemptions' under s 2 of the Act. Until recently, however, it would have been strongly arguable that the public interest limitation within the law of breach of confidence is more limited than that which applies generally under the Act (see Hansard HL, 14 November 2000, cols 176–177). The 'public interest' has in the past tended only to protect necessary disclosures to an appropriate recipient (such as the police or a regulatory authority) rather than to the public at large (see, for example, *Attorney-General v Guardian Newspapers Limited (No 2)* [1990] 1 AC 109, per Lord Griffiths). Decisions on the public interest under s 2, however, must be made on the presumption that the public generally have a right of access to information. However, recent cases concerning media intrusions into the private lives of celebrities have applied a much more expansive concept of the 'public interest', as a mechanism for balancing conflicting rights protected by the European Convention on Human Rights (see, for example, *Campbell v MGN Ltd* [2004] 2 WLR 1232, HL). Under the influence of such decisions, it is to be expected that applicants for information under the Act should be able to argue that the public interest requires disclosure of otherwise confidential information in a wider range of circumstances than previously. In this respect, it is particularly notable that the decision of the House of Lords in *Campbell* is premised upon an assumption that it is in the public interest to disclose information that corrects false information presented to the public by the person to whom an obligation of confidence is owed.

7.8.4 Information Obtained from Another Public Authority

Section 41 covers information which has been obtained by the public authority in confidence from another public authority and where the disclosure of that information would constitute an actionable breach of confidence (s 41(1)(a)). Thus, for example, if a private contractor designated as a public authority under s 5, were to provide information concerning its financial affairs in confidence to a local authority with which it had contracted to provide certain services, the local authority would be exempt from the duty to communicate that information under s 41(1).

The fact that information will often be exempt from disclosure under the Act where it has been passed in confidence from one public authority to another is controversial. There is a clear danger that one public authority will attempt to impose an obligation of confidence on another in order to avoid disclosure under the Act. However, there are a number of ways in which the possibility of abuse is restricted. First, it should be noted that s 81(2) generally prevents the imposition of a duty of confidence by one government department upon another from forming the basis of a claim to exemption under s 41. Section 81(2) does not, however, prevent reliance upon confidentiality in relation to information passing between government departments and Northern Ireland departments. Second, any public authority seeking to rely upon an action for breach of confidence must, unlike a non-public confidant, surmount an additional hurdle by demonstrating an initial substantial public interest in maintaining the confidence (*Attorney-General v Guardian Newspaper Limited (No 2)* [1990] 1 AC 109). Thus, the ambit of the defence is more limited in the case of public authority confidences. Third, it could be argued that the duty to offer advice and assistance under s 16 of the Act will generally oblige a public authority holding information under such an obligation of confidence to inform an applicant of the identity of the public authority to which the obligation of confidence is owed. This would allow an applicant to make a fresh application to that public authority for the information in question. The originating authority would not be entitled to rely upon s 41 in resisting disclosure. Note also the provisions of the Code of Practice made under s 45, which require public authorities to refuse to accept unjustified obligations of confidentiality (see Appendix 2, para 47).

7.8.5 No 'Reverse Freedom of Information'

'Reverse freedom of information' mechanisms established under overseas freedom of information legislation have been frequently employed in relation to applications for confidential information. As has been noted above, the Act contains no such mechanism and, therefore, a public authority is not obliged to consult a third party to whom, arguably, a duty of confidence is owed. However, consultation with such third parties may be required if an authority is to comply with the Code of Practice issued under s 45 (see paras 31–40).

7.8.6 The Duty to Confirm or Deny

Under s 41(2), the duty to confirm or deny is excluded only to the extent that confirmation or denial would itself constitute an actionable breach of confidence. This is unlikely to be the case where it is the subject-matter of information which is impressed with the duty of confidence. However, s 41(2) will apply where the very existence of information is confidential. The Information Commissioner has provided an example of a situation in which the duty to confirm or deny may well be excluded:

. . . [A] financial regulator might decline to confirm or deny that it has been provided with a confidential report on a company since to confirm that it even held a report would indicate that it harboured suspicions about the activities of that company. However, if it was already public knowledge that a report had been sent to it, there would be no breach of confidence in confirming receipt. In both cases, the regulator might not want to disclose the content of the report.

(Information Commissioner, Freedom of Information Awareness Guidance No 2, *Information provided in confidence*, www.informationcommissioner.gov.uk)

7.9 DISCLOSURE OTHERWISE PROHIBITED

Under s 44(1) of the Act, a public authority is exempt from the duty to communicate information where disclosure of that information:

(a) is prohibited by or under other legislation,

(b) is incompatible with a European Community obligation, or

(c) would constitute or be punishable as a contempt of court.

7.9.1 Disclosure Prohibited under other Legislation

There are numerous statutory provisions prohibiting the disclosure of information under certain circumstances. These derive both from primary and secondary legislation. The government has compiled a comprehensive list of such provisions as a step in the process of deciding whether their retention remains necessary (see Lord Chancellor's Department, *Second Report to Parliament on the Review of Legislation Governing the Disclosure of Information*, November 2002).

In addition to statutory provisions prohibiting disclosure, the Lord Chancellor's Department's Report also lists a number of statutes under which public authorities have *discretion* whether to disclose information or not. Such provisions are not covered by s 44 and, therefore, unless particular information falls under another exemption within Part II, must be regarded as impliedly repealed by the Act.

Many disclosures in breach of statutory provisions will in any event be exempt under other provisions of the Act. For example, disclosures prohibited under s 1 of the Official Secrets Act 1911 are highly likely to fall within one of the exemptions designed to secure national security, and disclosures prohibited under the Abortion Act 1967 may be covered by the exemption covering personal information (s 40). However, in other cases, there may be no such overlap. In those cases, the application of s 44 is problematic because it disturbs the balance between disclosure and non-disclosure generally established under the Act.

As noted above, the government has committed itself to a thorough review of statutory prohibitions on disclosure and, under s 75 of the Act, the Secretary of State has power by order to repeal or amend any such enactment for the purpose of removing or relaxing the prohibition. It is to be hoped that this power will be exercised vigorously at an early date in order to ensure that legislation governing the disclosure of information by public authorities is consistent and that s 44 does not unduly subvert the Act.

7.9.2 European Community Obligations

Prohibitions on the disclosure of information can also arise as a result of directly applicable European Community legislation. These could include regulations or, in some circumstances, directives which ought to have been implemented by the United Kingdom (for an example of a directive imposing duties of confidentiality on Member States, see Council Directive 90/220 on the deliberate release into the environment of genetically modified organisms). They could also arise as a result of prohibitions on disclosure required to ensure the proper functioning of Community bodies (see, for example, Commission Decision 94/90 [1994] OJ L46/58). An example of the latter form of prohibition would be that upon the disclosure of information held by the European Commission in connection with an enquiry which it is conducting into commercial activity suspected of breaching treaty provisions on competition.

7.9.3 Contempt of Court

Courts have inherent and statutory powers to restrict the disclosure of information concerning their own proceedings. Failure to comply with such restrictions may constitute contempt of court (see 9.2.4). A court, for example, may make an order prohibiting publication of details concerning a particular defendant in criminal proceedings under the Contempt of Court Act 1981, s 11(2). If a public authority were to breach such an order, it would be in contempt of court and, accordingly, any application to the authority under the Act for the disclosure of such information would be covered by the exemption in s 44.

For suggestions as to other ways in which disclosure of information by a public authority could give rise to proceedings for contempt of Court, see Coppel, P, *Information Rights* (London: Sweet & Maxwell, 2004) pp 703–706.

8

QUALIFIED EXEMPTIONS

8.1 INTRODUCTION

The remainder of the exemptions listed in Part II of the Freedom of Information Act 2000 are subject to a counter-balancing 'public interest' restriction. In this text, they are designated 'qualified exemptions'. Under s 2(1)(b) of the Act, a qualified exemption will only be effective in excluding the duty to confirm or deny where:

. . . in all the circumstances of the case, the public interest in maintaining the exclusion of the duty to confirm or deny outweighs the public interest in disclosing whether the public authority holds the information.

Similarly, under s 2(2)(b) of the Act, such an exemption will only be effective in excluding the duty to communicate information where:

. . . in all the circumstances of the case, the public interest in maintaining the exemption outweighs the public interest in disclosing the information.

Thus, decisions on the application of qualified exemptions must be taken in two stages. First, a public authority must determine whether or not information is covered by an exemption and then, even if it is covered, the authority must disclose the information unless the public interest favours non-disclosure. For further discussion of this assessment of the public interest, see 6.3 above.

As it may often be particularly difficult for a public authority to determine whether or not a request for information is covered by a qualified exemption, modifications to the usual procedures under the Act apply in such a case. Decisions on the public interest under a particular exemption must be taken within 'such time as is reasonable in all the circumstances' rather than within the usual 20-day period (s 10(3)). Where such decisions have to be taken in relation to historical information, the Act also imposes obligations of consultation upon public authorities (see 11.4).

8.2 INFORMATION INTENDED FOR FUTURE PUBLICATION

Under s 22(1) of the Act, a public authority does not have to communicate information where:

(a) the information is held by the public authority with a view to its publication, by the authority or any other person, at some future date (whether determined or not),

(b) the information was already held with a view to such publication at the time the request for information was made, and

(c) it is reasonable in all the circumstances that the information should be withheld from disclosure until the date referred to in paragraph (a).

The duty to confirm or deny is excluded where compliance with that duty would involve the disclosure of any information (whether or not already recorded) covered by s 22(1) (s 22(2)).

Public authorities may seek to rely upon this exemption where they wish to manage the release of information. The controversy surrounding the premature disclosure of the findings recorded in the Macpherson Report into the murder of Stephen Lawrence provides an example of such a situation. The exemption contained in s 22 prevents the media from using freedom of information legislation to gain premature access to such documents.

This exemption applies equally where information is to be published by the public authority itself or by a third party. Thus, for example, where a government department or university is holding research data which are to be published in a scholarly journal by an individual academic, that public authority may be exempt from the obligation to disclose such data under the Act.

Controversially, the intended future date for publication does not have to have been determined for this exemption to apply (s 22(1)(a)). However, a safeguard is provided for applicants by the fact that, under s 22(1)(c), the exemption will only apply where the delay before publication is 'reasonable'. The fact that s 22(1)(c) requires only that delay in publication 'until the date referred to in paragraph (a)' must be reasonable is rather odd. Paragraph (a) makes express reference to the possibility that this exemption may be effective whether a date for publication has been determined or not. Where a date has not yet been determined, s 22(1)(c) must therefore be interpreted to mean that the exemption will only apply where it is reasonable to postpone publication until an unspecified date.

It is not difficult to imagine circumstances in which it would be regarded as reasonable to exclude communication of information until a later publication date. This would presumably be so where a public authority delays publication in order to allow advance disclosure to those most directly affected by information (as in the case of the Macpherson Report) or to ensure that it has put in place administrative procedures to allow it to respond effectively to queries about published information. It will, however, not be possible to establish that delay is reasonable where it arises as a result of political embarrassment or administrative inefficiency.

An applicant may be able to argue that further delay in publication is unreasonable where inaccurate information is in circulation or where an urgent need for the information in question has developed. It seems that it is only the planned *date* of publication (where determined) that is relevant to an assessment of reasonableness under s 22(1)(c). It would not, therefore, be open for an applicant to argue that s 22 is inapplicable in a particular case because a public authority intends only to publish information in, for example, an expensive database. In such circumstances it may, however, be possible to argue that the public interest does not favour maintaining the exemption.

During Parliamentary debates on this provision, it was stated that, although s 22(1) refers to information held with a 'view to' publication, it will only apply where the authority has a settled intention to publish (Hansard HL, 19 October 2000, col 1245).

It should be remembered that s 22 is a qualified exemption and, thus, even where a public authority can establish that it is reasonable to withhold information from disclosure until later publication, the public interest may still favour disclosure. There is considerable potential for overlap between the factors relevant to an assessment of whether or not it is reasonable to delay publication and the factors relevant to an assessment of the balance of public interests in a particular case.

8.3 NATIONAL SECURITY

8.3.1 Scope of the Exemption

The absolute exemption covering information deriving from, or referring to, certain bodies responsible for security (s 23) has already been discussed above (at 7.3). However, even where that absolute exemption does not apply, a public authority is still exempt from the duty to communicate information where such exemption is 'required for the purpose of safeguarding national security' (s 24(1)). The duty to confirm or deny is also excluded where exemption from that duty is required for the purpose of safeguarding national security (s 24(2)). Public authorities will only need to rely upon this prejudice-based exemption where information neither derives from, nor relates to, any of the security bodies listed in s 23. It could, for example, apply to a request for information relating to safety precautions at nuclear power stations. While other exemptions could also apply to such a request (perhaps s 38 ('Health and safety'), for example), the certification procedures available under s 24 may make it more attractive to public authorities seeking to resist disclosure.

Historically, courts have been reluctant to question executive bodies' assessments of what is necessary in the interests of national security (see, for example, *Chandler v DPP* [1964] AC 763). However, more recently, it has been demonstrated that the judiciary will not simply accept executive assertions that information should be suppressed in the interests of national security (see, for example, *Lord Advocate v The Scotsman Publications Ltd* [1990] 1 AC 809). Some encouragement for a more sceptical approach can be found in the wording of s 24 itself, which only applies where exemption is '*required* for the purpose of safeguarding national security' (see Hansard HC, 5 April 2000, col 1060).

Nevertheless, this exemption may cover information which, while innocuous in its own right, could, when connected with other information, endanger national security. It has also been suggested that s 24 could function to exempt information that is, to some degree, in the public domain because formal disclosure by a public authority may authenticate information that was previously unconfirmed (Coppel, P, *Information Rights* (London: Sweet & Maxwell, 2004), pp 493–494). A public authority may also seek to argue that s 24 applies where disclosure of information would lead to the drying-up of sources of information and thereby, over time, endanger national security.

8.3.2 Ministerial Certificates under s 24

Where a 'Minister of the Crown' certifies that exemption from the duties to communicate information, or to confirm or deny, is required for the purpose of safeguarding national security, that certificate is to be taken as conclusive evidence of that fact (s 24(3)). Only certain senior ministers qualify as 'Ministers of the Crown' for the purposes of this provision (s 25(3)). An applicant who is aggrieved by the issue of such a certificate is entitled to appeal against it to the Information Tribunal (s 60). On the hearing of such an appeal, the Tribunal can quash the certificate where it finds that 'applying the principles applied by the court on an application for judicial review, the Minister did not have reasonable grounds for issuing the certificate' (s 60(3)). This is the standard of review which has been applied in judicial review proceedings and is a high hurdle for an applicant to surmount (the so-called test of '*Wednesbury*-unreasonableness', from *Associated Provincial Picture Houses v Wednesbury Corporation* [1948] 1 KB 223).

When a ministerial certificate is issued under s 24(3), that certificate need not specifically describe the information for which exemption is claimed. The information can instead be described 'by means of a general description' (s 24(4)). Thus, for example, a certificate could be issued covering all existing information concerning security arrangements at nuclear power stations in the United Kingdom. Such certificates can also be expressed 'to have prospective effect' and could therefore be issued in relation to all existing and future information concerning the security arrangements at nuclear power stations (s 24(4)). Where a certificate is issued by a public authority in relation to a general description of information, any other party to proceedings concerning a request under the Act may appeal to the Tribunal 'on the ground that the certificate does not apply to the information in question' (s 60(4)). Various evidential presumptions relating to certificates issued under s 24(3) are set out in s 25.

It is important to remember that the exemption provided by s 24 is a qualified exemption. Therefore, even though an applicant must appeal directly to the Information Tribunal, rather than to the Information Commissioner, against the issue of a certificate under s 24(3), he or she remains entitled to complain to the Information Commissioner about a public authority's assessment that the public interest favours maintenance of the exemption over disclosure of the requested information. An applicant's task in such circumstances may, however, be difficult. If it is necessary not to disclose information for the purpose of safeguarding national security, it seems likely that it will only be in rare cases that the Information Commissioner will be convinced that the public interest nevertheless favours disclosure.

8.4 DEFENCE

In addition to exemptions designed to ensure that disclosures do not threaten national security, the Act also contains a broader exemption designed to protect the United Kingdom's defences. Section 26(1) provides:

Information is exempt information if its disclosure under this Act would, or would be likely to, prejudice—

(a) the defence of the British Islands or of any colony, or

(b) the capability, effectiveness or security of any relevant forces.

Public authorities are also exempt from the duty to confirm or deny where compliance with that duty would, or would be likely to, prejudice any of the matters set out above (s 26(3)).

'Relevant forces' are defined as the armed forces of the Crown (or part thereof) and any forces co-operating with those forces (or part thereof) (s 26(2)). It should be noted that, while the Ministry of Defence and the armed forces of the Crown are themselves subject to the duties established in the Act, the 'special forces' and units assisting GCHQ are not subject to the Act (Sch 1, paras 1 and 6). Any information supplied by, or relating to, such forces is also exempt under s 23 (see 7.3).

Section 26 would, for example, be likely to exempt the Ministry of Defence from the duty to communicate information concerning the capabilities and combat-readiness of the United Kingdom's armed forces. It should, however, be noted that this exemption can also apply where information is held by public authorities other than the Ministry of Defence or the armed forces themselves.

The Information Commissioner has indicated that it may be necessary to ask a number of questions in order to assess whether 'prejudice' would be caused by a disclosure. Can the information in question be exploited by an enemy? Does the fact that an operation has been concluded mean that prejudice can no longer be caused? Is the same information already available from reputable sources in the public domain? ((Information Commissioner, Freedom of Information Awareness Guidance No 10, *The Defence Exemption*, www.informationcommissioner.gov.uk).

The inclusion of 'any forces co-operating with [the armed forces of the Crown]' within the definition of 'relevant forces' is interesting. The term 'co-operating' is potentially very broad and could be interpreted either to include only forces working with the United Kingdom's forces on a particular project or to include a much wider range of 'friendly' forces. Even in the more restricted sense, however, the exemption would cover information about the capabilities and vulnerabilities of forces working with United Kingdom forces on, for example, a joint peace-keeping mission. If a public authority were to receive a request for such information, the relevant public interest that would require consideration would be the interest of the public in the United Kingdom. The effect which such disclosure would be likely to have upon relations between the United Kingdom and that other state would, however, seem to be a relevant factor in the assessment of the public interest.

8.5 INTERNATIONAL RELATIONS

Within s 27 of the Act, there are two separate exemptions relating to international relations. The first is a 'prejudice-based' exemption and covers disclosures which would, or would be likely to, prejudice international relations. The second is a 'class-based' exemption covering information received in confidence from other states and international bodies.

8.5.1 Prejudice to International Relations

Under s 27(1), a public authority is exempt from the duty to communicate information where disclosure of that information would, or would be likely to, prejudice:

(a) relations between the United Kingdom and any other State,

(b) relations between the United Kingdom and any international organisation or international court,

(c) the interests of the United Kingdom abroad, or

(d) the promotion or protection by the United Kingdom of its interests abroad.

The duty to confirm or deny is also excluded to the extent that compliance with that duty would, or would be likely to, have any of these listed effects (s 27(4)(a)). Further definition of the terms 'international court', 'international organisation' and 'State' are provided in s 27(5).

This exemption is extremely broad (cf Official Secrets Act 1988, s 3). The 'interests of the United Kingdom abroad' and 'the promotion or protection by the United Kingdom of its interests abroad' are likely to prove particularly inviting to public authorities seeking to avoid the disclosure of information. In view of this danger, it will be important for the Information Commissioner to scrutinise closely public authorities seeking to rely on this exemption. In particular, it needs to be emphasised that this provision is designed to protect general national interests and not the interests of specific groups or bodies within the State.

8.5.2 Confidential Information Obtained from other States or International Bodies (s 27(2))

Under s 27(2) of the Act, a public authority is exempt from the duty to communicate information where that information is 'confidential information obtained from a State other than the United Kingdom or from an international organisation or international court'. The definitions of 'State', 'international organisation' and 'international court' are those set out in s 27(5). The duty to confirm or deny is also excluded to the extent that compliance with that duty:

. . . would involve the disclosure of any information (whether or not already recorded) which is confidential information obtained from a State other than the United Kingdom or from an international organisation or international court.

(s 27(4)(b))

The duty to disclose such confidential information would very often be excluded in any event under s 27(1). However, where the conditions set out in s 27(2) are satisfied, there is no need for the public authority to establish that specific prejudice would, or would be likely, to arise as a result of disclosure. It is presumed that prejudice will inevitably arise to our international relations if confidences owed to other States and bodies cannot be maintained (cf the parallel provision contained in the Official Secrets Act, s 3).

There is also an overlap between s 27(2) and the more general exemption covering information received in confidence (s 41; see 7.8). However, it is important to note that these two provisions are differently worded. Section 39 provides exemption where disclosure of information obtained from another person would 'constitute a breach of confidence actionable by that or any other person'. Section 27(2) is wider because, for its purposes:

. . . any information obtained from a State, organisation or court is confidential at any time while the terms on which it was obtained require it to be held in confidence or while the circumstances in which it was obtained make it reasonable for the State, organisation or court to expect that it will be so held.

(s 27(3))

This provision is therefore concerned only with the conditions under which information was *obtained*. Thus, for example, the fact that the information is already, to some degree, in the public domain will be irrelevant in establishing whether s 27(3) applies.

8.6 RELATIONS WITHIN THE UNITED KINGDOM

Section 28 of the Act provides exemption in certain circumstances to protect the relations between the devolved administrations of the United Kingdom. Under s 28(1), a public authority is exempt from the duty to communicate information where disclosure of that information:

. . . would, or would be likely to, prejudice relations between any administration in the United Kingdom and any other such administration.

For the purposes of this exemption, 'administration in the United Kingdom' is defined to include:

(a) the government of the United Kingdom,

(b) the Scottish Administration,

(c) the Executive Committee of the Northern Ireland Assembly, or

(d) the National Assembly of Wales.

The duty to confirm or deny is excluded where compliance with that duty would, or would be likely to, prejudice relations between the administrations as set out above (s 28(3)).

During the Parliamentary debates on this provision, interesting examples of its potential application were provided (see Hansard HL, 19 October 2000, col 1280). It was suggested that disclosure of a government department's 'thumbnail sketch of the strengths and weaknesses of the individual members of an executive' or of a government department's comments on a devolved administration's policy proposals or Acts may prejudice relations between the relevant devolved Assembly or Parliament and the United Kingdom government. Relevant prejudice would presumably also arise where a disclosure makes it less likely that a devolved body would provide a public authority with information in future.

Unlike the position under s 27 ('International relations'), there is no specific class-based exemption covering information received in confidence from another administration in the United Kingdom.

8.7 THE ECONOMY

Under s 29(1) of the Act, a public authority is exempt from the duty to communicate information where disclosure of that information:

. . . would, or would be likely to, prejudice—

(a) the economic interests of the United Kingdom or of any part of the United Kingdom, or

(b) the financial interests of any administration in the United Kingdom . . .

Again, as in the case of the exemption considered immediately above, 'administration in the United Kingdom' is defined to include the government of the United Kingdom, the Scottish Administration, the Executive Committee of the Northern Ireland Assembly and the National Assembly of Wales (s 29(1)(b)). The duty to confirm or deny is also excluded to the extent that compliance with that duty would, or would be likely to, prejudice any of the matters mentioned in s 29(1).

It is possible to envisage certain forms of information which are likely to fall within this exemption. For example, premature disclosure of governmental intentions with regard to taxation or to the disposal of substantial property holdings owned by the state would be likely to lead to prejudice to the economic interests of the United Kingdom. A disclosure that would be likely to lead to extensive and destabilising speculation would also seem likely to be regarded as prejudicial to such interests. Detailed guidance on the assessment of prejudice (and of the balance of public interests) in the context of this exemption has already been provided by the Information Commissioner (see Information Commissioner, *The Economy–Casework Guidance*, www.informationcommissioner. gov.uk).

However, sometimes it may be considerably harder for public authorities to prove that, in the long term, the disclosure of information will, or will be likely to, cause the specified forms of prejudice. The decision to release the minutes of the monthly meetings between the Governor of the Bank of England and the Chancellor of the Exchequer, for example, has not appeared to be detrimental to the national economic interest. Indeed, as the evidence presented by a public authority claiming prejudice to economic or financial interests may be particularly complex and speculative, the Information Commissioner ought to require a strong case of prejudice to be made out in the context of this provision.

During Parliamentary debates on this provision, clarification of the reasons for including 'the economic interests . . . of any part of the United Kingdom' within s 29(1) was provided. It was suggested that, where disclosure of information about a particular region of the country would be likely to lead to a diminution in inward investment in that region, the information would fall within s 29 (Hansard HL, 19 October 2000, col 1287).

8.8 INVESTIGATIONS AND PROCEEDINGS

Section 30 of the Act contains two distinct exemptions. The first (s 30(1)) covers information which has, at any time, been held for the purposes of specified *criminal* investigations and proceedings. The second (s 30(2)) covers information which has both been obtained for the purposes of a wider range of investigations or proceedings and relates to the obtaining of information from *confidential sources*.

8.8.1 Criminal Investigations and Proceedings (s 30(1))

Under s 30(1), a public authority is exempt from the duty to communicate information where that information has, at any time, been held for the purposes of:

(a) any investigation which the public authority has a duty to conduct with a view to it being ascertained—
   (i) whether someone should be charged with an offence, or
   (ii) whether a person charged with an offence is guilty of it,

(b) any investigation which is conducted by the authority and in the circumstances may lead to a decision by the authority to institute criminal proceedings which the authority has power to conduct, or

(c) any criminal proceedings which the authority has power to conduct.

The duty to confirm or deny is also excluded in relation to information which is (or if it were held by a public authority would be) exempt information as a result of the above provisions (s 30(3)).

Section 30(1) is a class exemption and is therefore not dependent on the ability of the public authority to establish that prejudice to any proceedings would, or would be likely to, arise as a result of disclosure. It provides comprehensive coverage of information connected with criminal proceedings and will, for example, mean that the police will not be required to disclose information concerning the extent of their enquiries in connection with a particular crime or information received from witnesses in an investigation. This exemption is designed to prevent the mechanism established under the Act from subverting the rules of disclosure within criminal proceedings. As such, it can be distinguished from comparable exemptions in freedom of information legislation in other jurisdictions, where the right of access to information has been used extensively as a means of obtaining disclosure in litigation.

It is not only the police, and the Crown Prosecution Service, which have duties and powers to conduct criminal proceedings and investigations. Other bodies, such as local authorities, the Environment Agency and HM Customs and Excise also have such powers and duties within their own areas of responsibility. In addition, under the Act, 'criminal proceedings' are expressly defined to include proceedings before a court-martial or other courts with statutory powers to handle cases concerning military discipline (s 30(5)). References to a 'public authority' in the provisions set out above must also be construed to include, as appropriate, officers of that authority and responsible government ministers (s 30(4)).

It is important to note that this exemption covers information held 'at any time' for the purposes described above. Thus, for example, information will fall within the exemption even where an investigation has been concluded. This feature of the exemption has received widespread criticism in the wake of significant controversies, such as those concerning BSE and the Paddington train crash, in which there have been suggestions that public authorities have not been sufficiently willing to disclose information acquired in the course of investigations. It is also contrary to the findings of the Macpherson Report which advised that information in the hands of prosecuting authorities should not be subject to such a 'class-based' exemption (1998, Cm 4262-I, ch. 47.9).

However, the fact that s 30(1) is a qualified exemption may go some way to meeting these criticisms. Where there is a substantial public interest in receiving information, or where the public interest in maintaining the exemption is reduced (for example, where an investigation has been concluded), a public authority will find it more difficult to rely successfully on s 30(1). Much will depend on the willingness of applicants to pursue public interest disclosure and the extent to which the Information Commissioner is willing to overrule public authorities on this issue.

In an assessment of the public interest under s 30, the Human Rights Act 1998 may sometimes be relevant. Where investigations or proceedings have not yet been concluded, the right to a fair trial under Article 6 of the European Convention may in some circumstances require that the public interest be interpreted against disclosure. In addition, it is important to note that information relating to individuals will often be covered by the exemption in s 40(2) ('Personal information'). That exemption is, generally, an absolute exemption.

Section 30(1), however, has an important restriction. It applies only to information relating to *specific* investigations or proceedings. It will not therefore apply to information of more general application, such as statistics on reported crime or on the effectiveness of particular investigating bodies.

8.8.2 Information Relating to the Obtaining of Information from Confidential Sources (s 30(2))

Under s 30(2), a public authority is exempt from the duty to communicate information where:

(a) [the information] was obtained or recorded by the authority for the purposes of its functions relating to—
   (i) investigations falling within subsection [30](1)(a) or (b),
   (ii) criminal proceedings which the authority has power to conduct,
   (iii) investigations . . . which are conducted by the authority for any of the purposes specified in section 31(2) and either by virtue of Her Majesty's prerogative or by virtue of powers conferred by or under any enactment, or
   (iv) civil proceedings which are brought by or on behalf of the authority and arise out of such investigations, and

(b) [the information] relates to the obtaining of information from confidential sources.

The duty to confirm or deny is excluded in relation to information falling within the above definition (s 30(3)). The definitions of 'criminal proceedings' and 'public authority' discussed above in relation to s 30(1) apply also to s 30(2). The 'purposes specified in s 31(2)' are listed at 8.9 below.

This exemption recognises the particular public interest in ensuring that information about confidential sources is not disclosed generally. It covers information acquired in connection with a wider range of investigations and proceedings than under s 30(1) (for example, civil proceedings such as those relating to the disqualification of company directors). Unlike s 30(1), the application of this exemption is not restricted to specific investigations or proceedings. Thus, for example, information volunteered to an officer of a prosecuting authority by a confidential source would be covered by s 30(2) whether or not it related to, or was applied to, any specific investigation or set of proceedings.

It is important to note that this exemption does not only cover the actual information received from a confidential source (which would, in any event, also be covered by s 41), but any information *relating to* the obtaining of information from confidential sources. Thus, for example, the exemption would (subject to the balance of public interests) seem to cover general information concerning appropriate methods for handling confidential sources and statistics concerning the number of such sources contacted by members of a particular police force.

8.9 LAW ENFORCEMENT

In addition to the 'class-based' exemption discussed above, s 31 of the Act provides an additional 'prejudice-based' exemption for information which is not exempt by virtue of s 30 but is nevertheless connected with a wide range of law enforcement functions. Under this provision, a public authority is exempt from the duty to communicate information where disclosure would, or would be likely to, prejudice:

(a) the prevention and detection of crime,

(b) the apprehension or prosecution of offenders,

(c) the administration of justice,

(d) the assessment or collection of any tax or duty or of any imposition of a similar nature,

(e) the operation of the immigration controls,

(f) the maintenance of security and good order in prisons or in other institutions where persons are lawfully detained,

(g) the exercise by any public authority of its functions for any of the purposes specified in subsection (2),

(h) any civil proceedings which are brought by or on behalf of a public authority and arise out of an investigation conducted, for any of the purposes specified in subsection (2), by or on behalf of the authority by virtue of Her Majesty's prerogative or by virtue of powers conferred by or under an enactment, or

(i) any inquiry held under the Fatal Accidents and Sudden Death Inquiries (Scotland) Act 1976 . . .

The purposes specified in subsection (2) encompass a wide range of law enforcement and regulatory functions. They are:

(a) the purpose of ascertaining whether any person has failed to comply with the law,

(b) the purpose of ascertaining whether any person is responsible for any conduct which is improper,

(c) the purpose of ascertaining whether circumstances which would justify regulatory action in pursuance of any enactment exist or may arise,

(d) the purpose of ascertaining a person's fitness or competence in relation to the management of bodies corporate or in relation to any profession or other activity which he is, or seeks to become, authorised to carry on,

(e) the purpose of ascertaining the cause of an accident,

(f) the purpose of protecting charities against misconduct or mismanagement . . . in their administration,

(g) the purpose of protecting the property of charities from loss or misapplication,

(h) the purpose of recovering the property of charities,

(i) the purpose of securing the health, safety and welfare of persons at work, and

(j) the purpose of protecting persons other than persons at work against risk to health or safety arising out of or in connection with the actions of persons at work.

The duty to confirm or deny is also excluded to the extent that compliance with that duty would, or would be likely to, prejudice any of the matters set out in s 31(1) above (s 31(3)).

It is not difficult to imagine how the premature release of information could prejudice the functions set out in s 31. Perhaps most obviously, such disclosure could result in the disruption of an investigation by the subject of that investigation. Prejudice to the listed functions could, however, arise in a number of other ways. For example, disclosure of the financial limits below which tax authorities do not investigate self-assessments could lead to prejudice to 'the assessment or collection of any tax or duty' as specified in s 31(1)(d) and disclosure of the registration numbers of unmarked police vehicles could prejudice 'the prevention or detection of crime' (s 31(1)(a)).

8.10 AUDIT FUNCTIONS

Section 33 of the Act applies only to public authorities which have functions in relation to either the audit of the accounts of other public authorities (s 33(1)(a)) or the examination of the economy, efficiency and effectiveness with which other public authorities use their resources in discharging their functions (s 33(1)(b)). Such public authorities are exempt from the duty to communicate information where the disclosure of such information would, or would be likely to, prejudice the exercise of these functions (s 33(2)).

It should be emphasised that this provision applies only to public authorities having audit functions in relation to *other* public authorities and therefore, for example, information relating to a local authority's internal audit will not fall within the exemption. The public authorities to which s 33(1)(a) has most obvious application are the National Audit Office (established under the National Audit Act 1983), equivalent bodies in the devolved administrations and the Audit Commission for Local Authorities and the National Health Service in England and Wales ('The Audit Commission'). The National Audit Office is an independent body responsible for reporting to Parliament on the economy, efficiency and effectiveness with which government departments, over 130 executive agencies (such as the Legal Services Commission and Regional Development Agencies) and many other public bodies (for example, the Metropolitan Police) spend public money. The Audit Commission has statutory auditing responsibility in relation to local authorities and NHS authorities.

Clearly, the value of the findings of such bodies could be significantly diminished if authorities under investigation had advance notice of all audit methodologies or of draft conclusions of the auditing bodies.

Many Audit Commission audits are in fact conducted under contract by private accountancy firms. Such firms would seem to be prime candidates for designation as public authorities for the purpose of the Act under s 5 (see 4.5.2).

Apart from those public authorities discussed above, which are clearly engaged in auditing activities, a wider range of bodies engaged in more general investigations or standards inspections may fall within the wording of s 31(1)(b). The Information Commissioner has suggested, for example, that bodies such as the Commission for Healthcare Audit and Inspection, HM Inspectorate of Prisons and Ofsted may be covered (see Information Commissioner, *The Audit Exemption–Casework Guidance*, www.informationcommissioner.gov.uk).

8.11 FORMULATION OF GOVERNMENT POLICY AND OTHER GOVERNMENTAL INTERESTS

Under s 35(1), information held by a government department, or by the National Assembly for Wales, is exempt from the duty to communicate information where it relates to:

(a) the formulation or development of government policy,

(b) Ministerial communications,

(c) the provision of advice by any of the Law Officers or any request for the provision of such advice, or

(d) the operation of any Ministerial private office.

The duty to confirm or deny is also excluded in relation to information which is (or if it were held by the public authority would be) exempt information under s 35(1) (s 35(2)).

Further definition of 'government policy', 'the Law Officers', 'Ministerial communications' and 'Ministerial private office' are provided in s 35(5). The definition of 'government department' throughout the Act includes Northern Ireland departments and any 'body or authority exercising statutory functions on behalf of the Crown' (s 84). This 'class-based' exemption, which is only available to government bodies and to the National Assembly of Wales, is designed to ensure that policy discussion can be conducted privately and without the disadvantages attendant upon 'government in a goldfish bowl'. The justification for such a provision is that, if policy advice and the consideration of policy options were not protected from disclosure, civil servants would be less frank in advising Ministers and consideration of policy options would be restricted. It is difficult to be sure whether this is actually true or not.

The most controversial aspect of this provision is the extremely broad exemption offered to information concerning 'the formulation or development of government policy' under s 35(1)(a). This exemption is broader than that which applied under the Code of Practice on Access to Government Information, which covered only information relating to policy and not *factual* information underlying policy discussions (*Code of Practice on Access to Government Information*, 2nd edn, 1997, Part II, para 2). Section 35(1)(a) covers all information relating to the 'formulation or development of government policy' even where a policy has finally been adopted (see s 35(2)).

As a result of Parliamentary pressure, some limitations upon the scope of the exemption have however been imposed. Under s 35(2), once a decision on government policy has been taken, any *statistical* information used to provide an informed background to the taking of the decision is not to be regarded as falling within s 35(1)(a) or (b). Distinguishing between 'statistics' and other forms of 'fact' will not be easy. This difficulty is alleviated to some degree by s 35(4), which provides that, in considering the balance of public interests in relation to an application for information covered by s 35(1)(a):

. . . regard shall be had to the particular public interest in the disclosure of factual information which has been used, or is intended to be used, to provide an informed background to decision-taking.

This provision provides a strong steer to public authorities, and to the Information Commissioner, in favour of the disclosure of such factual information. Indeed, such information should normally be disclosed (Hansard HL, 14 November 2000, col 156).

While the exemption contained in s 35(1)(a) is undoubtedly wide-ranging, it is not all-encompassing. It should be remembered that only information relating to the 'formulation or development of government policy' is covered.

Information concerning the execution of adopted policies or information concerning other procedural or administrative functions will not fall within the exemption.

8.12 PREJUDICE TO THE EFFECTIVE CONDUCT OF PUBLIC AFFAIRS

Section 36 of the Act applies only to information held by a public authority that is not otherwise exempt under the class-exemption contained in s 35. Under s 36(2), a public authority is exempt from the duty to communicate information where, in the reasonable opinion of a qualified person, disclosure of that information:

(a) would, or would be likely to, prejudice—
   (i) the maintenance of the convention of the collective responsibility of Ministers of the Crown, or
   (ii) the work of the Executive Committee of the Northern Ireland Assembly, or
   (iii) the work of the executive committee of the National Assembly for Wales,

(b) would, or would be likely to, inhibit—
   (i) the free and frank provision of advice, or
   (ii) the free and frank exchange of views for the purposes of deliberation, or

(c) would otherwise prejudice, or would be likely otherwise to prejudice, the effective conduct of public affairs.

The duty to confirm or deny is also excluded to the extent that, in the reasonable opinion of a qualified person, compliance with that duty would, or would be likely to, have any of the prejudicial effects set out in s 36(2).

In most instances, s 36 is a 'qualified exemption'. However, so far as it relates to information held by the House of Commons or the House of Lords, it is an absolute exemption and is not therefore subject to any 'public interest' limitation (see 7.6).

The rationale for this exemption is the same as that for s 35. However, its scope is broader, potentially applying to all public authorities and not just to central government. In addition, s 36(2)(c) has been described quite openly by the Act's promoters as a 'mopping-up' clause which will enable public authorities to resist disclosure in situations for which specific provision was not made when the legislation was drafted. It has been suggested, for example, that s 36(2)(c) would exempt a public examining body from the obligation to disclose communications between chief examiners and those responsible for drafting questions for public examinations (Hansard HL, 24 October 2000, col 311).

However, in order to ensure that the exemption is not abused by public authorities, restrictions have been placed upon its use. The exemption is 'prejudice-based' rather than 'class-based' and therefore any public authority seeking to rely on it must be able to demonstrate that the particular kinds of specified prejudice would, or would be likely to, arise as a result of compliance with the Act.

This task is made easier by the fact that, generally, the 'reasonable opinion of a qualified person' that such prejudice will, or will be likely to, arise will be sufficient. The only exception to this general position relates to 'statistical information', where a public authority must provide evidence of prejudice or likely prejudice (s 36(4)). In cases in which the reasonable opinion of a qualified person is sufficient to bring the exemption into effect, an applicant's ability to challenge a public authority's decision not to disclose particular information is significantly reduced. The Information Commissioner will only be able to overturn the opinion of the qualified person where that opinion is found to be unreasonable. In such a case, an applicant is again required to surmount the relatively high hurdle applied in judicial review proceedings.

For the purposes of s 36, the appropriate 'qualified person' for each type of public authority is specified in s 36(5). As a further restraint on the abuse of this exemption, the 'qualified person' in relation to many public authorities, must be either a Minister or a person authorised for the purposes of this section by a Minister (s 36(5)(o)).

8.13 COMMUNICATIONS WITH THE ROYAL FAMILY AND HONOURS

Under s 37 of the Act, a public authority is exempt from the duty to communicate information where information relates to:

(a) communications with Her Majesty, with other members of the Royal Family or with the Royal Household, or

(b) the conferring by the Crown of any honour or dignity.

(s 37(1))

The duty to confirm or deny is also excluded in relation to information which is (or if it were held by the public authority would be) covered by s 37(1) (s 37(2)).

Section 37(1)(a) encompasses all information which 'relates to' the specified forms of communication. Thus, for example, it will cover not only letters or other documents received from members of the Royal Family or Royal Household but also, for example, notes of a meeting between officials of a public authority and a member of the Royal Family or Royal Household. The award of honours and dignities (such as peerages) falls within the royal prerogative and is traditionally not under the scrutiny of Parliament.

121

8.14 HEALTH AND SAFETY

Under s 38 of the Act, a public authority is exempt from the duty to communicate information where disclosure of that information would, or would be likely to:

(a) endanger the physical or mental health of any individual, or

(b) endanger the safety of any individual.

The duty to confirm or deny is also excluded to the extent that compliance with that duty would, or would be likely, to have either of the effects mentioned in s 38(1) (s 38(2)). This provision bears similarities to a parallel exemption to the right of subject access under the Data Protection Act 1998 (see Data Protection (Subject Access Modification) (Health) Order 2000). However, that exemption excludes the right of subject access only where there is a risk of 'serious harm' arising as a result of disclosure. The use of the term 'endanger' does, however, suggest that only substantial and relatively immediate prejudice to the protected interests will bring the provision into play.

The danger to health and safety referred to in this provision could relate to the applicant, the supplier of information or to some other person. It could, for example, apply where a government department wishes to suppress information which it considers likely to hamper the effectiveness of a vaccination campaign. In some cases covered by s 38, the request for information will, in any event, fall within another exemption. For example, if a tabloid newspaper were to seek information concerning the identity or whereabouts of a particularly unpopular individual, such as a convicted paedophile, that information would in any event be likely to be exempt under s 40 ('Personal information').

Where the disclosure of information would endanger an individual's health or safety, it is possible that disclosure of that information by a public authority could violate that individual's rights under the European Convention on Human Rights (see, by analogy, *Osman v UK* (2000) 29 EHRR 245). In such a case, as a result of the Human Rights Act 1998, the 'public interest' would have to be interpreted against disclosure.

8.15 ENVIRONMENTAL INFORMATION

Section 39 of the Act is not designed to prevent individuals from obtaining access to environmental information. It merely aims to ensure that requests for such information are handled under specific regulations implementing the United Kingdom's international obligations on access to environmental information rather than under the Act itself. The relevant current regulations are the Environmental Information Regulations 2004, which came into force on 1 January 2005 (see Appendix 6). These implement Council Directive 2003/4 on public access to environmental information, which was itself passed to implement obligations assumed under the United Nations Economic Commission for Europe Convention on Access to Information, Public Participation in Decision Making and Access to Justice in Environmental Matters ('the Aarhus Convention'—ECE/CEP/43, adopted 25 June 1998).

Section 39(1) provides that a public authority is exempt from the duty to communicate information if the public authority is obliged by environmental information regulations to make the information available to the public in accordance with those regulations, or would be so obliged but for any exemption contained in the regulations. The duty to confirm or deny is also excluded in relation to such information (s 39(2)).

Under the Regulations, 'environmental information' is defined as:

. . . any information in written, visual, aural, electronic or any other material form on—

(a) the state of the elements of the environment, such as air and atmosphere, water, soil, land, landscape and natural sites including wetlands, coastal and marine areas, biological diversity and its components, including genetically modified organisms, and the interaction among these elements;

(b) factors, such as substances, energy, noise, radiation or waste, including radioactive waste, emissions, discharges and other releases into the environment, affecting or likely to affect the elements of the environment referred to in (a);

(c) measures (including administrative measures), such as policies, legislation, plans, programmes, environmental agreements, and activities referred to in (a) and (b) as well as measures or activities designed to protect those elements;

(d) reports on the implementation of environmental legislation;

(e) cost-benefit and other economic analyses and assumptions used within the framework of the measures and activities referred to in (c); and

(f) the state of human health and safety, including the contamination of the food chain, where relevant, conditions of human life, cultural sites and built structures inasmuch as they are or may be affected by the state of the elements of the environment referred to in (a) or, through those elements, by any of the matters referred to in (b) and (c).

The access right granted under reg 5 of the Environmental Information Regulations 2004 has been co-ordinated with the right of access under the Act. It applies only to information held by public authorities (defined according to a different method from that applying under the Act, see reg 2) and similar procedural provisions apply in relation to, for example, time limits for responding to requests (reg 5) and the duty to provide advice and assistance (reg 9). The Regulations also contain a series of exemptions to the right of access (reg 12).

However, there are also significant differences between the two regimes. For example, the circumstances in which a public authority will 'hold' environmental information differ from those applying under the Act (reg 3(2)) and any enactment that would have the effect of prohibiting the disclosure of information covered by the Regulations will not have effect (reg 5(6), cf s 44(1) of the Act). The scope of the exemptions under the two regimes also differs.

Finally, it should be noted that s 39 is a qualified exemption and, therefore, an applicant who is unable to obtain information under the Environmental Information Regulations (perhaps because the information is covered by an exemption under those Regulations) will be able to argue that, nevertheless, the public interest favours disclosure. In this regard, it is also important to bear in mind that the right of access to environmental information is, in certain circumstances, guaranteed by the European Convention on Human Rights (see, for example, *Guerra v Italy* (1998) 26 EHRR 357; see Chapter 1).

8.16 PERSONAL INFORMATION

Generally, the exemption for personal information provided under s 40 of the Act is an absolute exemption. This is necessarily so in order for the United Kingdom to comply with its obligations under the Data Protection Directive. However, in one respect, the exemption under s 40(2) (ie, the exemption relating to applications for 'personal data' by anyone other than the 'data subject') is a 'qualified exemption'. It is the view of the United Kingdom government that, in this one respect, it is possible to permit disclosure of information covered by the exemption in the public interest without breaching our obligations under the Directive (Hansard HL, 17 October 2000, col 903). The limited circumstances under which s 40 is a 'qualified exemption' arise when information falls within s 40(2) only because disclosure would breach s 10 of the Data Protection Act 1998. For further discussion of s 40, see 10.4 below.

8.17 LEGAL PROFESSIONAL PRIVILEGE

Under s 42(1) of the Act, a public authority is exempt from the duty to communicate information:

... in respect of which a claim to legal professional privilege or, in Scotland, to confidentiality of communications could be maintained in legal proceedings ...

The duty to confirm or deny is also excluded to the extent that compliance with that duty would disclose information (whether or not already recorded) in respect of which a claim of legal professional privilege (or confidentiality of communications) could be maintained in legal proceedings (s 42(2)).

Legal professional privilege has two distinct aspects. 'Litigation privilege' covers all communications if the predominant purpose of those communications relates to litigation. Legal privilege is also accorded, more generally, to communications between a client and his legal adviser for the purpose of the giving or obtaining of legal advice. In this latter case, the communications must be with a professional legal adviser in order to benefit from the privilege. The effect of legal professional privilege is to grant such communications immunity from disclosure in the course of legal proceedings.

Under the Act, this exemption will, for example, prevent an applicant from obtaining disclosure of legal advice provided to a public authority by a solicitor in private practice or an in-house lawyer. In the former case, the information contained in the advice would probably be covered by s 41 ('Information provided in confidence') in any event. This would not, however, be so in the latter case. Section 42 will not only cover information provided, or sought, by the public authority itself. It will also cover other legally privileged material which comes into the possession of a public authority.

Legal professional privilege is not absolute. There are certain circumstances in which the privilege can, or must, be overridden. For example, the privilege does not prevent disclosure where communications have been made for a fraudulent purpose (*R v Cox and Railton* (1884) 14 QBD 153) or where the privilege has been waived by a client (*Calcraft v Guest* [1898] 1 QB 759). Thus, in such exceptional circumstances, legal professional privilege could not be 'maintained in legal proceedings' and s 42 would not apply.

The fact that s 42 is a 'qualified exemption' and can therefore itself be 'overridden' in the public interest may encourage applicants to argue that legal professional privilege should not prevent access to information in a wider range of situations than the accepted exceptions to legal professional privilege. However, the very strong public interest served by the privilege and the relevance of Articles 6 and 8 of the European Convention in these circumstances mean that such arguments may be difficult to sustain.

8.18 COMMERCIAL INTERESTS

A public authority is exempt from the duty to communicate information where information 'constitutes a trade secret' (s 43(1)) or where disclosure of the requested information:

> ... would, or would be likely to, prejudice the commercial interests of any person (including the public authority holding it).

> (s. 43(2))

The duty to confirm or deny is also excluded to the extent that compliance with that duty would, or would be likely to, prejudice the interests specified in s 43(2). Thus there is no specific exemption of the duty to confirm or deny in relation to trade secrets. Presumably, this is because simple confirmation or denial is highly unlikely to result in the disclosure of a trade secret and because disclosure of a trade secret is likely to prejudice commercial interests and therefore be caught within s 43(2) in any event.

In some other jurisdictions, there is an important relationship between the exemption for third party commercial interests and 'reverse freedom of information' procedures. The absence of such procedures from the regime established under the Act has already been noted (see 6.5.2). However, the Code of Practice under s 45 requires consultation in a number of circumstances in which third party rights are affected (see paras 31–40).

8.18.1 Trade Secrets (s 43(1))

A typical example of a 'trade secret' would be secret know-how associated with the manufacture of a product or the secret formula used in the preparation of a perfume or drink. The designation 'trade secret' is most frequently used to identify commercial information protected by the obligation of confidence. However, there is no generally accepted definition of the term. One attempt at definition of the concept was offered by the House of Lords Select Committee which considered the draft Freedom of Information Bill. That Committee defined a 'trade secret' as 'information of commercial value which is protected by the law of confidence' (see *Report from the Select Committee appointed to consider the Draft Freedom of Information Bill*, 27 July 1998, para 45). For further detailed consideration of the meaning of 'trade secret', see Information Commissioner, *Freedom of Information Awareness Guide No 5, Commercial Interests*, pp 3–4.

Very often, information covered by s 43(2) will also be covered by s 41 ('Information provided in confidence'). However, it is important to note that there are some potentially significant distinctions between these two exemptions. A 'trade secret' remains a trade secret regardless of the manner in which it was obtained by the public authority. An actionable breach of confidence (as required under s 41) may not arise where information has, for example, been surreptitiously stolen rather than released in breach of an obligation of confidence. A trade secret, on the other hand, must have a certain *commercial* value, whereas disclosure of personal or governmental information is capable of giving rise to a breach of confidence. There will be a temptation for those submitting information to public authorities to declare that that information is confidential. While such actions may be successful in imposing an obligation of confidence upon an unwary (or complicit) public authority and thereby bringing information within the ambit of s 41, it is not possible to make information a trade secret simply by labelling it as such.

8.18.2 Commercial Interests (s 43(2))

Disclosure of a trade secret would also be likely to prejudice the commercial interests of the holder of that trade secret. However, the ambit of the 'prejudice-based' exemption contained in s 43(2) is considerably wider than s 43(1). Section 43(2) may, for example, exempt a public authority from the obligation to disclose valuable information which would not generally be described as a trade secret, such as pure scientific research data. It may also cover information which simply presents a person or body in a bad light. For example, it could strongly be argued that the disclosure of information showing mismanagement or dishonesty on the part of the directors of a public company would prejudice the commercial interests of that company. Clearly, exempting such information from disclosure under the Act is problematic and it will, in many such cases, be difficult for a public authority to persuade the Information Commissioner that the public interest favours maintenance of the exemption.

A public authority will be entitled to rely upon s 43(2) where disclosure of information would, or would be likely to, prejudice the commercial interests of the public authority itself. The potential for self-serving reliance upon the exemption in such circumstances is clearly great; particularly where so many public authorities are increasingly involved in commercial ventures. The Information Commissioner will need to be especially vigilant where public authorities seek to rely upon s 43(2) in relation to their own commercial interests. In particular, the Commissioner may wish to distinguish between prejudice to a true commercial interest and prejudice to some form of quasi-commercial interest created by 'internal market' mechanisms within public authorities (see Eagles, Taggart and Liddell, *Freedom of Information in New Zealand* (Auckland: OUP, 1992), p 314).

9

ENFORCEMENT

9.1 INTRODUCTION

The responsibility for monitoring the operation of the Freedom of Information Act 2000 and for enforcement of the obligations placed upon public authorities by the Act lies primarily with the Information Commissioner. If an applicant is dissatisfied with a public authority's response to an application for access to information, he or she is entitled to complain to the Commissioner, who has a range of enforcement powers. Ultimately, failure to comply with notices issued by the Commissioner is to be treated as though it were contempt of court. Appeals against the decisions of the Commissioner can, in some circumstances, be brought to the Information Tribunal, which has responsibility both for hearing appeals under the Act and under the Data Protection Act 1998. In this chapter, the enforcement procedures under the Act are explained in further detail.

However, before approaching the Commissioner the applicant should consider using the public authority's internal complaints and review mechanism. (See 5.11 above.) Part XII of the Code of Practice issued under s 45 of the Act provides more detailed guidance on the complaints procedure that authorities must have in place (see Appendix 2). The Code sets out the need for the procedure to deal with substantive applications and refusals to supply information.

Applicants who fail to take advantage of the internal complaints mechanism are likely to find that they cannot then make complaints to the Commissioner (see s 50(2)(a)).

9.2 THE INFORMATION COMMISSIONER

The first Information Commissioner was Elizabeth France, who was the Data Protection Commissioner until, as a result of the Act, that role was subsumed within the office of Information Commissioner (s 18(1)). Despite the change of nomenclature, the Commissioner's responsibilities with regard to data protection continue to be governed by the Data Protection Act 1998 (as amended by the Act; see Chapter 10). The current commissioner is Richard Thomas. He is thus at the head of two separate regimes providing for access to information. These two regimes have been established in a manner which is designed to be complementary. However, concern has been expressed that the same individual is responsible for supervising the enforcement of two Acts with potentially conflicting functions (ie, the promotion of openness in the case of the Act and the protection of privacy in the case of the Data Protection Act 1998) (see, for example, Hansard HL, 25 October 2000, col 431). Such conflicts are most likely to arise in relation to applications for information which make reference to individuals other than the applicant ('personal data' under the Data Protection Act). Those responsible for promoting the Act have countered such objections by arguing that, when conflicts between privacy and openness arise under the Act, it is better for a single person, rather than two separate office-holders, to adjudicate upon them. In any event, the chances of such conflicts arising are substantially diminished by the fact that, very often, applications for such information will be exempt under s 40 (see Chapter 10). In addition, as many applications are likely to encompass personal data and other information, there are advantages of convenience and user-friendliness in bringing the two roles together.

Freedom of information systems established elsewhere have also adopted a model under which responsibility for enforcement of access to information lies with a Commissioner or Ombudsman (see, for example, Ireland's Freedom of Information Act 1997 and New Zealand's Official Information Act 1982). Systems supervised by a Commissioner can be operated with a greater degree of informality and more cheaply than can a system under which courts adjudicate upon disputes about the right of access to information (as under the United States' Freedom of Information Act).

Under the Act, anyone who is dissatisfied with the way in which a public authority has responded to an application for information is entitled to make a complaint to the Commissioner. There are no procedural requirements for the making of such a complaint and no fee for invoking his powers of enforcement. The Information Commissioner is in a more powerful position than the Parliamentary Commissioner for Administration who, prior to the full implementation of the Act, was responsible for supervising the Open Government Code on Access to Information (see the discussion in Chapter 3). He can be contacted directly by anyone wishing to make a complaint under the Act (and not only via an MP as was the case with the Parliamentary Ombudsman) and can serve binding notices on public authorities failing to comply with their duties under the Act (see 9.2.2 below).

9.2.1 The Information Commissioner's Monitoring Responsibilities

Under the Act, the Commissioner has responsibility for monitoring public authorities' compliance with the obligations set out in the Act and with the advice contained in the Codes of Practice issued by the Home Secretary (under s 45) and the Lord Chancellor (under s 46).

Where the Commissioner finds that the practice of a particular authority does not conform with the Act or with that recommended in either of the Codes of Practice (either as a result of an assessment with a public authority's consent or otherwise), he can make a 'practice recommendation' (s 48). Such a practice recommendation must set out the steps which an authority is required to take to improve its practice (s 48(1)). It must be made in writing and must specify the particular provisions of the Codes of Practice with which the authority has failed to conform (s 48(2)). In order to establish whether or not there has been a lapse in good practice, the Commissioner can serve an information notice, requiring a public authority to furnish him with information necessary for his enquiry (s 51(1)(b) (see 9.2.2 below).

There are no formal sanctions for failure to comply with a practice recommendation. However, it is to be expected that fear of the adverse publicity deriving from a practice recommendation and subsequent reference in the Commissioner's Annual Report to Parliament (required under s 49) are likely to encourage compliance by authorities. In addition, where failure to observe good practice constitutes a failure by a public authority to comply with its duties under Part I of the Act, such non-compliance is likely to result in the service of an enforcement notice (see 9.2.2 below).

9.2.2 The Information Commissioner's Enforcement Responsibilities

Decision Notices
In addition to the monitoring responsibilities described above, the Commissioner has power to enforce the right of access to information established under Part I of the Act. These powers are set out in Part IV of the Act (ss 50–56). Where an applicant considers that a public authority has not complied with its obligations under Part I of the Act, he or she ('the complainant'):

... may apply to the Commissioner for a decision whether, in any specified respect, a request for information made by the complainant to a public authority has been dealt with in accordance with the requirements of Part I [of the Act].

(s 50(1))

Under this provision, complaints can be made in a number of different situations. Perhaps the most obvious example is where a public authority refuses to comply with either the duty to communicate information or the duty to confirm or deny in relation to a particular request. It may do so because it decides that the information is covered by one of the exemptions in Part II of the Act. Under the decision notice procedure, an applicant is able to challenge the public authority's refusal to disclose the information. For example, consider a hypothetical case in which a public authority refuses to communicate information on the grounds that to do so would be likely to prejudice the economic interests of the United Kingdom (s 29). In such circumstances, an applicant would be entitled to challenge the public authority's assessment of the likelihood of prejudice by complaining to the Commissioner that the public authority in question had failed to comply with its duty to communicate information under s 1(1)(b).

The extent to which the Information Commissioner is entitled to review the public authority's decision varies from exemption to exemption. For example, in the case of 'class-based' exemptions, such as that covering information accessible to the applicant by other means (s 21), the Commissioner's role is restricted to an assessment of whether or not the information is covered by the cited exemption. Where a public authority relies on s 21, the Commissioner would be entitled to decide that it had not complied with its duties under the Act where she considers that the information in question is not in fact reasonably accessible to the applicant. In the case of 'prejudice-based' exemptions (such as that covering information disclosure of which would be likely to prejudice the economic interests of the United Kingdom), the Commissioner is entitled to overrule a public authority's decision that disclosure of the information in question would have the requisite prejudicial effect.

Where an exemption is a 'qualified exemption', either 'class-based' or 'prejudice-based', the Information Commissioner can also review a public authority's decision that the public interest in non-disclosure outweighs the public interest in disclosure. In certain cases, however, the Commissioner's determination on this issue will not be final because it will be subject to ministerial 'override' under s 53 (see 9.2.3 below).

In the case of certain specific exemptions, the Commissioner's powers are also further restricted. For example, under s 36 ('Prejudice to effective conduct of public affairs'), information is exempt from disclosure where 'in the reasonable opinion of a qualified person' disclosure of the information would prejudice a series of listed interests. In such a case, the Commissioner's powers of review are limited to an assessment of the reasonableness of the decision of that 'qualified person'.

As has been seen, the Commissioner's jurisdiction to review decisions on the application of exemptions derives from his power to decide, under s 50, whether an information request has been dealt with in accordance with Part I of the Act. However, as a result of this power, other issues can also be raised by complainants. For example, where a public authority fails to comply with a request within the time-limits established under the Act (see 5.4 above), it will have failed to comply with its obligations under Part I and the Commissioner will be able to issue a decision notice to that effect. Complainants will also be able to ask the Commissioner to review, for example, the validity of a fees notice, a public authority's failure to communicate information in accordance with the complainant's preference or a decision not to communicate information because the costs of doing so exceed the appropriate limit (see further, Chapter 5).

On receipt of an application for a decision notice under s 50, the Commissioner must reach a decision unless it appears to him that the complainant has failed to exhaust any proper internal complaints procedure provided by the public authority in question, or there has been undue delay in bringing the case, or the complaint is frivolous or vexatious or has been withdrawn or abandoned (s 50(2)). Where any of these conditions are satisfied and, accordingly, the Information Commissioner is not required to make a decision, he must serve notice to this effect upon the complainant (s 50(3)(a)). Under the Code of Practice under s 45, a public authority is likely to be required to establish an internal complaints procedure (see Appendix 2, paras 52–63). The requirement for an applicant to exhaust internal complaints mechanisms where they exist provides an incentive for public authorities to put such procedures into operation. Where the handling of a complaint under an internal complaints procedure does not comply with the code of practice (perhaps, for example, as a result of undue delay), the complainant will be able to proceed directly to the Information Commissioner because s 50(2)(a) only prevents the Commissioner from making a decision where:

... the complainant has not exhausted any complaints procedure which is provided by the public authority in conformity with the code of practice under section 45.

When the Commissioner comes to a decision on a complaint, he must serve notice of that decision on the complainant and the relevant public authority (s 50(3)(b)). Where he decides that a public authority has, in some respect, failed to comply with its duties under Part I of the Act, the decision notice must specify the remedial steps required of the public authority, the period within which they must be taken and the procedures for appealing against the notice (s 50(4) and (5)). Where a decision notice requires a public authority to take action to remedy its breach and the public authority appeals against that notice, the requirement to take remedial action is suspended until the conclusion of the appeal proceedings (s 50(6)). Failure to comply with a decision notice issued by the Information Commissioner is treated as though it were contempt of court (see 9.2.4 below).

Information Notices (s 51)
The Information Commissioner may need further information in order to establish whether or not a public authority has complied with:

(a) its obligations arising under Part I of the Act; or

(b) the codes of practice made under ss 45 and 46 of the Act.

The need for further information could arise following receipt of an application for a decision under s 50 or in connection with an investigation instigated by the Commissioner. In either case, the Commissioner has the power to serve an information notice requiring the public authority to provide him with information within a specified period of time. The notice must explain why the particular information is required (s 51(2)). It must also contain particulars of the right to appeal against service of the notice (s 51(3)). The specified period within which the authority is required to respond to an information notice must not expire before the end of the period within which an appeal can be brought against the service of that notice (s 51(4)).

However, certain forms of information do not have to be supplied to the Commissioner in response to an information notice. Under s 51(5), there is no requirement to provide any information in respect of:

(a) any communication between a professional legal adviser and his client in connection with the giving of legal advice to the client with respect to his obligations, liabilities or rights under the Act, or

(b) any communication between a professional legal adviser and his client, or between such an adviser or his client and any other person, made in connection with or in contemplation of proceedings under or arising out of this Act (including proceedings before the Tribunal) and for the purposes of such proceedings.

It should be noted that this limitation relates only to client-lawyer communications concerning the operation of the Act and does not apply to all legally privileged material held by a public authority. Indeed, where a public authority seeks to resist disclosure of information under the Act on the grounds that it is covered by the exemption in s 42 ('Legal professional privilege'), the Commissioner will need to inspect privileged materials, in order to establish whether or not the exemption is made out.

For the purpose of s 51, 'information' is not restricted to 'information recorded in any form' as elsewhere in the Act but expressly includes 'unrecorded information' (s 51(8)). The inclusion of unrecorded information means that the Commissioner can, for example, require a public authority to provide evidence of its employees' recollections of relevant events.

Enforcement Notices (s 52)

Where the Information Commissioner is satisfied that a public authority has failed to comply with its obligations concerning the supply of information to an applicant, he has the power to serve an enforcement notice on that authority (s 52). This notice will require the authority to take the necessary steps to bring it into compliance within a specified period. Such a notice must contain a statement by the Commissioner that he is satisfied that the authority has failed to comply with its obligations with regard to the provision of information. It must give reasons for the Commissioner's belief that the public authority has not complied and explain that the authority has a right to appeal to the Information Tribunal (s 52(2)). Again, any time limit for compliance specified within the notice must not expire before the end of the period within which an appeal can be brought against the notice (s 52(3)).

The difference between a decision notice and an enforcement notice is that the former is served upon authorities that have made a wrongful decision under the Act, whereas the latter is served upon authorities which fail to make decisions themselves or refuse to comply with decisions made by the Commissioner.

9.2.3 Exception from Duty to Comply with a Decision Notice or an Enforcement Notice—the Ministerial 'Override' (s 53)

Generally, where a public authority fails to comply with a decision notice or an enforcement notice, the Information Commissioner will be able to instigate proceedings to ensure compliance (see 9.2.4 below). However, where the Information Commissioner has, in response to a complaint, decided that information covered by a qualified exemption should nevertheless be disclosed in the public interest, certain public authorities are entitled to 'overrule' his decision under s 53. This is a significant and controversial limitation on the enforcement powers of the Commissioner. The only authorities entitled to use the 'override' under s 53 are government departments, the National Assembly for Wales, and such other public authorities as are designated by order made by the Secretary of State (s 53(1)(a)).

Where either a decision notice or an enforcement notice is served upon such a public authority in the circumstances described above, that notice ceases to have effect if, within a specified period, an 'accountable person' gives the Commissioner a signed certificate stating that he has, on reasonable grounds, formed the opinion that the information ought not to be released under the Act (s 53(2)). The certificate must be served not later than the twentieth working day following either the service of the notice in question or, where an appeal against the notice has been taken to the Information Tribunal, from the determination of that appeal (s 53(2) and (4)). Where an 'accountable person' signs such a certificate in relation to a decision notice issued under s 50, that person must inform the complainant of his or her reasons for concluding that the public interest favours maintaining the exemption (s 53(6)). There is, however, no obligation to give such reasons where to do so would itself disclose exempt information (s 53(7)).

In some ways, the existence of a power such as that provided in s 53 undermines the whole mechanism of enforcement established by the Act. It is for this reason that the number of authorities entitled to exercise it is limited. A further safeguard against abuse of the power is provided by the requirement that any certificate issued under this provision must be signed by a member of the Cabinet, a Law Officer, or specific senior Ministers within the devolved administrations of Northern Ireland and Wales as appropriate (s 53(8)). A copy of any certificate issued under this provision must be laid before each House of Parliament, the Northern Ireland Assembly or National Assembly of Wales as appropriate (s 53(3)). A decision to issue a certificate will be subject to judicial review and the Information Commissioner will have *locus standi* to bring such proceedings (Hansard HL, 25 October 2000, col 436). It is also important to note that s 53 does not allow a public authority to escape compliance with an information notice.

The existence of ministerial override under s 53 caused considerable concern to be expressed during Parliamentary debates on the provision. In response to such concern, the Government offered assurances that the power would only be used *in extremis* and after consultation with the Cabinet (Hansard HC, 4 April 2000, col 922–25).

9.2.4 Failure to Comply with Notices Issued by the Information Commissioner (s 54)

Under the Act, unless a valid certificate under s 53 is issued, sanctions can be imposed upon any public authority that fails to take the steps specified in a decision notice, an information notice or an enforcement notice. Default is treated as contempt of court. The Information Commissioner is empowered to certify in writing to the court that the public authority in question has failed to comply with a notice (s 54(1)). Thereafter, the matter will be dealt with in the High Court as a civil contempt (s 54(3)). If contempt is established, the court has unlimited powers to fine a public authority or to sequestrate its assets. In addition, the court has the power to commit an individual in contempt to a period of imprisonment not exceeding two years. In the case of a corporate body, an order for committal to prison can be made against the officers of that body. The Crown cannot itself be found to be in contempt. However, individual government ministers can (see *M v Home Office* [1994] 1 AC 377). In such a case, the minister would not be subject to committal to prison or to financial penalty but could be required to pay the costs of the application.

Where a public authority makes a false statement intentionally or recklessly in 'purported compliance' with an information notice, it will be deemed to have failed to have complied with that notice and will thereafter be subject to proceedings equivalent to proceedings for contempt of court (s 54(2)). Thus, for example, if a local authority, in response to an information notice, falsely claims not to have a particular document, it will potentially be subject to the range of penalties available in contempt proceedings.

9.2.5 The Information Commissioner's Powers of Entry and Inspection

The Information Commissioner is, in certain circumstances, entitled to seek a warrant of entry and inspection from a circuit judge. Where issued, such a warrant can grant significant powers of entry and inspection to the Commissioner. The provisions governing the issue of such warrants are contained in Sch 3 to the

Act and are similar to those available under warrants issued under the Data Protection Act 1998.

9.2.6 Disclosure of Information to the Information Commissioner

Laws prohibiting or restricting the disclosure of information generally do not prevent a person from furnishing the Commissioner (or the Information Tribunal; see 9.3 below) with any 'information necessary for the discharge of their functions' under the Act (Sch 2, para 18 of the Act, extending Data Protection Act 1998, s 58). Thus, for example, a public authority could not refuse to pass information to the Commissioner or Tribunal on the grounds that it would breach an obligation of confidence or commit a contempt of court if it were to do so.

9.2.7 Disclosure of Information by the Information Commissioner

Under s 76 of the Act, the Information Commissioner is, in certain circumstances, entitled to disclose information which he holds under the Act, or under the Data Protection Act 1998, to persons listed in a table set out under s 76(1). The persons listed in the table are all ombudsmen of one form or another and are responsible for investigating the activities of public authorities. The Information Commissioner is able to release information to a listed ombudsman where it appears to him that the information relates to a matter falling within his or her investigatory jurisdiction.

However, current and former Commissioners and their staff or agents will commit a criminal offence if, without lawful authority, they disclose any information which they have acquired under, or for the purposes of, the Act (or under or for the purposes of the Data Protection Act 1998), where that information 'relates to an identified or identifiable individual or business' and is not otherwise available to the public (Sch 2, para 19 of the Act, extending s 59 of the Data Protection Act 1998 to cover information held in relation to applications under the Act). This 'gagging' provision exists because the Commissioner and his staff have privileged access to a huge volume of information of great sensitivity and it is desirable that the confidentiality of that information should be maintained. Disclosure of the information in accordance with the Commissioner's duties under the Act is not an offence because such disclosure is 'made with lawful authority'. The definition of the phrase 'with lawful authority' (to be found in s 59 of the Data Protection Act 1998, as amended) encompasses disclosures:

(a) made with the consent of the individual or the person carrying on the business;

(b) of information which were provided for the purpose of being made available to the public;

(c) made for the purposes of, and necessary for, the discharge of functions under the Act or under any European Community obligation;

(d) made for the purposes of any legal proceedings; and

(e) which are necessary in the public interest.

It is important to note that the Commissioner will himself be a public authority for the purposes of the Act. Accordingly, even where he himself is prohibited from voluntarily disclosing information acquired in connection with his responsibilities under the Act, it remains possible for another person to apply for that information under the Act. Any disclosure made by the Commissioner pursuant to such an application would be made with lawful authority and would not therefore fall within the amended s 59 of the 1998 Act.

9.3 THE INFORMATION TRIBUNAL

9.3.1 Introduction

Under the Act, appeals against notices served by the Commissioner are made to the Information Tribunal. This tribunal was formerly known as the Data Protection Tribunal and now has jurisdiction to hear appeals both under the Act and under the Data Protection Act 1998 (s 18 of the Act). The provisions of the Act dealing with appeals are contained in Part V (ss 57–61). Rules governing the procedure of the Tribunal are contained in Sch 6 to the Data Protection Act 1998. Schedule 4 to the Act also makes a number of changes to the rules governing the constitution of the Tribunal. These changes reflect the fact that it now has jurisdiction under the Act as well as under the Data Protection Act.

9.3.2 Appeals Against Notices Issued by the Information Commissioner

Where either a complainant or a public authority is dissatisfied with the fact that a decision notice has been served by the Information Commissioner, an appeal to the Information Tribunal is available. In addition, public authorities can appeal against the service upon them of either an information or an enforcement notice (s 57). On appeal, the Tribunal is entitled to consider whether the notice in question is lawful and/or whether the Information Commissioner, in serving the notice in question, has exercised his discretion correctly. The Tribunal is entitled to review any of the Commissioner's findings of fact (s 58(2)). The Tribunal can either allow the appeal or substitute any notice which the Commissioner could have made for the disputed notice.

Thus, for example, if the Tribunal finds that it was not reasonable for the Commissioner to have required a public authority to provide him with requested information, it can quash an information notice served on the authority.

Equally, if the Commissioner decides that particular information held by a public authority is covered by an exemption in Part II of the Act and serves a decision notice to that effect, a complainant can appeal against that notice to the Tribunal. Where the Tribunal grants an appeal by an applicant, it can issue an amended decision notice requiring the public authority to provide the information in question.

Appeals on points of law by any party to an appeal lie from the Information Tribunal to the High Court of Justice, the Court of Session or the High Court of Justice in Northern Ireland, depending upon the location of the relevant public authority (s 59).

9.3.3 Appeals Against National Security Certificates (s 60)

The Information Tribunal also has jurisdiction to hear appeals against the issuing of National Security Certificates under ss 23 or 24 of the Act. Under s 23 of the Act, information is exempt from disclosure if it was either supplied directly or indirectly by, or relates to, certain bodies responsible for national security (see 7.3 above). Where a Cabinet Minister or Law Officer certifies that a particular piece of information is covered by the exemption, the certificate to that effect is conclusive evidence of that fact (s 23(2)). Under s 24, information is exempt from the duties to confirm or deny and to communicate information where exemption is required for the purpose of safeguarding national security (see 8.3 above). Again, a certificate from a Cabinet Minister or Law Officer certifying that exemption is required for this purpose is to be taken as conclusive evidence of this fact. In this latter case, the certificate can be made in advance and can relate to information of a general description rather than to specific existing information.

Either the Information Commissioner or an applicant can bring an appeal against the issue of such a certificate to the Information Tribunal. Where the Tribunal finds that the information in question was not properly covered by the claimed exemption, it is entitled to quash the ministerial certificate. The standard of review differs depending upon whether the certificate has been issued under s 23 or s 24. Under s 23 (whether the information was in fact supplied by one of the listed agencies) the Tribunal can substitute its own view of this fact notwithstanding the 'conclusive evidence' process in s 23(2). Where a certificate has been issued under s 24, the Tribunal is only entitled to quash it where, on 'applying the principles applied by the court on an application for judicial review', the Tribunal considers that the Minister did not have reasonable grounds for issuing the certificate (s 60(3)).

Where a public authority claims that particular information is covered by a certificate made in relation to a general description of information under s 24(3), any other party can appeal to the Tribunal against this determination (s 60(4)). The Tribunal can overrule the public authority's decision (s 60(5)). A specific provision to this effect is necessary because, in such circumstances, it would not necessarily be appropriate simply to quash a certificate of general application, which is likely to be very general and issued in advance of any applications for information. The Tribunal dealing with personal data (previously the Data Protection Tribunal) has considered a challenge made under the Data Protection Act to a certificate based on national security. The two statutes on this point are identical except that the Security Service (as an institution) is not exempt under the Data Protection Act as it is under the Freedom of Information Act. The case concerned the Liberal Democrat MP, Norman Baker, who wanted to know if the Security Service (MI5) held information on him and, if so, whether he could have access to it. The certificate issued by the Home Secretary under the Data Protection Act purported to prevent this. He challenged the lawfulness of the certificate itself in the Data Protection Tribunal. The Tribunal quashed the certificate because it was too widely drawn. This led to certificates issued for the Intelligence Service (MI6) and GCHQ to be quashed as well (see *Baker v Secretary of State for the Home Department* [2001] UKHRR 1275).

In contrast with appeals against notices issued by the Information Commissioner (see 9.3.2 above), there is no further appeal against the decision of the Tribunal following an appeal against the issue of a National Security Certificate (see s 59).

9.3.4 Standard and Onus of Proof

The standard of proof that must be used by public authorities, the Commissioner and the Tribunal is the civil standard. It will not be sufficient for a public authority simply to argue that harm would arise for a disclosure without providing further detail (*Attorney General v Guardian Newspapers (No 2)* [1990] 1 AC 109).

In other jurisdictions the courts have decided that where there are ambiguities they should be resolved in favour of disclosure (see Australia: *Victoria Public Service Board v Wright* (1986) 160 CLR 145; Canada: *Maislin Industries Limited v Minister for Industry, Trade and Commerce* [1984] 1 FUNDED CLIENT 939; European Court of Justice: *Hautala v Council of the European Union* [2002] 1 WLR 1930).

9.4 THE ACT AND THE COURTS

9.4.1 Introduction

As has been seen in this chapter, the Act primarily relies upon enforcement by the Information Commissioner. Nevertheless, in addition to appeals from the Information Tribunal to the High Court on points of law and to proceedings for contempt of court where a public authority fails to comply with a notice issued by the Commissioner, there are certain other circumstances in which issues arising under the Act may have to be determined by a court.

9.4.2 Applications for Judicial Review

It will not be possible to bring proceedings for judicial review of many decisions made by the Information Commissioner or Information Tribunal. Routes of appeal are specified in the Act and any person or body wishing to seek review of such decisions will be expected to follow those routes in the first instance. However, where a party is aggrieved by some aspect of the Commissioner's activities which does not fall within the statutory appeal procedure, any challenge will have to be brought by means of an application for judicial review. Such an application could arise in relation to, for example, a claim that the Commissioner had erred procedurally, had acted beyond his jurisdiction or had acted unreasonably in making a practice recommendation under s 48.

In addition, applications for judicial review of the actions of other public bodies or office-holders under the Act may be made. For example, under s 53, certain public authorities can avoid complying with a notice issued by the Commissioner where an 'accountable person' (usually a member of the Cabinet) certifies that, in his or her opinion, the information is exempt from disclosure. There is no appeal to the Information Tribunal against the issuing of such a certificate. Any party dissatisfied with the issuing of such a certificate will be forced to make an application for judicial review. This will also be the route for challenges to the exercise of powers delegated to ministers under the Act; for example, powers to subject particular bodies to the duties arising under the Act (ss 4 and 5).

9.4.3 Criminal Offences

The Act creates a number of criminal offences. Perhaps the most significant is that under s 77, which applies to public authorities and to officers, employees or those under the direction of such an authority. Where a valid request for information has been made to a public authority, an offence will be committed where such a body or person:

... alters, defaces, erases, destroys or conceals any record held by the public authority, with the intention of preventing the disclosure by that authority of all, or any part, of the information to the communication of which the applicant would have been entitled.

(s 77(1))

This offence is a summary offence and is punishable by a fine (s 77(3)). A prosecution may be instituted by the Information Commissioner or by the Director of Public Prosecutions (or the Director of Public Prosecutions for Northern Ireland where appropriate) (s 77(4)).

Further criminal offences are also created under Sch 3, para 12 to the Act (obstructing the execution of a warrant granted to the Commissioner) and Sch 2, para 19 (improper disclosure of information by the Commissioner or his staff; see 9.2.7 above).

9.4.4 Private Law Actions

Under s 56 of the Act, it is provided that civil proceedings cannot be brought in relation to any 'failure to comply with any duty imposed by or under this Act'. Thus, for example, an individual who is dissatisfied with a public authority's failure to comply with a request for information cannot bypass the Act's enforcement mechanisms (and thereby also hope to obtain an award of damages) by bringing a civil claim for the tort of breach of statutory duty.

9.4.5 Third Parties

Other persons and organisations may have an interest in whether material is disclosed by a public authority to an applicant but the role of the third party is not particularly well catered for by the Act. Although the authority may have to seek the views of the third party before disclosure there is no duty on the authority to inform the third party of the outcome of the application or whether enforcement action or appeals are being instituted. The Commissioner also has no duty to consult the third party or advise him or her of the outcome.

Similarly the third party has no right to use the internal complaints mechanism or make applications to the Commissioner or the Tribunal. The third party will have to rely on judicial review of the authority, the Commissioner or the Tribunal to protect his or her interests. However there might be circumstances in which the third party might have a private law right which could be protected by an injunction.

10

PERSONAL INFORMATION AND DATA PROTECTION

10.1 INTRODUCTION

It has been predicted that the majority of applications for information under the Freedom of Information Act 2000 will be made by individuals seeking personal information concerning themselves. It is ironic, therefore, that such information is not generally available under the Act. Under the scheme established under the Act, such requests must be dealt with in accordance with the Data Protection Act 1998 (see 10.4 below).

The relationship between the Act and the 1998 Act is extremely complex. Indeed, it could be argued that it is undesirably over-complex. In addition to ensuring the mutual exclusivity of the two regimes described above, the Act makes a number of significant amendments to the 1998 Act. Most notably, it expands the range of data held by a public authority to which the right of access under the 1998 Act applies. It also modifies the enforcement procedures under the Act, with the result that a single office-holder, the Information Commissioner, and appeal tribunal, the Information Tribunal, now have jurisdiction over both data protection and freedom of information regimes.

In this chapter, the treatment of 'personal information' under the Act and the relationship between the Act and the 1998 Act is explored in greater detail. At 10.2, the regime established under the 1998 Act is outlined. An appreciation of the general scope of this legislation is essential for a full understanding of the issues discussed later in the chapter. Section 10.3 analyses the amendments made to the 1998 Act by the Act and 10.4 explores the manner in which applications for personal information must be handled under the Act. As indicated above, in general terms, where an application for personal information is received from the 'data subject' (ie, the person to whom the information relates), it is automatically to be treated as a request for personal data under the 1998 Act. By contrast, where an application for personal information is made by someone other than the 'data subject', that application is governed solely by the Act. However, the disclosure of personal information to someone other than the 'data subject' may infringe the data protection principles contained in the 1998 Act. Public authorities receiving such requests will, accordingly, often be exempt from their duties under the Act as a result of the exemption provided in s 40(2).

10.2 DATA PROTECTION ACT 1998

10.2.1 Introduction

The first data protection legislation in this jurisdiction, the Data Protection Act 1984, implemented the Council of Europe Data Protection Convention of 1981 (Treaty No 108). This Convention was inspired by a developing concern that individuals' privacy was threatened by the development of computerised means of storing and processing data. The 1984 Act provided individuals with a right of access to personal data of which they were the 'data subject' and also a right to object to certain forms of data processing by others. It obliged anyone processing data to comply with a number of 'data protection principles'. The 1998 Act (implementing the European Community Data Protection Directive (95/46/EC)) has, with effect from 1 March 2000, replaced the 1984 Act in its entirety. It expands the rights of data subjects and the obligations of those processing personal data. The main features of the Act are set out below. For a detailed analysis of data protection law, see Carey, P, *Data Protection: A Practical Guide to UK & EU Law* (Oxford: OUP, 2004).

10.2.2 'Personal Data'

The rights and obligations under the 1998 Act apply only to 'personal data'. Before amendment by the Act, the definition of 'data' under the 1998 Act, s 1(1) was restricted to:

information which—

(a) is being processed by means of equipment operating automatically in response to instructions given for that purpose,

(b) is recorded with the intention that it should be processed by means of such equipment.

(c) is recorded as part of a relevant filing system or with the intention that it should form part of a relevant filing system, or

(d) does not fall within paragraph (a), (b) or (c) but forms part of an accessible record.

Thus, even prior to amendment by the Act, the 1998 Act covered data which was processed either 'automatically' (ie, by computer) or, in certain cases, 'manually'. However, only limited classes of manually processed data were subject to the 1998 Act. As can be seen from the above definition, such data were required either to be recorded in a 'relevant filing system' or to form part of an 'accessible record' in order to fall within the scope of the Act. A 'relevant filing system' is defined in the 1998 Act, s 1(1) as a manually-processed:

... set of information relating to individuals to the extent that ... the set is structured, either by reference to individuals, or by reference to criteria relating to individuals in such a way that specific information relating to a particular individual is readily accessible.

In *Durant v Financial Service Authority* [2004] FSR 28, the Court of Appeal interpreted the phrase 'relevant filing system' restrictively, finding that:

... a 'relevant filing system' for the purpose of the Act, is limited to a system:

(1) in which the files forming part of it are structured or referenced in such a way as clearly to indicate at the outset of the search whether specific information capable of amounting to personal data of an individual requesting it ... is held within the system and, if so, in which file or files it is held; and

(2) which has, as part of its own structure or referencing mechanism, a sufficiently sophisticated and detailed means of readily indicating whether and where in an individual file or files specific criteria or information about the applicant can be readily located.

(per Auld LJ, at [50])

Thus, for example, a hand-written card index system, ordered by reference to individuals' surnames, may fall within this definition as long as it enables a searcher readily to find *personal* data relating to the data subject. However, a random file of correspondence received by an organisation within a particular month or year would not.

The only other class of data subject to the Act was data forming part of an 'accessible record' (s 1(1)(d)). An 'accessible record' is defined as a health record, an educational record or various other forms of local government record (DPA 1998, s 68). Such records are subject to the Act whether or not the information within them is contained in a 'relevant filing system'.

Within the categories of 'data' defined above, the rights and obligations established under the 1998 Act apply only to '*personal* data', which are defined as:

data which relate to a living individual who can be indentified—

(a) from those data, or

(b) from those data and other information which is in the possession of, or is likely to come into the possession of, the data controller,

and includes any expression of the opinion about the individual and any indication of the intentions of the data controller or any other person in respect of the individual.

Thus, for example, an individual's personnel, medical, educational or credit records or details held for the purpose of direct marketing, could satisfy this definition because they would constitute data from which a living individual could be identified.

In *Durant*, the Court of Appeal also provided guidance on the definition of *'personal* data' under the 1998 Act. In particular, it considered when data would 'relate to' an individual within the above definition. As in the case of 'relevant filing system' discussed above, a restrictive definition was approved. It was confirmed that not all data making reference to a data subject will be 'personal data'. In order to satisfy the definition, information must affect the privacy of the data subject, whether in his or her personal or family life, business or professional capacity (see *Durant v Financial Services Authority* [2003] FSR 28, at [28]).

In offering guidance following the *Durant* case, the Information Commissioner has suggested that the following forms of information would constitute 'personal data': information about an individual's medical history, salary, tax liabilities, bank statements or spending preferences. However, incidental reference to the fact that a particular individual was present at a meeting or an indication that a communication had been received by an individual would not, alone, constitute 'personal data' relating to that individual (see 'The *Durant* case and its impact on the interpretation of the Data Protection Act 1998', www.informationcommissioner.gov.uk).

10.2.3 Duties Imposed on Data Controllers by the 1998 Act

Prior to processing personal data, a 'data controller' must ensure that it has obtained an entry on a register maintained by the Information Commissioner ('Data Protection Commissioner' prior to amendment by the Act) (DPA 1998, ss 16–26). This procedure, known as 'notification', requires a 'data controller' to provide the Commissioner with certain information concerning its processing of personal data. A 'data controller' is defined as:

. . . a person who (either alone or jointly or in common with other persons) determines the purposes for which and the manner in which any personal data are, or are to be, processed.

Under the 1998 Act, the definition of 'processing' is extremely wide and encompasses almost any activity in relation to data, including, for example, 'obtaining', 'use' or even 'holding' of that data (DPA 1998, s 1(1)). Simply viewing data on a computer screen constitutes 'processing' for the purpose of the 1998 Act (thus plugging the lacuna in the 1984 Act identified by the House of Lords in *R v Brown* [1996] 1 AC 543).

Any processing of personal data by a data controller must comply with eight prescribed Data Protection Principles (DPA 1998, s 4). These principles require personal data to be:

(1) processed (defined to include 'obtained') fairly and lawfully;

(2) obtained only for specified and lawful purposes and not processed incompatibly with the specified purposes;

(3) adequate, relevant and not excessive for their purpose;

(4) accurate and up to date;

(5) not kept for longer than necessary;

(6) processed in accordance with the rights of data subjects (see below);

(7) secured against unauthorised or unlawful processing;

(8) not transferred to a country outside the EEA where there is inadequate protection for the data in that country.

Failure to comply with these principles may lead to the instigation of enforcement proceedings by the Commissioner (DPA 1998, ss 40–50). More onerous obligations are placed upon data controllers who are engaged in processing 'sensitive personal data', which are defined to include, amongst other things, information concerning an individual's racial or ethnic origin or political opinions (DPA 1998, s 2). The 1998 Act also created a series of criminal offences. These can be committed by, for example, processing personal data without notification (DPA 1998, s 21) and unlawful obtaining or disclosure of personal data (DPA 1998, s 55).

10.2.4 Rights of Data Subjects Under the 1998 Act

In addition to these obligations placed upon data controllers, 'data subjects' are provided with certain legally enforceable rights under the 1998 Act (DPA 1998, ss 7–14). These are:

(a) the right of access to personal data (s 7),

(b) the right to prevent processing likely to cause damage or distress (s 10),

(c) the right to prevent processing for direct marketing (s 11),

(d) certain rights relating to automated decision-making (s 12), and

(e) the right to have inaccurate data rectified, blocked, erased or destroyed (s 14).

For the purposes of understanding the relationship between the Act and the 1998 Act, the most important of these rights are the right of access to personal data and the right to prevent processing likely to cause damage or distress. A data subject is entitled to apply to court to enforce his or her rights and, in certain circumstances, to obtain compensation for damage resulting from a contravention of the data controller's obligation (DPA 1998, s 13).

10.2.5 Exemptions under the 1998 Act

As under the Act, however, there are a number of exemptions from the requirement to comply with the principles and rights provided by the 1998 Act. Some of these exemptions are permanent (DPA 1998, ss 27–39). For example, a data controller is exempt from some or all of the requirements of the 1998 Act where its processing is 'required for the purpose of safeguarding national security' (DPA 1998, s 28), where the data requested are otherwise available (DPA 1998, s 34) or where provision of data to a data subject would prejudice the prevention or detection of crime (DPA 1998, s 29(1)(a)). In addition to these permanent exemptions, the 1998 Act contains a series of transitional provisions designed to give data controllers time to prepare for full implementation of the Act (DPA 1998, Sch 8). Much manual processing of personal data will not be fully subject to the Act until 24 October 2007 (see DPA 1998, Sch 8. Part III).

10.3 AMENDMENTS TO THE DATA PROTECTION ACT 1998

In 10.2 above, the structure of the regime established under the 1998 Act has been outlined. The Act makes a number of important changes to this regime.

10.3.1 Extension of the Scope of the 1998 Act to Cover all 'Unstructured Personal Data' Held by a Public Authority

Before amendment by the Act, the 1998 Act generally covered only manually processed data stored in a 'structured' form. The only 'unstructured' data to which a right of access was granted were 'accessible records'. However, as a result of amendments made by the Act, all information held by a public authority falls within the scope of the 1998 Act (and is therefore subject to the right of access of the data subject). If the 1998 Act had not been extended in this way, an applicant would have had had a right of access to non-personal information held by a public authority under the Act regardless of the way in which it was stored, but would generally only have had access to personal information stored in a structured record.

This change has been effected by s 68 of the Act, which amends s 1(1) of the 1998 Act by bringing a further category of 'data' within the scope of that Act. This category (inserted as s 1(1)(e) in the 1998 Act) is defined as:

. . . recorded information held by a public authority which does not fall within the existing definitions of 'data' within any of paragraphs 1(1)(a) to 1(1)(d) of the 1998 Act].

(s. 68(2))

Thus, for example, Local Authority planning department files organised purely by reference to application or decision date would not have been covered by the 1998 Act prior to this amendment. They would not have formed part of a 'relevant filing system' for the purposes of s 1(1)(c) and would not have been 'accessible records' for the purpose of s 68 of the 1998 Act. However, they have now been brought within the ambit of the 1998 Act. Therefore, where such information constitutes 'personal data', it will be subject to the right of access under the 1998 Act (see 10.3.2).

For the purpose of this extended category of data, 'public authority' has the same meaning as it has under the Act (s 68(2)(b)). The circumstances in which information will be regarded as 'held by a public authority' under this provision are also the same as those applying generally under the Act (s 68(3)) (see 4.4.3). In the case of a 'public authority' having mixed public and private functions, the extension of the scope of the data protection legislation applies only to unstructured data related to those 'public' functions covered by the Act (s 68(3)).

10.3.2 Application of the Rights and Obligations Under the 1998 Act to the Extended Category of Data

Only certain of the 1998 Act's rights and obligations apply to the extended category of data (that is, data falling within the inserted s 1(1)(e) of the 1998 Act) (see s 70(1), inserting new s 33A(1) into the 1998 Act). These are:

- the right of subject access;
- the fourth data protection principle requiring information to be accurate, and where necessary, up to date;
- the right to rectify, block, erase or destroy inaccurate data;
- the sixth data protection principle to the extent that this requires data controllers to comply with data subjects' rights to access or to rectify, block, erase or destroy inaccurate data; and
- the right to compensation for damage arising as a result of a breach of a data subject's right of access to data or of the fourth data protection principle.

Thus, for example, under the amended 1998 Act, an individual data subject is (where data are held by a public authority and unless relevant exemptions apply) entitled to have access to personal data falling within s 1(1)(e) and to require the amendment of any inaccurate data (in accordance with s 14 of the 1998 Act). However, he or she has, for example, no right to prevent the use of such data for the purposes of direct marketing (DPA 1998, s 11) or to benefit from the 1998 Act's rights in relation to automated decision-taking (DPA 1998, s 12). Furthermore, a public authority data controller which is engaged in processing such data is not, for example, obliged to comply with the obligation not to retain such data for longer than is necessary for a specific purpose or purposes (as required under the fifth data protection principle).

10.3.3 Exemptions Applicable to the Extended Category of Data—Permanent and Transitional

Even where, prima facie, the rights of access under the 1998 Act apply to the extended category of data, a public authority is not obliged to grant access to personal data where they are covered by an exemption under the 1998 Act (DPA 1998, ss 27–39). Thus, for example, where personal data are processed only for journalistic, literary or artistic purposes, they may be exempt from the right of access under s 32 of the 1998 Act. The Act introduces an additional exemption which applies only to the extended category of data in the new s 1(1)(e). This exemption covers the processing of personal data relating to Crown personnel matters (DPA 1998, s 33A(2), as inserted by s 70(2) of the Act):

Personal data which fall within paragraph (e) of the definition of 'data' in section 1(1) and relate to appointments or removals, pay, discipline, superannuation or other personnel matters, in relation to—

(a) service in any of the armed forces of the Crown,
(b) service in any office or employment under the Crown or under any public authority, or
(c) service in any office or employment, or under any contract for services, in respect of which power to take action or to determine or approve the action taken, in such matters is vested in Her Majesty, any Minister of the Crown, the National Assembly for Wales, any Northern Ireland Minister (within the meaning of the Freedom of Information Act 2000) or any public authority, are also exempt from [all the duties and rights established under the 1998 Act].

The Act also contains transitional exemptions applying to the extended category of data during the 1998 Act's 'second transitional period' (ie, the period between 24 October 2001 and 23 October 2007). Such data are, during this period, also exempt from the fourth data protection principle (the duty to ensure that personal data are accurate and up to date) and the right to have inaccurate data rectified, blocked, erased or deleted (DPA 1998, Sch 8, para 14A, inserted by s 70(3) of the Act). During this second transitional period, a more limited transitional right to have inaccurate or incomplete data rectified, blocked, erased or destroyed and to require data controllers to cease holding data in a manner which is incompatible with legitimate purposes is provided by s 12A of the 1998 Act.

The extended category of data is excluded from the scope of the criminal offences created by s 55 of the 1998 Act. Under s 55, it is an offence to obtain or disclose, or to procure the disclosure, of personal data without the consent of the data controller. For the purposes of these offences, the definition of 'data' excludes data falling within s 1(1)(e) of the 1998 Act (DPA 1998, s 33A(1)(f), inserted by s 70(1) of the Act).

10.3.4 Procedural Conditions Applying to the Right of Access to the Extended Category of Data

The amendments to the 1998 Act contained in the Act impose conditions upon data subjects seeking access to personal data falling within the extended category of data (see s 69 of the Act, inserting s 9A into the 1998 Act). These conditions parallel those found in the Act itself and are designed to ensure that applications for access to unstructured personal data are not too burdensome for public authorities. A public authority is not obliged to provide access to unstructured personal data unless 'the request . . . contains a description of the data' (DPA 1998, s 9A(2)). Even where the data are described by the data subject, a public authority is not obliged to provide access to this form of data if the authority estimates that the cost of providing the information would exceed the 'appropriate amount' (DPA 1998, s 9A(3)). As with requests under the Act, the 'appropriate amount' is to be calculated in accordance with regulations made by the Secretary of State.

Where a public authority is able to inform a data subject whether it is processing his or her personal data at an estimated cost less than the 'appropriate amount', even though the estimated cost of supplying the data would exceed that amount, it must do so (DPA 1998, s 9A(4) as inserted by s 69(2)). These separable obligations parallel the dual duties to confirm or deny and to communicate information imposed by s 1(1) of the Act.

It should be noted that these procedural conditions apply only to data falling within the extended category of data (ie, data falling within the inserted s 1(1)(e) of the 1998 Act. Thus, for example, where a public authority holds data that is processed automatically or holds data in an 'accessible record', the usual procedural rules governing the access right under the 1998 Act will continue to apply.

10.3.5 The Jurisdiction of the Information Commissioner and the Information Tribunal

As explained in Chapter 9, the Data Protection Commissioner has been re-titled the Information Commissioner under the Act. This individual is now responsible for supervising both freedom of information and data protection regimes. In addition, the Data Protection Tribunal has been renamed the Information Tribunal, which has jurisdiction to hear appeals under both data protection and freedom of information legislation. As a result of these changes, a number of relatively minor amendments to the existing system of data protection enforcement have been required.

Thus, for example, the requirement that the members of the Data Protection Tribunal must be representative of the interests of data subjects and the interests of data controllers (DPA 1998, s 6(6)) has been amended to require additional representation for 'persons to represent the interests of those who make requests for information under the Freedom of Information Act 2000' and 'persons to represent the interests of public authorities' (Sch 2, para 16 to the Act). These consequential amendments are set out in full in Sch 2 to the Act.

10.3.6 Amendments to the Notification Requirements Under the 1998 Act

Under the 1998 Act, data controllers must generally notify the Commissioner that they intend to process personal data before doing so (DPA 1998, s 17). The Commissioner maintains a register of persons who have given such notification. A data controller is only exempt from the requirement to notify its activities where the sole purpose of processing is the maintenance of a public register, where the Secretary of State so orders or, in certain circumstances, where the data controller is engaged only in manual data processing (DPA 1998, s 17(2)–(4)).

In notifying the Commissioner, a data controller is required to provide the 'registrable particulars' listed in s 16 of the 1998 Act. Section 71 of the Act amends s 16(1) of the 1998 Act to add a further registrable particular to this list. Any notification provided by a public authority under the 1998 Act must include a statement that notification is being made by a 'public authority' under the Act. This requirement permits the Commissioner to identify bodies which are subject both to the Act and to the extended coverage of the 1998 Act.

10.4 REQUESTS FOR PERSONAL INFORMATION UNDER THE FREEDOM OF INFORMATION ACT 2000

10.4.1 Introduction

Under the Act, where an application for 'personal data' is made to a public authority by a 'data subject', the application must be handled under the 1998 Act rather than under the Act (s 40(1)).

Where an applicant other than the data subject makes an application for personal data, that application is handled under the Act. However, in the case of an application by such a third party, the requested information may after be exempt from the duty to disclose (s 40(2)).

10.4.2 Requests by 'Data Subjects' (s 40(1))

Section 40(1) of the Act states that:

Any information to which a request for information relates is exempt information if it constitutes personal data of which the applicant is the data subject.

This exemption is an 'absolute exemption' (see 6.2). 'Personal data' are defined by reference to s 1(1) of the 1998 Act (s 40(7)), which states:

data which relate to a living individual who can be identified—

(a) from those data, or
(b) from those data and other information which is in the possession of, or is likely to come into the possession of, the data controller, and includes any expression of the opinion about the individual and any indication of the intentions of the data controller or any other person in respect of the individual.

The effect of this exemption is not of course to deny an individual access to personal data. Rather, as is made clear in the Explanatory Notes which accompanied the Freedom of Information Bill:

The right to know whether [personal information relating to the applicant] is held, and if so to have access to it, is covered instead by the provisions of the Data Protection Act 1998.

Thus, for example, if an individual were to write to a local authority requesting access to the file kept on him by the authority's social services department, the authority would be exempt from both the duty to confirm or deny and the duty to communicate information under the Act. However, subject to any applicable exemptions, it would be required to provide access under the 1998 Act (DPA 1998, s 7). The applicant is not required to specify the particular enactment under which the information is sought and, therefore, on receipt of the application, the authority must simply process it in accordance with the appropriate regime.

In considering the effect of s 40, the decision of the Court of Appeal in *Durant* should be recalled (see 10.2.2 above). As a result of that decision, the exemption applies only to information affecting the privacy of the data subject. The simple fact that an individual is named in a record will not bring the exemption into effect and, as a result, a request for information in that record will continue to be governed by the Act rather than by the 1998 Act.

10.4.3 Requests by Third Parties (s 40(2))

An application for information by anyone other than the 'data subject' is to be dealt with under the Act. However, because the release of personal data to a third party raises issues of data privacy (and in many instances would breach the 1998 Act), broad exemptions apply to such requests under the Act (s 40(2)). These exemptions are defined by reference to the 1998 Act.

Section 40(2) provides that wherever an application for 'personal data' is made by someone other than the 'data subject', the information to which it relates is exempt from disclosure under the Act where either of two conditions are satisfied. These conditions are set out in s 40(3) and (4) respectively.

The First Condition (s 40(3))
The first condition provides for exemption where disclosure of the information by a public authority would contravene any of the data protection principles or, in the case of data falling within s 1(1)(a) to (d) of the 1998 Act, the right to prevent processing likely to cause damage or distress (DPA 1998, s 10). In fact, the release of personal data to third parties without consent may often breach the data protection principles. The first data protection principle, for example, requires personal data to be processed fairly and the second data protection principle requires that personal data must only be:

. . . obtained for one or more specified and lawful purposes, and shall not be further processed in any manner incompatible with that purpose or purposes.

Disclosure of personal data to a third party by a public authority will often breach these principles. In such circumstances, the public authority in question will not only be exempt from communicating information under s 40(2) but could be subject to enforcement proceedings under the 1998 Act if it were to do so.

The Information Commissioner has offered guidance on the scope of the exemption provided under s 40(2). He has suggested that the key question is likely to be: 'Would disclosure of the personal information in question be fair?' and that, in thinking about fairness, it will be important to distinguish between information that relates to the public life of an individual and information that relates to his or her private life:

An issue that will often arise is whether the Data Protection Act prevents the disclosure of information identifying members of staff. Applying the criteria suggested above, if the information requested consists of the names of officials, their grades, job functions or decisions which they have made in their official capacities, then disclosure would normally be made. On the other hand, information such as home addresses or internal disciplinary matters would not normally be disclosed. While it would be wrong to disclose bank account details of staff, it would be unlikely to be unfair to publish details of expenses incurred in the course of official business, information about pay bands, or, particularly in the case of senior staff, details of salaries.

(Information Commissioner, Freedom of Information Awareness Guidance No 1, *Personal Information*, www.informationcommissioner.gov.uk)

It is possible that public authorities could be tempted to rely too frequently upon s 40(2) as a reason for refusing disclosure of information. It should be remembered that, where personal data in a document can be obscured (or 'redacted'), the authority is not excused from the duty to release the rest of the information contained in the document. Authorities are also required to seek consent to the release of personal information wherever possible (see Code of Practice under s 45, paras 31–40).

In assessing whether a disclosure would breach the data protection principles, the transitional exemptions in Part III of Sch 8 to the 1998 Act (ie, transitional exemptions for the processing of manual data) are to be disregarded (s 40(6) of the Act).

The right to prevent processing likely to cause damage or distress under s 10 of the 1998 Act allows a data subject to serve notice upon a data controller requiring it to cease processing data on the grounds that such processing is likely to cause substantial damage or substantial distress to him or another. A data controller will breach this right if it fails to respond to the notice within a specified period. If, in its response, the data controller states that the notice served by the data subject is unjustified, the data subject is entitled to seek a court order requiring the data controller to comply with the notice.

The Second Condition (s 40(4))
The second condition provides for exemption where the information in question is exempt from the data subject's right of access under the 1998 Act, s 7(1)(c). Thus, even if communication of personal data to someone other than the data subject will not breach the data protection principles or any notice issued under s 10 of the 1998 Act, a public authority is not obliged to communicate it if it is covered by any of the exemptions to disclosure in the 1998 Act (see 10.3.3 above).

10.4.4 The Duty to Confirm or Deny

The duty to confirm or deny does not arise in relation to information which is (or if it were held by the public authority would be) exempt under s 40(1) of the Act (s 40(5)(a)). Thus, where an application for personal data is made by the data subject, a public authority is not obliged to comply with the duty to confirm or deny. Again, the request is governed entirely by the 1998 Act, which contains a parallel right 'to be informed by any data controller whether personal data of which that individual is the data subject are being processed by or on behalf of that data controller' (DPA 1998, s 7(1)(a)). Where an application for personal data is made by someone other than the data subject, the duty to confirm or deny is excluded if compliance with that duty would contravene any of the data protection principles or s 10 of the 1998 Act or where the data is exempt from disclosure under the 1998 Act (s 40(5) of the Act).

10.4.5 The Status of s 40

Section 40(1) of the Act is an absolute exemption. Section 40(2) is also an absolute exemption where disclosure of information in response to a third party request would contravene any of the data protection principles or where the data requested is covered by an exemption from the data subject's right of access under the 1998 Act. However, where s 40(2) comes into effect because disclosure of requested information would contravene the provisions of a notice given under s 10 of the 1998 Act, the exemption is a qualified exemption.

11

HISTORICAL RECORDS

11.1 INTRODUCTION

11.1.1 Special Rules for 'Historical Records'

Under the Freedom of Information Act 2000, information contained in 'historical records' is subject to a number of supplementary provisions (see Part VI of the Act (ss 62–67)). Records become historical records 30 years from the end of the year in which they were created (s 62(1)). These special rules apply because the disclosure of information contained in older records is less likely to be harmful to the public interest. Accordingly, information contained in historical records is covered by fewer exemptions under the Act than information contained in non-historical records (see 11.2 below).

11.1.2 Modification of Rules Relating to 'Public Records'

Prior to the coming into force of the Act, access to information contained in the historical records of government departments and certain other public authorities in England and Wales ('public records'), was governed by the Public Records Act 1958 ('the 1958 Act'). (In Northern Ireland, the position was governed by similar rules contained in the Public Records Act (Northern Ireland) 1923.) The 1958 Act established a scheme under which public records were usually transferred to a public records office (such as the Public Record Office at Kew) and made available to the public 30 years from the end of the year of their creation (20 years in Northern Ireland). Some public records of particular sensitivity remained closed even after the end of this period.

This scheme has been substantially modified by the Act. Following the coming into force of the Act, the 1958 Act continues to govern the *transfer* of public records to public record offices. However, the right of access to information held by *any* public authority, including information contained in public records subject to the 1958 Act, is now provided by the Act. In this chapter, the special rules applying to historical records are explained.

Many of these rules are designed to ensure the coordination of the rights introduced under the Act with the existing public records regime. In order fully to understand the position, it is therefore necessary to appreciate the effects of the 1958 Act (as amended). The regime established under the 1958 Act is outlined at 11.3 below.

11.1.3 Code of Practice made under s 46

Under s 46 of the Act, the Lord Chancellor must issue a Code of Practice:

... providing guidance to relevant authorities as to the practice which it would, in his opinion, be desirable for them to follow in connection with the keeping, management and destruction of their records.

Records management plays a vital role in freedom of information. If an authority were to wrongly destroy information or to store it in a way which made it difficult or impossible to identify when requested, the whole purpose of the Act would be subverted.

Under s 46 of the Act, the Lord Chancellor has issued a Code of Practice on the Management of Records. A copy of this can be found in Appendix 3.

11.2 INFORMATION CONTAINED IN HISTORICAL RECORDS—LIMITATION ON EXEMPTIONS UNDER THE ACT

Information contained in *any* historical record (ie, not just those records subject to the 1958 Act) is subject to fewer exemptions than information contained in non-historical records (see 11.2.1 below).

In addition, further restrictions are placed upon the application of exemptions to information contained in historical records which are also 'public records' under the 1958 Act (see 11.2.2 below).

11.2.1 Limitations on Exemptions Applying to All 'Historical Records' under the Act (s 63)

Exemptions expiring after 30 years (s 63(1) and (2))
From the moment that a record becomes a 'historical record' under the Act (see s 62(1)), public authorities are no longer entitled to rely upon the exemptions

listed below in order to resist compliance with the *duty to communicate information* contained in that record (s 63(1)):

(a) prejudice to relations between administrations within the United Kingdom (s 28);

(b) information held for the purpose of certain criminal investigations (s 30(1));

(c) court records (s 32);

(d) audit functions (s 33);

(e) formulation of government policy etc. (s 35);

(f) prejudice to the effective conduct of public affairs (s 36);

(g) communications with Her Majesty etc. (s 37(1)(a));

(h) legal professional privilege (s 42);

(i) commercial interests (s 43).

In addition, a public authority is not entitled to claim exemption from *the duty to confirm or deny* under any of the following provisions (s 63(2)):

(a) prejudice to the relations between the administrations within the United Kingdom (s 28(3));

(b) prejudice to audit functions (s 33(3));

(c) prejudice to the effective conduct of public affairs (s 36(3));

(d) legal professional privilege (s 42(2));

(e) prejudice to commercial interests (s 43(3)).

At first sight it may appear rather strange that the list of expired exemptions to the duty to communicate information is longer than the list relating to exemptions to the duty to confirm or deny. It would of course be absurd if a public authority were to be exempt from the duty to confirm or deny holding particular information and, at the same time, to be obliged to communicate that information.

On a closer look, however, this apparent anomaly disappears. The provisions which seem to be missing from the list of exemptions to the duty to confirm or deny are all 'class exemptions' (ss 30(3), 32(3), 35(3) and 37(2)). Such class exemptions to the duty to confirm or deny are uniformly expressed to exclude that duty in the case of *information which is exempt from the duty to communicate*. In the case of a historical record, where a particular 'class-based' exemption from the duty to communicate information no longer applies (in s 63(1)), the corresponding exemption from the obligation to confirm or deny also automatically ceases to be effective.

Thus, for example, consider the case of a local authority in possession of correspondence between a representative of that authority and a deceased member of the Royal Household. Where that correspondence does not yet satisfy the definition of a 'historical record', the local authority may (subject to the 'public interest') be able to rely upon the exemption in s 37(1)(a) in refusing to communicate the information contained in the correspondence. In addition, in those circumstances, the local authority would not have to confirm or deny whether it held such information, because s 37(2) provides that the 'duty to confirm or deny does not arise in relation to information which is . . . exempt information by virtue of s 37(1)'. However, as soon as that correspondence becomes a 'historical record', the relevant exemption from the duty to communicate the information (s 37(1)(a)) ceases to have effect as a result of s 63(1). Although the corresponding exemption from the duty to confirm or deny is not expressly excluded in the case of information held in a historical record, it will, nevertheless, automatically fall away.

In the above cases, reliance upon the relevant exemptions is excluded as soon as the record in which it is contained becomes a 'historical record'. In addition, after specified longer periods of time, certain other exemptions also fall away.

Exemptions Expiring after Periods Longer than 30 Years (s 63(3)–(5))
After the end of a period of 60 years from the end of the year in which a record was created, public authorities are no longer entitled to refuse to communicate information in reliance upon the exemption covering information relating to the conferring by the Crown of any honour or dignity (s 37(1)(b)). At that point, for the reasons given in the section above, the obligation to confirm or deny will also cease to apply in relation to such information (s 63(3)).

After the end of a period of 100 years from the end of the year in which a record was created, the exemptions set out in s 31 ('Law enforcement') will cease to apply both to the duty to confirm or deny and to the duty to communicate information under the Act (s 63(4) and (5)).

11.2.2 Further Limitations on Exemptions in the Case of 'Historical Records' Held in Public Records Offices (s 64)

Where a historical record is contained in either the Public Record Office or the Public Record Office of Northern Ireland, the exemptions contained in s 21 ('Information accessible to applicant by other means') and s 22 ('Information intended for future publication') cease to have effect (s 64(1)).

In addition, s 64(2) provides that, where a historical record is held in either the PRO or the PRO of Northern Ireland, the exemption covering information supplied by or relating to certain security bodies (s 23) is not to be construed as an 'absolute exemption'. Requests for disclosure of information contained in such records will not therefore automatically be excluded from the scope of the Act. They will instead be subject to the public interest test under s 2 of the Act (ie, the exemption will become a 'qualified exemption' (see 6.3 above)).

11.2.3 Inherent Restrictions on the Application of Exemptions to Information Contained in Historical Records

Even where particular exemptions within Part II of the Act are not expressly excluded in the case of historical records, their practical effectiveness is likely to be greatly reduced. This will be so in the case of those exemptions which apply whenever the disclosure of information would, or would be likely to, prejudice particular interests. As a record ages, it will become increasingly difficult for a public authority to demonstrate that relevant prejudice would, or would be likely to, arise as a result of disclosure of information contained in that record. For example, it seems unlikely that the disclosure of information contained in a record over 30 years old will very often be capable of causing prejudice to 'the economic interests of the United Kingdom' (s 29(1)(a)). This effect will also be apparent in the case of continuing exemptions subject to a 'public interest' test (ie, 'qualified exemptions'). As a record becomes older, it is likely to become more difficult for a public authority to demonstrate that the public interest in maintaining an exemption outweighs the public interest in disclosure.

In addition, certain continuing exemptions are, by their very nature, likely to be less potent in the case of 'historical records'. The exemption applying to 'personal information' (s 40) will frequently deny access to 'personal data' as defined under the Data Protection Act 1998 (see 10.4). Under the 1998 Act, the definition of 'personal data' applies only to data relating to a 'living individual' and will, therefore, be less likely to be satisfied as time passes. Those exemptions protecting information held under an obligation of confidence (ss 30(2), 41 and 43(1)) are also subject to an inherent trend towards obsolescence. Over time, information becomes more likely to enter the 'public domain' and, in any event, it has been established that the legally enforceable duty of confidence is itself of limited duration (see *Attorney-General v Jonathan Cape* [1975] 3 All ER 484).

11.3 PUBLIC RECORDS ACT 1958

11.3.1 Scope of the Legislation

Under the Public Records Act 1958, persons responsible for 'public records' must select records suitable for safe-keeping and transfer them to the Public Records Office (or other place of deposit of public records) not later than 30 years after their creation (PRA, s 3). The records are to be selected and transferred under the guidance of the Keeper of Public Records (an office established under s 2 of the 1958 Act). Overall responsibility for the public records regime under the 1958 Act currently lies with the Lord Chancellor (Public Records Act 1958, s 1). With the Historical Manuscripts Commission, the Public Records Office now forms part of the National Archives. However, for the purposes of the legislative scheme described in this chapter, the Public Records Office remains a separate body.

The first schedule to the 1958 Act lists the records falling within its scope. They are (with some exceptions, such as registers of births, deaths and marriages):

(a) the records of central government departments and of bodies controlled by such departments—such as the Legal Services Commission and National Health Service Authorities (Sch 1, Part I, paras 2 and 3);

(b) the records of numerous other public bodies—including the Criminal Cases Review Commission, the Imperial War Museum and the Information Commissioner (Sch 1, Part II, para 3); and

(c) the records of courts and tribunals (Sch 1, para 4).

Before amendment by the Act (see 11.1.2 above), the 1958 Act required that, unless records were retained by the public body or selected for continued closure (see 11.3.2 and 11.3.3 below respectively), they were to be 'opened' to the public at the Public Record Office (or other authorised place of deposit) at the beginning of the year following their thirtieth 'birthday' (Public Records Act 1958, s 5(1)).

As a result of this public records regime, the Public Record Office (PRO) has become a repository of fascinating information. It contains Shakespeare's will, Edward VIII's abdication instrument and the minutes of Churchill's War Cabinet. Each year, the disclosure of records under the '30-year rule' attracts considerable public attention. The 'New Year's Openings' in 2004 revealed interesting secret reports and correspondence concerning proposals to issue a commemorative 50 pence coin celebrating the United Kingdom's accession to the EEC and a scandal leading to the resignation of two cabinet ministers, Lord Lambton and Lord Jellicoe (see www.pro.gov.uk).

Not all records preserved under the public records legislation are held in the PRO at Kew. Some are held in other specialised places of deposit such as the National Sound Archive and the National Film and Television Archive. Also, other records of primarily local significance, such as local court and hospital records, are held in approved local archives.

Scotland and Northern Ireland have their own public records archives, the National Archives of Scotland and the Public Record Office of Northern Ireland respectively. Scottish public records fall outside the regimes established under both the Act and the 1958 Act and are thus not discussed in this chapter. As has been noted above, Northern Ireland has separate public records legislation making parallel provision to that in the 1958 Act. Northern Ireland authorities are also subject to the Act. Thus, the position discussed below applies, *mutatis mutandis*, to Northern Ireland. The Government of Wales Act 1998 contains a power to establish a records office for Wales (Government of Wales Act 1998, s 117). However, this power has not yet been exercised. Therefore, Welsh public records continue to be subject both to the Act and to the 1958 Act as amended.

11.3.2 Retention of Public Records by Public Bodies

Under the 1958 Act, a public body is, subject to the Lord Chancellor's approval, entitled to retain certain public records rather than transferring them to the Public Record Office or other place of deposit of public records. Legislative authority for the retention of public records is granted by a proviso to s 3(4) of the 1958 Act, which specifies that:

... any records may be retained after the [30-year] period if, in the opinion of the person who is responsible for them, they are required for *administrative purposes* or ought to be retained for *any other special reason* and, where that person is not the Lord Chancellor, the Lord Chancellor has been informed of the facts and given his approval. [emphasis added]

This provision is unaffected by the Act because it is concerned only with the *transfer* of physical control of the records in question and not with the conditions under which access to the information contained in the records is to be granted.

The majority of records retained by public bodies under this provision are held for administrative purposes—for example, plans and deeds to which the public body in question needs to make continued reference. The meaning of 'any other special reason' has been clarified by administrative guidance. The guidance currently applicable is to be found in the *Open Government* White Paper (1993, Cm 2290) and will continue in force under the Act. Under this guidance, a public body is permitted to retain records whose sensitivity is such that it is not possible to estimate when the record may be released. The power has been most frequently exercised in relation to records concerning national security.

Applications by public bodies to retain particular records beyond the 30-year period are scrutinised by an independent body whose role is to advise the Lord Chancellor on whether or not the applications should be accepted. This body, the Lord Chancellor's Advisory Council on Public Records, was established under s 1(2) of the 1958 Act and is chaired by the Master of the Rolls. Where a public record is retained by a public authority, applications for information under the Act must be made to that authority.

11.3.3 Continued Closure of Public Records by Public Bodies

Prior to amendment of the 1958 Act by the Act, a public body was entitled to seek 'extended closure' of a public record beyond the usual 30-year period (s 5(1) and (2), PRA). Detailed administrative criteria on the circumstances in which requests for 'extended closure' would be approved were periodically issued. The most recent set of criteria were published in the *Open Government* White Paper (1993, Cm 2290). The Lord Chancellor's approval was necessary for extended closure of public records and the Advisory Council was responsible for advising the Lord Chancellor whether applications by public bodies should be granted.

Under the Act, this system of 'extended closure' comes to an end. The duty to transfer public records to a public records office within the 30-year period remains (subject to the retention of certain records; see 11.3.2 above). However, the criteria under which access to the information in those records is to be provided are to be found in the Act itself.

If information is not covered by one of the Act's exemptions and if the Act's procedural requirements are satisfied, an applicant has a legal right of access to that information. This is the case whether information is held by a public record office or by any other public authority.

If, on transferring public records into the custody of the Keeper of Public Records, a public authority believes that information in those records remains exempt from disclosure under the Act, it can request that the information in question should not be opened to the public. In such circumstances, it is obliged to produce a schedule explaining why particular information should not be released (see the Lord Chancellor's Code of Practice on the Management of Records, Appendix 3, para 11). This schedule must be provided to the appropriate public records office and must be scrutinised by the Lord Chancellor's Advisory Council on Public Records. Ultimate responsibility for deciding whether to grant the public body's request for continued closure rests with the Lord Chancellor.

Under this amended system, members of the public will be able to challenge the continued closure of records in public record offices by making requests for access to the information contained in those records under the Act. Where a record office receives a request for information in public records which have not been opened for public access, it must consult with the relevant public body prior to releasing the information (see 11.4 below). Where an application for access to information under the Act is refused by a record office, the applicant can complain about that decision to the Information Commissioner in accordance with the enforcement procedures applying generally under the Act (see Chapter 9).

11.4 APPLICATIONS FOR ACCESS TO INFORMATION CONTAINED IN HISTORICAL DOCUMENTS

Where a 'historical record' is not subject to the 1958 Act (because it is held by a body which is not subject to the 1958 Act), the procedure for handling applications under the Act for access to information contained in that record is the same as that which applies in the case of non-historical records.

However, additional procedural provisions apply to applications for access to information contained in records covered by the 1958 Act. These have been enacted to ensure that consultation takes place between public authorities that would be affected by a particular disclosure. The effect of these provisions is explained below.

11.4.1 Duty to Consult before Refusing Access to Information Contained in Certain Historical Records Subject to the 1958 Act (s 65 of the Act)

This provision applies only to historical records which are subject to the Public Records Act 1958 but which are not 'transferred records' under the Act. 'Transferred records' are records which have been passed into the custody of the PRO or some other designated records authority (PRA, s 15(4)). Thus, s 65 applies to 'public records' which are retained by a public authority beyond the usual 30-year period set out in the 1958 Act (see 11.3.2 above).

Prior to refusing a request for access to information contained in such a record on the grounds that a qualified exemption applies, a public authority must consult either the Lord Chancellor or a Northern Ireland Minister as appropriate. This provision is designed to ensure that the public authority's assessment of the public interest in maintaining secrecy in older documents is subject to further scrutiny and can be properly supported.

11.4.2 Decision-making in Relation to Information Contained in Transferred Public Records (s 66 of the Act)

The decision-making procedure established under s 66 of the Act applies only to 'transferred public records' (see 11.4.1. above) which have not been designated as 'open records'. Where a record has already been designated as an 'open record' by the transferring public body, that body will already have decided that it is suitable for disclosure to the public and members of the public will have access to the information in question in an appropriate records office. Thus, s 66 applies to public records which have been transferred to the PRO or other authorised place of deposit, but which are not yet open to public scrutiny. Such records will generally be records which have either been approved for 'extended closure' under the regime applying prior to the Act or, after the coming into force of the Act, have been approved for continued closure in accordance with the procedure described in 11.3.3 above.

In the case of such 'transferred public records', responsibility for taking decisions about requests for access to information under the Act is divided between the 'responsible authority' for that particular record and the 'appropriate records authority'. The 'responsible authority' is the Minister, or other person, who is 'primarily concerned' with the information in question and is to be identified by either the Lord Chancellor or the Northern Ireland Minister as appropriate (s 15(5)). The 'appropriate records authority' will be either the PRO, the Lord Chancellor or the PRO of Northern Ireland, depending upon the place of deposit of the particular records (s 15(5)).

As the 'public authority' holding transferred public records, the appropriate records authority will receive requests under the Act for access to information in those transferred public records. Prior to determining whether or not a particular request is covered by an exemption, the appropriate records authority must consult the responsible authority (s 66(2)). Where a question arises as to whether or not particular information is covered by an *absolute* exemption (see 6.2 above), the decision whether or not the requested information falls within the scope of the exemption, rests, following consultation, with the appropriate records authority.

Where a question arises as to whether or not particular information is covered by a *qualified* exemption, the position is more complicated. Again, following consultation, the decision on whether or not information falls within a particular exemption rests with the appropriate records authority. However, the subsequent decision as to whether the public interest favours maintenance of the exemption rather than disclosure of the information is to be taken by the responsible authority (s 66(3) and (4)). Prior to refusing a request on the grounds that a 'qualified exemption' applies, the appropriate authority is also obliged to consult either the Lord Chancellor or a Northern Ireland Minister as appropriate (s 66(5)). This provides the same degree of external scrutiny as is provided by s 65 in the case of public records retained by public authorities (see 11.4.1 above).

Thus, for example, consider the case of historical records transferred from the Home Office to the PRO. A request for access to the information contained in those records under the Act will be made to the PRO because it will be the public authority holding that information. Before determining whether or not the information is covered by an exemption (for example, s 30(1) relating to criminal investigations and proceedings), the PRO is obliged to consult the Home Secretary (who is the 'responsible authority' in such circumstances). If, following consultation, the PRO decides that information does not fall within the scope of the exemption, it must communicate the information in accordance with its duties under s 1(1) of the Act. However, if, following consultation, it decides that the exemption applies to the information in question, responsibility for deciding whether or not the public interest in continued non-disclosure outweighs the public interest in disclosure rests with the Home Secretary. If the Home Secretary considers that the information should not be disclosed, he must consult the Lord Chancellor before refusing the request for access to the information. The procedures and time-limits for taking such decisions are set out in s 15 and are discussed at 11.4.3 below.

In some cases, transferred public records held by the PRO, or another appropriate records authority, will have originated from a public body which is not generally subject to the provisions of the Act. This could occur, for example, in the case of records deriving from public bodies such as courts or the Security Services. These bodies are subject to the 1958 Act but do not, generally, fall within the definition of 'public authority' for the purposes of the Act. In the case of records transferred by such bodies, the relevant body is to be treated as a public authority under the Act for the purpose of complying with the decision-making procedures described in this section (s 66(6)). That is, although not generally subject to the duties imposed upon public authorities under the Act, the body is required to act as the 'responsible body' in relation to requests for access to information contained in transferred public records for which it is responsible.

11.4.3 Obligation to Inform the 'Responsible Authority' of an Application for Access to 'Transferred Records' (s 15)

In order to enable the decision-making process described above to operate effectively, an appropriate records authority receiving a request for information which raises an issue as to the respective public interests in disclosure and non-disclosure, must send a copy of that request to the relevant responsible authority (s 15(1) and (2)). This provision applies whether or not the transferred public record is a historical record. It will therefore also cover records transferred to a records authority in advance of the date required under the 1958 Act. Thus, in the example given in 11.4.2 above, the PRO would be obliged to provide the Home Secretary with a copy of the 'request' in question in order to allow him to balance the respective public interests in disclosure and continued secrecy. While s 15 requires only a copy of the 'request' to be sent to the responsible authority, it will presumably also often be necessary for that authority to see the record itself (or a copy of that record) in order to come to a decision on the public interest. Public bodies have, in any event, the ability to borrow back public records from a records office under s 4(6) of the 1958 Act.

The appropriate records authority is required to send the copy of the request to the responsible authority within the usual period for compliance under the Act (ie, within 20 working days). On receipt of the copy of the request, the responsible authority is obliged to determine whether or not the information should be released within 'such time as is reasonable in all the circumstances' (s 15(3)). This provision reflects the general time limit for 'public interest' decisions under the Act (see 5.4 above).

Freedom of Information Act 2000 (as amended)

CHAPTER 36

ARRANGEMENT OF SECTIONS

PART I
ACCESS TO INFORMATION HELD BY
PUBLIC AUTHORITIES

170

Right to information

Refusal of request

The Information Commissioner and the Information Tribunal

FREEDOM OF INFORMATION ACT 2000*

2000 CHAPTER 36

An Act to make provision for the disclosure of information held by public authorities or by persons providing services for them and to amend the Data Protection Act 1998 and the Public Records Act 1958; and for connected purposes.

[30 November 2000]

BE IT ENACTED by the Queen's most Excellent Majesty, by and with the advice and consent of the Lords Spiritual and Temporal, and Commons, in this present Parliament assembled, and by the authority of the same, as follows:—

PART I
ACCESS TO INFORMATION HELD BY PUBLIC AUTHORITIES

Right to information

1. General right of access to information held by public authorities

(1) Any person making a request for information to a public authority is entitled—
    (a) to be informed in writing by the public authority whether it holds information of the description specified in the request, and
    (b) if that is the case, to have that information communicated to him.
(2) Subsection (1) has effect subject to the following provisions of this section and to the provisions of sections 2, 9, 12 and 14.
(3) Where a public authority—
    (a) reasonably requires further information in order to identify and locate the information requested, and
    (b) has informed the applicant of that requirement, the authority is not obliged to comply with subsection (1) unless it is supplied with that further information.
(4) The information—
    (a) in respect of which the applicant is to be informed under subsection (1)(a), or
    (b) which is to be communicated under subsection (1)(b),
    is the information in question held at the time when the request is received, except that account may be taken of any amendment or deletion made between that time and the time when the information is to be communicated under subsection (1)(b), being an amendment or deletion that would have been made regardless of the receipt of the request.
(5) A public authority is to be taken to have complied with subsection (1)(a) in relation to any information if it has communicated the information to the applicant in accordance with subsection (1)(b).

---

*Note the Act originally set out a number of functions for the Secretary of State. Subsequently it was amended and responsibilities passed to the Lord Chancellor. It has now been amended again and the responsibilities have reverted to the Secretary of State as a result of the Secretary of State for Constitutional Affairs Order 2003 SI 2003/1887.

(6) In this Act, the duty of a public authority to comply with subsection (1)(a) is referred to as 'the duty to confirm or deny'.

2. Effect of the exemptions in Part II

(1) Where any provision of Part II states that the duty to confirm or deny does not arise in relation to any information, the effect of the provision is that where either—
   (a) the provision confers absolute exemption, or
   (b) in all the circumstances of the case, the public interest in maintaining the exclusion of the duty to confirm or deny outweighs the public interest in disclosing whether the public authority holds the information,
   section 1(1)(a) does not apply.
(2) In respect of any information which is exempt information by virtue of any provision of Part II, section 1(1)(b) does not apply if or to the extent that—
   (a) the information is exempt information by virtue of a provision conferring absolute exemption, or
   (b) in all the circumstances of the case, the public interest in maintaining the exemption outweighs the public interest in disclosing the information.
(3) For the purposes of this section, the following provisions of Part II (and no others) are to be regarded as conferring absolute exemption—
   (a) section 21,
   (b) section 23,
   (c) section 32,
   (d) section 34,
   (e) section 36 so far as relating to information held by the House of Commons or the House of Lords,
   (f) in section 40—
      (i) subsection (1), and
      (ii) subsection (2) so far as relating to cases where the first condition referred to in that subsection is satisfied by virtue of subsection (3)(a)(i) or (b) of that section,
   (g) section 41, and
   (h) section 44.

3. Public authorities

(1) In this Act 'public authority' means—
   (a) subject to section 4(4), any body which, any other person who, or the holder of any office which—
      (i) is listed in Schedule 1, or
      (ii) is designated by order under section 5, or
   (b) a publicly-owned company as defined by section 6.
(2) For the purposes of this Act, information is held by a public authority if—
   (a) it is held by the authority, otherwise than on behalf of another person, or
   (b) it is held by another person on behalf of the authority.

4. Amendment of Schedule 1

(1) The Secretary of State may by order amend Schedule 1 by adding to that Schedule a reference to any body or the holder of any office which (in either case) is not for the

time being listed in that Schedule but as respects which both the first and the second conditions below are satisfied:

(2) The first condition is that the body or office—

    (a) is established by virtue of Her Majesty's prerogative or by an enactment or by subordinate legislation, or

    (b) is established in any other way by a Minister of the Crown in his capacity as Minister, by a government department or by the National Assembly for Wales.

(3) The second condition is—

    (a) in the case of a body, that the body is wholly or partly constituted by appointment made by the Crown, by a Minister of the Crown, by a government department or by the National Assembly for Wales, or

    (b) in the case of an office, that appointments to the office are made by the Crown, by a Minister of the Crown, by a government department or by the National Assembly for Wales.

(4) If either the first or the second condition above ceases to be satisfied as respects any body or office which is listed in Part VI or VII of Schedule 1, that body or the holder of that office shall cease to be a public authority by virtue of the entry in question.

(5) The Secretary of State may by order amend Schedule 1 by removing from Part VI or VII of that Schedule an entry relating to any body or office—

    (a) which has ceased to exist, or

    (b) as respects which either the first or the second condition above has ceased to be satisfied.

(6) An order under subsection (1) may relate to a specified person or office or to persons or offices falling within a specified description.

(7) Before making an order under subsection (1), the Secretary of State shall—

    (a) if the order adds to Part II, III, IV or VI of Schedule 1 a reference to—

        (i) a body whose functions are exercisable only or mainly in or as regards Wales, or

        (ii) the holder of an office whose functions are exercisable only or mainly in or as regards Wales,

    consult the National Assembly for Wales, and

    (b) if the order relates to a body which, or the holder of any office who, if the order were made, would be a Northern Ireland public authority, consult the First Minister and deputy First Minister in Northern Ireland.

(8) This section has effect subject to section 80.

(9) In this section 'Minister of the Crown' includes a Northern Ireland Minister.

5. Further power to designate public authorities

(1) The Secretary of State may by order designate as a public authority for the purposes of this Act any person who is neither listed in Schedule 1 nor capable of being added to that Schedule by an order under section 4(1), but who—

    (a) appears to the Secretary of State to exercise functions of a public nature, or

    (b) is providing under a contract made with a public authority any service whose provision is a function of that authority.

(2) An order under this section may designate a specified person or office or persons or offices falling within a specified description.

(3) Before making an order under this section, the Secretary of State shall consult every

person to whom the order relates, or persons appearing to him to represent such persons.

(4) This section has effect subject to section 80.

6. Publicly-owned companies

(1) A company is a 'publicly-owned company' for the purposes of section 3(1)(b) if—
  (a) it is wholly owned by the Crown, or
  (b) it is wholly owned by any public authority listed in Schedule 1 other than—
    (i) a government department, or
    (ii) any authority which is listed only in relation to particular information.

(2) For the purposes of this section—
  (a) a company is wholly owned by the Crown if it has no members except—
    (i) Ministers of the Crown, government departments or companies wholly owned by the Crown, or
    (ii) persons acting on behalf of Ministers of the Crown, government departments or companies wholly owned by the Crown, and
  (b) a company is wholly owned by a public authority other than a government department if it has no members except—
    (i) that public authority or companies wholly owned by that public authority, or
    (ii) persons acting on behalf of that public authority or of companies wholly owned by that public authority.

(3) In this section—
'company' includes any body corporate;
'Minister of the Crown' includes a Northern Ireland Minister.

7. Public authorities to which Act has limited application

(1) Where a public authority is listed in Schedule 1 only in relation to information of a specified description, nothing in Parts I to V of this Act applies to any other information held by the authority.

(2) An order under section 4(1) may, in adding an entry to Schedule 1, list the public authority only in relation to information of a specified description.

(3) The Secretary of State may by order amend Schedule 1—
  (a) by limiting to information of a specified description the entry relating to any public authority, or
  (b) by removing or amending any limitation to information of a specified description which is for the time being contained in any entry.

(4) Before making an order under subsection (3), the Secretary of State shall—
  (a) if the order relates to the National Assembly for Wales or a Welsh public authority, consult the National Assembly for Wales,
  (b) if the order relates to the Northern Ireland Assembly, consult the Presiding Officer of that Assembly, and
  (c) if the order relates to a Northern Ireland department or a Northern Ireland public authority, consult the First Minister and deputy First Minister in Northern Ireland.

(5) An order under section 5(1)(a) must specify the functions of the public authority

designated by the order with respect to which the designation is to have effect; and nothing in Parts I to V of this Act applies to information which is held by the authority but does not relate to the exercise of those functions.

(6) An order under section 5(1)(b) must specify the services provided under contract with respect to which the designation is to have effect; and nothing in Parts I to V of this Act applies to information which is held by the public authority designated by the order but does not relate to the provision of those services.

(7) Nothing in Parts I to V of this Act applies in relation to any information held by a publicly-owned company which is excluded information in relation to that company.

(8) In subsection (7) 'excluded information', in relation to a publicly-owned company, means information which is of a description specified in relation to that company in an order made by the Secretary of State for the purpose of this subsection.

(9) In this section 'publicly-owned company' has the meaning given by section 6.

8. Request for information

(1) In this Act any reference to a 'request for information' is a reference to such a request which—

    (a) is in writing,

    (b) states the name of the applicant and an address for correspondence, and

    (c) describes the information requested.

(2) For the purposes of subsection (1)(a), a request is to be treated as made in writing where the text of the request—

    (a) is transmitted by electronic means

    (b) is received in legible form, and

    (c) is capable of being used for subsequent reference.

9. Fees

(1) A public authority to whom a request for information is made may, within the period for complying with section 1(1), give the applicant a notice in writing (in this Act referred to as a 'fees notice') stating that a fee of an amount specified in the notice is to be charged by the authority for complying with section 1(1).

(2) Where a fees notice has been given to the applicant, the public authority is not obliged to comply with section 1(1) unless the fee is paid within the period of three months beginning with the day on which the fees notice is given to the applicant.

(3) Subject to subsection (5), any fee under this section must be determined by the public authority in accordance with regulations made by the Secretary of State.

(4) Regulations under subsection (3) may, in particular, provide—

    (a) that no fee is to be payable in prescribed cases,

    (b) that any fee is not to exceed such maximum as may be specified in, or determined in accordance with, the regulations, and

    (c) that any fee is to be calculated in such manner as may be prescribed by the regulations.

(5) Subsection (3) does not apply where provision is made by or under any enactment as to the fee that may be charged by the public authority for the disclosure of the information.

10. Time for compliance with request

(1) Subject to subsections (2) and (3), a public authority must comply with section 1(1) promptly and in any event not later than the twentieth working day following the date of receipt.

(2) Where the authority has given a fees notice to the applicant and the fee is paid in accordance with section 9(2), the working days in the period beginning with the day on which the fees notice is given to the applicant and ending with the day on which the fee is received by the authority are to be disregarded in calculating for the purposes of subsection (1) the twentieth working day following the date of receipt.

(3) If, and to the extent that—

    (a) section 1(1)(a) would not apply if the condition in section 2(1)(b) were satisfied, or

    (b) section 1(1)(b) would not apply if the condition in section 2(2)(b) were satisfied,

the public authority need not comply with section 1(1)(a) or (b) until such time as is reasonable in the circumstances; but this subsection does not affect the time by which any notice under section 17(1) must be given.

(4) The Secretary of State may by regulations provide that subsections (1) and (2) are to have effect as if any reference to the twentieth working day following the date of receipt were a reference to such other day, not later than the sixtieth working day following the date of receipt, as may be specified in, or determined in accordance with, the regulations.

(5) Regulations under subsection (4) may—

    (a) prescribe different days in relation to different cases, and

    (b) confer a discretion on the Commissioner.

(6) In this section—

'the date of receipt' means—

    (a) the day on which the public authority receives the request for information, or

    (b) if later, the day on which it receives the information referred to in section 1(3);

'working day' means any day other than a Saturday, a Sunday, Christmas Day, Good Friday or a day which is a bank holiday under the Banking and Financial Dealings Act 1971 in any part of the United Kingdom.

11. Means by which communication to be made

(1) Where, on making his request for information, the applicant expresses a preference for communication by any one or more of the following means, namely—

    (a) the provision to the applicant of a copy of the information in permanent form or in another form acceptable to the applicant,

    (b) the provision to the applicant of a reasonable opportunity to inspect a record containing the information, and

    (c) the provision to the applicant of a digest or summary of the information in permanent form or in another form acceptable to the applicant, the public authority shall so far as reasonably practicable give effect to that preference.

(2) In determining for the purposes of this section whether it is reasonably practicable to communicate information by particular means, the public authority may have regard to all the circumstances, including the cost of doing so.

(3) Where the public authority determines that it is not reasonably practicable to comply with any preference expressed by the applicant in making his request, the authority shall notify the applicant of the reasons for its determination.

(4) Subject to subsection (1), a public authority may comply with a request by communicating information by any means which are reasonable in the circumstances.

12. Exemption where cost of compliance exceeds appropriate limit

(1) Section 1(1) does not oblige a public authority to comply with a request for information if the authority estimates that the cost of complying with the request would exceed the appropriate limit.

(2) Subsection (1) does not exempt the public authority from its obligation to comply with paragraph (a) of section 1(1) unless the estimated cost of complying with that paragraph alone would exceed the appropriate limit.

(3) In subsection (1) and (2) 'the appropriate limit' means such amount as may be prescribed, and different amounts may be prescribed in relation to different cases.

(4) The Secretary of State may by regulations provide that, in such circumstances as may be prescribed, where two or more requests for information are made to a public authority—
   (a) by one person, or
   (b) by different persons who appear to the public authority to be acting in concert or in pursuance of a campaign,
the estimated cost of complying with any of the requests is to be taken to be the estimated total cost of complying with all of them.

(5) The Secretary of State may by regulations make provision for the purposes of this section as to the costs to be estimated and as to the manner in which they are to be estimated.

13. Fees for disclosure where cost of compliance exceeds appropriate limit

(1) A public authority may charge for the communication of any information whose communication—
   (a) is not required by section 1(1) because the cost of complying with the request for information exceeds the amount which is the appropriate limit for the purposes of section 12(1) and (2), and
   (b) is not otherwise required by law, such fee as may be determined by the public authority in accordance with regulations made by the Secretary of State.

(2) Regulations under this section may, in particular, provide—
   (a) that any fee is not to exceed such maximum as may be specified in, or determined in accordance with, the regulations, and
   (b) that any fee is to be calculated in such manner as may be prescribed by the regulations.

(3) Subsection (1) does not apply where provision is made by or under any enactment as to the fee that may be charged by the public authority for the disclosure of the information.

14. Vexatious or repeated requests

(1) Section 1(1) does not oblige a public authority to comply with a request for information if the request is vexatious.

(2) Where a public authority has previously complied with a request for information which was made by any person, it is not obliged to comply with a subsequent identical or substantially similar request from that person unless a reasonable interval has elapsed between compliance with the previous request and the making of the current request.

15. Special provisions relating to public records transferred to Public Record Office, etc.

(1) Where—
  (a) the appropriate records authority receives a request for information which relates to information which is, or if it existed would be, contained in a transferred public record, and
  (b) either of the conditions in subsection (2) is satisfied in relation to any of that information,
  that authority shall, within the period for complying with section 1(1), send a copy of the request to the responsible authority.

(2) The conditions referred to in subsection (1)(b) are—
  (a) that the duty to confirm or deny is expressed to be excluded only by a provision of Part II not specified in subsection (3) of section 2, and
  (b) that the information is exempt information only by virtue of a provision of Part II not specified in that subsection.

(3) On receiving the copy, the responsible authority shall, within such time as is reasonable in all the circumstances, inform the appropriate records authority of the determination required by virtue of subsection (3) or (4) of section 66.

(4) In this Act 'transferred public record' means a public record which has been transferred—
  (a) to the Public Record Office,
  (b) to another place of deposit appointed by the Lord Chancellor under the Public Records Act 1958, or
  (c) to the Public Record Office of Northern Ireland.

(5) In this Act—
  'appropriate records authority', in relation to a transferred public record means—
    (a) in a case falling within subsection (4)(a), the Public Record Office,
    (b) in a case falling within subsection (4)(b), the Lord Chancellor, and
    (c) in a case falling within subsection (4)(c), the Public Record Office of Northern Ireland;
  'responsible authority', in relation to a transferred public record, means—
  (a) in the case of a record transferred as mentioned in subsection (4)(a) or (b) from a government department in the charge of a Minister of the Crown, the Minister of the Crown who appears to the Lord Chancellor to be primarily concerned,
  (b) in the case of a record transferred as mentioned in subsection (4)(a) or (b) from any other person, the person who appears to the Lord Chancellor to be primarily concerned,
  (c) in the case of a record transferred to the Public Record Office of Northern Ireland from a government department in the charge of a Minister of the Crown, the Minister of the Crown who appears to the appropriate Northern Ireland Minister to be primarily concerned,
  (d) in the case of a record transferred to the Public Record Office of Northern

Ireland from a Northern Ireland department, the Northern Ireland Minister who appears to the appropriate Northern Ireland Minister to be primarily concerned, or

(e) in the case of a record transferred to the Public Record Office of Northern Ireland from any other person, the person who appears to the appropriate Northern Ireland Minister to be primarily concerned.

16. Duty to provide advice and assistance

(1) It shall be the duty of a public authority to provide advice and assistance, so far as it would be reasonable to expect the authority to do so, to persons who propose to make, or have made, requests for information to it.

(2) Any public authority which, in relation to the provision of advice or assistance in any case, conforms with the code of practice under section 45 is to be taken to comply with the duty imposed by subsection (1) in relation to that case.

Refusal of request

17. Refusal of request

(1) A public authority which, in relation to any request for information, is to any extent relying on a claim that any provision of Part II relating to the duty to confirm or deny is relevant to the request or on a claim that information is exempt information must, within the time for complying with section 1(1), give the applicant a notice which—

(a) states that fact,

(b) specifies the exemption in question, and

(c) states (if that would not otherwise be apparent) why the exemption applies.

(2) Where—

(a) in relation to any request for information, a public authority is, as respects any information, relying on a claim—

(i) that any provision of Part II which relates to the duty to confirm or deny and is not specified in section 2(3) is relevant to the request, or

(ii) that the information is exempt information only by virtue of a provision not specified in section 2(3), and

(b) at the time when the notice under subsection (1) is given to the applicant, the public authority (or, in a case falling within section 66(3) or (4), the responsible authority) has not yet reached a decision as to the application of subsection (1)(b) or (2)(b) of section 2,

the notice under subsection (1) must indicate that no decision as to the application of that provision has yet been reached and must contain an estimate of the date by which the authority expects that such a decision will have been reached.

(3) A public authority which, in relation to any request for information, is to any extent relying on a claim that subsection (1)(b) or (2)(b) of section 2 applies must, either in the notice under subsection (1) or in a separate notice given within such time as is reasonable in the circumstances, state the reasons for claiming—

(a) that, in all the circumstances of the case, the public interest in maintaining the exclusion of the duty to confirm or deny outweights the public interest in disclosing whether the authority holds the information, or

(b) that, in all the circumstances of the case, the public interest in maintaining the exemption outweighs the public interest in disclosing the information.

(4) A public authority is not obliged to make a statement under subsection (1)(c) or (3) if, or to the extent that, the statement would involve the disclosure of information which would itself be exempt information.

(5) A public authority which, in relation to any request for information, is relying on a claim that section 12 or 14 applies must, within the time for complying with section 1(1), give the applicant a notice stating that fact.

(6) Subsection (5) does not apply where—

(a) the public authority is relying on a claim that section 14 applies,

(b) the authority has given the applicant a notice, in relation to a previous request for information, stating that it is relying on such a claim, and

(c) it would in all the circumstances be unreasonable to expect the authority to serve a further notice under subsection (5) in relation to the current request.

(7) A notice under subsection (1), (3) or (5) must—

(a) contain particulars of any procedure provided by the public authority for dealing with complaints about the handling of requests for information or state that the authority does not provide such a procedure, and

(b) contain particulars of the right conferred by section 50.

The Information Commissioner and the Information Tribunal

18. The Information Commissioner and the Information Tribunal

(1) The Data Protection Commissioner shall be known instead as the Information Commissioner.

(2) The Data Protection Tribunal shall be known instead as the Information Tribunal.

(3) In this Act—

(a) the Information Commissioner is referred to as 'the Commissioner', and

(b) the Information Tribunal is referred to as 'the Tribunal'.

(4) Schedule 2 (which makes provision consequential on subsections (1) and (2) and amendments of the Data Protection Act 1998 relating to the extension by this Act of the functions of the Commissioner and the Tribunal) has effect.

(5) If the person who held office as Data Protection Commissioner immediately before the day on which this Act is passed remains in office as Information Commissioner at the end of the period of two years beginning with that day, he shall vacate his office at the end of that period.

(6) Subsection (5) does not prevent the re-appointment of a person whose appointment is terminated by that subsection.

(7) In the application of paragraph 2(4)(b) and (5) of Schedule 5 to the Data Protection Act 1998 (Commissioner not to serve for more than fifteen years and not to be appointed, except in special circumstances, for a third or subsequent term) to anything done after the passing of this Act, there shall be left out of account any term of office served by virtue of an appointment made before the passing of this Act.

Publication schemes

19. Publication schemes

(1) It shall be the duty of every public authority—
   (a) to adopt and maintain a scheme which relates to the publication of information by the authority and is approved by the Commissioner (in this Act referred to as a 'publication scheme'),
   (b) to publish information in accordance with its publication scheme, and
   (c) from time to time to review its publication scheme.

(2) A publication scheme must—
   (a) specify classes of information which the public authority publishes or intends to publish,
   (b) specify the manner in which information of each class is, or is intended to be, published, and
   (c) specify whether the material is, or is intended to be, available to the public free of charge or on payment.

(3) In adopting or reviewing a publication scheme, a public authority shall have regard to the public interest—
   (a) in allowing public access to information held by the authority, and
   (b) in the publication of reasons for decisions made by the authority.

(4) A public authority shall publish its publication scheme in such manner as it thinks fit.

(5) The Commissioner may, when approving a scheme, provide that his approval is to expire at the end of a specified period.

(6) Where the Commissioner has approved the publication scheme of any public authority, he may at any time give notice to the public authority revoking his approval of the scheme as from the end of the period of six months beginning with the day on which the notice is given.

(7) Where the Commissioner—
   (a) refuses to approve a proposed publication scheme, or
   (b) revokes his approval of a publication scheme, he must give the public authority a statement of his reasons for doing so.

20. Model publication schemes

(1) The Commissioner may from time to time approve, in relation to public authorities falling within particular classes, model publication schemes prepared by him or by other persons.

(2) Where a public authority falling within the class to which an approved model scheme relates adopts such a scheme without modification, no further approval of the Commissioner is required so long as the model scheme remains approved; and where such an authority adopts such a scheme with modifications, the approval of the Commissioner is required only in relation to the modifications.

(3) The Commissioner may, when approving a model publication scheme, provide that his approval is to expire at the end of a specified period.

(4) Where the Commissioner has approved a model publication scheme, he may at any time publish, in such manner as he thinks fit, a notice revoking his approval of the scheme as from the end of the period of six months begining with the day on which the notice is published.

(5) Where the Commissioner refuses to approve a proposed model publication scheme on the application of any person, he must give the person who applied for approval of the scheme a statement of the reasons for his refusal.

(6) Where the Commissioner refuses to approve any modifications under subsection (2), he must give the public authority a statement of the reasons for his refusal.

(7) Where the Commissioner revokes his approval of a model publication scheme, he must include in the notice under subsection (4) a statement of his reasons for doing so.

PART II
EXEMPT INFORMATION

21. Information accessible to applicant by other means

(1) Information which is reasonably accessible to the applicant otherwise than under section 1 is exempt information.

(2) For the purposes of subsection (1)—
  (a) information may be reasonably accessible to the applicant even though it is accessible only on payment, and
  (b) information is to be taken to be reasonably accessible to the applicant if it is information which the public authority or any other person is obliged by or under any enactment to communicate (otherwise than by making the information available for inspection) to members of the public on request, whether free of charge or on payment.

(3) For the purposes of subsection (1), information which is held by a public authority and does not fall within subsection (2)(b) is not to be regarded as reasonably accessible to the applicant merely because the information is available from the public authority itself on request, unless the information is made available in accordance with the authority's publication scheme and any payment required is specified in, or determined in accordance with, the scheme.

22. Information intended for future publication

(1) Information is exempt information if—
  (a) the information is held by the public authority with a view to its publication, by the authority or any other person, at some future date (whether determined or not),
  (b) the information was already held with a view to such publication at the time when the request for information was made, and
  (c) it is reasonable in all the circumstances that the information should be withheld from disclosure until the date referred to in paragraph (a).

(2) The duty to confirm or deny does not arise if, or to the extent that, compliance with section 1(1)(a) would involve the disclosure of any information (whether or not already recorded) which falls within subsection (1).

23. Information supplied by, or relating to, bodies dealing with seurity matters

(1) Information held by a public authority is exempt information if it was directly or indirectly supplied to the public authority by, or relates to, any of the bodies specified in subsection (3).

(2) A certificate signed by a Minister of the Crown certifying that the information to which it applies was directly or indirectly supplied by, or relates to, any of the bodies specified in subsection (3) shall, subject to section 60, be conclusive evidence of that fact.

(3) The bodies referred to in subsections (1) and (2) are—

(a) the Security Service,

(b) the Secret Intelligence Service,

(c) the Government Communications Headquarters,

(d) the special forces,

(e) the Tribunal established under section 65 of the Regulation of Investigatory Powers Act 2000,

(f) the Tribunal established under section 7 of the Interception of Communications Act 1985,

(g) the Tribunal established under section 5 of the Security Services Act 1989,

(h) the Tribunal established under section 9 of the Intelligence Services Act 1994,

(i) the Security Vetting Appeals Panel,

(j) the Security Commission,

(k) the National Criminal Intelligence Service, and

(l) the Service Authority for the National Criminal Intelligence Service.

(4) In subsection (3)(c) 'the Government Communications Headquarters' includes any unit or part of a unit of the armed forces of the Crown which is for the time being required by the Secretary of State to assist the Government Communications Headquarters in carrying out its functions.

(5) The duty to confirm or deny does not arise if, or to the extent that, compliance with section 1(1)(a) would involve the disclosure of any information (whether or not already recorded) which was directly or indirectly supplied to the public authority by, or relates to, any of the bodies specified in subsection (3).

24. National security

(1) Information which does not fall within section 23(1) is exempt information if exemption from section 1(1)(b) is required for the purpose of safeguarding national security.

(2) The duty to confirm or deny does not arise if, or to the extent that, exemption from section 1(1)(a) is required for the purpose of safeguarding national security.

(3) A certificate signed by a Minister of the Crown certifying that exemption from section 1(1)(b), or from section 1(1)(a) and (b), is, or at any time was, required for the purpose of safeguarding national security shall, subject to section 60, be conclusive evidence of that fact.

(4) A certificate under subsection (3) may identify the information to which it applies by means of a general description and may be expressed to have prospective effect.

25. Certificates under ss. 23 and 24: supplementary provisions

(1) A document purporting to be a certificate under section 23(2) or 24(3) shall be received in evidence and deemed to be such a certificate unless the contrary is proved.

(2) A document which purports to be certified by or on behalf of a Minister of the Crown as a true copy of a certificate issued by that Minister under section 23(2) or

24(3) shall in any legal proceedings be evidence (or. in Scotland, sufficient evidence) of that certificate.

(3) The power conferred by section 23(2) or 24(3) on a Minister of the Crown shall not be exercisable except by a Minister who is a member of the Cabinet or by the Attorney General, the Advocate General for Scotland or the Attorney General for Northern Ireland.

26. Defence

(1) Information is exempt information if its disclosure under this Act would, or would be likely to, prejudice—
   (a) the defence of the British Islands or of any colony, or
   (b) the capability, effectiveness or security of any relevant forces.
(2) In subsection (1)(b) 'relevant forces' means—
   (a) the armed forces of the Crown, and
   (b) any forces co-operating with those forces,
   or any part of any of those forces.
(3) The duty to confirm or deny does not arise if, or to the extent that, compliance with section 1(1)(a) would, or would be likely to, prejudice any of the matters mentioned in subsection (1).

27. International relations

(1) Information is exempt information if its disclosure under this Act would, or would be likely to, prejudice—
   (a) relations between the United Kingdom and any other State,
   (b) relations between the United Kingdom and any international organisation or international court,
   (c) the interests of the United Kingdom abroad, or
   (d) the promotion or protection by the United Kingdom of its interests abroad.
(2) Information is also exempt information if it is confidential information obtained from a State other than the United Kingdom or from an international organisation or international court.
(3) For the purposes of this section, any information obtained from a State, organisation or court is confidential at any time while the terms on which it was obtained require it to be held in confidence or while the circumstances in which it was obtained make it reasonable for the State, organisation or court to expect that it will be so held.
(4) The duty to confirm or deny does not arise if, or to the extent that, compliance with section 1(1)(a)—
   (a) would, or would be likely to, prejudice any of the matters mentioned in subsection (1), or
   (b) would involve the disclosure of any information (whether or not already recorded) which is confidential information obtained from a State other than the United Kingdom or from an international organisation or international court.
(5) In this section—
   'international court' means any international court which is not an international organisation and which is established—

(a) by a resolution of an international organisation of which the United Kingdom is a member, or

(b) by an international agreement to which the United Kingdom is a party;

'international organisation' means any international organisation whose members include any two or more States, or any organ of such an organisation;

'State' includes the government of any State and any organ of its government, and references to a State other than the United Kingdom include references to any territory outside the United Kingdom.

28. Relations within the United Kingdom

(1) Information is exempt information if its disclosure under this Act would, or would be likely to, prejudice relations between any administration in the United Kingdom and any other such administration.

(2) In subsection (1) 'administration in the United Kingdom' means—
(a) the government of the United Kingdom,
(b) the Scottish Administration,
(c) the Executive Committee of the Northern Ireland Assembly, or
(d) the National Assembly for Wales.

(3) The duty to confirm or deny does not arise if, or to the extent that, compliance with section 1(1)(a) would, or would be likely to, prejudice any of the matters mentioned in subsection (1).

29. The economy

(1) Information is exempt information if its disclosure under this Act would, or would be likely to, prejudice—
(a) the economic interests of the United Kingdom or of any part of the United Kingdom, or
(b) the financial interests of any administration in the United Kingdom, as defined by section 28(2).

(2) The duty to confirm or deny does not arise if, or to the extent that, compliance with section 1(1)(a) would, or would be likely to, prejudice any of the matters mentioned in subsection (1).

30. Investigations and proceedings conducted by public authorities

(1) Information held by a public authority is exempt information if it has at any time been held by the authority for the purposes of—
(a) any investigation which the public authority has a duty to conduct with a view to it being ascertained—
(i) whether a person should be charged with an offence, or
(ii) whether a person charged with an offence is guilty of it,
(b) any investigation which is conducted by the authority and in the circumstances may lead to a decision by the authority to institute criminal proceedings which the authority has power to conduct, or
(c) any criminal proceedings which the authority has power to conduct.

(2) Information held by a public authority is exempt information if—
(a) it was obtained or recorded by the authority for the purposes of its functions relating to—

      (i) investigations falling within subsection (1)(a) or (b),

      (ii) criminal proceedings which the authority has power to conduct,

      (iii) investigations (other than investigations falling within subsection (1)(a) or (b)) which are conducted by the authority for any of the purposes specified in section 31(2) and either by virtue of Her Majesty's prerogative or by virtue of powers conferred by or under any enactment, or

      (iv) civil proceedings which are brought by or on behalf of the authority and arise out of such investigations, and

   (b) it relates to the obtaining of information from confidential sources.

(3) The duty to confirm or deny does not arise in relation to information which is (or if it were held by the public authority would be) exempt information by virtue of subsection (1) or (2).

(4) In relation to the institution or conduct of criminal proceedings or the power to conduct them, references in subsection (1)(b) or (c) and subsection (2)(a) to the public authority include references—

   (a) to any officer of the authority,

   (b) in the case of a government department other than a Northern Ireland department, to the Minister of the Crown in charge of the department, and

   (c) in the case of a Northern Ireland department, to the Northern Ireland Minister in charge of the department.

(5) In this section—

'criminal proceedings' includes—

   (a) proceedings before a court-martial constituted under the Army Act 1955, the Air Force Act 1955 or the Naval Discipline Act 1957 [. . .]*

   (b) proceedings on dealing summarily with a charge under the Army Act 1955 or the Air Force Act 1955 or on summary trial under the Naval Discipline Act 1957,

   (c) proceedings before a court established by section 83ZA of the Army Act 1955, section 83ZA of the Air Force Act 1955 or section 52FF of the Naval Discipline Act 1957 (summary appeal courts),

   (d) proceedings before the Courts-Martial Appeal Court, and

   (e) proceedings before a Standing Civilian Court;

'offence' includes any offence under the Army Act 1955, the Air Force Act 1955 or the Naval Discipline Act 1957.

(6) In the application of this section to Scotland—

   (a) in subsection (1)(b), for the words from 'a decision' to the end there is substituted 'a decision by the authority to make a report to the procurator fiscal for the purpose of enabling him to determine whether criminal proceedings should be instituted',

   (b) in subsection (1)(c) and (2)(a)(ii) for 'which the authority has power to conduct' there is substituted 'which have been instituted in consequence of a report made by the authority to the procurator fiscal', and

   (c) for any reference to a person being charged with an offence there is substituted a reference to the person being prosecuted for the offence.

---

* Words repealed for Armed Forces Act (2001, C. A), Sch 7(1).

31. Law enforcement

(1) Information which is not exempt information by virtue of section 30 is exempt information if its disclosure under this Act would, or would be likely to, prejudice—

(a) the prevention or detection of crime,

(b) the apprehension or prosecution of offenders,

(c) the administration of justice,

(d) the assessment or collection of any tax or duty or of any imposition of a similar nature,

(e) the operation of the immigration controls,

(f) the maintenance of security and good order in prisons or in other institutions where persons are lawfully detained,

(g) the exercise by any public authority of its functions for any of the purposes specified in subsection (2),

(h) any civil proceedings which are brought by or on behalf of a public authority and arise out of an investigation conducted, for any of the purposes specified in subsection (2), by or on behalf of the authority by virtue of Her Majesty's prerogative or by virtue of powers conferred by or under an enactment, or

(i) any inquiry held under the Fatal Accidents and Sudden Deaths Inquiries (Scotland) Act 1976 to the extent that the inquiry arises out of an investigation conducted, for any of the purposes specified in subsection (2), by or on behalf of the authority by virtue of Her Majesty's prerogative or by virtue of powers conferred by or under an enactment.

(2) The purposes referred to in subsection (1)(g) to (i) are—

(a) the purpose of ascertaining whether any person has failed to comply with the law,

(b) the purpose of ascertaining whether any person is responsible for any conduct which is improper,

(c) the purpose of ascertaining whether circumstances which would justify regulatory action in pursuance of any enactment exist or may arise,

(d) the purpose of ascertaining a person's fitness or competence in relation to the management of bodies corporate or in relation to any profession or other activity which he is, or seeks to become, authorised to carry on,

(e) the purpose of ascertaining the cause of an accident,

(f) the purpose of protecting charities against misconduct or mismanagement (whether by trustees or other persons) in their administration,

(g) the purpose of protecting the property of charities from loss or misapplication,

(h) the purpose of recovering the property of charities,

(i) the purpose of securing the health, safety and welfare of persons at work, and

(j) the purpose of protecting persons other than persons at work against risk to health or safety arising out of or in connection with the actions of persons at work.

(3) The duty to confirm or deny does not arise if, or to the extent that, compliance with section 1(1)(a) would, or would be likely to, prejudice any of the matters mentioned in subsection (1).

32. Court records, etc.

(1) Information held by a public authority is exempt information if it is held only by virtue of being contained in—

(a) any document filed with, or otherwise placed in the custody of, a court for the purposes of proceedings in a particular cause or matter,

(b) any document served upon, or by, a public authority for the purposes of proceedings in a particular cause or matter, or

(c) any document created by—

(i) a court, or

(ii) a member of the administrative staff of a court,

for the purposes of proceedings in a particular cause or matter.

(2) Information held by a public authority is exempt information if it is held only by virtue of being contained in—

(a) any document placed in the custody of a person conducting an inquiry or arbitration, for the purposes of the inquiry or arbitration, or

(b) any document created by a person conducting an inquiry or arbitration, for the purposes of the inquiry or arbitration.

(3) The duty to confirm or deny does not arise in relation to information which is (or if it were held by the public authority would be) exempt information by virtue of this section.

(4) In this section—

(a) 'court' includes any tribunal or body exercising the judicial power of the State,

(b) 'proceedings in a particular cause or matter' includes any inquest or post-mortem examination,

(c) 'inquiry' means any inquiry or hearing held under any provision contained in, or made under, an enactment, and

(d) except in relation to Scotland, 'arbitration' means any arbitration to which Part I of the Arbitration Act 1996 applies.

33. Audit functions

(1) This section applies to any public authority which has functions in relation to—

(a) the audit of the accounts of other public authorities, or

(b) the examination of the economy, efficiency and effectiveness with which other public authorities use their resources in discharging their functions.

(2) Information held by a public authority to which this section applies is exempt information if its disclosure would, or would be likely to, prejudice the exercise of any of the authority's functions in relation to any of the matters referred to in subsection (1).

(3) The duty to confirm or deny does not arise in relation to a public authority to which this section applies if, or to the extent that, compliance with section 1(1)(a) would, or would be likely to, prejudice the exercise of any of the authority's functions in relation to any of the matters referred to in subsection (1).

34. Parliamentary privilege

(1) Information is exempt information if exemption from section 1(1)(b) is required for the purpose of avoiding an infringement of the privileges of either House of Parliament.

(2) The duty to confirm or deny does not apply if, or to the extent that, exemption from section 1(1)(a) is required for the purpose of avoiding an infringement of the privileges of either House of Parliament.

(3) A certificate signed by the appropriate authority certifying that exemption from section 1(1)(b), or from section 1(1)(a) and (b), is, or at any time was, required for the

purpose of avoiding an infringement of the privileges of either House of Parliament shall be conclusive evidence of that fact.

(4) In subsection (3) 'the appropriate authority' means—

    (a) in relation to the House of Commons, the Speaker of that House, and

    (b) in relation to the House of Lords, the Clerk of the Parliaments.

35. Formulation of government policy, etc.

(1) Information held by a government department or by the National Assembly for Wales is exempt information if it relates to—

    (a) the formulation or development of government policy,

    (b) Ministerial communications,

    (c) the provision of advice by any of the Law Officers or any request for the provision of such advice, or

    (d) the operation of any Ministerial private office.

(2) Once a decision as to government policy has been taken, any statistical information used to provide an informed background to the taking of the decision is not to be regarded—

    (a) for the purposes of subsection (1)(a), as relating to the formulation or development of government policy, or

    (b) for the purposes of subsection (1)(b), as relating to Ministerial communications.

(3) The duty to confirm or deny does not arise in relation to information which is (or if it were held by the public authority would be) exempt information by virtue of subsection (1).

(4) In making any determination required by section 2(1)(b) or (2)(b) in relation to information which is exempt information by virtue of subsection (1)(a), regard shall be had to the particular public interest in the disclosure of factual information which has been used, or is intended to be used, to provide an informed background to decision-taking.

(5) In this section—

'government policy' includes the policy of the Executive Committee of the Northern Ireland Assembly and the policy of the National Assembly for Wales;

'the Law Officers' means the Attorney General, the Solicitor General, the Advocate General for Scotland, the Lord Advocate, the Solicitor General for Scotland and the Attorney General for Northern Ireland;

'Ministerial communications' means any communications—

    (a) between Ministers of the Crown,

    (b) between Northern Ireland Ministers, including Northern Ireland junior Ministers, or

    (c) between Assembly Secretaries, including the Assembly First Secretary,

and includes, in particular, proceedings of the Cabinet or of any committee of the Cabinet, proceedings of the Executive Committee of the Northern Ireland Assembly, and proceedings of the executive committee of the National Assembly for Wales;

'Ministerial private office' means any part of a government department which provides personal administrative support to a Minister of the Crown, to a Northern Ireland Minister or a Northern Ireland junior Minister or any part of the administration of the National Assembly for Wales providing personal administrative support to the Assembly First Secretary or an Assembly Secretary;

'Northern Ireland junior Minister' means a member of the Northern Ireland Assembly appointed as a junior Minister under section 19 of the Northern Ireland Act 1998.

36. Prejudice to effective conduct of public affairs

(1) This section applies to—
    (a) information which is held by a government department or by the National Assembly for Wales and is not exempt information by virtue of section 35, and
    (b) information which is held by any other public authority.

(2) Information to which this section applies is exempt information if, in the reasonable opinion of a qualified person, disclosure of the information under this Act—
    (a) would, or would be likely to, prejudice—
        (i) the maintenance of the convention of the collective responsibility of Ministers of the Crown, or
        (ii) the work of the Executive Committee of the Northern Ireland Assembly, or
        (iii) the work of the executive committee of the National Assembly for Wales,
    (b) would, or would be likely to, inhibit—
        (i) the free and frank provision of advice, or
        (ii) the free and frank exchange of views for the purposes of deliberation, or
    (c) would otherwise prejudice, or would be likely otherwise to prejudice, the effective conduct of public affairs.

(3) The duty to confirm or deny does not arise in relation to information to which this section applies (or would apply if held by the public authority) if, or to the extent that, in the reasonable opinion of a qualified person, compliance with section 1(1)(a) would, or would be likely to, have any of the effects mentioned in subsection (2).

(4) In relation to statistical information, subsections (2) and (3) shall have effect with the omission of the words 'in the reasonable opinion of a qualified person'.

(5) In subsections (2) and (3) 'qualified person'—
    (a) in relation to information held by a government department in the charge of a Minister of the Crown, means any Minister of the Crown,
    (b) in relation to information held by a Northern Ireland department, means the Northern Ireland Minister in charge of the department,
    (c) in relation to information held by any other government department, means the commissioners or other person in charge of that department,
    (d) in relation to information held by the House of Commons, means the Speaker of that House,
    (e) in relation to information held by the House of Lords, means the Clerk of the Parliaments,
    (f) in relation to information held by the Northern Ireland Assembly, means the Presiding Officer,
    (g) in relation to information held by the National Assembly for Wales, means the Assembly First Secretary,
    (h) in relation to information held by any Welsh public authority other than the Auditor General for Wales, means—
        (i) the public authority, or
        (ii) any officer or employee of the authority authorised by the Assembly First Secretary,

(i) in relation to information held by the National Audit Office, means the Comptroller and Auditor General,

(j) in relation to information held by the Northern Ireland Audit Office, means the Comptroller and Auditor General for Northern Ireland,

(k) in relation to information held by the Auditor General for Wales, means the Auditor General for Wales.

(l) in relation to information held by any Northern Ireland public authority other than the Northern Ireland Audit Office, means—

    (i) the public authority, or

    (ii) any officer or employee of the authority authorised by the First Minister and deputy First Minister in Northern Ireland acting jointly,

(m) in relation to information held by the Greater London Authority, means the Mayor of London,

(n) in relation to information held by a functional body within the meaning of the Greater London Authority Act 1999, means the chairman of that functional body, and

(o) in relation to information held by any public authority not falling within any of paragraphs (a) to (n), means—

    (i) a Minister of the Crown,

    (ii) the public authority, if authorised for the purposes of this section by a Minister of the Crown, or

    (iii) any officer or employee of the public authority who is authorised for the purposes of this section by a Minister of the Crown.

(6) Any authorisation for the purposes of this section—

    (a) may relate to a specified person or to persons falling within a specified class,

    (b) may be general or limited to particular classes of case, and

    (c) may be granted subject to conditions.

(7) A certificate signed by the qualified person referred to in subsection (5)(d) or (e) above certifying that in his reasonable opinion—

    (a) disclosure of information held by either House of Parliament, or

    (b) compliance with section 1(1)(a) by either House, would, or would be likely to, have any of the effects mentioned in subsection (2) shall be conclusive evidence of that fact.

37. Communications with Her Majesty, etc. and honours

(1) Information is exempt information if it relates to—

    (a) communications with Her Majesty, with other members of the Royal Family or with the Royal Household, or

    (b) the conferring by the Crown of any honour or dignity.

(2) The duty to confirm or deny does not arise in relation to information which is (or if it were held by the public authority would be) exempt information by virtue of subsection (1).

38. Health and safety

(1) Information is exempt information if its disclosure under this Act would, or would be likely to—

    (a) endanger the physical or mental health of any individual, or

    (b) endanger the safety of any individual.

(2) The duty to confirm or deny does not arise if, or to the extent that, compliance with section 1(1)(a) would, or would be likely to, have either of the effects mentioned in subsection (1).

39. Environmental information

(1) Information is exempt information if the public authority holding it—
  (a) is obliged by environmental information regulations to make the information available to the public in accordance with the regulations, or
  (b) would be so obliged but for any exemption contained in the regulations.

(1A) In subsection (1) 'environmental information regulations' means—
  (a) regulations made under section 74, or
  (b) regulations made under section 2(2) of the European Communities Act 1972 for the purpose of implementing Community obligations public access to, and the dissemination of, information on the environment.

(2) The duty to confirm or deny does not arise in relation to information which is (or if it were held by the public authority would be) exempt information by virtue of subsection (1).

(3) Subsection (1)(a) does not limit the generality of section 21(1).

40. Personal information

(1) Any information to which a request for information relates is exempt information if it constitutes personal data of which the applicant is the data subject.

(2) Any information to which a request for information relates is also exempt information if—
  (a) it constitutes personal data which do not fall within subsection (1), and
  (b) either the first or the second condition below is satisfied.

(3) The first condition is—
  (a) in a case where the information falls within any of paragraphs (a) to (d) of the definition of 'data' in section 1(1) of the Data Protection Act 1998, that the disclosure of the information to a member of the public otherwise than under this Act would contravene—
    (i) any of the data protection principles, or
    (ii) section 10 of that Act (right to prevent processing likely to cause damage or distress), and
  (b) in any other case, that the disclosure of the information to a member of the public otherwise than under this Act would contravene any of the data protection principles if the exemptions in section 33A(1) of the Data Protection Act 1998 (which relate to manual data held by public authorities) were disregarded.

(4) The second condition is that by virtue of any provision of Part IV of the Data Protection Act 1998 the information is exempt from section 7(1)(c) of that Act (data subject's right of access to personal data).

(5) The duty to confirm or deny—
  (a) does not arise in relation to information which is (or if it were held by the public authority would be) exempt information by virtue of subsection (1), and
  (b) does not arise in relation to other information if or to the extent that either—
    (i) the giving to a member of the public of the confirmation or denial that would have to be given to comply with section 1(1)(a) would (apart from this Act) contravene any of the data protection principles or section 10 of the

Data Protection Act 1998 or would do so if the exemptions in section 33A(1) of that Act were disregarded, or

    (ii) by virtue of any provision of Part IV of the Data Protection Act 1998 the information is exempt from section 7(1)(a) of that Act (data subject's right to be informed whether personal data being processed).

(6) In determining for the purposes of this section whether anything done before 24 October 2007 would contravene any of the data protection principles, the exemptions in Part III of Schedule 8 to the Data Protection Act 1998 shall be disregarded.

(7) In this section—

'the data protection principles' means the principles set out in Part I of Schedule 1 to the Data Protection Act 1998, as read subject to Part II of that Schedule and section 27(1) of that Act;

'data subject' has the same meaning as in section 1(1) of that Act;

'personal data' has the same meaning as in section 1(1) of that Act.

41. Information provided in confidence

(1) Information is exempt information if—

    (a) it was obtained by the public authority from any other person (including another public authority), and

    (b) the disclosure of the information to the public (otherwise than under this Act) by the public authority holding it would constitute a breach of confidence actionable by that or any other person.

(2) The duty to confirm or deny does not arise if, or to the extent that, the confirmation or denial that would have to be given to comply with section 1(1)(a) would (apart from this Act) constitute an actionable breach of confidence.

42. Legal professional privilege

(1) Information in respect of which a claim to legal professional privilege or, in Scotland, to confidentiality of communications could be maintained in legal proceedings is exempt information.

(2) The duty to confirm or deny does not arise if, or to the extent that, compliance with section 1(1)(a) would involve the disclosure of any information (whether or not already recorded) in respect of which such a claim could be maintained in legal proceedings.

43. Commercial interests

(1) Information is exempt information if it constitutes a trade secret.

(2) Information is exempt information if its disclosure under this Act would, or would be likely to, prejudice the commercial interests of any person (including the public authority holding it).

(3) The duty to confirm or deny does not arise if, or to the extent that, compliance with section 1(1)(a) would, or would be likely to, prejudice the interests mentioned in subsection (2).

44. Prohibitions on disclosure

(1) Information is exempt information if its disclosure (otherwise than under this Act) by the public authority holding it—

    (a) is prohibited by or under any enactment,

    (b) is incompatible with any Community obligation, or

    (c) would constitute or be punishable as a contempt of court.

(2) The duty to confirm or deny does not arise if the confirmation or denial that would have to be given to comply with section 1(1)(a) would (apart from this Act) fall within any of paragraphs (a) to (c) of subsection (1).

PART III
GENERAL FUNCTIONS OF SECRETARY OF STATE, LORD CHANCELLOR AND INFORMATION COMMISSIONER

45. Issue of code of practice by Secretary of State

(1) The Secretary of State shall issue, and may from time to time revise, a code of practice providing guidance to public authorities as to the practice which it would, in his opinion, be desirable for them to follow in connection with the discharge of the authorities' functions under Part I.

(2) The code of practice must, in particular, include provision relating to—
   (a) the provision of advice and assistance by public authorities to persons who propose to make, or have made, requests for information to them,
   (b) the transfer of requests by one public authority to another public authority by which the information requested is or may be held,
   (c) consultation with persons to whom the information requested relates or persons whose interests are likely to be affected by the disclosure of information,
   (d) the inclusion in contracts entered into by public authorities of terms relating to the disclosure of information, and
   (e) the provision by public authorities of procedures for dealing with complaints about the handling by them of requests for information.

(3) The code may make different provision for different public authorities.

(4) Before issuing or revising any code under this section, the Secretary of State shall consult the Commissioner.

(5) The Secretary of State shall lay before each House of Parliament any code or revised code made under this section.

46. Issue of code of practice by Lord Chancellor

(1) The Lord Chancellor shall issue, and may from time to time revise, a code of practice providing guidance to relevant authorities as to the practice which it would, in his opinion, be desirable for them to follow in connection with the keeping, management and destruction of their records.

(2) For the purpose of facilitating the performance by the Public Record Office, the Public Record Office of Northern Ireland and other public authorities of their functions under this Act in relation to records which are public records for the purposes of the Public Records Act 1958 or the Public Records Act (Northern Ireland) 1923, the code may also include guidance as to—
   (a) the practice to be adopted in relation to the transfer of records under section 3(4) of the Public Records Act 1958 or section 3 of the Public Records Act (Northern Ireland) 1923, and
   (b) the practice of reviewing records before they are transferred under those provisions.

(3) In exercising his functions under this section, the Lord Chancellor shall have regard

to the public interest in allowing public access to information held by relevant authorities.

(4) The code may make different provision for different relevant authorities.

(5) Before issuing or revising any code under this section the Lord Chancellor shall consult—

(a) the Secretary of State,

(b) the Commissioner, and

(c) in relation to Northern Ireland, the appropriate Northern Ireland Minister.

(6) The Lord Chancellor shall lay before each House of Parliament any code or revised code made under this section.

(7) In this section 'relevant authority' means—

(a) any public authority, and

(b) any office or body which is not a public authority but whose administrative and departmental records are public records for the purposes of the Public Records Act 1958 or the Public Records Act (Northern Ireland) 1923.

47. General functions of Commissioner

(1) It shall be the duty of the Commissioner to promote the following of good practice by public authorities and, in particular, so to perform his functions under this Act as to promote the observance by public authorities of—

(a) the requirements of this Act, and

(b) the provisions of the codes of practice under sections 45 and 46.

(2) The Commissioner shall arrange for the dissemination in such form and manner as he considers appropriate of such information as it may appear to him expedient to give to the public—

(a) about the operation of this Act,

(b) about good practice, and

(c) about other matters within the scope of his functions under this Act, and may give advice to any person as to any of those matters.

(3) The Commissioner may, with the consent of any public authority, assess whether that authority is following good practice.

(4) The Commissioner may charge such sums as he may with the consent of the Secretary of State determine for any services provided by the Commissioner under this section.

(5) The Commissioner shall from time to time as he considers appropriate—

(a) consult the Keeper of Public Records about the promotion by the Commissioner of the observance by public authorities of the provisions of the code of practice under section 46 in relation to records which are public records for the purposes of the Public Records Act 1958, and

(b) consult the Deputy Keeper of the Records of Northern Ireland about the promotion by the Commissioner of the observance by public authorities of those provisions in relation to records which are public records for the purposes of the Public Records Act (Northern Ireland) 1923.

(6) In this section 'good practice', in relation to a public authority, means such practice in the discharge of its functions under this Act as appears to the Commissioner to be desirable, and includes (but is not limited to) compliance with the requirements of this Act and the provisions of the codes of practice under sections 45 and 46.

48. Recommendations as to good practice

(1) If it appears to the Commissioner that the practice of a public authority in relation to the exercise of its functions under this Act does not conform with that proposed in the codes of practice under sections 45 and 46, he may give to the authority a recommendation (in this section referred to as a 'practice recommendation') specifying the steps which ought in his opinion to be taken for promoting such conformity.

(2) A practice recommendation must be given in writing and must refer to the particular provisions of the code of practice with which, in the Commissioner's opinion, the public authority's practice does not conform.

(3) Before giving to a public authority other than the Public Record Office a practice recommendation which relates to conformity with the code of practice under section 46 in respect of records which are public records for the purposes of the Public Records Act 1958, the Commissioner shall consult the Keeper of Public Records.

(4) Before giving to a public authority other than the Public Record Office of Northern Ireland a practice recommendation which relates to conformity with the code of practice under section 46 in respect of records which are public records for the purposes of the Public Records Act (Northern Ireland) 1923, the Commissioner shall consult the Deputy Keeper of the Records of Northern Ireland.

49. Reports to be laid before Parliament

(1) The Commissioner shall lay annually before each House of Parliament a general report on the exercise of his functions under this Act.

(2) The Commissioner may from time to time lay before each House of Parliament such other reports with respect to those functions as he thinks fit.

PART IV
ENFORCEMENT

50. Application for decision by Commissioner

(1) Any person (in this section referred to as 'the complainant') may apply to the Commissioner for a decision whether, in any specified respect, a request for information made by the complainant to a public authority has been dealt with in accordance with the requirements of Part I.

(2) On receiving an application under this section, the Commissioner shall make a decision unless it appears to him—

    (a) that the complainant has not exhausted any complaints procedure which is provided by the public authority in conformity with the code of practice under section 45,

    (b) that there has been undue delay in making the application,

    (c) that the application is frivolous or vexatious, or

    (d) that the application has been withdrawn or abandoned.

(3) Where the Commissioner has received an application under this section, he shall either—

    (a) notify the complainant that he has not made any decision under this section as a result of the application and of his grounds for not doing so, or

    (b) serve notice of his decision (in this Act referred to as a 'decision notice') on the complainant and the public authority.

(4) Where the Commissioner decides that a public authority—

    (a) has failed to communicate information, or to provide confirmation or denial, in a case where it is required to do so by section 1(1), or

    (b) has failed to comply with any of the requirements of sections 11 and 17, the decision notice must specify the steps which must be taken by the authority for complying with that requirement and the period within which they must be taken.

(5) A decision notice must contain particulars of the right of appeal conferred by section 57.

(6) Where a decision notice requires steps to be taken by the public authority within a specified period, the time specified in the notice must not expire before the end of the period within which an appeal can be brought against the notice and, if such an appeal is brought, no step which is affected by the appeal need be taken pending the determination or withdrawal of the appeal.

(7) This section has effect subject to section 53.

51. Information notices

(1) If the Commissioner—

    (a) has received an application under section 50, or

    (b) reasonably requires any information—

        (i) for the purpose of determining whether a public authority has complied or is complying with any of the requirements of Part I, or

        (ii) for the purpose of determining whether the practice of a public authority in relation to the exercise of its functions under this Act conforms with that proposed in the codes of practice under section 45 and 46,

he may serve the authority with a notice (in this Act referred to as 'an information notice') requiring it, within such time as is specified in the notice, to furnish the Commissioner, in such form as may be so specified, with such information relating to the application, to compliance with Part I or to conformity with the code of practice as is so specified.

(2) An information notice must contain—

    (a) in a case falling within subsection (1)(a), a statement that the Commissioner has received an application under section 50, or

    (b) in a case falling within subsection (1)(b), a statement—

        (i) that the Commissioner regards the specified information as relevant for either of the purposes referred to in subsection (1)(b), and

        (ii) of his reasons for regarding that information as relevant for that purpose.

(3) An information notice must also contain particulars of the right of appeal conferred by section 57.

(4) The time specified in an information notice must not expire before the end of the period within which an appeal can be brought against the notice and, if such an appeal is brought, the information need not be furnished pending the determination or withdrawal of the appeal.

(5) An authority shall not be required by virtue of this section to furnish the Commissioner with any information in respect of—

(a) any communication between a professional legal adviser and his client in connection with the giving of legal advice to the client with respect to his obligations, liabilities or rights under this Act, or

(b) any communication between a professional legal adviser and his client, or between such an adviser or his client and any other person, made in connection with or in contemplation of proceedings under or arising out of this Act (including proceedings before the Tribunal) and for the purposes of such proceedings.

(6) In subsection (5) references to the client of a professional legal adviser include references to any person representing such a client.

(7) The Commissioner may cancel an information notice by written notice to the authority on which it was served.

(8) In this section 'information' includes unrecorded information.

52. Enforcement notices

(1) If the Commissioner is satisfied that a public authority has failed to comply with any of the requirements of Part I, the Commissioner may serve the authority with a notice (in this Act referred to as 'an enforcement notice') requiring the authority to take, within such time as may be specified in the notice, such steps as may be so specified for complying with those requirements.

(2) An enforcement notice must contain—

(a) a statement of the requirement or requirements of Part I with which the Commissioner is satisfied that the public authority has failed to comply and his reasons for reaching that conclusion, and

(b) particulars of the right of appeal conferred by section 57.

(3) An enforcement notice must not require any of the provisions of the notice to be complied with before the end of the period within which an appeal can be brought against the notice and, if such an appeal is brought, the notice need not be complied with pending the determination or withdrawal of the appeal.

(4) The Commissioner may cancel an enforcement notice by written notice to the authority on which it was served.

(5) This section has effect subject to section 53.

53. Exception from duty to comply with decision notice or enforcement notice

(1) This section applies to a decision notice or enforcement notice which—

(a) is served on—

(i) a government department,

(ii) the National Assembly for Wales, or

(iii) any public authority designated for the purposes of this section by an order made by the Secretary of State, and

(b) relates to a failure, in respect of one or more requests for information—

(i) to comply with section 1(1)(a) in respect of information which falls within any provision of Part II stating that the duty to confirm or deny does not arise, or

(ii) to comply with section 1(1)(b) in respect of exempt information.

(2) A decision notice or enforcement notice to which this section applies shall cease to have effect if, not later than the twentieth working day following the effective date, the accountable person in relation to that authority gives the Commissioner a certificate signed by him stating that he has on reasonable grounds formed the opinion that, in respect of the request or requests concerned, there was no failure falling within subsection (1)(b).

(3) Where the accountable person gives a certificate to the Commissioner under subsection (2) he shall as soon as practicable thereafter lay a copy of the certificate before—

   (a) each House of Parliament,

   (b) the Northern Ireland Assembly, in any case where the certificate relates to a decision notice or enforcement notice which has been served on a Northern Ireland department or any Northern Ireland public authority, or

   (c) the National Assembly for Wales, in any case where the certificate relates to a decision notice or enforcement notice which has been served on the National Assembly for Wales or any Welsh public authority.

(4) In subsection (2) 'the effective date', in relation to a decision notice or enforcement notice, means—

   (a) the day on which the notice was given to the public authority, or

   (b) where an appeal under section 57 is brought, the day on which that appeal (or any further appeal arising out of it) is determined or withdrawn.

(5) Before making an order under subsection (1)(a)(iii), the Secretary of State shall—

   (a) if the order relates to a Welsh public authority, consult the National Assembly for Wales,

   (b) if the order relates to the Northern Ireland Assembly, consult the Presiding Officer of that Assembly, and

   (c) if the order relates to a Northern Ireland public authority, consult the First Minister and deputy First Minister in Northern Ireland.

(6) Where the accountable person gives a certificate to the Commissioner under subsection (2) in relation to a decision notice, the accountable person shall, on doing so or as soon as reasonably practicable after doing so, inform the person who is the complainant for the purposes of section 50 of the reasons for his opinion.

(7) The accountable person is not obliged to provide information under subsection (6) if, or to the extent that, compliance with that subsection would involve the disclosure of exempt information.

(8) In this section 'the accountable person'—

   (a) in relation to a Northern Ireland department or any Northern Ireland public authority, means the First Minister and deputy First Minister in Northern Ireland acting jointly,

   (b) in relation to the National Assembly for Wales or any Welsh public authority, means the Assembly First Secretary, and

   (c) in relation to any other public authority, means—

      (i) a Minister of the Crown who is a member of the Cabinet, or

      (ii) the Attorney General, the Advocate General for Scotland or the Attorney General for Northern Ireland.

(9) In this section 'working day' has the same meaning as in section 10.

54. Failure to comply with notice

(1) If a public authority has failed to comply with—
  (a) so much of a decision notice as requires steps to be taken,
  (b) an information notice, or
  (c) an enforcement notice,
  the Commissioner may certify in writing to the court that the public authority has failed to comply with that notice.
(2) For the purposes of this section, a public authority which, in purported compliance with an information notice—
  (a) makes a statement which it knows to be false in a material respect, or
  (b) recklessly makes a statement which is false in a material respect, is to be taken to have failed to comply with the notice.
(3) Where a failure to comply is certified under subsection (1), the court may inquire into the matter and, after hearing any witness who may be produced against or on behalf of the public authority, and after hearing any statement that may be offered in defence, deal with the authority as if it had committed a contempt of court.
(4) In this section 'the court' means the High Court or, in Scotland, the Court of Session.

55. Powers of entry and inspection

Schedule 3 (powers of entry and inspection) has effect.

56. No action against public authority

(1) This Act does not confer any right of action in civil proceedings in respect of any failure to comply with any duty imposed by or under this Act.
(2) Subsection (1) does not affect the powers of the Commissioner under section 54.

PART V
APPEALS

57. Appeal against notices served under Part IV

(1) Where a decision notice has been served, the complainant or the public authority may appeal to the Tribunal against the notice.
(2) A public authority on which an information notice or an enforcement notice has been served by the Commissioner may appeal to the Tribunal against the notice.
(3) In relation to a decision notice or enforcement notice which relates—
  (a) to information to which section 66 applies, and
  (b) to a matter which by virtue of subsection (3) or (4) of that section falls to be determined by the responsible authority instead of the appropriate records authority,
  subsections (1) and (2) shall have effect as if the reference to the public authority were a reference to the public authority or the responsible authority.

58. Determination of appeals

(1) If on an appeal under section 57 the Tribunal considers—
  (a) that the notice against which the appeal is brought is not in accordance with the law, or

(b) to the extent that the notice involved an exercise of discretion by the Commissioner, that he ought to have exercised his discretion differently, the Tribunal shall allow the appeal or substitute such other notice as could have been served by the Commissioner; and in any other case the Tribunal shall dismiss the appeal.

(2) On such an appeal, the Tribunal may review any finding of fact on which the notice in question was based.

59. Appeals from decision of Tribunal

Any party to an appeal to the Tribunal under section 57 may appeal from the decision of the Tribunal on a point of law to the appropriate court; and that court shall be—

(a) the High Court of Justice in England if the address of the public authority is in England or Wales,

(b) the Court of Session if that address is in Scotland, and

(c) the High Court of Justice in Northern Ireland if that address is in Northern Ireland.

60. Appeals against national security certificate

(1) Where a certificate under section 23(2) or 24(3) has been issued—

(a) the Commissioner, or

(b) any applicant whose request for information is affected by the issue of the certificate,

may appeal to the Tribunal against the certificate.

(2) If on an appeal under subsection (1) relating to a certificate under section 23(2), the Tribunal finds that the information referred to in the certificate was not exempt information by virtue of section 23(1), the Tribunal may allow the appeal and quash the certificate.

(3) If on an appeal under subsection (1) relating to a certificate under section 24(3), the Tribunal finds that, applying the principles applied by the court on an application for judicial review, the Minister did not have reasonable grounds for issuing the certificate, the Tribunal may allow the appeal and quash the certificate.

(4) Where in any proceedings under this Act it is claimed by a public authority that a certificate under section 24(3) which identifies the information to which it applies by means of a general description applies to particular information, any other party to the proceedings may appeal to the Tribunal on the ground that the certificate does not apply to the information in question and, subject to any determination under subsection (5), the certificate shall be conclusively presumed so to apply.

(5) On any appeal under subsection (4), the Tribunal may determine that the certificate does not so apply.

61. Appeal proceedings

(1) Schedule 4 (which contains amendments of Schedule 6 to the Data Protection Act 1998 relating to appeal proceedings) has effect.

(2) Accordingly, the provisions of Schedule 6 to the Data Protection Act 1998 have effect (so far as applicable) in relation to appeals under this Part.

PART VI

HISTORICAL RECORDS AND RECORDS IN PUBLIC RECORD OFFICE OR
PUBLIC RECORD OFFICE OF NORTHERN IRELAND

62. Interpretation of Part VI

(1) For the purposes of this Part, a record becomes a 'historical record' at the end of the period of thirty years beginning with the year following that in which it was created.

(2) Where records created at different dates are for administrative purposes kept together in one file or other assembly, all the records in that file or other assembly are to be treated for the purposes of this Part as having been created when the latest of those records was created.

(3) In this Part 'year' means a calendar year.

63. Removal of exemptions: historical records generally

(1) Information contained in a historical record cannot be exempt information by virtue of section 28, 30(1), 32, 33, 35, 36, 37(1)(a), 42 or 43.

(2) Compliance with section 1(1)(a) in relation to a historical record is not to be taken to be capable of having any of the effects referred to in section 28(3), 33(3), 36(3), 42(2) or 43(3).

(3) Information cannot be exempt information by virtue of section 37(1)(b) after the end of the period of sixty years beginning with the year following that in which the record containing the information was created.

(4) Information cannot be exempt information by virtue of section 31 after the end of the period of one hundred years beginning with the year following that in which the record containing the information was created.

(5) Compliance with section 1(1)(a) in relation to any record is not to be taken, at any time after the end of the period of one hundred years beginning with the year following that in which the record was created, to be capable of prejudicing any of the matters referred to in section 31(1).

64. Removal of exemptions: historical records in public record offices

(1) Information contained in a historical record in the Public Record Office or the Public Record Office of Northern Ireland cannot be exempt information by virtue of section 21 or 22.

(2) In relation to any information falling within section 23(1) which is contained in a historical record in the Public Record Office or the Public Record Office of Northern Ireland, section 2(3) shall have effect with the omission of the reference to section 23.

65. Decisions as to refusal of discretionary disclosure of historical records

(1) Before refusing a request for information relating to information which is contained in a historical record and is exempt information only by virtue of a provision not specified in section 2(3), a public authority shall—

(a) if the historical record is a public record within the meaning of the Public Records Act 1958, consult the Lord Chancellor, or

   (b) if the historical record is a public record to which the Public Records Act (Northern Ireland) 1923 applies, consult the appropriate Northern Ireland Minister.

(2) This section does not apply to information to which section 66 applies.

66. Decisions relating to certain transferred public records

(1) This section applies to any information which is (or, if it existed, would be) contained in a transferred public record, other than information which the responsible authority has designated as open information for the purposes of this section.

(2) Before determining whether—

   (a) information to which this section applies falls within any provision of Part II relating to the duty to confirm or deny, or

   (b) information to which this section applies is exempt information, the appropriate records authority shall consult the responsible authority.

(3) Where information to which this section applies falls within a provision of Part II relating to the duty to confirm or deny but does not fall within any of the provisions of that Part relating to that duty which are specified in subsection (3) of section 2, any question as to the application of subsection (1)(b) of that section is to be determined by the responsible authority instead of the appropriate records authority.

(4) Where any information to which this section applies is exempt information only by virtue of any provision of Part II not specified in subsection (3) of section 2, any question as to the application of subsection (2)(b) of that section is to be determined by the responsible authority instead of the appropriate records authority.

(5) Before making by virtue of subsection (3) or (4) any determination that subsection (1)(b) or (2)(b) of section 2 applies, the responsible authority shall consult—

   (a) where the transferred public record is a public record within the meaning of the Public Records Act 1958, the Lord Chancellor, and

   (b) where the transferred public record is a public record to which the Public Records Act (Northern Ireland) 1923 applies, the appropriate Northern Ireland Minister.

(6) Where the responsible authority in relation to information to which this section applies is not (apart from this subsection) a public authority, it shall be treated as being a public authority for the purposes of Parts III, IV and V of this Act so far as relating to—

   (a) the duty imposed by section 15(3), and

   (b) the imposition of any requirement to furnish information relating to compliance with Part I in connection with the information to which this section applies.

67. Amendments of public records legislation

Schedule 5 (which amends the Public Records Act 1958 and the Public Records Act (Northern Ireland) 1923) has effect.

PART VII
AMENDMENTS OF DATA PROTECTION ACT 1998

Amendments relating to personal information held by public authorities

68. Extension of meaning of 'data'

(1) Section 1 of the Data Protection Act 1998 (basic interpretative provisions) is amended in accordance with subsections (2) and (3).

(2) In subsection (1)—

    (a) in the definition of 'data', the word 'or' at the end of paragraph (c) is omitted and after paragraph (d) there is inserted 'or (e) is recorded information held by a public authority and does not fall within any of paragraphs (a) to (d);', and

    (b) after the definition of 'processing' there is inserted—'public authority' has the same meaning as in the Freedom of Information Act 2000;'.

(3) After subsection (4) there is inserted—

'(5) In paragraph (e) of the definition of "data" in subsection (1), the reference to information "held" by a public authority shall be construed in accordance with section 3(2) of the Freedom of Information Act 2000.

'(6) Where section 7 of the Freedom of Information Act 2000 prevents Parts I to V of that Act from applying to certain information held by a public authority, that information is not to be treated for the purposes of paragraph (e) of the definition of "data" in subsection (1) as held by a public authority.'

(4) In section 56 of that Act (prohibition of requirement as to production of certain records), after subsection (6) there is inserted—

'(6A) A record is not a relevant record to the extent that it relates, or is to relate, only to personal data falling within paragraph (e) of the definition of "data" in section 1(1).'

(5) In the Table in section 71 of that Act (index of defined expressions) after the entry relating to processing there is inserted—

'public authority section 1(1)'.

69. Right of access to unstructured personal data held by public authorities

(1) In section 7(1) of the Data Protection Act 1998 (right of access to personal data), for 'sections 8 and 9' there is substituted 'sections 8, 9 and 9A'.

(2) After section 9 of that Act there is inserted—

'9A. Unstructured personal data held by public authorities

    (1) In this section "unstructured personal data" means any personal data falling within paragraph (e) of the definition of "data" in section 1(1), other than information which is recorded as part of, or with the intention that it should form part of, any set of information relating to individuals to the extent that the set is structured by reference to individuals or by reference to criteria relating to individuals.

    (2) A public authority is not obliged to comply with subsection (1) of section 7 in relation to any unstructured personal data unless the request under that section contains a description of the data.

(3) Even if the data are described by the data subject in his request, a public authority is not obliged to comply with subsection (1) of section 7 in relation to unstructured personal data if the authority estimates that the cost of complying with the request so far as relating to those data would exceed the appropriate limit.

(4) Subsection (3) does not exempt the public authority from its obligation to comply with paragraph (a) of section 7(1) in relation to the unstructured personal data unless the estimated cost of complying with that paragraph alone in relation to those data would exceed the appropriate limit.

(5) In subsections (3) and (4) "the appropriate limit" means such amount as may be prescribed by the Secretary of State by regulations, and different amounts may be prescribed in relation to different cases.

(6) Any estimate for the purposes of this section must be made in accordance with regulations under section 12(5) of the Freedom of Information Act 2000.'

(3) In section 67(5) of that Act (statutory instruments subject to negative resolution procedure), in paragraph (c), for 'or 9(3)' there is substituted ', 9(3) or 9A(5)'.

70. Exemptions applicable to certain manual data held by public authorities

(1) After section 33 of the Data Protection Act 1998 there is inserted—

'**33A. Manual data held by public authorities**

(1) Personal data falling within paragraph (e) of the definition of "data" in section 1(1) are exempt from—

    (a) the first, second, third, fifth, seventh and eighth data protection principles,

    (b) the sixth data protection principle except so far as it relates to the rights conferred on data subjects by sections 7 and 14,

    (c) sections 10 to 12,

    (d) section 13, except so far as it relates to damage caused by a contravention of section 7 or of the fourth data protection principle and to any distress which is also suffered by reason of that contravention,

    (e) Part III, and

    (f) section 55.

(2) Personal data which fall within paragraph (e) of the definition of "data" in section 1(1) and relate to appointments or removals, pay, discipline, superannuation or other personal matters, in relation to—

    (a) service in any of the armed forces of the Crown,

    (b) service in any office or employment under the Crown or under any public authority, or

    (c) service in any office or employment, or under any contract for services, in respect of which power to take action, or to determine or approve the action taken, in such matters is vested in Her Majesty, any Minister of the Crown, the National Assembly for Wales, any Northern Ireland Minister (within the meaning of the Freedom of Information Act 2000) or any public authority, are also exempt from the remaining data protection principles and the remaining provisions of Part II.'

(2) In section 55 of that Act (unlawful obtaining etc. of personal data) in subsection (8) after 'section 28' there is inserted 'or 33A'.

(3) In Part III of Schedule 8 to that Act (exemptions available after 23 October 2001 but before 24 October 2007) after paragraph 14 there is inserted—

'**14A.**
(1) This paragraph applies to personal data which fall within paragraph (e) of the definition of "data" in section 1(1) and do not fall within paragraph 14(1)(a), but does not apply to eligible manual data to which the exemption in paragraph 16 applies.
(2) During the second transitional period, data to which this paragraph applies are exempt from—
  (a) the fourth data protection principle, and
  (b) section 14(1) to (3).'
(4) In Schedule 13 to that Act (modifications of Act having effect before 24 October 2007) in subsection (4)(b) of section 12A to that Act as set out in paragraph 1, after 'paragraph 14' there is inserted 'or 14A'.

71. Particulars registrable under Part III of Data Protection Act 1998

In section 16(1) of the Data Protection Act 1998 (the registrable particulars), before the word 'and' at the end of paragraph (f) there is inserted—
'(ff) where the data controller is a public authority, a statement of that fact,'.

72. Availability under Act disregarded for purpose of exemption

In section 34 of the Data Protection Act 1998 (information available to the public by or under enactment), after the word 'enactment' there is inserted 'other than an enactment contained in the Freedom of Information Act 2000'.

Other amendments

73. Further amendments of Data Protection Act 1998

Schedule 6 (which contains further amendments of the Data Protection Act 1998) has effect.

PART VIII
MISCELLANEOUS AND SUPPLEMENTAL

74. Power to make provision relating to environmental information

(1) In this section 'the Aarhus Convention' means the Convention on Access to Information, Public Participation in Decision-making and Access to Justice in Environmental Matters signed at Aarhus on 25 June 1998.
(2) For the purposes of this section 'the information provisions' of the Aarhus Convention are Article 4, together with Articles 3 and 9 so far as relating to that Article.
(3) The Secretary of State may be regulations make such provision as he considers appropriate—
  (a) for the purpose of implementing the information provisions of the Aarhus Convention or any amendment of those provisions made in accordance with Article 14 of the Convention, and

(b) for the purpose of dealing with matters arising out of or related to the implementation of those provisions or of any such amendment.

(4) Regulations under subsection (3) may in particular—

(a) enable charges to be made for making information available in accordance with the regulations,

(b) provide that any obligation imposed by the regulations in relation to the disclosure of information is to have effect notwithstanding any enactment or rule of law.

(c) make provision for the issue by the Secretary of State of a code of practice,

(d) provide for sections 47 and 48 to apply in relation to such a code with such modifications as may be specified,

(e) provide for any of the provisions of Parts IV and V to apply, with such modifications as may be specified in the regulations, in relation to compliance with any requirement of the regulations, and

(f) contain such transitional or consequential provision (including provision modifying any enactment) as the Secretary of State considers appropriate.

(5) This section has effect subject to section 80.

75. Power to amend or repeal enactments prohibiting disclosure of information

(1) If, with respect to any enactment which prohibits the disclosure of information held by a public authority, it appears to the Secretary of State that by virtue of section 44(1)(a) the enactment is capable of preventing the disclosure of information under section 1, he may by order repeal or amend the enactment for the purpose of removing or relaxing the prohibition.

(2) In subsection (1)—

'enactment' means—

(a) any enactment contained in an Act passed before or in the same Session as this Act, or

(b) any enactment contained in Northern Ireland legislation or subordinate legislation passed or made before the passing of this Act;

'information' includes unrecorded information.

(3) An order under this section may do all or any of the following

(a) make such modifications of enactments as, in the opinion of the Secretary of State, are consequential upon, or incidental to, the amendment or repeal of the enactment containing the prohibition;

(b) contain such transitional provisions and savings as appear to the Secretary of State to be appropriate;

(c) make different provision for different cases.

76. Disclosure of information between Commissioner and ombudsmen

(1) The Commissioner may disclose to a person specified in the first column of the Table below any information obtained by, or furnished to, the Commissioner under or for the purposes of this Act or the Data Protection Act 1998 if it appears to the Commissioner that the information relates to a matter which could be the subject of an investigation by that person under the enactment specified in relation to that person in the second column of that Table.

TABLE

Ombudsman	Enactment
The Parliamentary Commissioner for Administration.	The Parliamentary Commissioner Act 1967 (c. 13).
The Health Service Commissioner for England.	The Health Service Commissioners Act 1993 (c. 46).
The Health Service Commissioner for Wales.	The Health Service Commissioners Act 1993 (c. 46).
The Health Service Commissioner for Scotland.	The Health Service Commissioners Act 1993 (c. 46).
A Local Commissioner as defined by section 23(3) of the Local Government Act 1974.	Part III of the Local Government Act 1974 (c. 7).
The Commissioner for Local Administration in Scotland.	Part II of the Local Government (Scotland) Act 1975 (c. 30).
The Scottish Parliamentary Commissioner for Administration.	The Scotland Act 1998 (Transitory and Transitional Provisions) (Complaints of Maladministration) Order 1999 (SI 1999/ 1351).
The Welsh Administration Ombudsman.	Schedule 9 to the Government of Wales Act 1998 (c. 38).
The Northern Ireland Commissioner for Complaints.	The Commissioner for Complaints (Northern Ireland) Order 1996 (SI 1996/1297 (NI 7)).
The Assembly Ombudsman for Northern Ireland.	The Ombudsman (Northern Ireland) Order 1996 (SI 1996/1298 (NI 8)).

(2) Schedule 7 (which contains amendments relating to information disclosed to ombudsmen under subsection (1) and to the disclosure of information by ombudsmen to the Commissioner) has effect.

77. Offence of altering etc. records with intent to prevent disclosure

(1) Where—
   (a) a request for information has been made to a public authority, and
   (b) under section 1 of this Act or section 7 of the Data Protection Act 1998, the applicant would have been entitled (subject to payment of any fee) to communication of any information in accordance with that section, any person to whom this subsection applies is guilty of an offence if he alters, defaces, blocks, erases, destroys or conceals any record held by the public authority, with the intention of preventing the disclosure by that authority of all, or any part, of the information to the communication of which the applicant would have been entitled.

(2) Subsection (1) applies to the public authority and to any person who is employed by, is an officer of, or is subject to the direction of, the public authority.

(3) A person guilty of an offence under this section is liable on summary conviction to a fine not exceeding level 5 on the standard scale.

(4) No proceedings for an offence under this section shall be instituted—

(a) in England or Wales, except by the Commissioner or by or with the consent of the Director of Public Prosecutions;

(b) in Northern Ireland, except by the Commissioner or by or with the consent of the Director of Public Prosecutions for Northern Ireland.

78. Saving for existing powers

Nothing in this Act is to be taken to limit the powers of a public authority to disclose information held by it.

79. Defamation

Where any information communicated by a public authority to a person ('the applicant') under section 1 was supplied to the public authority by a third person, the publication to the applicant of any defamatory matter contained in the information shall be privileged unless the publication is shown to have been made with malice.

80. Scotland

(1) No order may be made under section 4(1) or 5 in relation to any of the bodies specified in subsection (2); and the power conferred by section 74(3) does not include power to make provision in relation to information held by any of those bodies.

(2) The bodies referred to in subsection (1) are—

(a) the Scottish Parliament,

(b) any part of the Scottish Administration,

(c) the Scottish Parliamentary Corporate Body, or

(d) any Scottish public authority with mixed functions or no reserved functions (within the meaning of the Scotland Act 1998).

81. Application to government departments, etc.

(1) For the purposes of this Act each government department is to be treated as a person separate from any other government department.

(2) Subsection (1) does not enable—

(a) a government department which is not a Northern Ireland department to claim for the purposes of section 41(1)(b) that the disclosure of any information by it would constitute a breach of confidence actionable by any other government department (not being a Northern Ireland department), or

(b) a Northern Ireland department to claim for those purposes that the disclosure of information by it would constitute a breach of confidence actionable by any other Northern Ireland department.

(3) A government department is not liable to prosecution under this Act, but section 77 and paragraph 12 of Schedule 3 apply to a person in the public service of the Crown as they apply to any other person.

(4) The provisions specified in subsection (3) also apply to a person acting on behalf of either House of Parliament or on behalf of the Northern Ireland Assembly as they apply to any other person.

82. Orders and regulations

(1) Any power of the Secretary of State to make an order or regulations under this Act shall be exercisable by statutory instrument.

(2) A statutory instrument containing (whether alone or with other provisions)—
(a) an order under section 5, 7(3) or (8), 53(1)(a)(iii) or 75, or
(b) regulations under section 10(4) or 74(3),
shall not be made unless a draft of the instrument has been laid before, and approved by a resolution of, each House of Parliament.

(3) A statutory instrument which contains (whether alone or with other provisions)—
(a) an order under section 4(1), or
(b) regulations under any provision of this Act not specified in subsection (2)(b),
and which is not subject to the requirement in subsection (2) that a draft of the instrument be laid before and approved by a resolution of each House of Parliament, shall be subject to annulment in pursuance of a resolution of either House of Parliament.

(4) An order under section 4(5) shall be laid before Parliament after being made.

(5) If a draft of an order under section 5 or 7(8) would, apart from this subsection, be treated for the purposes of the Standing Orders of either House of Parliament as a hybrid instrument, it shall proceed in that House as if it were not such an instrument.

83. Meaning of 'Welsh public authority'

(1) In this Act 'Welsh public authority' means—
(a) any public authority which is listed in Part II, III, IV or VI of Schedule 1 and whose functions are exercisable only or mainly in or as regards Wales, other than an excluded authority, or
(b) any public authority which is an Assembly subsidiary as defined by section 99(4) of the Government of Wales Act 1998.

(2) In paragraph (a) of subsection (1) 'excluded authority' means a public authority which is designated by the Secretary of State by order as an excluded authority for the purposes of that paragraph.

(3) Before making an order under subsection (2), the Secretary of State shall consult the National Assembly for Wales.

84. Interpretation

In this Act, unless the context otherwise requires—
'applicant', in relation to a request for information, means the person who made the request;
'appropriate Northern Ireland Minister' means the Northern Ireland Minister in charge of the Department of Culture, Arts and Leisure in Northern Ireland;
'appropriate records authority', in relation to a transferred public record, has the meaning given by section 15(5);
'body' includes an unincorporated association;
'the Commissioner' means the Information Commissioner;
'decision notice' has the meaning given by section 50;
'the duty to confirm or deny' has the meaning given by section 1(6);
'enactment' includes an enactment contained in Northern Ireland legislation;
'enforcement notice' has the meaning given by section 52;

'executive committee', in relation to the National Assembly for Wales, has the same meaning as in the Government of Wales Act 1998;

'exempt information' means information which is exempt information by virtue of any provision of Part II;

'fees notice' has the meaning given by section 9(1);

'government department' includes a Northern Ireland department, the Northern Ireland Court Service and any other body or authority exercising statutory functions on behalf of the Crown, but does not include—

(a) any of the bodies specified in section 80(2),

(b) the Security Service, the Secret Intelligence Service or the Government Communications Headquarters, or

(c) the National Assembly for Wales;

'information' (subject to sections 51(8) and 75(2)) means information recorded in any form;

'information notice' has the meaning given by section 51;

'Minister of the Crown' has the same meaning as in the Ministers of the Crown Act 1975;

'Northern Ireland Minister' includes the First Minister and deputy First Minister in Northern Ireland;

'Northern Ireland public authority' means any public authority, other than the Northern Ireland Assembly or a Northern Ireland department, whose functions are exercisable only or mainly in or as regards Northern Ireland and relate only or mainly to transferred matters;

'prescribed' means prescribed by regulations made by the Secretary of State;

'public authority' has the meaning given by section 3(1);

'public record' means a public record within the meaning of the Public Records Act 1958 or a public record to which the Public Records Act (Northern Ireland) 1923 applies;

'publication scheme' has the meaning given by section 19;

'request for information' has the meaning given by section 8;

'responsible authority', in relation to a transferred public record, has the meaning given by section 15(5);

'the special forces' means those units of the armed forces of the Crown the maintenance of whose capabilities is the responsibility of the Director of Special Forces or which are for the time being subject to the operational command of that Director;

'subordinate legislation' has the meaning given by subsection (1) of section 21 of the Interpretation Act 1978, except that the definition of that term in that subsection shall have effect as if 'Act' included Northern Ireland legislation;

'transferred matter', in relation to Northern Ireland, has the meaning given by section 4(1) of the Northern Ireland Act 1998;

'transferred public record' has the meaning given by section 15(4);

'the Tribunal' means the Information Tribunal;

'Welsh public authority' has the meaning given by section 83.

85. Expenses

There shall be paid out of money provided by Parliament—
    (a) any increase attributable to this Act in the expenses of the Secretary of State in respect of the Commissioner, the Tribunal or the members of the Tribunal,
    (b) any administrative expenses of the Secretary of State attributable to this Act,
    (c) any other expenses incurred in consequence of this Act by a Minister of the Crown or government department or by either House of Parliament, and
    (d) any increase attributable to this Act in the sums which under any other Act are payable out of money so provided.

86. Repeals

Schedule 8 (repeals) has effect.

87. Commencement

(1) The following provisions of this Act shall come into force on the day on which this Act is passed—
    (a) sections 3 to 8 and Schedule 1,
    (b) section 19 so far as relating to the approval of publication schemes,
    (c) section 20 so far as relating to the approval and preparation by the Commissioner of model publication schemes,
    (d) section 47(2) to (6),
    (e) section 49,
    (f) section 74,
    (g) section 75,
    (h) sections 78 to 85 and this section,
    (i) paragraphs 2 and 17 to 22 of Schedule 2 (and section 18(4) so far as relating to those paragraphs),
    (j) paragraph 4 of Schedule 5 (and section 67 so far as relating to that paragraph),
    (k) paragraph 8 of Schedule 6 (and section 73 so far as relating to that paragraph),
    (l) Part I of Schedule 8 (and section 86 so far as relating to that Part), and
    (m) so much of any other provision of this Act as confers power to make any order, regulations or code of practice.
(2) The following provisions of this Act shall come into force at the end of the period of two months beginning with the day on which this Act is passed—
    (a) section 18(1),
    (b) section 76 and Schedule 7,
    (c) paragraphs 1(1), 3(1), 4, 6, 7, 8(2), 9(2), 10(a), 13(1) and (2), 14(a) and 15(1) and (2) of Schedule 2 (and section 18(4) so far as relating to those provisions), and
    (d) Part II of Schedule 8 (and section 86 50 far as relating to that Part).
(3) Except as provided by subsections (1) and (2), this Act shall come into force at the end of the period of five years beginning with the day on which this Act is passed or on such day before the end of that period as the Secretary of State may be order appoint; and different days may be appointed for different purposes.
(4) An order under subsection (3) may contain such transitional provisions and savings (including provisions capable of having effect after the end of the period referred to in that subsection) as the Secretary of State considers appropriate.

(5) During the twelve months beginning with the day on which this Act is passed, and during each subsequent complete period of twelve months in the period beginning with that day and ending with the first day on which all the provisions of this Act are fully in force, the Secretary of State shall—
   (a) prepare a report on his proposals for bringing fully into, force those provisions of this Act which are not yet fully in force, and
   (b) lay a copy of the report before each House of Parliament.

88. Short title and extent

(1) This Act may be cited as the Freedom of Information Act 2000.
(2) Subject to subsection (3), this Act extends to Northern Ireland.
(3) The amendment or repeal of any enactment by this Act has the same extent as that enactment.

SCHEDULES

SCHEDULE 1   **Section 3(1)(a)(i)**
PUBLIC AUTHORITIES

PART I
GENERAL

1. Any government department.
2. The House of Commons.
3. The House of Lords.
4. The Northern Ireland Assembly.
5. The National Assembly for Wales.
6. The armed forces of the Crown, except—
   (a) the special forces, and
   (b) any unit or part of a unit which is for the time being required by the Secretary of State to assist the Government Communications Headquarters in the exercise of its functions.

PART II
LOCAL GOVERNMENT

England and Wales

7. A local authority within the meaning of the Local Government Act 1972, namely—
   (a) in England, a county council, a London borough council, a district council or a parish council,
   (b) in Wales, a county council, a county borough council or a community council.
8. The Greater London Authority.
9. The Common Council of the City of London, in respect of information held in its capacity as a local authority, police authority or port health authority.

10. The Sub-Treasurer of the Inner Temple or the Under-Treasurer of the Middle Temple, in respect of information held in his capacity as a local authority.
11. The Council of the Isles of Scilly.
12. A parish meeting constituted under section 13 of the Local Government Act 1972.
13. Any charter trustees constituted under section 246 of the Local Government Act 1972.
14. A fire authority constituted by a combination scheme under section 5 or 6 of the Fire Services Act 1947.
15. A waste disposal authority established by virtue of an order under section 10(1) of the Local Government Act 1985.
16. A port health authority constituted by an order under section 2 of the Public Health (Control of Disease) Act 1984.
17. A licensing planning committee constituted under section 119 of the Licensing Act 1964.
18. An internal drainage board which is continued in being by virtue of section 1 of the Land Drainage Act 1991.
19. A joint authority established under Part IV of the Local Government Act 1985 (fire services, civil defence and transport).
20. The London Fire and Emergency Planning Authority.
21. A joint fire authority established by virtue of an order under section 42(2) of the Local Government Act 1985 (reorganisation of functions).
22. A body corporate established pursuant to an order under section 67 of the Local Government Act 1985 (transfer of functions to successors of residuary bodies, etc.).
23. A body corporate established pursuant to an order under section 22 of the Local Government Act 1992 (residuary bodies).
24. The Broads Authority established by section 1 of the Norfolk and Suffolk Broads Act 1988.
25. A joint committee constituted in accordance with section 102(1)(b) of the Local Government Act 1972.
26. A joint board which is continued in being by virtue of section 263(1) of the Local Government Act 1972.
27. A joint authority established under section 21 of the Local Government Act 1992.
28. A Passenger Transport Executive for a passenger transport area within the meaning of Part II of the Transport Act 1968.
29. Transport for London.
30. The London Transport Users Committee.
31. A joint board the constituent members of which consist of any of the public authorities described in paragraphs 8, 9, 10, 12, 15, 16, 20 to 31, 57 and 58.
32. A National Park authority established by an order under section 63 of the Environment Act 1995.
33. A joint planning board constituted for an area in Wales outside a National Park by an order under section 2(1B) of the Town and Country Planning Act 1990.
34. A magistrates' court committee established under section 27 of the Justices of the Peace Act 1997.
35. The London Development Agency.
35A. A local fisheries Committee for a sea fisheries district established under section 1 of the Sea Fisheries Regulation Act 1966.

213

Northern Ireland

36. A district council within the meaning of the Local Government Act (Northern Ireland) 1972.

PART III

THE NATIONAL HEALTH SERVICE

England and Wales

36A. A Strategic Health Authority established under section 8 of the National Health Service Act 1977.

37. A Health Authority established under section 8 of the National Health Service Act 1977.

38. A special health authority established under section 11 of the National Health Service Act 1977.

39. A primary care trust established under section 16A of the National Health Service Act 1977.

39A. A Local Health Board established under section 16BA of the National Health Service Act 1977.

40. A National Health Service trust established under section 5 of the National Health Service and Community Care Act 1990.

40A. An NHS foundation trust.

41. A Community Health Council established under section 20 of the National Health Service Act 1977.

41A. A Patients' Forum established under section 15 of the National Health Service Reform and Health Care Professions Act 2002.

42. The Dental Practice Board constituted under regulations made under section 37 of the National Health Service Act 1977.

43. The Public Health Laboratory Service Board constituted under Schedule 3 to the National Health Service Act 1977.

43A. Any person providing primary medical services or primary dental services—
   (a) in accordance with arrangements made under section 28C of the National Health Service Act 1977; or
   (b) under a contract under section 28K or 28Q of that Act.

44. Any person providing general medical services, general dental services, general ophthalmic services or pharmaceutical services under Part II of the National Health Service Act 1977, in respect of information relating to the provision of those services.

45. Any person providing personal medical services or personal dental services under arrangements made under section 28C of the National Health Service Act 1977, in respect of information relating to the provision of those services.

45A. Any person providing local pharmaceutical services under—
   (a) a pilot scheme established under section 28 of the Health and Social Care Act 2001; or
   (b) an LPS scheme established under Schedule 8A to the National Health Service Act 1977 (c 49),
   in respect of information relating to the provision of those services.

45B. The Commission for Patient and Public Involvement in Health.

Northern Ireland

46. A Health and Social Services Board established under Article 16 of the Health and Personal Social Services (Northern Ireland) Order 1972.
47. A Health and Social Services Council established under Article 4 of the Health and Personal Social Services (Northern Ireland) Order 1991.
48. A Health and Social Services Trust established under Article 10 of the Health and Personal Social Services (Northern Ireland) Order 1991.
49. A special agency established under Article 3 of the Health and Personal Social Services (Special Agencies) (Northern Ireland) Order 1990.
50. The Northern Ireland Central Services Agency for the Health and Social Services established under Article 26 of the Health and Personal Social Services (Northern Ireland) Order 1972.
51. Any person providing general medical services, general dental services, general ophthalmic services or pharmaceutical services under Part VI of the Health and Personal Social Services (Northern Ireland) Order 1972, in respect of information relating to the provision of those services.

PART IV
MAINTAINED SCHOOLS AND OTHER EDUCATIONAL INSTITUTIONS

England and Wales

52. The governing body of—
    (a) a maintained school, as defined by section 20(7) of the School Standards and Framework Act 1998, or
    (b) a maintained nursery school, as defined by section 22(9) of that Act.
53.— (1) The governing body of —
    (a) an institution within the further education sector,
    (b) a university receiving financial support under section 65 of the Further and Higher Education Act 1992,
    (c) an institution conducted by a higher education corporation,
    (d) a designated institution for the purposes of Part II of the Further and Higher Education Act 1992 as defined by section 72(3) of that Act, or
    (e) any college, school, hall or other institution of a university which falls within paragraph (b).
    (2) In sub-paragraph (1)—
    (a) 'governing body' is to be interpreted in accordance with subsection (1) of section 90 of the Further and Higher Education Act 1992 but without regard to subsection (2) of that section,
    (b) in paragraph (a), the reference to an institution within the further education sector is to be construed in accordance with section 91(3) of the Further and Higher Education Act 1992,

(c) in paragraph (c), 'higher education corporation' has the meaning given by section 90(1) of that Act, and

(d) in paragraph (e) 'college' includes any institution in the nature of a college.

Northern Ireland

54.—(1) The managers of—

(a) a controlled school, voluntary school or grant-maintained integrated school within the meaning of Article 2(2) of the Education and Libraries (Northern Ireland) Order 1986, or

(b) a pupil referral unit as defined by Article 87(1) of the Education (Northern Ireland) Order 1998.

(2) In sub-paragraph (1) 'managers' has the meaning given by Article 2(2) of the Education and Libraries (Northern Ireland) Order 1986.

55.—(1) The governing body of—

(a) a university receiving financial support under Article 30 of the Education and Libraries (Northern Ireland) Order 1993,

(b) a college of education maintained in pursuance of arrangements under Article 66(1) or in respect of which grants are paid under Article 66(2) or (3) of the Education and Libraries (Northern Ireland) Order 1986, or

(c) an institution of further education within the meaning of the Further Education (Northern Ireland) Order 1997.

(2) In sub-paragraph (1) 'governing body' has the meaning given by Article 30(3) of the Education and Libraries (Northern Ireland) Order 1993.

56. Any person providing further education to whom grants, loans or other payments are made under Article 5(1)(b) of the Further Education (Northern Ireland) Order 1997.

PART V
POLICE

England and Wales

57. A police authority established under section 3 of the Police Act 1996.

58. The Metropolitan Police Authority established under section 5B of the Police Act 1996.

59. A chief officer of police of a police force in England or Wales.

Northern Ireland

60. The Northern Ireland Policing Board.

61. The Chief Constable of the Police Service of Northern Ireland.

Miscellaneous

62. The British Transport Police.
63. The Ministry of Defence Police established by section 1 of the Ministry of Defence Police Act 1987.
64. Any person who—
    (a) by virtue of any enactment has the function of nominating individuals who may be appointed as special constables by justices of the peace, and
    (b) is not a public authority by virtue of any other provision of this Act, in respect of information relating to the exercise by any person appointed on his nomination of the functions of a special constable.

PART VI
OTHER PUBLIC BODIES AND OFFICES: GENERAL

The Adjudication Panel for Wales.
The Adjudicator for the Inland Revenue and Customs and Excise.
The Administration of Radioactive Substances Advisory Committee.
The Adult Learning Inspectorate.
The Advisory Board on Restricted Patients.
The Advisory Board on the Registration of Homeopathic Products.
The Advisory Committee for Disabled People in Employment and Training.
The Advisory Committee for the Public Lending Right.
The Advisory Committee on Advertising.
The Advisory Committee on Animal Feedingstuffs.
The Advisory Committee on Borderline Substances.
The Advisory Committee on Business and the Environment.
The Advisory Committee on Business Appointments.
The Advisory Committee on Conscientious Objectors.
The Advisory Committee on Consumer Products and the Environment.
The Advisory Committee on Dangerous Pathogens.
The Advisory Committee on Distinction Awards.
An Advisory Committee on General Commissioners of Income Tax.
The Advisory Committee on the Government Art Collection
The Advisory Committee on Hazardous Substances.
The Advisory Committee on Historic Wreck Sites.
An Advisory Committee on Justices of the Peace in England and Wales.
The Advisory Committee on the Microbiological Safety of Food.
The Advisory Committee on Novel Foods and Processes.
The Advisory Committee on Organic Standards.
The Advisory Committee on Overseas Economic and Social Research.
The Advisory Committee on Packaging.
The Advisory Committee on Pesticides.
The Advisory Committee on Releases to the Environment.
The Advisory Committee on Statute Law.
The Advisory Committee on Telecommunications for the Disabled and Elderly.
The Advisory Committee on Historical Manuscripts.
The Advisory Council on Libraries.
The Advisory Council on the Misuse of Drugs.

The Advisory Council on Public Records.
The Advisory Group on Hepatitis.
The Advisory Group on Medical Countermeasures.
The Advisory Panel on Beacon Councils.
The Advisory Panel on Standards for the Planning Inspectorate.
The Aerospace Committee.
An Agricultural Dwelling House Advisory Committee.
An Agricultural Wages Board for England and Wales.
An Agricultural Wages Committee.
The Agriculture and Environment Biotechnology Commission.
The Airborne Particles Expert Group.
The Alcohol Education and Research Council.
The All-Wales Medicines Strategy Group.
The Ancient Monuments Board for Wales.
The Animal Procedures Committee.
The Animal Welfare Advisory Committee.
The Architects Registration Board.
The Armed Forces Pay Review Body.
The Arts Council of England.
The Arts Council of Wales.
The Audit Commission for Local Authorities and the National Health Service in England and Wales.
The Auditor General for Wales.
The Authorised Conveyancing Practitioners Board.
The Bank of England, in respect of information held for purposes other than those of its functions with respect to—
  (a) monetary policy,
  (b) financial operations intended to support financial institutions for the purposes of maintaining stability, and
  (c) the provision of private banking services and related services.
The Better Regulation Task Force.
The Biotechnology and Biological Sciences Research Council.
Any Board of Visitors established under section 6(2) of the Prison Act 1952.
The Britain-Russia Centre and East-West Centre.
The British Association for Central and Eastern Europe.
The British Broadcasting Corporation, in respect of information held for purposes other than those of journalism, art or literature.
The British Coal Corporation.
The British Council.
The British Educational Communications and Technology Agency.
The British Hallmarking Council.
The British Library.
The British Museum.
The British Pharmacopoeia Commission.
The British Potato Council.
The British Railways Board.
British Shipbuilders.
The British Tourist Authority.

The British Waterways Board.

The British Wool Marketing Board.

The Broadcasting Standards Commission.

The Building Regulations Advisory Committee.

The Business Incubation Fund Investment Panel.

The Care Council for Wales.

The Central Advisory Committee on War Pensions.

The Central Police Training and Development Authority.

The Central Rail Users' Consultative Committee.

The Certification Officer.

The Channel Four Television Corporation, in respect of information held for purposes other than those of journalism, art or literature.

The Chemical Weapons Convention National Authority Advisory Committee.

The Children and Family Court Advisory and Support Service.

The Children's Commissioner for Wales.

The Civil Aviation Authority.

The Civil Justice Council.

The Civil Procedure Rule Committee.

The Civil Service Appeal Board.

The Civil Service Commissioners.

The Coal Authority.

The Commission for Architecture and the Built Environment.

The Commission for Health Improvement.

The Commission for Healthcare Audit and Inspection, in respect of information held for purposes other than those of its functions exercisable by virtue of paragraph 5(a)(i) of the Care Standards Act 2000.

The Commission for Local Administration in England.

The Commission for Local Administration in Wales.

The Commission for Racial Equality.

The Commission for Social Care Inspection, in respect of information held for purposes other than those of its functions exercisable by virtue of paragraph 5(a)(ii) of the Care Standards Act 2000.

The Commission for the New Towns.

The Commissioner for Integrated Transport.

The Commissioner for Public Appointments.

The Commissioners for Northern Lighthouses.

The Committee for Monitoring Agreements on Tobacco Advertising and Sponsorship.

The Committee of Investigation for Great Britain.

The Committee on Agricultural Valuation.

The Committee on Carcinogenicity of Chemicals in Food, Consumer Products and the Environment.

The Committee on Chemicals and Materials of Construction For Use in Public Water Supply and Swimming Pools.

The Committee on Medical Aspects of Food and Nutrition Policy.

The Committee on Medical Aspects of Radiation in the Environment.

The Committee on Mutagenicity of Chemicals in Food, Consumer Products and the Environment.

The Committee on Radioactive Waste Management.

The Committee on Safety of Devices.

The Committee on Standards in Public Life.

The Committee on Toxicity of Chemicals in Food, Consumer Products and the Environment.

The Committee on the Medical Effects of Air Pollutants.

The Committee on the Safety of Medicines.

The Commonwealth Scholarship Commission in the United Kingdom.

Communications for Business.

The Community Development Foundation.

The Competition Commission, in relation to information held by it otherwise than as a tribunal.

The Competition Service.

The Construction Industry Training Board.

Consumer Communications for England.

The Consumer Council for Postal Services.

The Consumer Panel established under section 16 of the Communications Act 2003.

The consumers' committee for Great Britain appointed under section 19 of the Agricultural Marketing Act 1958.

The Council for the Regulation of Health Care Professionals.

The Council for the Central Laboratory of the Research Councils.

The Council for Science and Technology.

The Council on Tribunals.

The Countryside Agency.

The Countryside Council for Wales.

The Covent Garden Market Authority.

The Criminal Cases Review Commission.

The Criminal Injuries Compensation Appeals Panel, in relation to information held by it otherwise than as a tribunal.

The Criminal Injuries Compensation Authority.

The Criminal Justice Consultative Council.

The Crown Court Rule Committee.

The Dartmoor Steering Group and Working Party.

The Darwin Advisory Committee.

The Defence Nuclear Safety Committee.

The Defence Scientific Advisory Council.

The Design Council.

The Diplomatic Service Appeal Board.

The Disability Employment Advisory Committee.

The Disability Living Allowance Advisory Board.

The Disability Rights Commission.

The Disabled Persons Transport Advisory Committee.

The Distributed Generation Co-ordinating Group.

The East of England Industrial Development Board.

The Economic and Social Research Council.

The Electoral Commission.

The Engineering Construction Industry Training Board.

The Engineering and Physical Sciences Research Council.

English Nature.

The English Sports Council.
The English Tourist Board.
The Environment Agency.
The Equal Opportunities Commission.
The Ethnic Minority Business Forum.
The Expert Advisory Group on AIDS.
The Expert Group on Cryptosporidium in Water Supplies.
An Expert Panel on Air Quality Standards.
The Export Guarantees Advisory Council.
The Family Proceedings Rules Committee.
The Farm Animal Welfare Council.
The Financial Reporting Advisory Board.
The Financial Services Authority.
The Fire Services Examination Board.
The Firearms Consultative Committee.
The Food Advisory Committee.
Food from Britain.
The Football Licensing Authority.
The Fuel Cell Advisory Panel.
The Fuel Poverty Advisory Group.
The Gaming Board for Great Britain.
The Gas and Electricity Consumer Council.
The Gene Therapy Advisory Committee.
The General Chiropractic Council.
The General Dental Council.
The General Medical Council.
The General Osteopathic Council.
The General Social Care Council.
The General Teaching Council for England.
The General Teaching Council for Wales.
The General Testing and Insurance Committee.
The Government Hospitality Advisory Committee for the Purchase of Wine.
The Government Chemist.
The Great Britain-China Centre.
The Health Professions Council.
The Health and Safety Commission.
The Health and Safety Executive.
The Health Service Commissioner for England.
The Health Service Commissioner for Wales.
The Hearing Aid Council.
Her Majesty's Chief Inspector of Education and Training in Wales or Prif Arolygydd
    Ei Mawrhydi dros Addysg a Hyfforddiant yng Nghymru.
Her Majesty's Commissioners for Judicial Appointments.
The Higher Education Funding Council for England.
The Higher Education Funding Council for Wales.
The Historic Buildings Council for Wales.
The Historic Buildings and Monuments Commission for England.
The Historic Royal Palaces Trust.

The Home-Grown Cereals Authority.

The Horserace Betting Levy Board.

The Horserace Totalisator Board.

The Horticultural Development Council.

Horticulture Research International.

The House of Lords Appointments Commission.

Any housing action trust established under Part III of the Housing Act 1988.

The Housing Corporation.

The Human Fertilisation and Embryology Authority.

The Human Genetics Commission.

The Immigration Services Commissioner.

The Imperial War Museum.

The Independent Advisory Group on Teenage Pregnancy.

The Independent Board of Visitors for Military Corrective Training Centres.

The Independent Case Examiner for the Child Support Agency.

The Independent Living Funds.

The Independent Police Complaints Commission.

The Independent Review Panel for Advertising.

The Independent Review Panel for Borderline Products.

The Independent Scientific Group on Cattle Tuberculosis.

The Independent Television Commission.

The Industrial Development Advisory Board.

The Industrial Injuries Advisory Council.

The Information Commissioner.

The Inland Waterways Amenity Advisory Council.

The Insolvency Rules Committee.

The Integrated Administration and Controls System Appeals Panel.

The Intellectual Property Advisory Committee.

Investors in People UK.

The Joint Committee on Vaccination and Immunisation.

The Joint Nature Conservation Committee.

The Joint Prison/Probation Accreditation Panel.

The Judicial Studies Board.

The Know-How Fund Advisory Board.

The Land Registration Rule Committee.

The Law Commission.

The Learning and Skills Council for England.

The Legal Services Commission.

The Legal Services Complaints Commissioner.

The Legal Services Consultative Panel.

The Legal Services Ombudsman.

The Local Government Boundary Commission for Wales.

The Local Government Commission for England.

A Local probation board established under section 4 of the Criminal Justice and Court Services Act 2000.

The London and South East Industrial Development Board.

The London Pensions Fund Authority.

The Low Pay Commission.

The Magistrates' Courts Rules Committee.
The Marshall Aid Commemoration Commission.
The Measurement Advisory Committee.
The Meat and Livestock Commission.
The Medical Research Council.
The Medicines Commission.
The Milk Development Council.
The Millennium Commission.
The Museum of London.
The National Army Museum.
The National Audit Office.
The National Biological Standards Board (UK).
The National Care Standards Commission.
The National Consumer Council.
The National Council for Education and Training in Wales.
The National Crime Squad.
The National Employers' Liaison Committee.
The National Employment Panel.
The National Endowment for Science, Technology and the Arts.
The National Expert Group on Transboundary Air Pollution.
The National Forest Company.
The National Gallery.
The National Heritage Memorial Fund.
The National Library of Wales.
The National Lottery Charities Board.
The National Lottery Commission.
The National Maritime Museum.
The National Museum of Science and Industry.
The National Museums and Galleries of Wales.
The National Museums and Galleries on Merseyside.
The National Portrait Gallery.
The National Radiological Protection Board.
The Natural Environment Research Council.
The Natural History Museum.
The New Deal Task Force.
The New Opportunities Fund.
The North East Industrial Development Board.
The North West Industrial Development Board.
The Nuclear Research Advisory Council.
The Nursing and Midwifery Council.
The Occupational Pensions Regulatory Authority.
The Office of Communications.
The Office of Government Commerce.
The Office of Manpower Economics.
The Oil and Pipelines Agency.
The OSO Board.
The Overseas Service Pensions Scheme Advisory Board.
The Panel on Standards for the Planning Inspectorate.

The Parliamentary Boundary Commission for England.
The Parliamentary Boundary Commission for Scotland.
The Parliamentary Boundary Commission for Wales.
The Parliamentary Commissioner for Administration.
The Parole Board.
The Particle Physics and Astronomy Research Council.
The Pensions Compensation Board.
The Pensions Ombudsman.
The Pesticide Residues Committee.
The Pesticides Forum.
The Pharmacists' Review Panel.
The Poisons Board.
The Police Advisory Board for England and Wales.
The Police Information Technology Organisation.
The Police Negotiating Board.
The Political Honours Scrutiny Committee.
The Postgraduate Medical Education and Training Board.
The Post Office.
The Prison Service Pay Review Body.
The Property Advisory Group.
The Public Private Partnership Agreement Arbiter.
The Qualifications, Curriculum and Assessment Authority for Wales.
The Qualifications Curriculum Authority.
The Race Education and Employment Forum.
The Race Relations Forum.
The Radio Authority.
The Radioactive Waste Management Advisory Committee.
Any Rail Passengers' Committee established under section 2(2) of the Railways Act 1993.
A Regional Cultural Consortium.
Any regional development agency established under the Regional Development Agencies
    Act 1998, other than the London Development Agency.
Any regional flood defence committee.
The Registrar of Occupational and Personal Pension Schemes.
The Registrar of Public Lending Right.
Remploy Ltd.
The Renewable Energy Advisory Committee.
Resource: The Council for Museums, Archives and Libraries.
The Review Board for Government Contracts.
The Review Body for Nursing Staff, Midwives, Health Visitors and Professions Allied to
    Medicine.
The Review Body on Doctors and Dentists Remuneration.
The Reviewing Committee on the Export of Works of Art.
The Royal Air Force Museum.
The Royal Armouries.
The Royal Botanic Gardens, Kew.
The Royal Commission on Ancient and Historical Monuments of Wales.
The Royal Commission on Environmental Pollution.
The Royal Commission on Historical Manuscripts.

The Royal Hospital at Chelsea.

The Royal Military College of Science Advisory Council.

The Royal Mint Advisory Committee on the Design of Coins, Medals, Seals and Decorations.

The School Teachers' Review Body.

The Scientific Advisory Committee on Nutrition.

The Scientific Committee on Tobacco and Health.

The Scottish Committee of the Council on Tribunals.

The Sea Fish Industry Authority.

The Security Industry Authority.

The Senior Salaries Review Body.

The Sentencing Advisory Panel.

The Service Authority for the National Crime Squad.

Sianel Pedwar Cymru, in respect of information held for purposes other than those of journalism, art or literature.

Sir John Soane's Museum.

The Small Business Council.

The Small Business Investment Task Force.

The Social Care Institute for Excellence.

The social fund Commissioner appointed under section 65 of the Social Security Administration Act 1992.

The Social Security Advisory Committee.

The Social Services Inspectorate for Wales Advisory Group.

The South West Industrial Development Board.

The Specialist Advisory Committee on Antimicrobid Research.

The Spongiform Encephalopathy Advisory Committee.

The Sports Council for Wales.

The Standards Board for England.

The Standing Advisory Committee on Industrial Property.

The Standing Advisory Committee on Trunk Road Assessment.

The Standing Dental Advisory Committee.

The Standing Nursing and Midwifery Advisory Committee.

The Standing Medical Advisory Committee.

The Standing Pharmaceutical Advisory Committee.

The Statistics Commission.

The Steering Committee on Pharmacy Postgraduate Education.

The Strategic Investment Board.

Strategic Rail Authority.

The subsidence adviser appointed under section 46 of the Coal Industry Act 1994.

The Substance Misuse Advisory Panel.

The Sustainable Development Commission.

The Sustainable Energy Policy Advisory Board.

The Tate Gallery.

The Teacher Training Agency.

The Technical Advisory Board.

The Theatres Trust.

The Traffic Commissioners, in respect of information held by them otherwise than as a tribunal.

The Treasure Valuation Committee.
The UK Advisory Panel for Health Care Workers Infected with Bloodborne Viruses.
The UK Chemicals Stakeholder Forum.
The UK Sports Council.
The United Kingdom Atomic Energy Authority.
The United Kingdom Xenotransplantation Interim Regulatory Authority.
The Unlinked Anonymous Serosurveys Steering Group.
The Unrelated Live Transplant Regulatory Authority.
The Urban Regeneration Agency.
The Valuation Tribunal Service.
The Veterinary Products Committee.
The Veterinary Residues Committee.
The Victoria and Albert Museum.
The Wales Centre for Health.
The Wales Tourist Board.
The Wallace Collection.
The War Pensions Committees.
The Water Regulations Advisory Committee.
The Welsh Administration Ombudsman.
The Welsh Committee for Professional Development of Pharmacy.
The Welsh Dental Committee.
The Welsh Development Agency.
The Welsh Industrial Development Advisory Board.
The Welsh Language Board.
The Welsh Medical Committee.
The Welsh Nursing and Midwifery Committee.
The Welsh Optometric Committee.
The Welsh Pharmaceutical Committee.
The Welsh Scientific Advisory Committee.
The Westminster Foundation for Democracy.
The West Midlands Industrial Development Board.
The Wilton Park Academic Council.
The Wine Standards Board of the Vintners' Company.
The Women's National Commission.
The Yorkshire and the Humber and East Midlands Industrial Development Board.
The Youth Justice Board for England and Wales.
The Zoos Forum.

PART VII
OTHER PUBLIC BODIES AND OFFICES: NORTHERN IRELAND

An Advisory Committee on General Commissioners of Income Tax (Northern Ireland).
An Advisory Committee established under paragraph 25 of the Health and Personal Social Services (Northern Ireland) Order 1972.
The Advisory Committee on Justices of the Peace in Northern Ireland.
The Advisory Committee on Juvenile Court Lay Panel (Northern Ireland).

The Advisory Committee on Pesticides for Northern Ireland.

The Agricultural Research Institute of Northern Ireland.

The Agricultural Wages Board for Northern Ireland.

The Arts Council of Northern Ireland.

The Assembly Ombudsman for Northern Ireland.

The Attorney General for Northern Ireland.

The Belfast Harbour Commissioners.

The Board of Trustees of National Museums and Galleries of Northern Ireland.

Boards of Visitors and Visiting Committees.

The Boundary Commission for Northern Ireland.

A central advisory committee established under paragraph 24 of the Health and Personal Social Services (Northern Ireland) Order 1972.

The Certification Officer for Northern Ireland.

The Charities Advisory Committee.

The Chief Electoral Officer for Northern Ireland.

The Chief Inspector of Criminal Justice in Northern Ireland.

The Civil Service Commissioners for Northern Ireland.

Comhairle na Gaelscolaíochta.

Commissioner for Children and Young People for Northern Ireland.

The Commissioner for Public Appointments for Northern Ireland.

The Construction Industry Training Board.

The consultative Civic Forum referred to in section 56(4) of the Northern Ireland Act 1998.

The Council for Catholic Maintained Schools.

The Council for Nature Conservation and the Countryside.

The County Court Rules Committee (Northern Ireland).

The Criminal Injuries Compensation Appeals Panel for Northern Ireland, in relation to information held by it otherwise than as a tribunal.

A development corporation established under Part III of the Strategic Investment and Regeneration of Sites (Northern Ireland) Order 2003.

The Disability Living Allowance Advisory Board for Northern Ireland.

The Distinction and Meritorious Service Awards Committee.

A district policing partnership.

The Drainage Council for Northern Ireland.

An Education and Library Board established under Article 3 of the Education and Libraries (Northern Ireland) Order 1986.

Enterprise Ulster.

The Equality Commission for Northern Ireland.

The Family Proceedings Rules Committee (Northern Ireland).

The Fire Authority for Northern Ireland.

The Fisheries Conservancy Board for Northern Ireland.

The General Consumer Council for Northern Ireland.

The General Teaching Council for Northern Ireland.

The Governors of the Armargh Observatory and Planetarium.

The Harbour of Donaghadee Commissioners.

The Health and Safety Agency for Northern Ireland.

The Historic Buildings Council.

The Historic Monuments Council.

The Independent Assessor of Military Complaints Procedures in Northern Ireland.

The Independent Reviewer of the Northern Ireland (Emergency Provisions) Act.

The Independent Commissioner for Holding Centres.

Invest Northern Ireland.

The Labour Relations Agency.

The Laganside Corporation.

The Law Reform Advisory Committee for Northern Ireland.

The Lay Observer for Northern Ireland.

The Legal Aid Advisory Committee (Northern Ireland).

The Life Sentence Review Commissioners appointed under Article 3 of the Life Sentences (Northern Ireland) Order 2001.

The Livestock & Meat Commission for Northern Ireland.

The Local Government Staff Commission.

The Londonderry Port and Harbour Commissioners.

The Magistrates' Courts Rules Committee (Northern Ireland).

The Mental Health Commission for Northern Ireland.

The Northern Ireland Advisory Committee on Telecommunications.

The Northern Ireland Audit Office.

The Northern Ireland Building Regulations Advisory Committee.

The Northern Ireland Civil Service Appeal Board.

The Northern Ireland Commissioner for Complaints.

The Northern Ireland Community Relations Council.

The Northern Ireland Council for the Curriculum, Examinations and Assessment.

The Northern Ireland Crown Court Rules Committee.

The Northern Ireland Economic Council.

The Northern Ireland Fishery Harbour Authority.

The Northern Ireland Higher Education Council.

The Northern Ireland Housing Executive.

The Northern Ireland Human Rights Commission.

The Northern Ireland Insolvency Rules Committee.

The Northern Ireland Judicial Appointments Commission.

The Northern Ireland Law Commission.

The Northern Ireland Legal Services Commission.

The Northern Ireland Local Government Officers' Superannuation Committee.

The Northern Ireland Museums Council.

The Northern Ireland Pig Production Development Committee.

The Northern Ireland Practice and Education Council for Nursing and Midwifery.

The Northern Ireland Social Care Council.

The Northern Ireland Supreme Court Rules Committee.

The Northern Ireland Tourist Board.

The Northern Ireland Transport Holding Company.

The Northern Ireland Water Council.

The Parades Commission.

The Police Ombudsman for Northern Ireland.

The Probation Board for Northern Ireland.

The Rural Development Council for Northern Ireland.

The Sentence Review Commissioners appointed under section 1 of the Northern Ireland (Sentences) Act 1998.

The social fund Commissioner appointed under Article 37 of the Social Security (Northern Ireland) Order 1998.

The Sports Council for Northern Ireland.

The Staff Commission for Education and Library Boards.

The Statistics Advisory Committee.

The Statute Law Committee for Northern Ireland.

Ulster Supported Employment Ltd.

The Warrenpoint Harbour Authority.

The Waste Management Advisory Board.

The Youth Council for Northern Ireland.

SCHEDULE 2   **Section 18(4)**
THE COMMISSIONER AND THE TRIBUNAL

PART I
PROVISION CONSEQUENTIAL ON s. 18(1) AND (2)

General

1.—(1) Any reference in any enactment, instrument or document to the Data Protection Commissioner or the Data Protection Registrar shall be construed, in relation to any time after the commencement of section 18(1), as a reference to the Information Commissioner.

(2) Any reference in any enactment, instrument or document to the Data Protection Tribunal shall be construed, in relation to any time after the commencement of section 18(2), as a reference to the Information Tribunal.

2.—(1) Any reference in this Act or in any instrument under this Act to the Commissioner shall be construed, in relation to any time before the commencement of section 18(1), as a reference to the Data Protection Commissioner.

(2) Any reference in this Act or in any instrument under this Act to the Tribunal shall be construed, in relation to any time before the commencement of section 18(2), as a reference to the Data Protection Tribunal.

Public Records Act 1958 (c. 51)

3.—(1) In Part II of the Table in paragraph 3 of Schedule 1 to the Public Records Act 1958 (definition of public records), the entry relating to the Data Protection Commissioner is omitted and there is inserted at the appropriate place—
'Information Commissioner.'

(2) In paragraph 4(1) of that Schedule, for paragraph (nn) there is substituted—
'(nn) records of the Information Tribunal;'.

Parliamentary Commissioner Act 1967 (c. 13)

4. In Schedule 2 to the Parliamentary Commissioner Act 1967 (departments etc.

subject to investigation), the entry relating to the Data Protection Commissioner is omitted and there is inserted at the appropriate place—
'Information Commissioner'.

5. In Schedule 4 to that Act (tribunals exercising administrative functions), for the entry relating to the Data Protection Tribunal there is substituted—
'Information Tribunal constituted under section 6 of the Data Protection Act 1998.'

Superannuation Act 1972 (c. 11)

6. In Schedule 1 to the Superannuation Act 1972 (employment with superannuation scheme), for 'Data Protection Commissioner' there is substituted 'Information Commissioner'.

Consumer Credit Act 1974 (c. 39)

7. In section 159 of the Consumer Credit Act 1974 (correction of wrong information), in subsections (7) and (8)(b), for 'Data Protection Commissioner', in both places where it occurs, there is substituted 'Information Commissioner'.

House of Commons Disqualification Act 1975 (c. 24)

8.—(1) In Part II of Schedule 1 to the House of Commons Disqualification Act 1975 (bodies whose members are disqualified), the entry relating to the Data Protection Tribunal is omitted and there is inserted at the appropriate place—
'The Information Tribunal'.

(2) In Part III of that Schedule (disqualifying offices), the entry relating to the Data Protection Commissioner is omitted and there is inserted at the appropriate place—
'The Information Commissioner'.

Northern Ireland Assembly Disqualification Act 1975 (c. 25)

9.—(1) In Part II of Schedule 1 to the Northern Ireland Assembly Disqualification Act 1975 (bodies whose members are disqualified), the entry relating to the Data Protection Tribunal is omitted and there is inserted at the appropriate place—
'The Information Tribunal'.

(2) In Part III of that Schedule (disqualifying offices), the entry relating to the Data Protection Commissioner is omitted and there is inserted at the appropriate place—
'The Information Commissioner'.

Tribunals and Inquiries Act 1992 (c. 53)

10. In paragraph 14 of Part I of Schedule 1 to the Tribunals and Inquiries Act 1992 (tribunals under direct supervision of Council on Tribunals)—

(a) in sub-paragraph (a), for 'The Data Protection Commissioner' there is substituted 'The Information Commissioner', and

(b) for sub-paragraph (b) there is substituted—

'(b) the Information Tribunal constituted under that section, in respect of its jurisdiction under—

(i) section 48 of that Act, and

(ii) section 57 of the Freedom of Information Act 2000.'

Judicial Pensions and Retirement Act 1993 (c. 8)

11. In Schedule 5 to the Judicial Pensions and Retirement Act 1993 (retirement provisions: the relevant offices), in the entry relating to the chairman and deputy chairman of the Data Protection Tribunal, for 'the Data Protection Tribunal' there is substituted 'the Information Tribunal'.

12. In Schedule 7 to that Act (retirement dates: transitional provisions), in paragraph 5(5)(xxvi) for 'the Data Protection Tribunal' there is substituted 'the Information Tribunal'.

Data Protection Act 1998 (c. 29)

13.—(1) Section 6 of the Data Protection Act 1998 (the Data Protection Commissioner and the Data Protection Tribunal) is amended as follows.

(2) For subsection (1) there is substituted—

'(1) For the purposes of this Act and of the Freedom of Information Act 2000 there shall be an officer known as the Information Commissioner (in this Act referred to as "the Commissioner").'

(3) For subsection (3) there is substituted—

'(3) For the purposes of this Act and of the Freedom of Information Act 2000 there shall be a tribunal known as the Information Tribunal (in this Act referred to as "the Tribunal").'

14. In section 70(1) of that Act (supplementary definitions)—

(a) in the definition of 'the Commissioner', for 'the Data Protection Commissioner' there is substituted 'the Information Commissioner', and

(b) in the definition of 'the Tribunal', for 'the Data Protection Tribunal' there is substituted 'the Information Tribunal'.

15.—(1) Schedule 5 to that Act (the Data Protection Commissioner and the Data Protection Tribunal) is amended as follows.

(2) In paragraph 1(1), for 'Data Protection Commissioner' there is substituted 'Information Commissioner'.

(3) Part III shall cease to have effect.

PART II
AMENDMENTS RELATING TO EXTENSION OF FUNCTIONS OF
COMMISSIONER AND TRIBUNAL

Interests represented by lay members of Tribunal

16. In section 6(6) of the Data Protection Act 1998 (lay members of Tribunal)—
   (a) for the word 'and' at the end of paragraph (a) there is substituted—
      '(aa) persons to represent the interests of those who make requests for information under the Freedom of Information Act 2000,', and
   (b) after paragraph (b) there is inserted 'and
      (bb) persons to represent the interests of public authorities.'

Expenses incurred under this Act excluded in calculating fees

17. In section 26(2) of that Act (fees regulations), in paragraph (a)—
   (a) after 'functions' there is inserted 'under this Act', and
   (b) after 'Tribunal' there is inserted 'so far as attributable to their functions under this Act'.

Information provided to Commissioner or Tribunal

18. In section 58 of that Act (disclosure of information to Commissioner or Tribunal), after 'this Act' there is inserted 'or the Freedom of Information Act 2000'.
19.—(1) Section 59 of that Act (confidentiality of information) is amended as follows.
(2) In subsections (1) and (2), for 'this Act', wherever occurring, there is substituted 'the information Acts'.
(3) After subsection (3) there is inserted—
   '(4) In this section "the information Acts" means this Act and the Freedom of Information Act 2000.'

Deputy commissioners

20.—(1) Paragraph 4 of Schedule 5 to that Act (officers and staff) is amended as follows.
(2) In sub-paragraph (1)(a), after 'a deputy commissioner' there is inserted 'or two deputy commissioners'.
(3) After sub-paragraph (1) there is inserted—
   '(1A) The Commissioner shall, when appointing any second deputy commissioner, specify which of the Commissioner's functions are to be performed, in the circumstances referred to in paragraph 5(1), by each of the deputy commissioners.'

Exercise of Commissioner's functions by others

21.—(1) Paragraph 5 of Schedule 5 to that Act (exercise of functions of Commissioner during vacancy etc.) is amended as follows.

(2) In sub-paragraph (1)—

(a) after 'deputy commissioner' there is inserted 'or deputy commissioners', and

(b) after 'this Act' there is inserted 'or the Freedom of Information Act 2000'.

(3) In sub-paragraph (2) after 'this Act' there is inserted 'or the Freedom of Information Act 2000'.

Money

22. In paragraph 9(1) of Schedule 5 to that Act (money) for 'or section 159 of the Consumer Credit Act 1974' there is substituted ',under section 159 of the Consumer Credit Act 1974 or under the Freedom of Information Act 2000'.

SCHEDULE 3   **Section 55**

POWERS OF ENTRY AND INSPECTION

Issue of warrants

1.—(1) If a circuit judge is satisfied by information on oath supplied by the Commissioner that there are reasonable grounds for suspecting—

(a) that a public authority has failed or is failing to comply with—

(i) any of the requirements of Part I of this Act,

(ii) so much of a decision notice as requires steps to be taken, or

(iii) an information notice or an enforcement notice, or

(b) that an offence under section 77 has been or is being committed, and that evidence of such a failure to comply or of the commission of the offence is to be found on any premises specified in the information, he may, subject to paragraph 2, grant a warrant to the Commissioner.

(2) A warrant issued under sub-paragraph (1) shall authorise the Commissioner or any of his officers or staff at any time within seven days of the date of the warrant—

(a) to enter and search the premises.

(b) to inspect and seize any documents or other material found there which may be such evidence as is mentioned in that sub-paragraph, and

(c) to inspect, examine, operate and test any equipment found there in which information held by the public authority may be recorded.

2.—(1) A judge shall not issue a warrant under this Schedule unless he is satisfied—

(a) that the Commissioner has given seven days' notice in writing to the occupier of the premises in question demanding access to the premises, and

(b) that either—

(i) access was demanded at a reasonable hour and was unreasonably refused, or

(ii) although entry to the premises was granted, the occupier unreasonably refused to comply with a request by the Commissioner or any of the Commissioner's officers or staff to permit the Commissioner or the officer or member of staff to do any of the things referred to in paragraph 1(2), and

(c) that the occupier, has, after the refusal, been notified by the Commissioner of the application for the warrant and has had an opportunity of being heard by the judge on the question whether or not it should be issued.

(2) Sub-paragraph (1) shall not apply if the judge is satisfied that the case is one of urgency or that compliance with those provisions would defeat the object of the entry.

3. A judge who issues a warrant under this Schedule shall also issue two copies of it and certify them clearly as copies.

Execution of warrants

4. A person executing a warrant issued under this Schedule may use such reasonable force as may be necessary.

5. A warrant issued under this Schedule shall be executed at a reasonable hour unless it appears to the person executing it that there are grounds for suspecting that the evidence in question would not be found if it were so executed.

6.—(1) If the premises in respect of which a warrant is issued under this Schedule are occupied by a public authority and any officer or employee of the authority is present when the warrant is executed, he shall be shown the warrant and supplied with a copy of it; and if no such officer or employee is present a copy of the warrant shall be left in a prominent place on the premises.

(2) If the premises in respect of which a warrant is issued under this Schedule are occupied by a person other than a public authority and he is present when the warrant is executed, he shall be shown the warrant and supplied with a copy of it; and if that person is not present a copy of the warrant shall be left in a prominent place on the premises.

7.—(1) A person seizing anything in pursuance of a warrant under this Schedule shall give a receipt for it if asked to do so.

(2) Anything so seized may be retained for so long as is necessary in all the circumstances but the person in occupation of the premises in question shall be given a copy of anything that is seized if he so requests and the person executing the warrant considers that it can be done without undue delay.

Matters exempt from inspection and seizure

8. The powers of inspection and seizure conferred by a warrant issued under this Schedule shall not be exercisable in respect of information which is exempt information by virtue of section 23(1) or 24(1).

9.—(1) Subject to the provisions of this paragraph, the powers of inspection and seizure conferred by a warrant issued under this Schedule shall not be exercisable in respect of—

(a) any communication between a professional legal adviser and his client in connection with the giving of legal advice to the client with respect to his obligations, liabilities or rights under this Act, or

(b) any communication between a professional legal adviser and his client, or between such an adviser or his client and any other person, made in connection with or in contemplation of proceedings under or arising out of this Act (including proceedings before the Tribunal) and for the purposes of such proceedings.

(2) Sub-paragraph (1) applies also to—

(a) any copy or other record of any such communication as is there mentioned, and

(b) any document or article enclosed with or referred to in any such communication if made in connection with the giving of any advice or, as the case may be, in connection with or in contemplation of and for the purposes of such proceedings as are there mentioned.

(3) This paragraph does not apply to anything in the possession of any person other than the professional legal adviser or his client or to anything held with the intention of furthering a criminal purpose.

(4) In this paragraph references to the client of a professional legal adviser include references to any person representing such a client.

10. If the person in occupation of any premises in respect of which a warrant is issued under this Schedule objects to the inspection or seizure under the warrant of any material on the grounds that it consists partly of matters in respect of which those powers are not exercisable, he shall, if the person executing the warrant so requests, furnish that person with a copy of so much of the material in relation to which the powers are exercisable.

Return of warrants

11. A warrant issued under this Schedule shall be returned to the court from which it was issued—
(a) after being executed, or
(b) if not executed within the time authorised for its execution; and the person by whom any such warrant is executed shall make an endorsement on it stating what powers have been exercised by him under the warrant.

Offences

12. Any person who—
(a) intentionally obstructs a person in the execution of a warrant issued under this Schedule, or
(b) fails without reasonable excuse to give any person executing such a warrant such assistance as he may reasonably require for the execution of the warrant,
is guilty of an offence.

Vessels, vehicles etc.

13. In this Schedule 'premises' includes any vessel, vehicle, aircraft or hovercraft, and references to the occupier of any premises include references to the person in charge of any vessel, vehicle, aircraft or hovercraft.

Scotland and Northern Ireland

14. In the application of this Schedule to Scotland—
(a) for any reference to a circuit judge there is substituted a reference to the sheriff, and
(b) for any reference to information on oath there is substituted a reference to evidence on oath.

15. In the application of this Schedule to Northern Ireland—
    (a) for any reference to a circuit judge there is substituted a reference to a county court judge, and
    (b) for any reference to information on oath there is substituted a reference to a complaint on oath.

SCHEDULE 4   **Section 61(1)**

APPEAL PROCEEDINGS: AMENDMENTS OF SCHEDULE 6 TO DATA PROTECTION ACT 1998

Constitution of Tribunal in national security cases

1. In paragraph 2(1) of Schedule 6 to the Data Protection Act 1998 (constitution of Tribunal in national security cases), at the end there is inserted 'or under section 60(1) or (4) of the Freedom of Information Act 2000'.
2. For paragraph 3 of that Schedule there is substituted—
    '3. The Tribunal shall be duly constituted—
    (a) for an appeal under section 28(4) or (6) in any case where the application of paragraph 6(1) is excluded by rules under paragraph 7, or
    (b) for an appeal under section 60(1) or (4) of the Freedom of Information Act 2000,
    if it consists of three of the persons designated under paragraph 2(1), of whom one shall be designated by the Lord Chancellor to preside.'

Constitution of Tribunal in other cases

3.—(1) Paragraph 4 of that Schedule (constitution of Tribunal in other cases) is amended as follows.
   (2) After sub-paragraph (I) there is inserted—
    '(1A) Subject to any rules made under paragraph 7, the Tribunal shall be duly constituted for an appeal under section 57(1) or (2) of the Freedom of Information Act 2000 if it consists of—
    (a) the chairman or a deputy chairman (who shall preside), and
    (b) an equal number of the members appointed respectively in accordance with paragraphs (aa) and (bb) of section 6(6).'
   (3) In sub-paragraph (2), after '(1)' there is inserted 'or (1A)'.

Rules of procedure

4.—(1) Paragraph 7 of that Schedule (rules of procedure) is amended as follows.
   (2) In sub-paragraph (1), for the words from 'regulating' onwards there is substituted 'regulating—
    (a) the exercise of the rights of appeal conferred—
       (i) by sections 28(4) and (6) and 48, and
       (ii) by sections 57(1) and (2) and section 60(1) and (4) of the Freedom of Information Act 2000, and

(b) the practice and procedure of the Tribunal.'

(3) In sub-paragraph (2), after paragraph (a) there is inserted—

'(aa) for the joinder of any other person as a party to any proceedings on an appeal under the Freedom of Information Act 2000,

(ab) for the hearing of an appeal under this Act with an appeal under the Freedom of Information Act 2000,'.

SCHEDULE 5   **Section 67**
AMENDMENTS OF PUBLIC RECORDS LEGISLATION

PART I
AMENDMENTS OF PUBLIC RECORDS ACT 1958

Functions of Advisory Council on Public Records

1.   In section 1 of the Public Records Act 1958 (general responsibility of the Lord Chancellor for public records), after subsection (2) there is inserted—

'(2A) The matters on which the Advisory Council on Public Records may advise the Lord Chancellor include matters relating to the application of the Freedom of Information Act 2000 to information contained in public records which are historical records within the meaning of Part VI of that Act.'

Access to public records

2.—(1) Section 5 of that Act (access to public records) is amended in accordance with this paragraph.

(2) Subsections (1) and (2) are omitted.

(3) For subsection (3) there is substituted—

'(3) It shall be the duty of the Keeper of Public Records to arrange that reasonable facilities are available to the public for inspecting and obtaining copies of those public records in the Public Record Office which fall to be disclosed in accordance with the Freedom of Information Act 2000.'

(4) Subsection (4) and, in subsection (5), the words from 'and subject to' to the end are omitted.

3.   Schedule 2 of that Act (enactments prohibiting disclosure of information obtained from the public) is omitted.

Power to extend meaning of 'public records'

4.   In Schedule 1 to that Act (definition of public records) after the Table at the end of paragraph 3 there is inserted—

'3A.—(1) Her Majesty may by Order in Council amend the Table at the end of paragraph 3 of this Schedule by adding to either Part of the Table an entry relating to any body or establishment—

(a) which, at the time when the Order is made, is specified in Schedule 2 to the

Parliamentary Commissioner Act 1967 (departments, etc. subject to investigation), or

(b) in respect of which an entry could, at that time, be added to Schedule 2 to that Act by an Order in Council under section 4 of that Act (which confers power to amend that Schedule).

(2) An Order in Council under this paragraph may relate to a specified body or establishment or to bodies or establishments falling within a specified description.

(3) An Order in Council under this paragraph shall be subject to annulment in pursuance of a resolution of either House of Parliament.'

PART II
AMENDMENT OF PUBLIC RECORDS ACT (NORTHERN IRELAND) 1923

5. After section 5 of the Public Records Act (Northern Ireland) 1923 (deposit of documents in Record Office by trustees or other persons) there is inserted—

'**5A. Access to public records**

It shall be the duty of the Deputy Keeper of the Records of Northern Ireland to arrange that reasonable facilities are available to the public for inspecting and obtaining copies of those public records in the Public Record Office of Northern Ireland which fall to be disclosed in accordance with the Freedom of Information Act 2000.'

SCHEDULE 6   **Section 73**
FURTHER AMENDMENTS OF DATA PROTECTION ACT 1998

Request by data controller for further information

1. In section 7 of the Data Protection Act 1998 (right of access to personal data), for subsection (3) there is substituted—

'(3) Where a data controller—

(a) reasonably requires further information in order to satisfy himself as to the identity of the person making a request under this section and to locate the information which that person seeks, and

(b) has informed him of that requirement, the data controller is not obliged to comply with the request unless he is supplied with that further information.'

Parliament

2. After section 35 of that Act there is inserted—

'**35A. Parliamentary privilege**

Personal data are exempt from—

(a) the first data protection principle, except to the extent to which it requires compliance with the conditions in Schedules 2 and 3,

(b)   the second, third, fourth and fifth data protection principles,

(c)   section 7, and

(d)   sections 10 and 14(1) to (3),

if the exemption is required for the purpose of avoiding an infringement of the privileges of either House of Parliament.'

3.   After section 63 of that Act there is inserted—

'63A.   Application to Parliament

(1)   Subject to the following provisions of this section and to section 35A, this Act applies to the processing of personal data by or on behalf of either House of Parliament as it applies to the processing of personal data by other persons.

(2)   Where the purposes for which and the manner in which any personal data are, or are to be, processed are determined by or on behalf of the House of Commons, the data controller in respect of those data for the purposes of this Act shall be the Corporate Officer of that House.

(3)   Where the purposes for which and the manner in which any personal data are, or are to be, processed are determined by or on behalf of the House of Lords, the data controller in respect of those data for the purposes of this Act shall be the Corporate Officer of that House.

(4)   Nothing in subsection (2) or (3) is to be taken to render the Corporate Officer of the House of Commons or the Corporate Officer of the House of Lords liable to prosecution under this Act, but section 55 and paragraph 12 of Schedule 9 shall apply to a person acting on behalf of either House as they apply to any other person.'

4.   In Schedule 2 to that Act (conditions relevant for the purposes of the first data protection principle: processing of any personal data) in paragraph 5 after paragraph (a) there is inserted—

'(aa)   for the exercise of any functions of either House of Parliament,'.

5.   In Schedule 3 to that Act (conditions relevant for the purposes of the first data protection principle: processing of sensitive personal data) in paragraph 7 after paragraph (a) there is inserted—

'(aa)   for the exercise of any functions of either House of Parliament,'.

Honours

6.   In Schedule 7 to that Act (miscellaneous exemptions) in paragraph 3(b) (honours) after 'honour' there is inserted 'or dignity'.

Legal professional privilege

7.   In paragraph 10 of that Schedule (legal professional privilege), for the words 'or, in Scotland, to confidentiality as between client and professional legal adviser,' there is substituted 'or, in Scotland, to confidentiality of communications'.

Extension of transitional exemption

8.   In Schedule 14 to that Act (transitional provisions), in paragraph 2(1) (which confers transitional exemption from the prohibition on processing without registration on

those registered under the Data Protection Act 1984) the words 'or, if earlier, 24 October 2001' are omitted.

SCHEDULE 7   Section 76(2)

DISCLOSURE OF INFORMATION BY OMBUDSMEN

The Parliamentary Commissioner for Administration

1. At the end of section 11 of the Parliamentary Commissioner Act 1967 (provision for secrecy of information) there is inserted—

    '(5) Information obtained from the Information Commissioner by virtue of section 76(1) of the Freedom of Information Act 2000 shall be treated for the purposes of subsection (2) of this section as obtained for the purposes of an investigation under this Act and, in relation to such information, the reference in paragraph (a) of that subsection to the investigation shall have effect as a reference to any investigation.'

2. After section 11A of that Act there is inserted—

    '11AA. Disclosure of information by Parliamentary Commissioner to Information Commissioner

    (1) The Commissioner may disclose to the Information Commissioner any information obtained by, or furnished to, the Commissioner under or for the purposes of this Act if the information appears to the Commissioner to relate to—

    (a) a matter in respect of which the Information Commissioner could exercise any power conferred by—

    (i) Part V of the Data Protection Act 1998 (enforcement),

    (ii) section 48 of the Freedom of Information Act 2000 (practice recommendations), or

    (iii) Part IV of that Act (enforcement), or

    (b) the commission of an offence under—

    (i) any provision of the Data Protection Act 1998 other than paragraph 12 of Schedule 9 (obstruction of execution of warrant), or

    (ii) section 77 of the Freedom of Information Act 2000 (offence of altering etc. records with intent to prevent disclosure).

    (2) Nothing in section 11(2) of this Act shall apply in relation to the disclosure of information in accordance with this section.'

The Commissions for Local Administration in England and Wales

3. In section 32 of the Local Government Act 1974 (law of defamation, and disclosure of information) after subsection (6) there is inserted—

    '(7) Information obtained from the Information Commissioner by virtue of section 76 of the Freedom of Information Act 2000 shall be treated for the purposes of subsection (2) above as obtained for the purposes of an investigation under this Part of this Act and, in relation to such information, the reference in paragraph (a) of that subsection to the investigation shall have effect as a reference to any investigation.'

240

4. After section 33 of that Act there is inserted—

'33A. Disclosure of information by Local Commissioner to Information Commissioner

(1) A Local Commissioner may disclose to the Information Commissioner any information obtained by, or furnished to, the Local Commissioner under or for the purposes of this Part of this Act if the information appears to the Local Commissioner to relate to—

    (a) a matter in respect of which the Information Commissioner could exercise any power conferred by—

        (i) Part V of the Data Protection Act 1998 (enforcement),

        (ii) section 48 of the Freedom of Information Act 2000 (practice recommendations), or

        (iii) Part IV of that Act (enforcement), or

    (b) the commission of an offence under—

        (i) any provision of the Data Protection Act 1998 other than paragraph 12 of Schedule 9 (obstruction of execution of warrant), or

        (ii) section 77 of the Freedom of Information Act 2000 (offence of altering etc. records with intent to prevent disclosure).

(2) Nothing in section 32(2) of this Act shall apply in relation to the disclosure of information in accordance with this section.'

The Health Service Commissioners

5. At the end of section 15 of the Health Service Commissioners Act 1993 (confidentiality of information) there is inserted—

'(4) Information obtained from the Information Commissioner by virtue of section 76 of the Freedom of Information Act 2000 shall be treated for the purposes of subsection (1) as obtained for the purposes of an investigation and, in relation to such information, the reference in paragraph (a) of that subsection to the investigation shall have effect as a reference to any investigation.'

6. After section 18 of that Act there is inserted—

'18A. Disclosure of information to Information Commissioner

(1) The Health Service Commissioner for England or the Health Service Commissioner for Wales may disclose to the Information Commissioner any information obtained by, or furnished to, the Health Service Commissioner under or for the purposes of this Act if the information appears to the Health Service Commissioner to relate to—

    (a) a matter in respect of which the Information Commissioner could exercise any power conferred by—

        (i) Part V of the Data Protection Act 1998 (enforcement),

        (ii) section 48 of the Freedom of Information Act 2000 (practice recommendations), or

        (iii) Part IV of that Act (enforcement), or

    (b) the commission of an offence under—

        (i) any provision of the Data Protection Act 1998 other than paragraph 12 of Schedule 9 (obstruction of execution of warrant), or

(ii) section 77 of the Freedom of Information Act 2000 (offence of altering etc. records with intent to prevent disclosure).

(3) Nothing in section 15 (confidentiality of information) applies in relation to the disclosure of information in accordance with this section.'

The Welsh Administration Ombudsman

7. In Schedule 9 to the Government of Wales Act 1998 (the Welsh Administration Ombudsman), at the end of paragraph 25 (confidentiality of information) there is inserted—

'(5) Information obtained from the Information Commissioner by virtue of section 76 of the Freedom of Information Act 2000 shall be treated for the purposes of sub-paragraph (1) as obtained for the purposes of an investigation and, in relation to such information, the reference in paragraph (a) of that subsection to the investigation shall have effect as a reference to any investigation.'

8. After paragraph 27 of that Schedule there is inserted—

'Disclosure of information to Information Commissioner

28.—(1) The Welsh Administration Ombudsman may disclose to the Information Commissioner any information obtained by, or furnished to, the Welsh Administration Ombudsman under or for the purposes of this Schedule if the information appears to the Welsh Administration Ombudsman to relate to—

(a) a matter in respect of which the Information Commissioner could exercise any power conferred by—

   (i) Part V of the Data Protection Act 1998 (enforcement),

   (ii) section 48 of the Freedom of Information Act 2000 (practice recommendations), or

   (iii) Part IV of that Act (enforcement), or

(b) the commission of an offence under—

   (i) any provision of the Data Protection Act 1998 other than paragraph 12 of Schedule 9 (obstruction of execution of warrant), or

   (ii) section 77 of the Freedom of Information Act 2000 (offence of altering etc. records with intent to prevent disclosure).

(2) Nothing in paragraph 25(1) applies in relation to the disclosure of information in accordance with this paragraph.'

The Northern Ireland Commissioner for complaints

9. At the end of Article 21 of the Commissioner for Complaints (Northern Ireland) Order 1996 (disclosure of information by Commissioner) there is inserted—

'(5) Information obtained from the Information Commissioner by virtue of section 76 of the Freedom of Information Act 2000 shall be treated for the purposes of paragraph (1) as obtained for the purposes of an investigation under this Order and, in relation to such information, the reference in paragraph (1)(a) to the investigation shall have effect as a reference to any investigation.'

10. After that Article there is inserted—

'21A. Disclosure of information to Information Commissioner

(1) The Commissioner may disclose to the Information Commissioner any information obtained by, or furnished to, the Commissioner under or for the purposes of this Order if the information appears to the Commissioner to relate to—

(a) a matter in respect of which the Information Commissioner could exercise any power conferred by—

(i) Part V of the Data Protection Act 1998 (enforcement),

(ii) section 48 of the Freedom of Information Act 2000 (practice recommendations), or

(iii) Part IV of that Act (enforcement), or

(b) the commission of an offence under—

(i) any provision of the Data Protection Act 1998 other than paragraph 12 of Schedule 9 (obstruction of execution of warrant), or

(ii) section 77 of the Freedom of Information Act 2000 (offence of altering etc. records with intent to prevent disclosure).

(2) Nothing in Article 21(1) applies in relation to the disclosure of information in accordance with this Article.'

The Assembly Ombudsman for Northern Ireland

11. At the end of Article 19 of the Ombudsman (Northern Ireland) Order 1996 there is inserted—

'(5) Information obtained from the Information Commissioner by virtue of section 76 of the Freedom of Information Act 2000 shall be treated for the purposes of paragraph (1) as obtained for the purposes of an investigation under this Order and, in relation to such information, the reference in paragraph (1)(a) to the investigation shall have effect as a reference to any investigation.'

12. After that Article there is inserted—

'19A. Disclosure of information to Information Commissioner

(1) The Ombudsman may disclose to the Information Commissioner any information obtained by, or furnished to, the Ombudsman under or for the purposes of this Order if the information appears to the Ombudsman to relate to—

(a) a matter in respect of which the Information Commissioner could exercise any power conferred by—

(i) Part V of the Data Protection Act 1998 (enforcement),

(ii) section 48 of the Freedom of Information Act 2000 (practice recommendations), or

(iii) Part IV of that Act (enforcement), or

(b) the commission of an offence under—

(i) any provision of the Data Protection Act 1998 other than paragraph 12 of Schedule 9 (obstruction of execution of warrant), or

(ii) section 77 of the Freedom of Information Act 2000 (offence of altering etc. records with intent to prevent disclosure).

(2) Nothing in Article 19(1) applies in relation to the disclosure of information in accordance with this Article.'

The Commissioner for Local Administration in Scotland

13. [. . .]

SCHEDULE 8
REPEALS

PART I
REPEAL COMING INTO FORCE ON PASSING OF ACT

Chapter	Short title	Extent of repeal
1998 c. 29.	The Data Protection Act 1998.	In Schedule 14, in paragraph 2(1), the words 'or, if earlier, 24 October 2001'.

PART II
REPEALS COMING INTO FORCE IN ACCORDANCE WITH SECTION 87(2)

Chapter	Short title	Extent of repeal
1958 c. 51.	The Public Records Act 1958.	In Schedule 1, in Part II of the Table in paragraph 3, the entry relating to the Data Protection Commissioner.
1967 c. 13.	The Parliamentary Commissioner Act 1967.	In Schedule 2, the entry relating to the Data Protection Commissioner.
1975 c. 24.	The House of Commons Disqualification Act 1975.	In Schedule 1, in Part III, the entry relating to the Data Protection Commissioner.
1975 c. 25.	The Northern Ireland Assembly Disqualification Act 1975.	In Schedule 1, in Part III, the entry relating to the Data Protection Commissioner.
1998 c. 29.	The Data Protection Act 1998.	In Schedule 5, Part III. In Schedule 15, paragraphs 1(1), 2, 4, 5(2) and 6(2)

PART III
REPEALS COMING INTO FORCE IN ACCORDANCE WITH SECTION 87(3)

Chapter	Short title	Extent of repeal
1958 c. 51.	The Public Records Act 1958.	In section 5, subsections (1), (2) and (4) and, in subsection (5), the words from 'and subject to' to the end. Schedule 2.
1975 c. 24.	The House of Commons Disqualification Act 1975.	In Schedule 1, in Part II, the entry relating to the Data Protection Tribunal.
1975 c. 25.	The Northern Ireland Assembly Disqualification Act 1975.	In Schedule 1, in Part II, the entry relating to the Data Protection Tribunal.
1998 c. 29.	The Data Protection Act 1998.	In section 1(1), in the definition of 'data', the word 'or' at the end of paragraph (c). In Schedule 15, paragraphs 1(2) and (3), 3, 5(1) and 6(1).

Lord Chancellor's Code of Practice on the Discharge of Public Authorities' Functions under Part I of the Freedom of Information Act 2000

The Lord Chancellor, after consulting the Information Commissioner, issues the following Code of Practice pursuant to section 45 of the Act.

Laid before Parliament on 20 November 2002 pursuant to section 45(5) of the Freedom of Information Act 2000.

I Introduction

1. This code of practice outlines to public authorities the practice which it would, in the opinion of the Lord Chancellor, be desirable for them to follow in connection with the discharge of their functions under Part I (Access to information held by public authorities) of the Freedom of Information Act 2000 ('the Act').

2. The aims of the Code are to:
   - facilitate the disclosure of information under the Act by setting out good administrative practice that it is desirable for public authorities to follow when handling requests for information, including, where appropriate, the transfer of a request to a different authority;
   - protect the interests of applicants by setting out standards for the provision of advice which it would be good practice to make available to them and to encourage the development of effective means of complaining about decisions taken under the Act;
   - ensure that the interests of third parties who may be affected by any decision to disclose information are considered by the authority by setting standards for consultation; and
   - ensure that authorities consider the implications for Freedom of Information before agreeing to confidentiality provisions in contracts and accepting information in confidence from a third party more generally.

3. Although there is a statutory duty on the Lord Chancellor to issue the Code, the provisions of the Code themselves do not have statutory force. However, authorities are expected to abide by the Code unless there are good reasons, capable of being justified to the Information Commissioner, why it would be inappropriate to do so. The statutory requirements for dealing with requests for information are contained in the Act and regulations made under it and public authorities must comply with these statutory provisions at all times. However, section 47 of the Act places a duty

on the Information Commissioner to promote the following of good practice by public authorities ('good practice' includes compliance with the provisions of the Code), and section 48 of the Act enables the Information Commissioner to issue a 'practice recommendation' to a public authority if it appears to him that the practice of the authority does not conform with that proposed in the Code. Further, section 16 of the Act places a duty on public authorities to provide advice and assistance to applicants and potential applicants. Authorities will have complied with this duty in any particular case if they have conformed with the Code in relation to the provision of advice or assistance in that case.

4. Words and expressions used in this Code have the same meaning as the same words and expressions used in the Act.

II The provision of advice and assistance to persons making requests for information

5. Every public authority should be ready to provide advice and assistance, including but not necessarily limited to the steps set out below, to those who propose to make, or have made requests to it, in order to facilitate their use of the Act. The duty on the public authority is to provide advice and assistance 'so far as it would be reasonable to expect the authority to do so'. Any public authority which conforms with this Code in relation to the provision of advice and assistance in any case will be taken to comply with this duty in relation to that case.

6. Public authorities should publish their procedures for dealing with requests for information. These procedures may include what the public authority's usual procedure will be where it does not hold the information requested. (See also VI—*'Transferring requests for information'*) It may also alert potential applicants to the fact that the public authority may need to consult other public authorities and/or third parties in order to reach a decision on whether the requested information can be released, and therefore alert potential applicants that they may wish to be notified before any transfer of request or consultation is made and if so, they should say so in their applications. (See also VII—*'Consultation with third parties'*.) The procedures should include an address or addresses (including an e-mail address where possible) to which applicants may direct requests for information or for assistance. A telephone number should also be provided, where possible that of a named individual who can provide assistance. These procedures should be referred to in the authority's publication scheme.

7. Staff working in public authorities in contact with the public should bear in mind that not everyone will be aware of the Act, or Regulations made under it, and they will need to draw these to the attention of potential applicants who appear unaware of them.

8. A request for information under the Act's general right of access must be made in writing (which includes a request transmitted by electronic means which is received in legible form and is capable of being used for subsequent reference). Where a person is unable to frame their request in writing, the public authority should ensure that appropriate assistance is given to enable that person to make a request for information. Depending on the circumstances, appropriate assistance might include:

- advising the person that another person or agency (such as a Citizens Advice Bureau) may be able to assist them with the application, or make the application on their behalf;

- in exceptional circumstances, offering to take a note of the application over the telephone and then send the note to the applicant for confirmation (in which case the written note of the telephone request, once verified by the applicant and returned, would constitute a written request for information and the statutory time limit for reply would begin when the written confirmation was received).

This list is not exhaustive, and public authorities should be flexible in offering advice and assistance most appropriate to the circumstances of the applicant.

9. Where the applicant does not describe the information sought in a way which would enable the public authority to identify or locate it, or the request is ambiguous, the authority should, as far as practicable, provide assistance to the applicant to enable him or her to describe more clearly the information requested. Authorities should be aware that the aim of providing assistance is to clarify the nature of the information sought, not to determine the aims or motivation of the applicant. Care should be taken not to give the applicant the impression that he or she is obliged to disclose the nature of his or her interest or that he or she will be treated differently if he or she does. It is important that the applicant is contacted as soon as possible, preferably by telephone, fax or e-mail, where more information is needed to clarify what is sought.

10. Appropriate assistance in this instance might include:
- providing an outline of the different kinds of information which might meet the terms of the request;
- providing access to detailed catalogues and indexes, where these are available, to help the applicant ascertain the nature and extent of the information held by the authority;
- providing a general response to the request setting out options for further information which could be provided on request;

This list is not exhaustive, and public authorities should be flexible in offering advice and assistance most appropriate to the circumstances of the applicant.

11. In seeking to clarify what is sought public authorities should bear in mind that applicants cannot reasonably be expected to possess identifiers such as a file reference number, or a description of a particular record, unless this information is made available by the authority for the use of applicants.

12. If, following the provision of such assistance, the applicant still fails to describe the information requested in a way which would enable the authority to identify and locate it, the authority is not expected to seek further clarification. The authority should disclose any information relating to the application which has been successfully identified and found for which it does not wish to claim an exemption. It should also explain to the applicant why it cannot take the request any further and provide details of the authority's complaints procedure and the applicant's rights under section 50 of the Act (see '*Complaints Procedure*' in section XII below).

13. Where the applicant indicates that he or she is not prepared to pay the fee notified in any fees notice given to the applicant, the authority should consider whether there is any information that may be of interest to the applicant that is available free of charge.

14. Where an authority is not obliged to comply with a request for information because, under section 12(1) and regulations made under section 12(4), the cost of complying would exceed the 'appropriate limit' (i.e. cost threshold), and where the public

authority is not prepared to comply on a discretionary basis because of the cost of doing so, the authority should consider providing an indication of what information could be provided within the cost ceiling.

15. An authority is not expected to provide assistance to applicants whose requests are vexatious within the meaning of section 14 of the Act.

III Handling requests for information which appear to be part of an organised campaign

16. Where an authority is not required to comply with a number of related requests because, under section 12(1) and regulations made under section 12(4), the cumulative cost of complying with the requests would exceed the 'appropriate limit' (i.e. cost threshold) prescribed in Fees Regulations, the authority should consider whether the information could be disclosed in another, more cost-effective, manner. For example, the authority should consider if the information is such that publication on the authority's website, and a brief notification of the website reference to each applicant, would bring the cost within the appropriate limit.

IV Timeliness in dealing with requests for information

17. Public authorities are required to comply with all requests for information promptly and they should not delay responding until the end of the 20 working day period under section 10(1) if the information could reasonably have been provided earlier.

18. Public authorities should aim to make *all* decisions within 20 working days, including in cases where a public authority needs to consider where the public interest lies in respect of an application for exempt information. However, it is recognised there will be some instances where it will not be possible to deal with such an application within 20 working days. Although there is no statutory time limit on the length of time the authority may take to reach a decision where the public interest must be considered, it must, under section 17(2), give an estimate of the date by which it expects to reach such a decision. In these instances, authorities are expected to give estimates which are realistic and reasonable in the circumstances of the particular case, taking account, for example, of the need to consult third parties where this is necessary. Public authorities are expected to comply with their estimates unless there are good reasons not to. If the public authority exceeds its estimate, it should apologise to the applicant and explain the reason(s) for the delay. If a public authority finds, while considering the public interest, that the estimate given is proving unrealistic, it should keep the applicant informed. Public authorities should keep a record of instances where estimates are exceeded, and where this happens more than occasionally, take steps to identify the problem and rectify it.

V Charging fees

19. The Act does not require charges to be made, but public authorities have discretion to charge applicants a fee in accordance with Fees Regulations made under sections 9, 12 and 13 of the Act in respect of requests made under the general right of access.

20. The Fees Regulations do not apply:
   - to material made available under a publication scheme under section 19;

- to information which is reasonably accessible to the applicant by other means within the meaning of the exemption provided for at section 21; or
- where provision is made by or under any enactment as to the fee that may be charged by the public authority for disclosure of the information as provided in sections 9(5) and 13(3) of the Act'.

Public authorities should ensure that any charges they make in cases falling outside those covered by the Fees Regulations are in accordance with any relevant legislation and are within the terms of any relevant guidance which has been issued or approved by HM Treasury and which is applicable to the public authority, or any relevant guidance issued or approved by the Northern Ireland Department of Finance and Personnel applicable to devolved public bodies in Northern Ireland.

VI Transferring requests for information

21. A request can only be transferred where a public authority receives a request for information which it does not hold, within the meaning of section 3(2) of the Act, but which is held by another public authority. If a public authority in receipt of a request holds some of the information requested, a transfer can only be made in respect of the information it does not hold (but is held by another public authority).

22. Public authorities should bear in mind that 'holding' information includes holding a copy of a record produced or supplied by another person or body (but does not extend to holding a record on behalf of another person or body as provided for in section 3(2)(a) of the Act).

23. The authority receiving the initial request must always process it in accordance with the Act in respect of such information relating to the request as it holds. The authority should also advise the applicant that it does not hold part of the requested information, or all of it, whichever applies. But before doing this, the authority must be certain as to the extent of the information relating to the request which it holds itself.

24. If the authority to whom the original request was made believes that some or all of the information requested is held by another public authority, the authority should consider what would be the most helpful way of assisting the applicant with his or her request. In most cases this is likely to involve:
    - contacting the applicant and informing him or her that the information requested may be held by another public authority;
    - suggesting that the applicant re-applies to the authority which the original authority believes to hold the information;
    - providing him or her with contact details for that authority.

25. However, in some cases the authority to whom the original request is made may consider it to be more appropriate to transfer the request to another authority in respect of the information which it does not hold. In such cases, the authority should consult the other authority with a view to ascertaining whether it does hold the information and, if so, consider whether it should transfer the request to it. A request (or part of a request) should not be transferred without confirmation by the second authority that it holds the information.

26. Before transferring a request for information to another authority, the authority should consider:

- whether a transfer is appropriate; and if so
- whether the applicant is likely to have any grounds to object to the transfer;

If the authority reasonably concludes that the applicant is not likely to object, it may transfer the request without going back to the applicant, but should tell him or her it has done so.

27. Where there are reasonable grounds to believe an applicant is likely to object, the authority should only transfer the request to another authority with his or her consent. If the authority is in any doubt, it may prefer contact the applicant with a view to suggesting that he or she makes a new request to the other authority, as in *paragraph 23* above.

28. Where a request or part of a request is transferred from one public authority to another, the receiving authority must comply with its obligations under Part I of the Act in the same way as it would for a request that is received direct from an applicant. The time for complying with such a request will be measured from the day that the receiving authority receives the request.

29. All transfers of requests should take place as soon as is practicable, and the applicant should be informed as soon as possible once this has been done.

30. Where a public authority is unable either to advise the applicant which public authority holds, or may hold, the requested information or to facilitate the transfer of the request to another authority (or considers it inappropriate to do so) it should consider what advice, if any, it can provide to the applicant to enable him or her to pursue his or her request.

VII Consultation with third parties

31. In some cases the disclosure of information pursuant to a request may affect the legal rights of a third party, for example where information is subject to the common law duty of confidence or where it constitutes 'personal data' within the meaning of the Data Protection Act 1998 ('the DPA'). Public authorities must always remember that unless an exemption provided for in the Act applies in relation to any particular information, they will be obliged to disclose that information in response to a request.

32. Where a disclosure of information cannot be made without the consent of a third party (for example, where information has been obtained from a third party and in the circumstances the disclosure of the information without their consent would constitute an actionable breach of confidence such that the exemption at section 41 of the Act would apply), the authority should consult that third party with a view to seeking their consent to the disclosure, unless such a consultation is not practicable, for example because the third party cannot be located or because the costs of consulting them would be disproportionate.

33. Where information constitutes 'personal data' within the meaning of the DPA, public authorities should have regard to section 40 of the Act which makes detailed provision for cases in which a request relates to such information and the interplay between the Act and the DPA in such cases.

34. Where the interests of the third party which may be affected by a disclosure do not give rise to legal rights, consultation may still be appropriate.

35. Consultation should take place where:
    - the views of the third party may assist the authority to determine whether an exemption under the Act applies to the information requested; or

- the views of the third party may assist the authority to determine where the public interest lies under section 2 of the Act.

36. A public authority may consider that consultation is not appropriate where the cost of consulting with third parties would be disproportionate. In such cases, the authority should consider what is the most reasonable course of action for it to take in light of the requirements of the Act and the individual circumstances of the request.

37. Consultation will be unnecessary where:
   - the public authority does not intend to disclose the information relying on some other legitimate ground under the terms of the Act;
   - the views of the third party can have no effect on the decision of the authority, for example, where there is other legislation preventing or requiring the disclosure of this information;
   - no exemption applies and so under the Act's provisions, the information must be provided.

38. Where the interests of a number of third parties may be affected by a disclosure and those parties have a representative organisation which can express views on behalf of those parties, the authority may, if it considers consultation appropriate, consider that it would be sufficient to consult that representative organisation. If there is no representative organisation, the authority may consider that it would be sufficient to consult a representative sample of the third parties in question.

39. The fact that the third party has not responded to consultation does not relieve the authority of its duty to disclose information under the Act, or its duty to reply within the time specified in the Act.

40. In all cases, it is for the public authority, not the third party (or representative of the third party) to determine whether or not information should be disclosed under the Act. A refusal to consent to disclosure by a third party does not, in itself, mean information should be withheld.

VIII Freedom of information and public sector contracts

41. When entering into contracts public authorities should refuse to include contractual terms which purport to restrict the disclosure of information held by the authority and relating to the contract beyond the restrictions permitted by the Act. Public authorities cannot 'contract out' of their obligations under the Act. Unless an exemption provided for under the Act is applicable in relation to any particular information, a public authority will be obliged to disclose that information in response to a request, regardless of the terms of any contract.

42. When entering into contracts with non-public authority contractors, public authorities may be under pressure to accept confidentiality clauses so that information relating to the terms of the contract, its value and performance will be exempt from disclosure. Public authorities should reject such clauses wherever possible. Where, exceptionally, it is necessary to include non-disclosure provisions in a contract, an option could be to agree with the contractor a schedule of the contract which clearly identifies information which should not be disclosed. But authorities will need to take care when drawing up any such schedule, and be aware that any restrictions on disclosure provided for could potentially be overridden by their obligations under the Act, as described in the paragraph above.

43. In any event, public authorities should not agree to hold information 'in confidence' which is not in fact confidential in nature. Authorities should be aware that the exemption provided for in section 41 only applies if information has been obtained by a public authority from another person, and the disclosure of the information to the public, otherwise than under the Act would constitute a breach of confidence actionable by that, or any other person.

44. Any acceptance of such confidentiality provisions must be for good reasons and capable of being justified to the Commissioner.

45. It is for the public authority to disclose information pursuant to the Act, and not the non-public authority contractor. However, the public authority may wish to protect from disclosure by the contractor, by appropriate contractual terms, information which the authority has provided to the contractor which would clearly be exempt from disclosure under the Act, by appropriate contractual terms. In order to avoid unnecessary secrecy, any such constraints should be drawn as narrowly as possible, and according to the individual circumstances of the case. Apart from such cases, public authorities should not impose terms of secrecy on contractors.

46. Section 5(1)(b) of the Act empowers the Lord Chancellor to designate as public authorities for the purposes of the Act, persons (or bodies) who provide under a contract made with a public authority, any service whose provision is a function of that authority. Thus, some non-public authority contractors will be regarded as public authorities within the meaning of the Act, although only in respect of the services provided under the contract. As such, and to that extent, the contractor will be required to comply with the Act like any other public authority.

IX Accepting information in confidence from third parties

47. A public authority should only accept information from third parties in confidence if it is necessary to obtain that information in connection with the exercise of any of the authority's functions and it would not otherwise be provided. In addition, public authorities should not agree to hold information received from third parties 'in confidence' which is not confidential in nature. Again, acceptance of any confidentiality provisions must be for good reasons, capable of being justified to the Commissioner.

X Consultation with devolved administrations

48. Public authorities should consult with the relevant devolved administration before disclosing information provided by or directly concerning that administration, except where:
  • the views of the devolved administration can have no effect on the decision of the authority (for example where there is other legislation requiring the disclosure of the information), or there is no applicable exemption so the information must be disclosed under the Act; or
  • in the circumstances, consultation would be disproportionate.

49. Similarly, the devolved administrations should consult with the relevant non-devolved public authority before disclosing information provided by or directly concerning that authority, except where the views of the public authority can have no

effect on the decision whether to disclose, or where consultation would be disproportionate in the circumstances.

XI Refusal of request

50. Where a request for information is refused in reliance on an exemption, the Act requires that the authority notifies the applicant which exemption has been claimed, and if it would otherwise not be apparent, why that exemption applies. Public authorities should not (subject to the proviso in section 17(4) i.e. if the statement would involve the disclosure of information which would itself be exempt information) merely paraphrase the wording of the exemption. The Act also requires authorities, when withholding information (other than under an 'absolute' exemption), to state the reasons for claiming that the public interest in maintaining the exemption outweighs the public interest in disclosure. Public authorities should specify the public interest factors (for and against disclosure) which they have taken into account before reaching the decision (again, subject to the proviso in section 17(4)).

51. For monitoring purposes public authorities should keep a record of all applications where either all or part of the requested information is withheld. In addition to a record of the numbers of applications involved where information is withheld, senior managers in each public authority need information on each case to determine whether cases are being properly considered, and whether the reasons for refusals are sound. This could be done by requiring all staff who refuse a request for information to forward the details to a central point in the organisation for collation. Details of information on complaints about applications which have been refused (see XII— 'Complaints procedure' below) could be collected at the same central point.

XII Complaints procedure

52. Each public authority should have a complaints procedure in place by the date that its duties in respect of the publication scheme provisions of the Act come into effect. The complaints procedure may then be used by any person who perceives that the authority is not complying with its publication scheme. If the matter cannot be dealt with satisfactorily on an informal basis, the public authority should inform such persons if approached by them of the details of its internal complaints procedure, and how to contact the Information Commissioner, if the complainant wishes to write to him about the matter. The authority should also explain that although the complainant cannot apply to the Commissioner for a decision under section 50 of the Act, the Commissioner may investigate the matter at his discretion.

53. When the provisions of the Act relating to the general right of access come into force, the complaints procedure will also be required for dealing with complaints from people who consider that their request has not been properly handled, or who are otherwise dissatisfied with the outcome of the consideration of their request, and where the issue is such that it cannot be resolved informally in discussion with the official dealing with the request. If a public authority has failed to introduce a complaints procedure, an applicant is entitled, under the Act, to complain directly to the Commissioner.

54. When communicating any decision made in relation to a request under the Act's

general right of access, public authorities are obliged, under section 17(7) of the Act notify the applicant of their rights of complaint. They should provide details of their own complaints procedure, including how to make a complaint and inform the applicant of the right to complain to the Commissioner under section 50 if he or she is still dissatisfied following the authority's review.

55. Any written reply from the applicant (including one transmitted by electronic means) expressing dissatisfaction with an authority's response to a valid request for information should be treated as a complaint, as should any written communication from a person who perceives the authority is not complying with its publication scheme. These communications should be handled in accordance with the authority's complaints procedure, even if, in the case of a request for information under the general right of access, the applicant does not state his or her desire for the authority to review their decision or their handling of the application.

56. The complaints procedure should be a fair and impartial means of dealing with handling problems and reviewing decisions taken pursuant to the Act, including decisions taken about where the public interest lies in respect of exempt information. It should be possible to reverse or otherwise amend decisions previously taken. Complaints procedures should be clear and not unnecessarily bureaucratic. They should be capable of producing a prompt determination of the complaint.

57. Where the complaint concerns a request for information under the general right of access, the review should be handled by a person who was not a party to the original decision, where this is practicable. If this is not possible (for example in a very small public authority), the circumstances should be explained to the applicant. Where the decision on the application was taken by someone in a position where a review cannot realistically be undertaken (e.g. a Minister), the public authority may consider whether to waive the internal review procedure (and inform the applicant if this is what is decided), so that the applicant is free to approach the Commissioner.

58. In all cases, complaints should be acknowledged and the complainant should be informed of the authority's target date for determining the complaint. Where it is apparent that determination of the complaint will take longer than the target time (for example because of the complexity of the particular case), the authority should inform the applicant and explain the reason for the delay. The complainant should always be informed of the outcome of his or her complaint.

59. Authorities may set their own target times for dealing with complaints but these should be reasonable, defensible, and subject to regular review. Each public authority should publish its target times for determining complaints and information as to how successful it is with meeting those targets.

60. Records should be kept of all complaints and of their outcome. Authorities should have procedures in place for monitoring complaints and for reviewing, and, if necessary, amending, procedures for dealing with requests for information where such action is indicated by more than occasional reversals of initial decisions.

61. Where the outcome of a complaint is that information should be disclosed which was previously withheld, the information in question should be disclosed as soon as practicable and the applicant should be informed how soon this will be.

62. Where the outcome of a complaint is that the procedures within an authority have not been properly followed by the authority's staff, the authority should apologise to the applicant. The authority should also take appropriate steps to prevent similar errors occurring in future.

63. Where the outcome of a complaint is that an initial decision to withhold information is upheld, or is otherwise in the authority's favour, the applicant should be informed of his or her right to apply to the Commissioner, and be given details of how to make an application, for a decision on whether the request for information has been dealt with in accordance with the requirements of Part I of the Act.

Lord Chancellor's Code of Practice on the Management of Records under the Freedom of Information Act 2000

CODE OF PRACTICE

ON (1) THE MANAGEMENT OF RECORDS BY PUBLIC AUTHORITIES
AND (2) THE TRANSFER AND REVIEW OF PUBLIC RECORDS UNDER
THE FREEDOM OF INFORMATION ACT 2000

The Lord Chancellor, after consulting the Information Commissioner and the appropriate Northern Ireland Minister issues the following Code of Practice pursuant to section 46 of the Freedom of Information Act.

Laid before Parliament on 20 November 2002 pursuant to section 46(6) of the Freedom of Information Act 2000.

Introduction

1. The aims of the Code are:
    (1) to set out practices which public authorities and bodies subject to the Public Records Act 1958 and the Public Records Act (NI) 1923 should follow in relation to the creation, keeping, management and destruction of their records (Part One of the Code), and
    (2) to describe the arrangements which public record bodies should follow in reviewing public records and transferring them to the Public Record Office or to places of deposit or to the Public Record Office of Northern Ireland (Part Two of the Code).
2. This Code refers to records in all technical or physical formats.
3. Part One of the Code provides a framework for the management of records of public authorities and bodies subject to the Public Records Act 1958 and the Public Records Act (NI) 1923, and Part Two deals with the review and transfer of public records. More detailed guidance on both themes may be obtained from published standards. Those which support the objectives of this Code most directly are listed at Annex A.
4. Words and expressions used in this Code have the same meaning as the same words and expressions used in the FOIA.

PART ONE: RECORDS MANAGEMENT

5. Functional Responsibility

5.1   The records management function should be recognised as a specific corporate programme within an authority and should receive the necessary levels of organisational support to ensure effectiveness. It should bring together responsibilities for records in all formats, including electronic records, throughout their life cycle, from planning and creation through to ultimate disposal. It should have clearly defined responsibilities and objectives, and the resources to achieve them. It is desirable that the person, or persons, responsible for the records management function should also have either direct responsibility or an organisational connection with the person or persons responsible for freedom of information, data protection and other information management issues.

6. Policy

6.1   An authority should have in place an overall policy statement, endorsed by top management and made readily available to staff at all levels of the organisation, on how it manages its records, including electronic records.

6.2   This policy statement should provide a mandate for the performance of all records and information management functions. In particular, it should set out an authority's commitment to create, keep and manage records which document its principal activities. The policy should also outline the role of records management and its relationship to the authority's overall strategy; define roles and responsibilities including the responsibility of individuals to document their actions and decisions in the authority's records, and to dispose of records; provide a framework for supporting standards, procedures and guidelines; and indicate the way in which compliance with the policy and its supporting standards, procedures and guidelines will be monitored.

6.3   The policy statement should be reviewed at regular intervals (at least once every three years) and, if appropriate, amended to maintain its relevance.

7. Human Resources

7.1   A designated member of staff of appropriate seniority should have lead responsibility for records management within the authority. This lead role should be formally acknowledged and made known throughout the authority.

7.2   Staff responsible for records management should have the appropriate skills and knowledge needed to achieve the aims of the records management programme. Responsibility for all aspects of record keeping should be specifically defined and incorporated in the role descriptions or similar documents.

7.3   Human resource policies and practices in organisations should address the need to recruit and retain good quality staff and should accordingly support the records management function in the following areas:
- the provision of appropriate resources to enable the records management function to be maintained across all of its activities;
- the establishment and maintenance of a scheme, such as a competency framework, to identify the knowledge, skills and corporate competencies required in records and information management;

- the regular review of selection criteria for records management posts to ensure currency and compliance with best practice;
- the regular analysis of training needs;
- the establishment of a professional development programme for records management staff;
- the inclusion in induction training programmes for all new staff of an awareness of records issues and practices.

8. Active Records Management

Record creation

8.1 Each operational/business unit of an authority should have in place an adequate system for documenting its activities. This system should take into account the legislative and regulatory environments in which the authority works.

8.2 Records of a business activity should be complete and accurate enough to allow employees and their successors to undertake appropriate actions in the context of their responsibilities, to
- facilitate an audit or examination of the business by anyone so authorised,
- protect the legal and other rights of the authority, its clients and any other person affected by its actions, and
- provide authenticity of the records so that the evidence derived from them is shown to be credible and authoritative.

8.3 Records created by the authority should be arranged in a record keeping system that will enable the authority to obtain the maximum benefit from the quick and easy retrieval of information.

Record keeping

8.4 Installing and maintaining an effective records management programme depends on knowledge of what records are held, in what form they are made accessible, and their relationship to organisational functions. An information survey or record audit will meet this requirement, help to promote control over the records, and provide valuable data for developing records appraisal and disposal procedures.

8.5 Paper and electronic record keeping systems should contain metadata (descriptive and technical documentation) to enable the system and the records to be understood and to be operated efficiently, and to provide an administrative context for effective management of the records.

8.6 The record-keeping system, whether paper or electronic, should include a set of rules for referencing, titling, indexing and, if appropriate, security marking of records. These should be easily understood and should enable the efficient retrieval of information.

Record maintenance

8.7 The movement and location of records should be controlled to ensure that a record can be easily retrieved at any time, that any outstanding issues can be dealt with, and that there is an auditable trail of record transactions.

8.8 Storage accommodation for current records must be clean and tidy, and it should prevent damage to the records. Equipment used for current records should provide storage which is safe from unauthorised access and which meets fire regulations, but which allows maximum accessibility to the information commensurate with its frequency of use. When records are no longer required for the conduct of current business, their placement in a designated records centre rather than in offices is a more economical and efficient way to store them. Procedures for handling records should take full account of the need to preserve important information.

8.9 A contingency or business recovery plan should be in place to provide protection for records which are vital to the continued functioning of the authority.

9. Disposal Arrangements

9.1 It is particularly important under FOI that the disposal of records—which is here defined as the point in their lifecycle when they are either transferred to an archive or destroyed—is undertaken in accordance with clearly established policies which have been formally adopted by authorities and which are enforced by properly authorised staff.

Record closure

9.2 Records must be closed as soon as they have ceased to be of active use other than for reference purposes. As a general rule, files should be closed after five years and, if action continues, a further file should be opened. An indication that a file of paper records or folder of electronic records has been closed should be shown on the record itself as well as noted in the index or database of the files/folders. Wherever possible, information on the intended disposal of electronic records should be included in the metadata when the record is created.

9.3 The storage of closed records awaiting disposal should follow accepted standards relating to environment, security and physical organisation.

Appraisal planning and documentation

9.4 In order to make their disposal policies work effectively and for those to which the FOIA applies to provide the information required under FOI legislation, authorities need to have in place systems for managing appraisal and for recording the disposal decisions made. An assessment of the volume and nature of records due for disposal, the time taken to appraise records, and the risks associated with destruction or delay in appraisal will provide information to support an authority's resource planning and workflow arrangements.

9.5 An appraisal documentation system will ensure consistency in records appraisal and disposal. It should show what records are designated for destruction, the authority under which they are to be destroyed and when they are to be destroyed. It should also provide background information on the records, such as legislative provisions, functional context and physical arrangement. This information will provide valuable data for placing records selected for preservation into context and will enable future records managers to provide evidence of the operation of their selection policies.

Record selection

9.6 Each authority should maintain a selection policy which states in broad terms the functions from which records are likely to be selected for permanent preservation and the periods for which other records should be retained. The policy should be supported by or linked to disposal schedules which should cover all records created, including electronic records. Schedules should be arranged on the basis of series or collection and should indicate the appropriate disposal action for all records (e.g. review after x years; destroy after y years).

9.7 Records selected for permanent preservation and no longer in regular use by the authority should be transferred as soon as possible to an archival institution that has adequate storage and public access facilities (see Part Two of this Code for arrangements for bodies subject to the Public Records Acts).

9.8 Records not selected for permanent preservation and which have reached the end of their administrative life should be destroyed in as secure a manner as is necessary for the level of confidentiality or security markings they bear. A record of the destruction of records, showing their reference, description and date of destruction should be maintained and preserved by the records manager. Disposal schedules would constitute the basis of such a record.

9.9 If a record due for destruction is known to be the subject of a request for information, destruction should be delayed until disclosure has taken place or, if the authority has decided not to disclose the information, until the complaint and appeal provisions of the FOIA have been exhausted.

10. Management of Electronic Records

10.1 The principal issues for the management of electronic records are the same as those for the management of any record. They include, for example the creation of authentic records, the tracking of records and disposal arrangements. However, the means by which these issues are addressed in the electronic environment will be different.

10.2 Effective electronic record keeping requires:
- a clear understanding of the nature of electronic records;
- the creation of records and metadata necessary to document business processes: this should be part of the systems which hold the records;
- the maintenance of a structure of folders to reflect logical groupings of records;
- the secure maintenance of the integrity of electronic records;
- the accessibility and use of electronic records for as long as required (which may include their migration across systems);

- the application of appropriate disposal procedures, including procedures for archiving; and
- the ability to cross reference electronic records to their paper counterparts in a mixed environment.

10.3 Generic requirements for electronic record management systems are set out in the 1999 Public Record Office statement *Functional Requirements and Testing of Electronic Records Management Systems.* (*see*: http:// www.pro.gov.uk/ recordsmanagement/eros/invest.htm). Authorities are encouraged to use these as a model when developing their specifications for such systems.

10.4 Audit trails should be provided for all electronic information and documents. They should be kept securely and should be available for inspection by authorised personnel. The BSI document *Principles of Good Practice for Information Management (PD0010)* recommends audits at predetermined intervals for particular aspects of electronic records management.

10.5 Authorities should seek to conform to the provisions of BSI DISC PD0008—*A Code of Practice for Legal Admissibility and Evidential Weight of Information Stored Electronically (2nd edn)*—especially for those records likely to be required as evidence.

PART TWO: REVIEW AND TRANSFER OF PUBLIC RECORDS

11.1 This part of the Code relates to the arrangements which authorities should follow to ensure the timely and effective review and transfer of public records. Accordingly, it is relevant only to authorities which are subject to the Public Records Acts 1958 and 1967 or to the Public Records Act (NI) 1923. The general purpose of this part of the Code is to facilitate the performance by the Public Record Office, the Public Record Office of Northern Ireland and other public authorities of their functions under the Freedom of Information Act.

11.2 Under the Public Records Acts, records selected for preservation may be transferred either to the Public Record Office or to places of deposit appointed by the Lord Chancellor. This Code applies to all such transfers. For guidance on which records may be transferred to which institution, and on the disposition of UK public records relating to Northern Ireland, see the Public Record Office *Acquisition Policy* (1998) and the Public Record Office *Disposition Policy* (2000).

11.3 In reviewing records for public release, authorities should ensure that public records become available to the public at the earliest possible time in accordance with the FOIA.

11.4 Authorities which have created or are otherwise responsible for public records should ensure that they operate effective arrangements to determine
(a) which records should be selected for permanent preservation; and
(b) which records should be released to the public.
These arrangements should be established and operated under the supervision of the Public Record Office or, in Northern Ireland, in conjunction with the Public Record Office of Northern Ireland. The objectives and

arrangements for the review of records for release are described in greater detail below.

11.5 In carrying out their review of records for release to the public, authorities should observe the following points:

11.5.1 transfer to the Public Record Office must take place by the time the records are 30 years old, unless the Lord Chancellor gives authorisation for them to be retained for a longer period of time (see section 3(4) of the Public Records Act 1958). By agreement with the Public Record Office, transfer and release may take place before 30 years;

11.5.2 review—for selection and release—should therefore take place before the records in question are 30 years old.

11.5.3 in Northern Ireland transfer under the Public Records Act (NI) 1923 to the Public Record Office of Northern Ireland is normally at 20 years.

11.6 In the case of records to be transferred to the Public Record Office or to a place of deposit appointed under section 4 of the Public Records Act 1958, or to the Public Record Office of Northern Ireland, the purpose of the review of records for release to the public is to:

- consider which information must be available to the public on transfer because no exemptions under the FOIA apply;
- consider which information must be available to the public at 30 years because relevant exemptions in the FOIA have ceased to apply;
- consider whether the information must be released in the public interest, notwithstanding the application of an exemption under the FOIA; and
- consider which information merits continued protection in accordance with the provisions of the FOIA.

11.7 If the review results in the identification of specified information which the authorities consider ought not to be released under the terms of the FOIA, the authorities should prepare a schedule identifying this information precisely, citing the relevant exemption(s), explaining why the information may not be released and identifying a date at which either release would be appropriate or a date at which the case for release should be reconsidered where the information is environmental information to which the exemption at section 39 of the FOIA applies, the schedule should cite the appropriate exception in the Environmental Information Regulations. This schedule must be submitted to the Public Record Office or, in Northern Ireland, to the Public Record Office of Northern Ireland prior to transfer which must be before the records containing the information are 30 years old (in the case of the Public Record Office) or 20 years old (in the case of the Public Record Office of Northern Ireland). Authorities should consider whether parts of records might be released if the sensitive information were blanked out.

11.8 In the first instance, the schedule described in 11.7 is to be submitted to the Public Record Office for review and advice. The case in favour of withholding the records for a period longer than 30 years is than considered by the Advisory Council. The Advisory Council may respond as follows:

(a) by accepting that the information may be withheld for longer than 30 years and earmarking the records for release or re-review at the date identified by the authority;

   (b) by accepting that the information may be withheld for longer than 30 years but asking the authority to reconsider the later date designated for release or re-review;

   (c) by questioning the basis on which it is deemed that the information may be withheld for longer than 30 years and asking the authority to reconsider the case;

   (d) by advising the Lord Chancellor if it is not satisfied with the responses it receives from authorities on particular cases;

   (e) by taking such other action as it deems appropriate within its role as defined in the Public Records Act.

In Northern Ireland there are separate administrative arrangements requiring that schedules are submitted to a Sensitivity Review Group consisting of representatives of different departments. The Sensitivity Review Group has the role of advising public authorities as to the appropriateness or otherwise of releasing records.

11.9   For the avoidance of doubt, none of the actions described in this Code affects the statutory rights of access established under the FOIA. Requests for information in public records transferred to the Public Record Office or to a place of deposit appointed under section 4 of the Public Records Act 1958 or to the Public Record Office of Northern Ireland will be dealt with on a case by case basis in accordance with the provisions of the FOIA.

11.10 Where records are transferred to the Public Record Office or a place of deposit before they are 30 years old, they should be designated by the transferring department or agency for immediate release unless an exemption applies: there will be no formal review of these designations.

11.11 When an exemption has ceased to apply under section 63 of the FOIA the records will become automatically available to researchers on the day specified in the finalised schedule (i.e. the schedule after it has been reviewed by the Advisory Council). In other cases, if the authority concerned wishes further to extend the period during which the information is to be withheld in accordance with the FOIA, it should submit a further schedule explaining the sensitivity of the information. This is to be done before the expiry of the period stated in the earlier schedule. The Public Record Office and Advisory Council will then review the schedule in accordance with the process described in paragraph 11.8 above. In Northern Ireland, Ministerial approval is required for any further extension of the stated period.

11.12 In reviewing records an authority may identify those which are appropriate for retention within the department, after they are 30 years old, under section 3(4) of the Public Records Act 1958. Applications must be submitted to the Public Record Office for review and advice. The case in favour of retention beyond the 30 year period will then be considered by the Advisory Council. The Advisory Council will consider the case for retaining individual records unless there is already in place a standing authorisation by the Lord Chancellor for the retention of a whole category of records. It will consider such applications on the basis of the guidance in chapter 9 of the White Paper *Open Government* (Cm 2290, 1993) or subsequent revisions of government policy on retention.

ANNEX A

STANDARDS ACCEPTED IN RECORDS MANAGEMENT

British Standards (BSI)

BS 4783	Storage, transportation and maintenance of media for use in data processing and information storage
BS 7799	Code of practice for information security management
BS ISO 15489-1	Information and Documentation—Records Management—Part 1: General
BSI DISC PD 0008	Code of practice for legal admissibility and evidential weight of information stored on electronic document management systems
BSI DISC PD0010	Principles of good practice for information management
BSI DISC PD0012	Guide to the practical implications of the Data Protection Act 1998

Public Record Office standards for the management of public records

The Public Record Office publishes standards, guidance and toolkits on the management of public records, in whatever format, covering their entire life cycle. They are available on the Public Record Office website (www.pro.gov.uk/recordsmanagement).

APPENDIX 4

Extracts from Hansard

This appendix contains a selection of some of the statements made by introducing ministers during the Parliamentary debates on the Freedom of Information Act 2000.

For reasons of space, we have given only the ministerial rationale underlying individual sections. It is hoped that these extracts will illuminate the intended effect of some of the provisions of the Act and may even, in one or two cases, be admissible under the rule in *Pepper* v *Hart* [1993] AC 593.

For statements of the overall aims of the Act, see the speeches of Jack Straw on Second Reading in the House of Commons (Hansard HC, 7 December 1999, col. 714–728) and Lord Falconer of Thoroton on Second Reading in the House of Lords (Hansard HL, 20 April, col. 823–830).

ACCESS TO INFORMATION—RIGHTS AND DUTIES

Relationship between the Act and the Human Rights Act 1998

House of Commons, Second Reading
Hansard HC, 7 December 1999, col. 719–720
The Secretary of State for the Home Department (Mr Jack Straw)

The [Human Rights Act 1998] sets out the European Convention's statement of basic rights. Some of those rights are absolute—such as that provided in article 3, guaranteeing freedom from torture or degrading treatment. The rights with which we have had to wrestle in the Freedom of Information Bill are not absolutes, but have to be balanced one with another. Article 10 gives a right to freedom of expression, but that has to be set against article 8 on the right to respect for a private life.

We have therefore sought in the Bill to secure a balance between the right to information needed for the proper exercise of the freedom of expression and the—directly conflicting—right of individuals to protection of information about themselves; the rights that institutions, including commercial companies, should have to proper confidentiality; and the need for any organisation, including the Government, to be able to formulate its collective policies in private.

Reasons for not including a purpose clause

House of Commons, Report and Third Reading
Hansard HC, 4 April 2000, col. 844
The Parliamentary Under-Secretary of State for the Home Department (Mr Mike O'Brien)

We want the [Act] to express our view that the citizen should have a right to know, and I do not think that we need a purpose clause to make the [Act] do what we want it to do.

. . . I have heard the arguments, including the recommendation of the Select Committee on Public Administration, that a purpose clause can be used to show clearly which of two or more competing values should be uppermost when a decision is made. However, I do not think that a purpose clause . . . is appropriate, and I shall set out precisely why.

One must assume that such a clause would be given legislative effect by the commissioner, the tribunal and the courts, so it would change the balance of rights that the Bill seeks to achieve. It is not possible to say that in every case one right should trump another. The right of access to information must be balanced against the right to privacy and confidentiality. Too strong a presumption in favour of disclosure for certain purposes, however worthy, over other competing rights to privacy or confidentiality could lead us into conflict, perhaps with the Human Rights Act.

. . . .

Openness does not have a monopoly on righteousness. Privacy and confidentiality have their proper place, and the right of the public to know must not place an unnecessary burden on business or undermine the proper and efficient running of government in the public interest.

Intended coverage of the Act

House of Lords, Committee Stage
Hansard HL, 17 October 2000, col. 951
The Minister of State, Cabinet Office (Lord Falconer of Thoroton)

I want to be clear about the Government's intentions in respect of coverage under the Bill. We have produced a Bill which provides rights of access to information held by an astonishingly wide range of public sector bodies. It is right that the public should have that access. It is our intention that the normal and proper course of action would be that, whenever the Secretary of State becomes aware of the creation of a new public authority, he should seek to ensure that it is brought in as quickly as he reasonably can. In some cases that would be achieved through the primary legislation setting up the new body. In other cases there will be no need to take action because it will be covered by one of the generic descriptions in Parts I to V of Schedule 1. In some instances the Secretary of State would need to use the order-making powers in [ss. 4 and 5], but as lists in Parts VI and VII of Schedule 1 show, many of the bodies which might be brought in under the order-making power of [s. 4] may be relatively or absolutely small bodies and offices. Many others which will fall to be considered under the [s. 4] powers may be working groups to task forces set up with a limited lifespan or having no real independent character from their parent or sponsoring department. Comparable considerations are likely to apply in the exercise of the [s. 5] powers.

We believe it is sensible that in those circumstances the Secretary of State should have some discretion to consider the full facts and implications of listing for FoI purposes before proceeding to make an order—not so that information can be withheld from the public, because in almost every case it is likely that the information will be available from another authority, but because it would be irresponsible to designate all those meeting the broad criteria as public authorities without regard to other relevant considerations.

Power to amend schedule 1 to limit application of the Act in the case of certain public authorities (s. 7(3))

House of Commons, Report and Third Reading

Hansard HC, 4 April 2000, col. 880–1
The Parliamentary Under-Secretary of State for the Home Department (Mr Mike O'Brien)

The BBC will be a public authority subject to the Bill's provisions. The BBC is particularly relevant here because its journalists will be able to claim an exemption from the provisions of freedom of information in respect of material held for the purposes of journalism, art or literature.

What if a court decision were to conclude that for particular purposes of definition areas that we might feel should remain the confidential prerogative of the journalists should be subject to freedom of information, and the journalists had to disclose their sources? I suspect that the BBC journalists would not be too happy about it and would want the Government to be able to act to deal with the situation [by using the power under s. 7(3).]

. . .

I shall give another example of the power's ability to vary or limit the description of information caught by the Bill. The Bank of England might decide to expand its financial activities to include insurance. The bank is already included in schedule 1 because of some of its functions. A decision would need to be made about whether to include the new business. Without the provisions, we could not make such a decision.

The hon. Member for Somerton and Frome (Mr. Heath) said that orders under [s. 7] to remove information from the scope of the Bill were retrospective. That is not the case.

Publication schemes

House of Lords, Report
Hansard HL, 14 November 2000, col. 199
The Parliamentary Secretary, Lord Chancellor's Department (Lord Bach)

My Lords, requiring public authorities to publish their publication schemes in both paper and electronic forms and to make them available to the public free of charge might seem at first sight—even at second sight—laudable attempts to promote maximum openness and the maximum public access to information. There are, however, some sound reasons to doubt whether these proposals would achieve what the noble Lord [Lord Lucas] hopes that they will achieve.

First, we have to bear in mind that this legislation will apply to a vast range of authorities. What would involve a minimal cost to a large government department or even a medium-sized local authority might represent a sizeable additional expense for a school or a parish council. Requiring bodies such as these to publish in both paper and electronic form could involve considerable outlay on new IT equipment and possibly extra staff to operate it, making it even more difficult to justify telling them to provide the publication scheme to the public free of charge. I question whether the House wants to see this kind of cost imposed on a small business, without its being allowed to increase its revenue in some way.

No one wants public authorities to use charging as a way of defeating the new culture and the drive towards greater openness that the Bill genuinely seeks to achieve. The Government are confident that public authorities will not wish to embarrass themselves by making people pay unreasonably for copies of their publication schemes. We have made it clear all along that we expect public authorities to bear most of the additional cost of freedom of information and there is no reason to suppose that that will not apply in the area of the legislative framework.

Perhaps I may remind the House that all publication schemes will have to have the approval of the information commissioner. She is bound to question any unreasonable proposals with regard to charging. She will also be best placed to judge what is the most appropriate form for the publication of these schemes in individual cases.

House of Lords, Third Reading
Hansard HL, 22 November 2000, col. 819
The Minister of State, Cabinet Office (Lord Falconer of Thoroton)

If the information commissioner thinks that an authority is not making appropriate use of electronic communication in a given set of circumstnaces, she can require the authority to include the necessary provisions in its scheme.

APPLICATIONS FOR INFORMATION—PROCEDURE

Urgent applications

House of Lords, Third Reading
Hansard HL, 22 November 2000, col. 840
The Minister of State, Cabinet Office (Lord Falconer of Thoroton)

[W]hat happens when . . . information is needed urgently? . . .

The position under the [Act] is that a public authority must inform the applicant within 20 working days if it is not going to comply with the request. At the same time, if the public interest test applies by virtue of [s. 2], then the public authority must inform the applicant of its determination under that clause or it must indicate when it is going to determine that beyond the 20 days; and if the applicant disagrees with that length of time, the applicant can go to the information commissioner and complain about the length of time.

Obviously, under the Bill there must be a period of time within which the public authority has time to comply with the request. As regards appeals procedures, . . . domestic complaints procedures must be exhausted first—for example, local authority complaints procedures—when there has not been a disclosure. Whether or not there is a provision in relation to those for urgency will depend upon the individual procedure.

The information commissioner's code of practice will say that applications should be dealt with promptly and, if there is good reason why it should be dealt with urgently, no doubt that will be taken into account in determining how quickly to deal with the individual complaint or appeal against a particular ruling by a public authority.

That is as far as I can take it. Inevitably, there must be some period of time within which both public authorities and information commissioners are allowed to deal with the applications, Of course, if the applicant has a particular reason for needing the information urgently, no doubt that will be taken into account when the application is being considered.

No requirement to give real name

House of Lords, Committee Stage
Hansard HL, 14 November 2000, col. 183–4
The Parliamentary Secretary, Lord Chancellor's Department (Lord Bach)

My Lords, the internet age has dawned. The Freedom of Information Bill makes provision for an application to be purpose blind. It requires that an application must apply in writing, which includes any electronic application, and provide an address. These are commonsense provisions which are necessary to ensure that a public authority can carry out its statutory duty to communicate information to that applicant. The Bill assumes that an applicant will wish to give his real name, but nothing requires him or her to do so or to use any particular name. He can call himself Father Christmas, or even Ralph Lucas, if he desires.

Desirability of keeping to time estimates for public
interest decisions on qualified exemptions

House of Lords, Report
Hansard HL, 14 November 2000, col. 189
The Parliamentary Under-Secretary of State, Home Office (Lord Bassam of Brighton)

Failure to provide an estimate of time would mean there was failure to comply with the requirements of Part I of the Bill. The commissioner would therefore be able to issue an enforcement notice under [s. 52], or a decision notice under [s. 50(3)]. . . . [T]he Government make a commitment to add a reference in the Secretary of State's code of practice under [s. 45] to the desirability of complying with estimates given. Failure to comply with the estimate would render the authority liable to a practice recommendation from the commissioner under [s. 48].

Availability of judicial review of decisions not to release
information on grounds of excessive cost (s. 12)

House of Lords, Report
Hansard HL, 14 November 2000, col. 193
The Parliamentary Under-Secretary of State, Home Office (Lord Bassam of Brighton)

. . . I can understand why the noble Lord might wish to ensure that information which is in the public interest should be made public irrespective of cost. . . .

269

... Nothing in the Bill prevents a public authority from disclosing such information. That is a point that I made clear when we considered the matter in Committee. Where a public authority has the power to disclose information, it would be required to do so under administrative law; and when asked to disclose such information, in so doing to balance the costs of disclosure with the public interest. We feel that that is the sensible way in which to approach this issue, rather than the blanket disapplication of exemption provided for in [s. 12]—regardless of the implications for the public authority. Indeed, those implications would be real and could from time to time be very substantial.

EXEMPTIONS—GENERAL ISSUES

The meaning of 'prejudice'

House of Commons, Report and Third Reading
Hansard HC, 5 April 2000, col. 1067
The Parliamentary Under-Secretary of State for the Home Department (Mr Mike O'Brien)

... The Government have consistently stated their view that prejudice means prejudice that is 'actual, real or of substance'. Prejudice is an ordinary word that is found without qualification in many pieces of legislation. It is a word that is familiar to the courts as well as to others involved with the day-to-day interpreting of legislation.

House of Lords, Second Reading
Hansard HL, 20 April 2000, col. 827
The Minister of State, Cabinet Office (Lord Falconer of Thoroton)

... I want to emphasise the strength of the prejudice test. Prejudice is a term used in other legislation relating to the disclosure of information. It is a term well understood by the courts and the public. It is not a weak test. The commissioner will have the power to overrule an authority if she feels that any prejudice caused by a disclosure would be trivial or insignificant. She will ensure that an authority must point to prejudice which is 'real, actual or of substance'. We do not think that reliance on undefined terms such as 'substantial' or 'significant' is a sensible way forward. We do not know how they will be interpreted by the commissioner or the courts. We can never deliver absolute certainty, but we can avoid making uncertainty worse by adding ill-defined terminology into the Bill.

Public interest—interpretation

House of Lords, Third Reading
Hansard HL, 22 November 2000, col. 831
The Minister of State, Cabinet Office (Lord Falconer of Thoroton)

... [I]n the case of a piece of information to which an exemption applies but which also falls under the provisions of [s. 2], it is necessary for the public authority to consider in each case whether or not the [s. 2] discretion requires disclosure of the document or the information. It has to be considered on a case-by-case basis.

House of Lords, Committee Stage
Hansard HL, 17 October 2000, col. 921
The Minister of State, Cabinet Office (Lord Falconer of Thoroton)

As far as public interest between disclosure on the other hand and the maintenance of exemption on the other is concerned, it has to be looked at objectively. One looks at the impact of disclosure, that is, making it public. What is the impact of the exemption being maintained? That should be looked at objectively rather than in terms of whatever the motive may be of the person applying. That does not mean that the motive of the person applying may not coincide with factors that could be relevant to what damage may be done and what assistance could be served by making the matter public. But individual motives will not be relevant to that.

House of Lords, Report
Hansard HL, 14 November 2000, col. 224
The Minister of State, Cabinet Office (Lord Falconer of Thoroton)

The noble Viscount's [Viscount Colville of Culross] amendment quite properly deals with the question: does the fact that a long period of time has elapsed since the event occurred on which information is now required affect the exercise of the public interest discretion under [s. 2]? The reply to that is: of course the age of the information will be a relevant consideration when deciding where the public interest lies under the provisions of [s. 2]. Plainly, that will be the case.

Redaction

House of Lords, Committee Stage
Hansard HL, 14 November 2000, col. 224
The Minister of State, Cabinet Office (Lord Falconer of Thoroton)

We have been discussing whether the Bill in effect permits partial disclosure. It will in fact require that when some of the information that is requested is exempt but other information is not. The right of access in [s. 1] involves information that is recorded in any form. That means that the right of access attaches to the content of documents or records rather than to the documents or records themselves. When a document contains a mixture of disclosable and non-disclosable information, the disclosable information must be communicated to the applicant.

On the point about summarisation, [s. 11] states that when applicants have a preference for one of certain specified means in which they wish the information to be communicated to them, the authority shall, so far as is reasonably practicable, give effect to that preference. The means specified involve copying of the information, inspection, or a digest or summary of the information. If the applicant requests a copy of the document that contains the information or to inspect the actual document, [s. 11] requires the authority to give effect to that preference so far as is reasonably practicable to do so. That includes 'blanking out' information, such as names that cannot be disclosed. Similarly, if the applicant has requested a digest or summary of the information, the authority must also comply with that request, if it is reasonable to do so.

ABSOLUTE EXEMPTIONS

Certificates under s. 23 and s. 24

House of Lords, Committee Stage
Hansard HL, 19 October 2000, col. 1259
The Minister of State, Cabinet Office (Lord Falconer of Thoroton)

The noble Lord, Lord Lucas, then raised the question of whether the exemption certificate could ever conceivably be itself exempt under any such exemption. I cannot conceive that that would be the case. The purpose of the evidential certificate proving the exemption is that it is intended to be produced in public to the information commissioner or to the appropriate authority. I cannot conceive that it could be exempt because it is intended to be made, in effect, public.

House of Lords, Committee Stage
Hansard HL, 17 October 2000, col. 902
The Minister of State, Cabinet Office (Lord Falconer of Thoroton)

It is necessary to exclude the operation of the public interest test in relation to information held by Parliament and exempt by virtue of [s. 36] as, although disclosure of such information may not technically constitute a breach of parliamentary privilege, the effective conduct of Parliament is so closely connected with it that the same consideration applies. For example, something that might prejudice the conduct of parliamentary affairs but not be a breach of parliamentary privilege is advice from the Clerks of the House to the Speaker. Another example is advice from officials of the House to Members of the House. Neither of those would fall into the category of parliamentary privilege but disclosure under freedom of information could prejudice the affairs of Parliament. It is for Parliament alone to consider whether to disclose such information.

Interpretation of the exemption for information provided in confidence (s. 41)

House of Lords, Committee Stage
Hansard HL, 25 October 2000, col. 416
The Minister of State, Cabinet Office (Lord Falconer of Thoroton)

Simply to put at the top of a document 'Confidential' does not make the disclosure of that document by anyone actionable in breach of confidence. 'Actionable' means that one can go to court and vindicate a right in confidence in relation to that document or information. It means being able to go to court and win.

On the question of confidence, one could be given a document or information in confidence. As time went by, it could cease to be confidential; for example, because the information was published elsewhere. The issue has to be tested at the point the application is made under the Freedom of Information Act. There is a two-pronged test in [s. 41]; first, the information has to be obtained in confidence by the public authority; and, secondly, its disclosure would give rise to an actionable breach of confidence by the public authority. So the information must be confidential from the start and it must still be an actionable breach of confidence to disclose it at the time the application is made under the terms of the [Act].

House of Lords, Committee Stage
Hansard HL, 17 October 2000, col. 928
The Minister of State, Cabinet Office (Lord Falconer of Thoroton)

. . . [Section 2] refers to a public interest in disclosing a particular fact. In relation to the common law test and confidentiality, the courts say that on the face of it someone has a right to keep that information confidential but ask, despite that confidentiality, whether there is a public interest in disclosing the information at large. I am sure that lawyers could fine tune the differences between the two tests but they are in substance sufficiently close. In order to establish whether the exemption applies, consideration must be given as to whether common law public interest applies.

QUALIFIED EXEMPTIONS

Information intended for future publication (s. 22)

House of Lords, Committee Stage
Hansard HL, 19 October 2000, col. 1244–5
The Parliamentary Under-Secretary of State, Home Office (Lord Bassam of Brighton)

[Section 22] provides an exemption from the duty to provide information where there is a present intention to publish and it is reasonable to withhold the information until publication. The applicant should be told of that intention and would be expected to await formal publication. The requirement of reasonableness, which is a fair test, effectively prevents this exemption being used simply as a device to avoid publishing something which might cause embarrassment to Ministers. In order for this requirement to be satisfied, there must be a clear commitment on the part of the authority to publish the information at some defined point in the future, as well as, by definition, a real reason for the withholding of the information.

National security (s. 24)

House of Commons, Report and Third Reading
Hansard HC, 5 April 2000, col. 1060
The Parliamentary Under-Secretary of State for the Home Department (Mr Mike O'Brien)

The exemption applies only when it is required; the test is of necessity, not desirability. The clause is drafted in similar terms to section 28 of the Data Protection Act 1998. The two provisions have the same purpose. It is therefore sensible for them to be drafted in similar language. Any difference in approach between the provisions could lead to them being interpreted differently.

Defence (s. 26)

House of Lords, Committee Stage
Hansard HL, 19 October 2000, col. 1252
The Minister of State, Cabinet Office (Lord Falconer of Thoroton)

The public authority is not obliged to communicate the information if it falls in any one of the exemptions. Each one of the exemptions has its own justification. . . . The exception to the duty to confirm or deny in every case is a logical adjunct of the existence of the exemption.

The clearest and easiest example is endangering the defence of the realm. You do not have to communicate information which endangers the defence of the realm. Nor do you have to confirm or deny whether such information exists when, if you did confirm or deny its existence, that in itself would endanger the defence of the realm. I give the obvious example. 'Do you have detailed information concerning the chemical warfare capacities of the following countries?'; and then a list of countries is given. It could well damage the defence of the realm if one indicated the extent to which one had that information.

The economy (s. 29)

House of Lords, Committee Stage
Hansard HL, 19 October 2000, col. 1287
The Minister of State, Cabinet Office (Lord Falconer of Thoroton)

We believe that the freedom of information regime should not require disclosure of information which would harm the economic interests of the United Kingdom generally or a part of the United Kingdom. . . . Perhaps I may give a brief example. Public authorities such as the DTI may hold documents which set out the advantages and disadvantages of investing in different regions. If that type of information were disclosed to an overseas business organisation which was contemplating setting up a factory in the UK, the organisation may be put off its proposed investment.

Relations within the United Kingdom (s. 28)

House of Lords, Committee Stage
Hansard HL, 19 October 2000, col. 1280
The Minister of State, Cabinet Office (Lord Falconer of Thoroton)

The noble Lords, Lord Mackay of Ardbrecknish and Lord Hunt, asked for examples of where the exemption might apply where it is not covered by [ss. 35 or 36]. I shall give two examples. First, let us suppose that there was kept in a government department a thumbnail sketch of the strengths and weaknesses of the individual members of an executive. That would not assist relations between the devolved Assembly or Parliament and the UK Government. It would not be caught by [s. 35] and it probably would not be caught by [s. 36]. A second example might be comments within a government department on a devolved administration's policy proposals or Acts.

Investigations and proceedings (s. 30)

House of Lords, Committee Stage
Hansard HL, 24 October 2000, col. 274
The Minister of State, Cabinet Office (Lord Falconer of Thoroton)

I should like to take this opportunity to say a few words about [s. 30(1)(b)]. In our discussions last Thursday, I made the point that non-criminal investigations into safety matters or accidents, for example, were not covered by the class exemption in [s. 30]. That is, of course, correct However, subsection (1)(b) includes investigations by an authority into matters which may lead to a decision being taken by that authority to institute criminal proceedings, even if no such proceedings are eventually taken. To cite two examples: accident investigations where criminal proceedings are a possible outcome, or environmental health reports into compliance with food safety would fall within this subsection.

Concern has been expressed that this would mean that the public may be denied information about serious health issues or the causes of accidents, even where criminal proceedings are not taken. I do not believe that this will be the case as the public interest test in [s. 2] of the Bill would come into play. If there were no criminal prosecution in the case, I am sure that the public interest in knowing of health risks or the causes of accidents would outweigh the public interest in maintaining exemption.

Formulation of government policy (s. 35)

House of Commons, Report and Third Reading
Hansard HC, 5 April 2000, col. 1026–28
The Secretary of State for the Home Department (Mr Jack Straw)

As I shall explain to the House in a moment, the Government face a genuine difficulty in putting together a form of words that separates what I think people are talking about—basic statistical data, which are already published; although there are not much such data, there are some—from the analysis of that data and policy advice, which people accept, for reasons that everyone understands, should not be published immediately.

. . .

The word 'fact' encompasses a huge sphere of human activity. 'Words and Phrases Legally Defined' states:

Everything in the cosmos is a fact or a phenomenon.

Occasionally, there are arguments—perhaps I should say happy and comradely discussions—in Cabinet Committees and between Ministers. Although those arguments themselves will be an expression of opinion, it will be a fact that those arguments occurred.

. . .

As is well known, discussions are being held between departmental spending Ministers and the Treasury on bids for the next spending round, which will be announced in July. A huge amount of the information that has been submitted, on paper, to PSX—which is the Cabinet Committee concerned—is factual information on the costs of the various bids submitted by Ministers or on the analysis of that information. The conclusion of those

Cabinet discussions will be made public very soon, in July 2000, in the statement of my right hon. Friend the Chancellor of the Exchequer and in the public spending White Paper that will be published with that statement.

. . . [T]here is no way in which a Minister can say that the type of information in the bid letters that I have submitted, or in the briefing that is in my folder for meetings with colleagues, is opinion. It is not opinion: it is raw fact and raw data, and, at best, analysis of them.

. . .

It is easy to say that such matters are easily defined, but much more difficult to define them. That is the difficulty, and that is at the heart of the issue. We are arguing about what is a fact. If my hon. Friend applies himself not only to the Oxford English Dictionary, but to 'Words and Phrases Legally Defined', he will discover that there is no complete separation between a fact and an opinion. It is—in fact—a bit like Venn Diagrams, in which there is certainly separation at the extremes, but a large area in the middle where things can be both fact and opinion. Additionally, a fact can be made out of the existence of an opinion.

House of Lords, Committee Stage
Hansard HL, 24 October 2000, col. 299
The Minister of State, Cabinet Office (Lord Falconer of Thoroton)

It is pretty easy to identify what is a statistic: you know a statistic when you see it. As to what is a fact or an opinion, that is a much harder question to answer.

House of Lords, Report
Hansard HL, 14 November 2000, col. 156–7
The Minister of State, Cabinet Office (Lord Falconer of Thoroton)

. . . Factual information has to be disclosed unless there is a good reason not to do so. It is possible to envisage occasions—which will be very rare—when such factual information might not be disclosed. An example is where a government department decides to sell off an asset; it has advice as to what the asset is worth; it is going to negotiate for the sale of the asset; the policy decision is taken; it would be wrong to disclose advice in relation to the value of the asset. I should have thought that anyone would agree with that.

House of Lords, Third Reading
Hansard HL, 22 November 2000, col. 832
The Minister of State, Cabinet Office (Lord Falconer of Thoroton)

I believe that it is impossible satisfactorily to distinguish pure analysis of information from advice which is to be given based on that information. The noble Lord, Lord Mackay of Ardbrecknish, made that point. For example, analysis of data could relate to collation of statistical data or the expression of such data in other ways in order that it be more easily understood. The Government believe that it would be exceedingly difficult for a public authority to make a case for withholding this type of information.

House of Lords, Committee Stage
Hansard HL, 24 October 2000, col. 297
The Minister of State, Cabinet Office (Lord Falconer of Thoroton)

I also emphasise that the Government believe that factual information used to provide an informed background to decision-taking will normally be disclosed.

The 'reasonable opinion of a qualified person' (s. 36)

House of Lords, Committee Stage
Hansard HL, 24 October 2000, col. 306
The Minister of State, Cabinet Office (Lord Falconer of Thoroton)

The information commissioner decides at stage one whether any reasonable qualified person could come to the conclusion that there was prejudice. She can intervene at that stage only on the judicial review basis. If she concludes that no reasonable qualified person could come to the conclusion that there was prejudice under [s. 36], she can override the decision and require disclosure.

. . . [I]f the public authority decides against disclosure, having balanced the reasons for the exemption against the public interest in disclosure under [s. 36], the information commissioner can form her own view. That is pretty clear.

ENFORCEMENT

Effect of a practice recommendation

House of Lords, Committee Stage
Hansard HL, 17 October 2000, col. 944
The Parliamentary Under-Secretary of State, Home Office (Lord Bassam of Brighton)

I said that I would return to the issue of enforcement. I fully accept that compliance with the published codes of practice would not be enforceable in the courts in the same way that a statutory duty might be. As the provision is drafted, the information commissioner has the power to look at compliance and issue practice recommendations. I believe it would be an exceptional authority which wilfully ignored such a recommendation, particularly given the commissioner's powers to name and shame in any report that she might make to Parliament. An additional point is that the code of practice could be referred to in any test case which was the subject of judicial review. The powers of naming and shaming should not be underestimated in regard to public sector bodies keen to keep the confidence of the public they serve.

Disclosure of practice recommendations

House of Lords, Committee Stage
Hansard HL, 25 October 2000, col. 433
The Parliamentary Under-Secretary of State, Home Office (Lord Bassam of Brighton)

. . . nothing in the [Act] requires that information contained in a practice recommenda-tion is exempt. We believe it is likely that the commissioner will wish to summarise any recommendations she may have made when she makes her annual report to Parliament, as required under [s. 49(1)]. It would be open to her to refer directly to such a recommendation in that report, or in any other report that she might decide to make under the provisions of [s. 49(2)]. To that extent, much of the information relating to practice recommendations will be routinely made available to the public.

The information commissioner is herself a public authority for the purposes of freedom of information. A member of the public would, therefore, be entitled to request that the commissioner, or the relevant public authority, should disclose information that she or it held which is contained in a practice recommendation.

Prohibition on disclosure by Information Commissioner and her staff

House of Lords, Committee Stage
Hansard HL, 19 October 2000, col. 1225–6
The Parliamentary Under-Secretary of State, Home Office (Lord Bassam of Brighton)

The Government believe that it would be unworkable for the commissioner and her staff to have a situation where Section 59 [of the Data Protection Act 1998] applied to one regime but not to another. We have said that we believe the vast majority of requests for information, and consequently complaints to the commissioner, will involve both personal and non-personal information. Information obtained by the commissioner will not, therefore, fall neatly under one regime or the other. Given this, there is no practical way to apply Section 59 to one regime and not the other.

We are aware that the Data Protection Commissioner regards Section 59 of the Data Protection Act 1998 as overly restrictive. We have also accepted the strength of the argument for an amendment to the Bill to allow information to be shared by and between the commissioner and certain other investigatory bodies and have tabled amendments that will achieve that.

Nothing in the Freedom of Information [Act] would prevent the release by the information commissioner of information about the handling of complaints where that disclosure was made with the consent of the individual or company to whom the information relates, obtained in accordance with Section 59 of the Data Protection Act 1998.

However, where a person or company declines to give such consent, it is right that the information commissioner should not be able to overrule that view and routinely disclose such information. Given the commissioner's power to require disclosure of information for the purposes of an investigation . . . it is right that authorities must have confidence that such information will not be disclosed.

Furthermore, the commissioner can, and annually must, report to Parliament about the exercise of her functions under the [Act]. Any disclosure of information in such reports would be done for the purposes of, and as is necessary for, the exercise of the commissioner's functions, and would therefore have lawful authority. There would be no offence under Section 59.

The ministerial 'over-ride' (s. 53)

House of Commons, Report and Third Reading
Hansard HL, 4 April 2000, col. 922–4
The Secretary of State for the Home Department (Mr Jack Straw)

It is neither possible nor necessary to write into the [Act] that the decisions made by a Cabinet Minister must be made only after consultation and agreement with all of his or her Cabinet colleagues—not least because some of the decisions are quasi-judicial. In practice, it would be an extremely unwise Cabinet Minister who chose to issue an exemption certificate amounting to a veto of a decision made by the commissioner to order disclosure without consulting his or her Cabinet colleagues. That might lead to that Cabinet Minister's speedy demise and the receipt of his or her P45 by return of post.

To reinforce those arrangements, I propose that there should be written into the ministerial code—which is a published document available in the Library of the House and, I believe, on the internet—guidance on how decisions relating to Executive exemption certificates should be made and the way in which other colleagues should be consulted, other than on quasi-judicial decisions.

. . .

I do not believe that there will be many occasions when a Cabinet Minister—with or without the backing of his colleagues—will have to explain to the House or publicly, as necessary, why he decided to require information to be held back which the commissioner said should be made available.

. . .

This regime will not be used all that often, and only in extremis.

House of Lords, Committee Stage
Hansard HL, 25 October 2000, col. 442–3
The Minister of State, Cabinet Office (Lord Falconer of Thoroton)

[T]he executive override is limited in application. It will be available only on the signature of a senior member of the Government. Although, for reasons that I shall explain in a moment, it cannot be put on the face of the [Act], it is intended that the exercise of the override should occur only after consultation within the Cabinet. Its use will be subject on the face of the [Act] to a clear duty to explain the circumstances. We can be sure that this House and the other place will hold such signatories accountable for their actions and that they will also be accountable in court pursuant to judicial review proceedings.

. . .

The government amendments do not make provision on the face of the Bill for the certificate to be authorised by a Cabinet Minister acting collectively with Cabinet-rank colleagues. That point was raised in another place and my right honourable friend the Home Secretary said that he would consider it. In legislation passed by Parliament it is the Minister who is the decision-taker. As Members of the Committee are aware, when so acting, the Minister is bound by the convention of collective responsibility. The concept of a statutory duty to consult between Cabinet colleagues is not one which fits within that convention and it would disturb it in ways which we could not predict if we were to write such a provision into the Bill. I want to make it quite clear that guidance to Ministers will require that when acting as the 'accountable person', they should consult Cabinet colleagues before signing a certificate.

PERSONAL INFORMATION AND DATA PROTECTION

Reasons why 'personal information' unavailable under the Act

House of Commons, Report and Third Reading
Hansard HC, 4 April 2000, col. 920
The Secretary of State for the Home Department (Mr Jack Straw)

The [Data Protection Act 1998] protects private information while the Freedom of Information Bill is there to bring information out into the public. There is a natural and profound tension between the two and they are, in a sense, different sides of the same coin. If information is protected under the Data Protection Act, we cannot possibly get into the situation where there is, none the less, a discretion in the public interest to break what is a fundamental obligation not to disclose that information. That would not only be wrong and against the Data Protection Act, but against European Community law, a point that will appeal considerably to the hon. Member for Aldridge Brownhills (Mr. Shepherd). In addition—this point will appeal to the whole House—disclosure of such information would break the European convention on human rights. I am happy to say that that convention has the genuine approbation of the whole House.

Council of Europe: Recommendation Rec(2002)2 of the Committee of Ministers to Member States on Access to Official Documents

(*Adopted by the Committee of Ministers on 21 February 2002 at the 784th meeting of the Ministers' Deputies*)

The Committee of Ministers, under the terms of Article 15.*b* of the Statute of the Council of Europe,

Considering that the aim of the Council of Europe is to achieve greater unity between its members for the purpose of safeguarding and realising the ideals and principles which are their common heritage;

Bearing in mind, in particular, Article 19 of the Universal Declaration of Human Rights, Articles 6, 8 and 10 of the European Convention on Human Rights and Fundamental Freedoms, the United Nations Convention on Access to Information, Public Participation in Decision-making and Access to Justice in Environmental Matters (adopted in Aarhus, Denmark, on 25 June 1998) and the Convention for the Protection of Individuals with regard to Automatic Processing of Personal Data of 28 January 1981 (ETS No. 108); the Declaration on the freedom of expression and information adopted on 29 April 1982; as well as Recommendation No. R (81) 19 on the access to information held by public authorities, Recommendation No. R (91) 10 on the communication to third parties of personal data held by public bodies; Recommendation No. R (97) 18 concerning the protection of personal data collected and processed for statistical purposes and Recommendation No. R (2000) 13 on a European policy on access to archives;

Considering the importance in a pluralistic, democratic society of transparency of public administration and of the ready availability of information on issues of public interest;

Considering that wide access to official documents, on a basis of equality and in accordance with clear rules:
- allows the public to have an adequate view of, and to form a critical opinion on, the state of the society in which they live and on the authorities that govern them, whilst encouraging informed participation by the public in matters of common interest;
- fosters the efficiency and effectiveness of administrations and helps maintain their integrity by avoiding the risk of corruption;

– contributes to affirming the legitimacy of administrations as public services and to strengthening the public's confidence in public authorities;

Considering therefore that the utmost endeavour should be made by member states to ensure availability to the public of information contained in official documents, subject to the protection of other rights and legitimate interests;

Stressing that the principles set out hereafter constitute a minimum standard, and that they should be understood without prejudice to those domestic laws and regulations which already recognise a wider right of access to official documents;

Considering that, whereas this instrument concentrates on requests by individuals for access to official documents, public authorities should commit themselves to conducting an active communication policy, with the aim of making available to the public any information which is deemed useful in a transparent democratic society,

Recommends the governments of member states to be guided in their law and practice by the principles set out in this recommendation.

I. Definitions

For the purposes of this recommendation:

'public authorities' shall mean:
  (i)   government and administration at national, regional or local level;
  (ii) natural or legal persons insofar as they perform public functions or exercise administrative authority and as provided for by national law.

'official documents' shall mean all information recorded in any form, drawn up or received and held by public authorities and linked to any public or administrative function, with the exception of documents under preparation.

II. Scope

1. This recommendation concerns only official documents held by public authorities. However, member states should examine, in the light of their domestic law and practice, to what extent the principles of this recommendation could be applied to information held by legislative bodies and judicial authorities.
2. This recommendation does not affect the right of access or the limitations to access provided for in the Convention for the Protection of Individuals with regard to Automatic Processing of Personal Data.

III. General principle on access to official documents

Member states should guarantee the right of everyone to have access, on request, to official documents held by public authorities. This principle should apply without discrimination on any ground, including that of national origin.

IV. Possible limitations to access to official documents

1. Member states may limit the right of access to official documents. Limitations should be set down precisely in law, be necessary in a democratic society and be proportionate to the aim of protecting:
  (i)   national security, defence and international relations;
  (ii) public safety;
  (iii) the prevention, investigation and prosecution of criminal activities;

(iv) privacy and other legitimate private interests;

(v) commercial and other economic interests, be they private or public;

(vi) the equality of parties concerning court proceedings;

(vii) nature;

(viii) inspection, control and supervision by public authorities;

(ix) the economic, monetary and exchange rate policies of the state;

(x) the confidentiality of deliberations within or between public authorities during the internal preparation of a matter.

2. Access to a document may be refused if the disclosure of the information contained in the official document would or would be likely to harm any of the interests mentioned in paragraph 1, unless there is an overriding public interest in disclosure.

3. Member states should consider setting time limits beyond which the limitations mentioned in paragraph 1 would no longer apply.

V. Requests for access to official documents

1. An applicant for an official document should not be obliged to give reasons for having access to the official document.

2. Formalities for requests should be kept to a minimum.

VI. Processing of requests for access to official documents

1. A request for access to an official document should be dealt with by any public authority holding the document.

2. Requests for access to official documents should be dealt with on an equal basis.

3. A request for access to an official document should be dealt with promptly. The decision should be reached, communicated and executed within any time limit which may have been specified beforehand.

4. If the public authority does not hold the requested official document it should, wherever possible, refer the applicant to the competent public authority.

5. The public authority should help the applicant, as far as possible, to identify the requested official document, but the public authority is not under a duty to comply with the request if it is a document which cannot be identified.

6. A request for access to an official document may be refused if the request is manifestly unreasonable.

7. A public authority refusing access to an official document wholly or in part should give the reasons for the refusal.

VII. Forms of access to official documents

1. When access to an official document is granted, the public authority should allow inspection of the original or provide a copy of it, taking into account, as far as possible, the preference expressed by the applicant.

2. If a limitation applies to some of the information in an official document, the public authority should nevertheless grant access to the remainder of the information it contains. Any omissions should be clearly indicated. However, if the partial version of the document is misleading or meaningless, such access may be refused.

3. The public authority may give access to an official document by referring the applicant to easily accessible alternative sources.

VIII. Charges for access to official documents

1. Consultation of original official documents on the premises should, in principle, be free of charge.
2. A fee may be charged to the applicant for a copy of the official document, which should be reasonable and not exceed the actual costs incurred by the public authority.

IX. Review procedure

1. An applicant whose request for an official document has been refused, whether in part or in full, or dismissed, or has not been dealt with within the time limit mentioned in Principle VI.3 should have access to a review procedure before a court of law or another independent and impartial body established by law.
2. An applicant should always have access to an expeditious and inexpensive review procedure, involving either reconsideration by a public authority or review in accordance with paragraph 1 above.

X. Complementary measures

1. Member states should take the necessary measures to:
    (i)   inform the public about its rights of access to official documents and how that right may be exercised;
    (ii)   ensure that public officials are trained in their duties and obligations with respect to the implementation of this right;
    (iii) ensure that applicants can exercise their right.
2. To this end, public authorities should in particular:
    (i)   manage their documents efficiently so that they are easily accessible;
    (ii)   apply clear and established rules for the preservation and destruction of their documents;
    (iii) as far as possible, make available information on the matters or activities for which they are responsible, for example by drawing up lists or registers of the documents they hold.

XI. Information made public at the initiative of the public authorities

A public authority should, at its own initiative and where appropriate, take the necessary measures to make public information which it holds when the provision of such information is the interest of promoting the transparency of public administration and efficiency within administrations or will encourage informed participation by the public in matters of public interest.

APPENDIX 6

The Environmental Information Regulations 2004

ARRANGEMENT OF REGULATIONS

Whereas a draft of these Regulations has been approved by resolution of each House of Parliament in pursuance of paragraph 2(2) of Schedule 2 to the European Communities Act 1972.

Now, therefore, the Secretary of State, being a Minister designated for the purposes of section 2(2) of the European Communities Act 1972 in relation to freedom of access to, and dissemination of, information on the environment held by or for public authorities or other bodies, in exercise of the powers conferred on her by that section makes the following regulations:

PART 1

Introductory

Citation and commencement

1. These Regulations may be cited as the Environmental Information Regulations 2004 and shall come into force on 1st January 2005.

Interpretation

2. (1) In these Regulations—
    'the Act' means the Freedom of Information Act 2000;
    'applicant', in relation to a request for environmental information, means the person who made the request;
    'appropriate records authority' in relation to a transferred public record, has the same meaning as in section 15(5) of the Act;
    'the Commissioner' means the Information Commissioner;
    'the Directive' means Council Directive 2003/4/EC on public access to environmental information and repealing Council Directive 90/313/EEC;
    'environmental information' has the same meaning as in Article 2(1) of the Directive, namely any information in written, visual, aural, electronic or any other material form on—

(a) the state of the elements of the environment, such as air and atmosphere, water, soil, land, landscape and natural sites including wetlands, coastal and marine areas, biological diversity and its components, including genetically modified organisms, and the interaction among these elements;

(b) factors, such as substances, energy, noise, radiation or waste, including radioactive waste, emissions, discharges and other releases into the environment, affecting or likely to affect the elements of the environment referred to in (a);

(c) measures (including administrative measures), such as policies, legislation, plans, programmes, environmental agreements, and activities affecting or likely to affect the elements and factors referred to in (a) and (b) as well as measures or activities designed to protect those elements;

(d) reports on the implementation of environmental legislation;

(e) cost-benefit and other economic analyses and assumptions used within the framework of the measures and activities referred to in (c); and

(f) the state of human health and safety, including the contamination of the food chain, where relevant, conditions of human life, cultural sites and built structures inasmuch as they are or may be affected by the state of the elements of the environment referred to in (a) or, through those elements, by any of the matters referred to in (b) and (c);

'historical record' has the same meaning as in section 62(1) of the Act;

'public authority' has the meaning given by paragraph (2);

'public record' has the same meaning as in section 84 of the Act;

'responsible authority', in relation to a transferred public record, has the same meaning as in section 15(5) of the Act;

'Scottish public authority' means—

(a) a body referred to in section 80(2) of the Act; and

(b) insofar as not such a body, a Scottish public authority as defined in section 3 of the Freedom of Information (Scotland) Act 2002(a);

'transferred public record' has the same meaning as in section 15(4) of the Act; and

'working day' has the same meaning as in section 10(6) of the Act.

(2) Subject to paragraph (3), 'public authority' means—

(a) government departments;

(b) any other public authority as defined in section 3(1) of the Act, disregarding for this purpose the exceptions in paragraph 6 of Schedule 1 to the Act, but excluding—

(i) any body or office-holder listed in Schedule 1 to the Act only in relation to information of a specified description; or

(ii) any person designated by Order under section 5 of the Act;

(c) any other body or other person, that carries out functions of public administration; or

(d) any other body or other person, that is under the control of a person falling within sub-paragraphs (a), (b) or (c) and—

(i) has public responsibilities relating to the environment;

(ii) exercises functions of a public nature relating to the environment; or

(iii) provides public services relating to the environment.

(3) Except as provided by regulation 12(10) a Scottish public authority is not a 'public authority' for the purpose of these Regulations.

(4) The following expressions have the same meaning in these Regulations as they have in the Data Protection Act 1998(a), namely—

    (a) 'data' except that for the purposes of regulation 12(3) and regulation 13 a public authority referred to in the definition of data in paragraph (e) of section 1(1) of that Act means a public authority within the meaning of these Regulations;

    (b) 'the data protection principles';

    (c) 'data subject'; and

    (d) 'personal data'.

(5) Except as provided by this regulation, expressions in these Regulations which appear in the Directive have the same meaning in these Regulations as they have in the Directive.

(6) The following expressions have the same meaning in these Regulations as they have in the Data Protection Act 1998, namely—

    (a) 'data' except that for the purposes of regulation 12(3) and regulation 13, a public authority referred to in the definition of data in paragraph (e) of section 1(1) of that Act means a public authority within the meaning of these Regulations;

    (b) 'the data protection principles';

    (c) 'data subject'; and

    (d) 'personal data'.

(7) Subject to paragraphs (1) and (2), expressions in these Regulations which appear in the Directive have the same meaning in these Regulations as they have in the Directive.

Application

3. (1) Subject to paragraphs (3) and (4), these Regulations apply to public authorities.

(2) For the purposes of these Regulations, environmental information is held by a public authority if the information—

    (a) is in its possession and it has been produced or received by the authority; or

    (b) is held by another person on behalf of the authority.

(3) These Regulations shall not apply to any public authority to the extent that it is acting in a judicial or legislative capacity.

(4) These Regulations shall not apply to either House of Parliament to the extent required for the purpose of avoiding an infringement of the privileges of either House.

(5) For the purposes of these Regulations each government department is to be treated as a person separate from any other government department for the purposes of Parts 2, 4 and 5 of these Regulations.

PART 2

Access to Environmental Information held by Public Authorities

Dissemination of environmental information

4. (1) Subject to paragraph (3), a public authority shall in respect of environmental information that it holds—
    (a) progressively make the information available to the public by electronic means which are easily accessible; and
    (b) take reasonable steps to organize the information relevant to its functions with a view to the active and systematic dissemination to the public of the information.
   (2) For the purposes of paragraph (1) the use of electronic means to make information available or to organize information shall not be required in relation to information collected before 1st January 2005 in non-electronic form.
   (3) Paragraph (1) shall not extend to making available or disseminating information which a public authority would be entitled to refuse to disclose under regulation 12.
   (4) The information under paragraph (1) shall include at least—
    (a) the information referred to in Article 7(2) of the Directive; and
    (b) facts and analyses of facts which the public authority considers relevant and important in framing major environmental policy proposals.

Duty to make available environmental information on request

5. (1) Subject to paragraph (3) and in accordance with paragraphs (2), (4) (5) and (6) and the remaining provisions of this Part and Part 3 of these Regulations, a public authority that holds environmental information shall make it available on request.
   (2) Information shall be made available under paragraph (1) as soon as possible and no later than 20 working days after the date of receipt of the request.
   (3) To the extent that the information requested includes personal data of which the applicant is the data subject, paragraph (1) shall not apply to those personal data.
   (4) For the purposes of paragraph (1), where the information made available is compiled by the public authority it shall be up to date, accurate and comparable, so far as the public authority reasonably believes.
   (5) Where a public authority makes available information in paragraph (b) of the definition of environmental information, and the applicant so requests, the public authority shall, insofar as it is able to do so, either inform the applicant of the place where information can be found on the measurement procedures, including methods of analysis, sampling, and pre-treatment of samples, used in compiling the information, or refer the applicant to the standardised procedures used.
   (6) Any enactment or rule of law that would prevent the disclosure of information in accordance with these Regulations shall not apply.

Form and format of information

6. (1) Where an applicant requests that the information be made available in a particular form or format, a public authority shall make it so available, unless—

    (a) it is reasonable for it to make the information available in another form or format; or

    (b) the information is already publicly available and easily accessible to the applicant in another form or format.

(2) If the information is not made available in the form or format requested, the public authority shall—

    (a) explain the reason for its decision as soon as possible and no later than 20 working days after the date of receipt of the request for the information;

    (b) provide the explanation in writing if the applicant so requests; and

    (c) inform the applicant of the provisions of regulation 11 and of the enforcement and appeal provisions of the Act applied by regulation 18.

Extension of time

7. (1) Where a request is made under regulation 5, the public authority may extend a period of no later than 20 working days referred to in the provisions in paragraph (2) to a period of no later than 40 working days if it reasonably believes that the complexity or volume of the information requested means that it is impracticable either to comply with the request within the earlier period or to make a decision to refuse to do so.

(2) The following provisions are those referred to in paragraph (1)—

    (a) regulation 5(2);

    (b) regulation 6(2)(a); and

    (c) regulation 14(2).

(3) Where paragraph (1) applies the public authority shall notify the applicant accordingly as soon as possible and no later than 20 working days after the date of receipt of the request.

Charging

8. (1) Subject to paragraphs (2) to (8), where a public authority makes information available to an applicant in accordance with regulation 5(1), the authority may charge the applicant for making the information available.

(2) A public authority shall not make any charge for allowing an applicant—

    (a) to access any public registers or lists of environmental information held by the public authority; or

    (b) to examine the information requested at the place which the public authority makes available for that examination.

(3) A charge under paragraph (1) shall not exceed an amount which the public authority is satisfied is a reasonable amount.

(4) A public authority may require advance payment of a charge for making environmental information available and if it does it shall, no later than 20 working days after the date of receipt of the request for the information, notify the applicant of this requirement and of the amount of the advance payment.

(5) Where a public authority has notified an applicant under paragraph (4) that advance payment is required, the public authority is not required—

(a) to make available the information requested; or

(b) to comply with regulations 6 or 14,

unless the charge is paid no later than 60 working days after the date on which it gave the notification.

(6) The period beginning with the day on which the notification of advance payment is made and ending on the day on which that payment is received by the public authority is to be disregarded for the purposes of determining the period of no later than 20 working days referred to in the provisions in paragraph (7), including any extension to those periods under regulation 7(1).

(7) The provisions referred to in paragraph (6) are

(a) regulation 5(2);

(b) regulation 6(2)(a); and

(c) regulation 14(2).

(8) A public authority shall publish and make available to applicants—

(a) a schedule of its charges; and

(b) information on the circumstances in which a charge may be levied or waived.

Advice and assistance

9. (1) A public authority shall provide advice and assistance, so far as it would be reasonable to expect the authority to do so, to applicants and prospective applicants.

(2) Where a public authority decides that an applicant has formulated a request in too general a manner, it shall—

(a) ask the applicant as soon as possible and in any event no later than 20 working days after the date of receipt of the request, to provide more particulars in relation to the request; and

(b) assist the applicant in providing those particulars.

(3) Where a code of practice has been made under regulation 16, and to the extent that a public authority conforms to that code in relation to the provision of advice and assistance in a particular case, it shall be taken to have complied with paragraph (1) in relation to that case.

(4) Where paragraph (2) applies, in respect of the provisions in paragraph (5), the date on which the further particulars are received by the public authority shall be treated as the date after which the period of no later than 20 working days referred to in those provisions shall be calculated.

(5) The provisions referred to in paragraph (4) are

(a) regulation 5(2);

(b) regulation 6(2)(a); and

(c) regulation 14(2).

Transfer of a request

10. (1) Where a public authority that receives a request for environmental information does not hold the information requested but believes that another public authority or a Scottish public authority holds the information, the public authority shall either—

    (a) transfer the request to the other public authority or Scottish public authority; or

    (b) supply the applicant with the name and address of that authority,

and inform the applicant accordingly with the refusal sent under regulation 14(1).

(2) Where a request is transferred to a public authority, for the purposes of the provisions referred to in paragraph (3) the request is received by that public authority on the date on which it receives the transferred request.

(3) The provisions referred to in paragraph (2) are

    (a) regulation 5(2);

    (b) regulation 6(2)(a); and

    (c) regulation 14(2).

Representations and reconsideration

11. (1) Subject to paragraph (2), an applicant may make representations to a public authority in relation to the applicant's request for environmental information if it appears to the applicant that the authority has failed to comply with a requirement of these Regulations in relation to the request.

(2) Representations under paragraph (1) shall be made in writing to the public authority no later than 40 working days after the date on which the applicant believes that the public authority has failed to comply with the requirement.

(3) The public authority shall on receipt of the representations and free of charge—

    (a) consider them and any supporting evidence produced by the applicant; and

    (b) decide if it has complied with the requirement.

(4) A public authority shall notify the applicant of its decision under paragraph (3) as soon as possible and no later than 40 working days after the date of receipt of the representations.

(5) Where the public authority decides that it has failed to comply with these Regulations in relation to the request, the notification under paragraph (4) shall include a statement of—

    (a) the failure to comply;

    (b) the action the authority has decided to take to comply with the requirement; and

    (c) the period within which that action is to be taken.

PART 3

Exceptions to the Duty to Disclose Environmental Information

Exceptions to the duty to disclose environmental information

12. (1) Subject to paragraphs (2), (3) and (9), a public authority may refuse to disclose environmental information requested if—

    (a) an exception to disclosure applies under paragraphs (4) or (5); and

    (b) in all the circumstances of the case, the public interest in maintaining the exception outweighs the public interest in disclosing the information.

(2) A public authority shall apply a presumption in favour of disclosure.

(3) To the extent that the information requested includes personal data of which the applicant is not the data subject, the personal data shall not be disclosed otherwise than in accordance with regulation 13.

(4) For the purposes of paragraph (1)(a), a public authority may refuse to disclose information to the extent that—

(a) it does not hold that information when an applicant's request is received;

(b) the request for information is manifestly unreasonable;

(c) the request for information is formulated in too general a manner and the public authority has complied with its duty under regulation 9;

(d) the request relates to material which is still in the course of completion, to unfinished documents or to incomplete data; or

(e) the request involves the disclosure of internal communications.

(5) For the purposes of paragraph (1)(a), a public authority may refuse to disclose information to the extent that its disclosure would adversely affect—

(a) international relations, defence, national security or public safety;

(b) the course of justice, the ability of a person to receive a fair trial or the ability of a public authority to conduct an inquiry of a criminal or disciplinary nature;

(c) intellectual property rights;

(d) the confidentiality of the proceedings of that or any other public authority where such confidentiality is provided by law;

(e) the confidentiality of commercial or industrial information where such confidentiality is provided by law to protect a legitimate economic interest;

(f) the interests of the person who provided the information where that person—

(i) was not under, and could not have been put under, any legal obligation to supply it to that or any other public authority,

(ii) did not supply it in circumstances such that that or any other public authority is entitled apart from these Regulations to disclose it, and

(iii) has not consented to its disclosure; or

(g) the protection of the environment to which the information relates.

(6) For the purposes of paragraph (1), a public authority may respond to a request by neither confirming nor denying whether such information exists and is held by the public authority, whether or not it holds such information, if that confirmation or denial would involve the disclosure of information which would adversely affect any of the interests referred to in paragraph (5)(a) and would not be in the public interest under paragraph (1)(b).

(7) For the purposes of a response under paragraph (6), whether information exists and is held by the public authority is itself the disclosure of information.

(8) For the purposes of paragraph 4(e), internal communications include communications between government departments.

(9) To the extent that the environmental information to be disclosed relates to information on emissions, a public authority shall not be entitled to refuse to disclose that information under an exception referred to in paragraphs (5)(d) to (g).

(10) For the purposes of paragraphs (5)(b) and (d), reference to a public authority shall include reference to a Scottish public authority.

(11) Nothing in these Regulations shall authorise a refusal to make available any environmental information contained in or otherwise held with other information which is withheld by virtue of these Regulations unless it is not reasonably capable of being separated from the other information for the purpose of making available that information.

Personal data

13. (1) To the extent that the information requested includes personal data of which the applicant is not the data subject and as respects which either the first or second condition below is satisfied, a public authority shall not disclose the personal data.

(2) The first condition is—

  (a) in a case where the information falls within any of paragraphs (a) to (d) of the definition of 'data' in section 1(1) of the Data Protection Act 1998, that the disclosure of the information to a member of the public otherwise than under these Regulations would contravene—

    (i) any of the data protection principles; or

    (ii) section 10 of that Act (right to prevent processing likely to cause damage or distress) and in all the circumstances of the case, the public interest in not disclosing the information outweighs the public interest in disclosing it, and

  (b) in any other case, that the disclosure of the information to a member of the public otherwise than under these Regulations would contravene any of the data protection principles if the exemptions in section 33A(1) of the Data Protection Act 1998 (which relate to manual data held by public authorities) were disregarded.

(3) The second condition is that by virtue of any provision of Part IV of the Data Protection Act 1998 the information is exempt from section 7(1) of that Act and in all the circumstances of the case, the public interest in not disclosing the information outweighs the public interest in disclosing it.

(4) In determining whether anything done before 24th October 2007 would contravene any of the data protection principles, the exemptions in Part III of Schedule 8 to the Data Protection Act 1998 shall be disregarded.

(5) For the purposes of this regulation, a public authority may respond to a request by neither confirming nor denying whether such information exists and is held by the public authority, whether or not it holds such information, to the extent that—

  (a) the giving to a member of the public of the confirmation or denial would contravene any of the data protection principles or section 10 of the Data Protection Act 1998 or would do so if the exemptions in section 33A(1) of that Act were disregarded; or

  (b) by virtue of any provision of Part IV of the Data Protection Act 1998, the information is exempt from section 7(1)(a) of that Act.

Refusal to disclose information

14. (1) If a request for environmental information is refused by a public authority under regulations 12(1) or 13(1), the refusal shall be made in writing and comply with the following provisions of this regulation.

(2) The refusal shall be made as soon as possible and no later than 20 working days after the date of receipt of the request.

(3) The refusal shall specify the reasons not to disclose the information requested, including—

    (a) any exception relied on under regulations 12(4), 12(5) or 13; and

    (b) the matters the public authority considered in reaching its decision with respect to the public interest under regulation 12(1)(b) or, where these apply, regulations 13(2)(a)(ii) or 13(3).

(4) If the exception in regulation 12(4)(d) is specified in the refusal, the authority shall also specify, if known to the public authority, the name of any other public authority preparing the information and the estimated time in which the information will be finished or completed.

(5) The refusal shall inform the applicant—

    (a) that he can make representations to the public authority under regulation 11; and

    (b) of the enforcement and appeal provisions of the Act applied by regulation 18.

Ministerial certificates

15. (1) A Minister of the Crown may certify that a refusal to disclose information under regulation 12(1) is because the disclosure—

    (a) would adversely affect national security; and

    (b) would not be in the public interest under regulation 12(1)(b).

(2) For the purposes of paragraph (1)—

    (a) a Minister of the Crown may designate a person to certify the matters in that paragraph on his behalf; and

    (b) a refusal to disclose information under regulation 12(1) includes a response under regulation 12(6).

(3) A certificate issued in accordance with paragraph (1)—

    (a) shall be conclusive evidence of the matters in that paragraph; and

    (b) may identify the information to which it relates in general terms.

(4) A document purporting to be a certificate under paragraph (1) shall be received in evidence and deemed to be such a certificate unless the contrary is proved.

(5) A document which purports to be certified by or on behalf of a Minister of the Crown as a true copy of a certificate issued by that Minister under paragraph (1) shall in any legal proceedings be evidence (or, in Scotland, sufficient evidence) of that certificate.

(6) In paragraphs (1), (2) and (5), a 'Minister of the Crown' has the same meaning as in section 25(3) of the Act.

PART 4

Code of Practice and Historical Records

Issue of a code of practice and functions of the Commissioner

16. (1) The Secretary of State may issue, and may from time to time revise, a code of practice providing guidance to public authorities as to the practice which it would, in the Secretary of State's opinion, be desirable for them to follow in connection with the discharge of their functions under these Regulations.

(2) The code may make different provision for different public authorities.

(3) Before issuing or revising any code under this regulation, the Secretary of State shall consult the Commissioner.

(4) The Secretary of State shall lay before each House of Parliament any code issued or revised under this regulation.

(5) The general functions of the Commissioner under section 47 of the Act and the power of the Commissioner to give a practice recommendation under section 48 of the Act shall apply for the purposes of these Regulations as they apply for the purposes of the Act but with the modifications specified in paragraph (6).

(6) For the purposes of the application of sections 47 and 48 of the Act to these Regulations, any reference to—

(a) public authority is a reference to a public authority within the meaning of these Regulations;

(b) the requirements or operation of the Act, or functions under the Act, includes a reference to the requirements or operation of these Regulations, or functions under these Regulations; and

(c) a code of practice made under section 45 of the Act includes a reference to a code of practice made under this regulation.

Historical and transferred public records

17. (1) Where a request relates to information contained in a historical record other than one to which paragraph (2) applies and the public authority considers that it may be in the public interest to refuse to disclose that information under regulation 12(1)(b), the public authority shall consult—

(a) the Lord Chancellor, if it is a public record within the meaning of the Public Records Act 1958; or

(b) the appropriate Northern Ireland Minister, if it is a public record to which the Public Records Act (Northern Ireland) 1923 applies,

before it decides whether the information may or may not be disclosed.

(2) Where a request relates to information contained in a transferred public record, other than information which the responsible authority has designated as open information for the purposes of this regulation, the appropriate records authority shall consult the responsible authority on whether there may be an exception to disclosure of that information under regulation 12(5).

(3) If the appropriate records authority decides that such an exception applies—

(a) subject to paragraph (4), a determination on whether it may be in the public interest to refuse to disclose that information under regulation 12(1)(b) shall be made by the responsible authority;

(b) the responsible authority shall communicate its determination to the appropriate records authority within such time as is reasonable in all the circumstances; and

(c) the appropriate records authority shall comply with regulation 5 in accordance with that determination.

(4) Where a responsible authority is required to make a determination under paragraph (3), it shall consult—

(a) the Lord Chancellor, if the transferred public record is a public record within the meaning of the Public Records Act 1958; or

(b) the appropriate Northern Ireland Minister, if the transferred public record is a public record to which the Public Records Act (Northern Ireland) 1923 applies,

before it determines whether the information may or may not be disclosed.

(5) A responsible authority which is not a public authority under these Regulations shall be treated as a public authority for the purposes of—

(a) the obligations of a responsible authority under paragraphs (3)(a) and (b) and (4); and

(b) the imposition of any requirement to furnish information relating to compliance with regulation 5.

PART 5

Enforcement, Offences and Revocation

Enforcement and appeal provisions

18.—(1) The enforcement and appeals provisions of the Act shall apply for the purposes of these Regulations as they apply for the purposes of the Act but with the modifications specified in this regulation.

(2) In this regulation, 'the enforcement and appeals provisions of the Act' means—

(a) Part IV of the Act (enforcement), including Schedule 3 (powers of entry and inspection) which has effect by virtue of section 55 of the Act; and

(b) Part V of the Act (appeals).

(3) Part IV of the Act shall not apply in any case where a certificate has been issued in accordance with regulation 15(1).

(4) For the purposes of the application of the enforcement and appeals provisions of the Act—

(a) for any reference to—

(i) 'this Act' there shall be substituted a reference to 'these Regulations'; and

(ii) 'Part I' there shall be substituted a reference to 'Parts 2 and 3 of these Regulations';

(b) any reference to a public authority is a reference to a public authority within the meaning of these Regulations;

(c) for any reference to the code of practice under section 45 of the Act (issue of a code of practice by the Secretary of State) there shall be substituted a reference to any code of practice issued under regulation 16(1);

    (d) in section 50(4) of the Act (contents of decision notice)—
        (i) in paragraph (a) for the reference to 'section 1(1)' there shall be substituted a reference to 'regulation 5(1)'; and
        (ii) in paragraph (b) for the references to 'sections 11 and 17' there shall be substituted references to 'regulations 6, 11 or 14';
    (e) in section 56(1) of the Act (no action against public authority) for the words 'This Act does not confer' there shall be substituted the words 'These Regulations do not confer';
    (f) in section 57(3)(a) of the Act (appeal against notices served under Part IV) for the reference to 'section 66' of the Act (decisions relating to certain transferred public records) there shall be substituted a reference to 'regulations 17(2) to (5)';
    (g) in paragraph 1 of Schedule 3 to the Act (issue of warrants) for the reference to 'section 77' (offence of altering etc. records with intent to prevent disclosure) there shall be substituted a reference to 'regulation 19'; and
    (h) in paragraph 8 of Schedule 3 to the Act (matters exempt from inspection and seizure) for the reference to 'information which is exempt information by virtue of section 23(1) or 24(1)' (bodies and information relating to national security) there shall be substituted a reference to 'information whose disclosure would adversely affect national security'.

(5) In section 50(4)(a) of the Act (contents of decision notice) the reference to confirmation or denial applies to a response given by a public authority under regulation 12(6) or regulation 13(5).

(6) Section 53 of the Act (exception from duty to comply with decision notice or enforcement notice) applies to a decision notice or enforcement notice served under Part IV of the Act as applied to these Regulations on any of the public authorities referred to in section 53(1)(a); and in section 53(7) for the reference to 'exempt information' there shall be substituted a reference to 'information which may be refused under these Regulations'.

(7) Section 60 of the Act (appeals against national security certificate) shall apply with the following modifications—
    (a) for the reference to a certificate under section 24(3) of the Act (national security) there shall be substituted a reference to a certificate issued in accordance with regulation 15(1);
    (b) subsection (2) shall be omitted; and
    (c) in subsection (3), for the words, 'the Minister did not have reasonable grounds for issuing the certificate' there shall be substituted the words 'the Minister or person designated by him did not have reasonable grounds for issuing the certificate under regulation 15(1)'.

(8) A person found guilty of an offence under paragraph 12 of Schedule 3 to the Act (offences relating to obstruction of the execution of a warrant) is liable on summary conviction to a fine not exceeding level 5 on the standard scale.

(9) A government department is not liable to prosecution in relation to an offence under paragraph 12 of Schedule 3 to the Act but that offence shall apply to a person in the public service of the Crown and to a person acting on behalf of either House of Parliament or on behalf of the Northern Ireland Assembly as it applies to any other person.

(10) Section 76(1) of the Act (disclosure of information between Commissioner and

ombudsmen) shall apply to any information obtained by, or furnished to, the Commissioner under or for the purposes of these Regulations.

Offence of altering records with intent to prevent disclosure

19. (1) Where—
   (a) a request for environmental information has been made to a public authority under regulation 5; and
   (b) the applicant would have been entitled (subject to payment of any charge) to that information in accordance with that regulation,
   any person to whom this paragraph applies is guilty of an offence if he alters, defaces, blocks, erases, destroys or conceals any record held by the public authority, with the intention of preventing the disclosure by that authority of all, or any part, of the information to which the applicant would have been entitled.

   (2) Subject to paragraph (5), paragraph (1) applies to the public authority and to any person who is employed by, is an officer of, or is subject to the direction of, the public authority.

   (3) A person guilty of an offence under this regulation is liable on summary conviction to a fine not exceeding level 5 on the standard scale.

   (4) No proceedings for an offence under this regulation shall be instituted—
   (a) in England and Wales, except by the Commissioner or by or with the consent of the Director of Public Prosecutions; or
   (b) in Northern Ireland, except by the Commissioner or by or with the consent of the Director of Public Prosecutions for Northern Ireland.

   (5) A government department is not liable to prosecution in relation to an offence under paragraph (1) but that offence shall apply to a person in the public service of the Crown and to a person acting on behalf of either House of Parliament or on behalf of the Northern Ireland Assembly as it applies to any other person.

Amendment

20.—(1) Section 39 of the Act is amended as follows.
   (2) In Subsection (1)(a), for 'regulations under section 74' there is substituted 'environmental information regulations'.
   (3) After subsection (1) there is inserted—
   '(1A) In subsection (1) "environmental information regulations" means—
   (a) regulations made under section 74, or
   (b) regulations made under section 2(2) of the European Communities Act 1972 for the purpose of implementing any Community obligation relating to public access to, and the dissemination of, information on the environment.'

Revocation

21. The following are revoked—
   (a) The Environmental Information Regulations 1992 and the Environmental Information (Amendment) Regulations 1998 except insofar as they apply to Scottish public authorities; and

(b)   The Environmental Information Regulations (Northern Ireland) 1993 and the Environmental Information (Amendment) Regulations (Northern Ireland) 1998.

Index